S0-BWO-232

Italian Literature
in Translation

JAMES E. MILLER, JR.
Professor of English, University
of Chicago. Awarded Fulbright to Italy, 1958–1959.
President of the National Council of
Teachers of English, 1970.
Author of *Quests Surd and Absurd: Essays in American
Literature,* and other works.

ROBERT O'NEAL
Humanities Coordinator for the Indiana
Humanities Project. Former Professor and Chairman of
the English Department, San Antonio College.
Author of *Teachers' Guide to World Literature
for the High School* and contributor of articles
to professional publications.

HELEN M. McDONNELL
Chairman, English Department,
Ocean Township High School, Oakhurst, New Jersey.
Chairman of the Committee on Comparative and
World Literature, National Council of Teachers of English.
Contributor of articles to professional publications.

*Introductory Essay
Translation: The Art of Failure
by John Ciardi*

SCOTT, FORESMAN AND COMPANY

Editorial Director / LEO B. KNEER

Development / MARGARET RAUSCH
with Ghia Brenner, Dorothy Koeber, and Fitzgerald Higgins

Design / ROBERT AMFT

The authors and editors of *Italian Literature in Translation*
wish to express their appreciation to the following teachers.
Acting as reader-consultants, they chose from the many
selections submitted to them those that they believed were most
relevant to the interests and needs of today's youth. They tested
their opinions against classroom use and contributed ideas
that evolved during the give-and-take of class discussion.

SISTER EUGENE FOX, S.C.
Denver, Colorado

MR. RONALD MIDKIFF
Rome, Georgia

MR. THOMAS GAGE
Concord, California

MR. ELMER E. MOORE, JR.
Dobbs Ferry, New York

MRS. JEANNE LUCKETT
Jackson, Mississippi

MR. ROBERT ROMANO
Wilmington, Massachusetts

MRS. ELIZABETH DRUM MCDOWELL
Nashville, Tennessee

COVER: 15th century Italian Textile. *Courtesy of The Art Institute of Chicago.*
FRONTISPIECE AND ILLUSTRATIONS: Adapted from eighteenth-
century Italian peasant embroidery.

ISBN: 0–673–10238–6

1976 Impression

12345678910–KPK–85848382818079787776

CONTENTS

Italian Literature

Translation: The Art of Failure

by JOHN CIARDI

A translator's explanation of his method has no choice but to be an apology for failure. Frost may have been right when he said that "poetry is what disappears in translation." For a translator to dream of success would be overweening: what he tries for is no more than the best possible failure.

"Translation" is, in any case, the wrong word for the process of rendering a piece of writing from one language to another. The idea contained in "translation" smacks too much of that contained in "transliteration"—it seems to assume that there exists in Language A some word that will equal any given word in Language B, and that the translator need only find the equivalent word and put it in place, allowing of course for something called idiom.

But such an assumption ignores the nature of words. Semanticists claim, as a basic tenet, that no word ever means exactly the same thing twice—and that tenet takes no thought of crossing a language boundary. A look at a few of the ways in which words refuse to be exactly equivalent to other words is much to the point in identifying the translator's real work, and, by the way, in identifying one element of the poetic process. Words are complex things. We tend, in general usage, to consider only

---

John Ciardi was born in Medford, Massachusetts, and has taught at several universities, including principally Rutgers. He has served as poetry editor of the Saturday Review, *and has published many volumes of poetry. His translation of Dante's* Divine Comedy *into the modern American idiom has tended to make all previous English translations obsolete.*

the top slice of a given word. Poets, on the other hand, are likely to use words in depth: they are interested, among other things, in the images locked inside a word, in its muscularity, in its history, in its connotations, and in its levels of usage. As soon as one begins to hunt the American-English language for words that are equivalent *in depth* to Italian words, he learns that whatever he does manage to get across the language boundary will not be got across by any simple one-for-one transliteration.

The American word "daisy," for example, labels the same flower the French intend by *la marguerite* and the Italians by *la margherita,* or at least approximately so (a botanist might be quick to say that the varieties of the European daisy are distinct from those of the American daisy). Nevertheless, those are the words one would naturally use in these three tongues for labeling any particular daisy. Semantically, that is to say, the denotations are reasonably firm.

But words consist of much more than denotation. Every word has a certain muscularity. That is to say, it involves certain speech muscles. Certainly any man who is word-sensitive is likely to linger over the difference between the long-drawn Italian *carina* and the common, though imprecise, American usage "cute" when applied to an attractive child. The physical gestures the two words invite are at least as different as the Italian child's goodbye wave (*"Fa ciao, carina"*) with the palm of the hand up, and the American child's ("Wave bye-bye") with the back of the hand up. The very difference in ethnic concept between two peoples moves the words about in their mouths. As I once wrote in a poem I am not moved to cherish particularly but whose point remains:

> My mother facing a day in Avellino
> Tasted it: *una dolce giornata.*
>
> My wife's mother in Protestant Missouri
> Judges it: *it is a good day.*

There are two distinct kinds of muscularity. Other kinds could certainly be adduced. And all must function in the effort one must make to find truly equivalent language.

Every word, moreover, has a history. Sometimes the history changes out from under the word very rapidly. English "broadcast" once meant specifically "a way of sowing" and was borrowed by radio as an analogy. Meanwhile, new machines all but eliminated the old methods of broadcast-sowing, and the word has just about lost all farm connotation. What to do then when, to shift examples, one language uses a word denoting anxiety whose essential meaning is based on the history of medieval torture, when the only word in another language that will render that denotation is based on the history of, say, the internal-combustion engine? Pure hypotheticals, to be sure, but how does one find equivalents in any language for such English words as "billingsgate," or "to burke," or "boycott"—words whose meanings are inseparable from the local scene and local history in which the English language evolved?

Every word has an image locked into its roots. The English word "daisy" is a contraction of the earlier "day's eye," which is to say "the eye of day"—a lovely root image. *Marguerite* and *margherita* release a root connotation of all girls named Margaret/Marguerite/Margherita—and bless them all as lovely images. Behind that first suggestion, too, lies the true root of the Greek *margaron,* meaning "pearl"—another fine image. But what happened to "day's eye"? Not that there is any point here in arguing which is the more attractive root image. The point is simply that they are different. What then does one do for equivalent words?

And to point out only one more of many possibilities within the nature of words, every word connotes a certain level of usage. Italian *antipatico,* for example, is so common a usage that it falls readily from the lips of even very small children, whereas English "antipathetic" is a relatively learned word, and certainly not one for the normal nursery. What weight does one give this element of word usage in seeking equivalents?

Normally, we use words as simple things, paying attention to one, or at most two, levels of their meaning. But once the other levels of a word are allowed into consideration, no word is a simple thing. It becomes a complex. But if a single word is a complex, then a phrase is a complex of complexes, and a line is a complex of complexes of complexes, and a stanza, and a poem are . . . and so forth and so on.

I have now translated (or, rather, "rendered in English") two-thirds of *The Divine Comedy*. I don't honestly know how to make a theory of translation out of such musings and bewilderments as these. All I can truthfully say is that such equivalence as I have managed has happened by feel, and that I am more comfortable within specifications than I am in trying to defend theories that distort under every effort to state them.

I began to peck away at Dante because I could find no translation that satisfied my sense of the original. Let nothing in that statement imply that I have now satisfied my sense. When I read the original with my rendering in mind I have no choice but to feel sad. When I read any other translation with my rendering in mind, I feel relatively happy. No one, of course, should trust my sense of it, but I must. Who else's sense can I trust?

In looking at other translations I was distressed by the fact that none of them seemed to be using what I understood to be Dante's vulgate. They seemed rather to fall into literary language, the very sort of thing Dante took such pains to avoid. And none of them, above all else, gave me a satisfying sense of Dante's pace, which is to say, the rate at which the writing reveals itself to the reader.

I began to experiment out of curiosity. I rendered a number of Cantos in *terza rima* and satisfied myself that it could not do. English is a rhyme-poor language. It was obvious to me that the price of forcing that third rhyme into place in English was ruinous to the language. There are approximately 4,500 lines in each third of *The Divine Comedy*. One must find 1,500 triple rhymes to render each third into *terza rima,* and English has no such resources. Mechanically, it can be done, but not in anything approximating spoken American-English. I could see what wrestling agonies I had put into my own efforts in order to force the language around to that third rhyme, and the same agonies are immediately visible in every extant version in *terza rima.*

Abandoning all thought of *terza rima,* I tried blank verse. But there the language and its movement went askew on another characteristic of English verse. The blank-verse paragraph in English, as nearly as I can determine, runs to an average of about fourteen lines. (Interestingly, the paragraph of Pope's couplets runs to about the same average.) If one thinks of the structure of pauses in a poem as subtotaling points, I take that fact of English poetry to mean that blank verse pauses to complete its subthoughts about once every fourteen lines. But Dante sets his pauses (which is to say, his periods, or more usually his semicolons, or sometimes his commas) every three lines, and I take that fact to be, above all else, what determines the pace and sparseness of Dante's writing. If the fundamental unit runs from ten to twenty lines, there is room for all sorts of digression or even self-indulgence. An extra line or two, an extra image or two, an extra flourish or two, are easily possible. But if one is forcing his lines to some sort of summary every three lines, that fact must work to squeeze out all flab. Dante does, to be sure, write any number of run-on tercets, but the three-line unit remains firm as the rigorous basic measure of his way of writing. This writing is of bone and sinew.

I went on to experiment at all sorts of other possibilities. In another effort at *terza rima* I tried assonantal rhyming. Assonance may yet be a possibility for someone else. I can only report that I do not favor it as an English rhyme method. For a time I tried English couplets, thinking they might be made to render an Italian tercet: they cannot, at least not as a sustained measure. I tried various sorts of ballad stanzas: they had no hope of being for anything but the wastebasket. Then I hit on what I may as well call "dummy *terza rima,*" which is to say, I kept the three-line unit but rhymed only the first and third lines. And with that it began to happen, at least for me. I could persuade myself that what came was reasonably English, reasonably poetry, and reasonably faithful to Dante's pace and to his special way of using language. What is reasonable can, of course,

12   *Introduction*

include an awareness of failure, but I could begin to believe this was a good enough failure to be worth investing in.

I had no theory at that point—only a feeling. And I still have no theory I can securely defend. The rest was trial and error, something like learning to walk a tightrope: if one can only manage to grab the rope when he falls, and if he can then manage to get back up, and if he falls only forward, there is always the possibility that he will make it to the other side. To let a single example do for all, the process can be illustrated from Canto VIII of the "Purgatorio," which reads, in the original:

> Ben discerneva in lor la testa bionda;
> Ma nella faccia l'occhio si smarria
> Come virtù ch'a troppo si confonda.

The passage is part of the description of two angels that descend to Dante and his companions in the Valley of the Negligent Rulers. It is a simple enough passage as Dante goes, and almost any man with a sense of Latin roots can puzzle out most of the meaning. *Virtù* (virtue) in the Latin sense of "faculty/power/ability/generative force" (cf. "by virtue of the power invested in me") is perhaps the one word that might trip the unwary. How is one to render such a passage? In Pidgin-Literal it might read:

> Well was I discerning in them the head blond
> but in their faces my eye was dazed
> like a faculty which is overcome by excess.

But though such a rendering is approximately idiomatic, phrase by phrase, the sequence of phrases is not really intelligible as a communication in English. The passage is still in no spoken tongue, but, rather, in an unspeakable hodgepodge neither Italian nor English. So one might work toward a more speakable, which is to say, communicable, equivalent:

> I saw clearly that their heads were blond,
> but looking into the faces my eyes grew dazed
> like an overstimulated faculty of the senses.

That begins to be closer, but now one runs into a peculiarity of the way Dante describes the workings of his senses. If one has been reading from the beginning of *The Divine Comedy* he is used to this way Dante has of describing such matters. Dante often describes the workings of his eyes as if he could focus on, say, the forehead of a distant figure, seeing nothing else, and as if he then had deliberately to move his eyes downward in order to focus on the figure's nose. It is some such thing he is saying here: staring at the angels he can see that their hair is blond, but when he looks down from their hair to their faces, his eyes grow dazzled, overstimulated by the light that shines from them. Obviously, it would be impossible, at any distance, not to be entirely blinded by such light, and the literalist has firm grounds for arguing that Dante could not have seen either the hair or the faces of the angels. Such a device must be accepted by the reader as a well-established mannerism.

With that much understood, then, the passage may be simplified. Were one simply communicating Dante's thought in an English prose paraphrase it might be stated: "I could make out clearly that their hair was blond, but when I focused on their faces, my eyes were dazzled by the excess of light they gave forth."

Let the rendering remain ragged: it contains the essential intent. But the passage is written as poetry and it must be rendered within meter, rhyme, and in a language sufficient to its emotional intent. After much scratching and scrambling for a rhyme (and it sometimes happens that the very rhyme you want has been used in the preceding tercet and may not, therefore, be repeated so soon) I came up with the following:

> I could distinctly see their golden hair,
>> but my eyes drew back defeated from their faces
>> like a sense perceiving more than it can bear.

Such a rendering covers the law perhaps, and at times I have been forced to leave some of Dante in no better state than that, but certainly it is nothing to be satisfied with. I especially do not like the feel of that last line in English. As nearly as I can say it, the English word choice is being forced from Dante's Italian rather than being developed in sequence by the normal flow of English.

Whereupon, after more floundering I came to rest on:

I could see clearly that their hair was gold,
    but my eyes drew back bedazzled from their faces,
    defeated by more light than they could hold.

It is simple enough to see that there are all sorts of things literally wrong with such a passage. The original says "the head" and the passage says "hair." There is nothing, at least explicitly, in the original that says the eye "drew back." *Virtù* has disappeared, and "defeated" is certainly not the same thing as "confounded."

When the charge is put in those terms, I have no defense and very little, if any, theory on which to base a defense. Nor any hope of arguing that I have achieved a perfect rendering. All I can really argue, as lamely as need be, is that within the essential failure, this final version *feels* enough like the original, and *feels* enough like English poetry (or at least verse) to allow me to conclude that I have probably caught it as well as I shall be able to. There must be some theory of translation implicit in these feelings, but in practice I suspect any translation turns out to be a long series of such individual cases, each met on its own grounds, and that each is finally settled by *feel*. What has any poet to trust more than the *feel* of the thing? Theory concerns him only until he picks up his pen, and it begins to concern him again as soon as he lays it down. But when the pen is in his hand he has to write by itch and twitch, though certainly his itch and twitch are intimately conditioned by all his past itching and twitching, and by all his past theorizing about them.

Dante Alighieri[1] (1265–1321)

DIVINA COMMEDIA

"*Vexilla regis prodeunt inferni*
   verso di noi: però dinanzi mira,"
   disse il maestro mio, "se tu il discerni."

Come quando una grossa nebbia spira,
5   o quando l'emisperio nostro annotta
   par da lungi un molin che il vento gira:

veder mi parve un tal 'dificio allotta;
   poi per lo vento mi ristrinsi retro
   al duca mio, chè non li era altra grotta.

10   Già era, e con paura il metto in metro,
   là dove l'ombre eran tutte coperte,
   e trasparean come festuca in vetro.

Altre sono a giacere, altre stanno erte,
   quella col capo e quella con le pinate;
15   altra, com' arco, il volto a' piedi inverte.

Quando noi fummo fatti tanto avante,
   ch'al mio maestro piacque di mostrarmi
   la creatura ch'ebbe il bel sembiante,

dinanzi mi si tolse, e fe' restarmi,
20   "Ecco Dite," dicendo, "ed ecco il loco,
   ove convien che di fortezza t'armi."

Com'io divenni allor gelato e fioco,
   nol domandar, lettor, ch' io non lo scrivo,
   però ch'ogni parlar sarebbe poco.

---

1. *Alighieri,* (ä lē'gyer'ē).

Dante's DIVINE COMEDY is an allegorical epic describing a journey through Hell, Purgatory, and Heaven. The poem is divided into three parts, or canticles: the Inferno, *the* Purgatorio, *and the* Paradiso.

The protagonist of the poem is Dante himself. Midway through his life he finds himself lost in the Dark Wood of Error. His path out is blocked by three beasts, symbolizing various aspects of worldliness. He is in despair when the spirit of the poet Virgil appears to him. Virgil, symbolizing human reason, has been sent to lead Dante from error. But their way is to be a long and hard one. Together they must first travel through Hell. Hell is a vast pit, divided into levels, or circles, *to which the damned are assigned for punishments appropriate to their crimes. The guilt of the sinners and their sufferings increase as they descend, until finally they arrive at Cocytus, the Ninth Circle, occupied by Satan himself.*

from THE INFERNO: CANTO XXXIV

Translated from the Italian by
John Ciardi

"On march the banners of the King of Hell,"
   my Master said. "Toward us. Look straight ahead:
   can you make him out at the core of the frozen shell?"

Like a whirling windmill seen afar at twilight,
5   or when a mist has risen from the ground—
   just such an engine rose upon my sight

stirring up such a wild and bitter wind
    I cowered for shelter at my Master's back,
    there being no other windbreak I could find.

10 I stood now where the souls of the last class
    (with fear my verses tell it) were covered wholly;
    they shone below the ice like straws in glass.

Some lie stretched out; others are fixed in place
    upright, some on their heads, some on their soles;
15   another, like a bow, bends foot to face.

When we had gone so far across the ice
    that it pleased my Guide to show me the foul creature
    which once had worn the grace of Paradise,

he made me stop, and, stepping aside, he said:
20   "Now see the face of Dis! [2] This is the place
    where you must arm your soul against all dread."

Do not ask, Reader, how my blood ran cold
    and my voice choked up with fear. I cannot write it:
    this is a terror that cannot be told.

25 I did not die, and yet I lost life's breath:
    imagine for yourself what I became,
    deprived at once of both my life and death.

The Emperor of the Universe of Pain
    jutted his upper chest above the ice;
30   and I am closer in size to the great mountain

the Titans make around the central pit,
    than they to his arms. Now, starting from this part,
    imagine the whole that corresponds to it!

If he was once as beautiful as now
35   he is hideous, and still turned on his Maker,
    well may he be the source of every woe!

---

2. *Dis,* Satan.

With what a sense of awe I saw his head
  towering above me! for it had three faces:
  one was in front, and it was fiery red;

40 the other two, as weirdly wonderful,
  merged with it from the middle of each shoulder
  to the point where all converged at the top of the skull;

the right was something between white and bile;
  the left was about the color that one finds
45 on those who live along the banks of the Nile.

Under each head two wings rose terribly,
  their span proportioned to so gross a bird:
  I never saw such sails upon the sea.

They were not feathers—their texture and their form
50 were like a bat's wings—and he beat them so
  that three winds blew from him in one great storm:

it is these winds that freeze all Cocytus.[3]
  He wept from his six eyes, and down three chins
  the tears ran mixed with bloody froth and pus.

55 In every mouth he worked a broken sinner
  between his rake-like teeth. Thus he kept three
  in eternal pain at his eternal dinner.

For the one in front the biting seemed to play
  no part at all compared to the ripping: at times
60 the whole skin of his back was flayed away.

"That soul that suffers most," explained my Guide,
  "is Judas Iscariot, he who kicks his legs
  on the fiery chin and has his head inside.

Of the other two, who have their heads thrust forward,
65 the one who dangles down from the black face
  is Brutus: note how he writhes without a word.

---

3. *Cocytus* (kō sī′təs), one of the rivers of Hell.

And there, with the huge and sinewy arms, is the
    soul
    of Cassius.—But the night is coming on
    and we must go, for we have seen the whole."

70 Then, as he bade, I clasped his neck, and he,
    watching for a moment when the wings
    were opened wide, reached over dexterously

and seized the shaggy coat of the king demon;
    then grappling matted hair and frozen crusts
75 from one tuft to another, clambered down.

When we had reached the joint where the great
    thigh
    merges into the swelling of the haunch,
    my Guide and Master, straining terribly,

turned his head to where his feet had been
80 and began to grip the hair as if he were climbing;
    so that I thought we moved toward Hell again.

"Hold fast!" my Guide said, and his breath came
    shrill
    with labor and exhaustion. "There is no way
    but by such stairs to rise above such evil."

85 At last he climbed out through an opening
    in the central rock, and he seated me on the rim;
    then joined me with a nimble backward spring.

I looked up, thinking to see Lucifer
    as I had left him, and I saw instead
90 his legs projecting high into the air.

Now let all those whose dull minds are still vexed
    by failure to understand what point it was
    I had passed through, judge if I was perplexed.

"Get up. Up on your feet," my Master said.
95   "The sun already mounts to middle tierce,[4]
   and a long road and hard climbing lie ahead."

It was no hall of state we had found there,
   but a natural animal pit hollowed from rock
   with a broken floor and a close and sunless air.

100 "Before I tear myself from the Abyss,"
   I said when I had risen, "O my Master,
   explain to me my error in all this:

where is the ice? and Lucifer—how has he
   been turned from top to bottom: and how can the sun
105   have gone from night to day so suddenly?"

And he to me: "You imagine you are still
   on the other side of the center where I grasped
   the shaggy flank of the Great Worm of Evil

which bores through the world—you *were* while I climbed
      down,
110   but when I turned myself about, you passed
   the point to which all gravities are drawn.

You are under the other hemisphere where you stand;
   the sky above us is the half opposed
   to that which canopies the great dry land.

115 Under the mid point of that other sky
   the Man who was born sinless and who lived
   beyond all blemish, came to suffer and die.

You have your feet upon a little sphere
   which forms the other face of the Judecca.
120   There it is evening when it is morning here.

---

4. *tierce* (tirs), the third of the canonical hours, or nine A.M.

And this gross Fiend and Image of all Evil
　　who made a stairway for us with his hide
　　is pinched and prisoned in the ice-pack still.

On this side he plunged down from heaven's height,
125　　and the land that spread here once hid in the sea
　　and fled North to our hemisphere for fright;

and it may be that moved by that same fear,
　　the one peak [5] that still rises on this side
　　fled upward leaving this great cavern here.

130 Down there, beginning at the further bound
　　of Beelzebub's [6] dim tomb, there is a space
　　not known by sight, but only by the sound

of a little stream descending through the hollow
　　it has eroded from the massive stone
135　　in its endlessly entwining lazy flow."

My Guide and I crossed over and began
　　to mount that little known and lightless road
　　to ascend into the shining world again.

He first, I second, without thought of rest
140　　we climbed the dark until we reached the point
　　where a round opening brought in sight the blest

and beauteous shining of the Heavenly cars.
And we walked out once more beneath the Stars.

---

5. *the one peak,* Purgatory, pictured by Dante as a mountain. **6.** *Beelzebub,* Satan.

from THE INFERNO: CANTO XXXIV

*Translated from the Italian by
Henry Wadsworth Longfellow*

"*Vexilla Regis prodeunt Inferni*
Towards us; therefore look in front of thee,"
   My Master said, "If thou discernest him."
As, when there breathes a heavy fog, or when
5   Our hemisphere is darkening into night,
   Appears far off a mill the wind is turning,
Methought that such a building then I saw;
   And, for the wind, I drew myself behind
   My Guide, because there was no other shelter.
10 Now was I, and with fear in verse I put it,
   There where the shades were wholly covered up,
   And glimmered through like unto straws in glass.
Some prone are lying, others stand erect,
   This with the head, and that one with the soles;
15   Another, bow-like, face to feet inverts.
When in advance so far we had proceeded,
   That it my Master pleased to show to me
   The creature who once had the beauteous semblance,
He from before me moved and made me stop,
20   Saying: "Behold Dis, and behold the place
   Where thou with fortitude must arm thyself."
How frozen I became and powerless then,
   Ask it not, Reader, for I write it not,
   Because all language would be insufficient.
25 I did not die, and I alive remained not;
   Think for thyself now, hast thou aught of wit,
   What I became, being of both deprived.
The Emperor of the kingdom dolorous

From his mid-breast forth issued from the ice;

30   And better with a giant I compare
Than do the giants with those arms of his;
    Consider now how great must be that whole,
    Which unto such a part conforms itself.
Were he as fair once, as he now is foul,

35   And lifted up his brow against his Maker,
    Well may proceed from him all tribulation.
    O, what a marvel it appeared to me,
    When I beheld three faces on his head!
    The one in front, and that vermilion was;

40 Two were the others, that were joined with this
    Above the middle part of either shoulder,
    And they were joined together at the crest;
And the right-hand one seemed 'twixt white and yellow;
    The left was such to look upon as those

45   Who come from where the Nile falls valleyward.
Underneath each came forth two mighty wings,
    Such as befitting were so great a bird;
    Sails of the sea I never saw so large.
No feathers had they, but as of a bat

50   Their fashion was; and he was waving them,
    So that three winds proceeded forth therefrom.
Thereby Cocytus wholly was congealed.
    With six eyes did he weep, and down three chins
    Trickled the tear-drops and the bloody drivel.

55 At every mouth he with his teeth was crunching
    A sinner, in the manner of a brake,
    So that he three of them tormented thus.
To him in front the biting was as naught
    Unto the clawing, for sometimes the spine

60   Utterly stripped of all the skin remained.
"That soul up there which has the greatest pain,"
    The Master said, "is Judas Iscariot;
    With head inside, he plies his legs without.
Of the two others, who head downward are,

65   The one who hangs from the black jowl is Brutus;

See how he writhes himself, and speaks no word.
And the other, who so stalwart seems, is Cassius.
    But night is reascending, and 'tis time
That we depart, for we have seen the whole."
70 As seemed him good, I clasped him round the neck,
    And he the vantage seized of time and place,
    And when the wings were opened wide apart,
He laid fast hold upon the shaggy sides;
    From fell to fell descended downward then
75   Between the thick hair and the frozen crust.
When we were come to where the thigh revolves
    Exactly on the thickness of the haunch,
    The Guide, with labor and with hard-drawn breath,
Turned round his head where he had had his legs,
80   And grappled to the hair, as one who mounts,
    So that to Hell I thought we were returning.
"Keep fast thy hold, for by such stairs as these,"
    The Master said, panting as one fatigued,
    "Must we perforce depart from so much evil."
85 Then through the opening of a rock he issued,
    And down upon the margin seated me;
    Then tow'rds me he outstretched his wary step.
I lifted up mine eyes and thought to see
    Lucifer in the same way I had left him;
90   And I beheld him upward hold his legs.
And if I then became disquieted,
    Let stolid people think who do not see
    What the point is beyond which I had passed.
"Rise up," the Master said, "upon thy feet;
95   The way is long, and difficult the road,
    And now the sun to middle-tierce returns."
It was not any palace corridor
    There where we were, but dungeon natural,
    With floor uneven and unease of light.
100 "Ere from the abyss I tear myself away,
    My Master," said I when I had arisen,
    "To draw me from an error speak a little;

Where is the ice? and how is this one fixed
Thus upside down? and how in such short time
105 From eve to morn has the sun made his transit?"
And he to me: "Thou still imaginest
Thou art beyond the centre, where I grasped
The hair of the fell worm, who mines the world.
That side thou wast, so long as I descended;
110 When round I turned me, thou didst pass the point
To which things heavy draw from every side,
And now beneath the hemisphere, art come
Opposite that which overhangs the vast
Dry-land, and 'neath whose cope was put to death
115 The Man who without sin was born and lived.
Thou hast thy feet upon the little sphere
Which makes the other face of the Judecca.
Here it is morn when it is evening there;
And he who with his hair a stairway made us
120 Still fixed remaineth as he was before.
Upon this side he fell down out of heaven;
And all the land, that whilom here emerged,
For fear of him made of the sea a veil,
And came to our hemisphere; and peradventure
125 To flee from him, what on this side appears
Left the place vacant here, and back recoiled."
A place there is below, from Beelzebub
As far receding as the tomb extends,
Which not by sight is known, but by the sound
130 Of a small rivulet, that there descendeth
Through chasm within the stone, which it has gnawed
With course that winds about and slightly falls.
The Guide and I into that hidden road
Now entered, to return to the bright world;
135 And without care of having any rest
We mounted up, he first and I the second,
Till I beheld through a round aperture
Some of those beauteous things which Heaven doth bear;
Thence we came forth to rebehold the stars.

Vittorio Alfieri [1] (1749–1803)

THE FREE MAN

Translated from the Italian by
A. Michael de Luca

A man of sentiment, of courage, born free;
    He reveals himself at once by unmistakable signs.
    He boldly tilts, now against corruption, then against
        tyrants;
    His countenance is bare, but the rest of him is armed.
5 Though imbued with lofty messages, disdainfully fearless,
    He cloisters himself within his own silence.
    The infamy of others brings a flush to his cheek;
    Nor does he ever seek the company of despots.
He may sometimes yield, but he will not serve the corrupt
        times.
10   He is hated and feared by rulers
    And no less by slavish and ignoble souls.
Conscious of his own purpose, such a man does not deign
    To manifest the wrath that righteously seethes within
        him;
    His bearing alone is a lesson against servitude.

"The Free Man" by Vittorio Alfieri, translated by A. Michael de Luca from SELECTIONS FROM ITALIAN POETRY by A. Michael de Luca and William Giuliano. Copyright © 1966 by Harvey House, Inc. Reprinted by permission of Evelyn Singer Agency.

1. *Alfieri* (äl fye′ rē).

Corrado Alvaro (1895–1955)

THE RUBY

THE DAILY PAPERS had recorded one of those news items that
keep a town in a buzz of excitement for a whole day and finally
make a circuit of the world. A ruby as big as a hazelnut, a
famous stone, bearing a famous name, and said to be of enormous value, had disappeared. An Indian prince, on a visit to a
North American city, had been wearing this jewel as an orna-
ment. He had suddenly become aware of his loss after a journey
he had made in a taxi that had set him down—incognito—at a
hotel in the suburbs, for he had managed to evade the attention
of both his private bodyguard and the police. The flying squad
was mobilized, the entire city awoke the following morning to a
knowledge of the loss, and right up to midday hundreds of
people cherished the hope of finding the celebrated stone in their
own street. One of those waves of optimism and excitement had
fallen on the town; the kind of feeling you get when the opulence
of one individual enriches everybody else's hopes. The prince
had not been very forthcoming in his statement to the police, but
it ruled out any possibility that the lady accompanying him could
have been responsible for the loss. They were not, therefore, to
try and locate her. The taxi driver came forward to testify that

"The Ruby" by Corrado Alvaro from MODERN ITALIAN SHORT
STORIES edited by W. J. Strachan. Published by Eyre & Spottiswoode.
Reprinted by permission of Associated Book Publishers (International)
Ltd. and Aldo Garzanti Editore S.A.S.

he had driven the Indian wearing his precious turban, and stated that he had deposited him and the lady in front of a hotel in the suburbs. The lady was a European, and the only thing that distinguished her was a magnificent diamond, the size of a pea, which she wore in her left nostril after the manner of certain wealthy Indians. This detail distracted the attention of the public for a while from the missing ruby and whetted their curiosity still more. The driver, after making a thorough search of the interior of the vehicle, checked up on the "fares" he had driven during the early hours of the morning in question; they had been a business man, a foreigner whom he had taken down to the port and who was evidently sailing for Europe, and a woman. The foreigner, recognizable as an Italian, had emerged from one of the houses where emigrants lived in a colony; he had been wearing a pair of trousers of generous width such as are popular with emigrants, rough, thick-soled shoes of a type nowadays seen only among people of that social class, and a hard hat set above a thin, clean-shaven face, seamed with wrinkles. His luggage consisted of a heavy suitcase secured with stout cord and one other weighty box which appeared to be made of steel. He had embarked that same day, but any suspicion that might have alighted on him was immediately dispelled when it was realized that he had behaved as though he was riding in a taxi for the first time in his life. He had not managed to close the door properly and had hugged the front window all the time, possibly so as to avoid being suddenly jerked backward into the road, and he had gazed at the streets with the air of one who is leaving a town perhaps forever. The driver reserved his attention rather for the man who, on leaving the suburban hotel, had taken the taxi immediately after the prince and had given orders to be driven to the Italian workmen's quarter, at which point his place had been taken by the foreigner. The fare in question, of whom he had given a description and who must have been a local resident, was searched for in vain. Furthermore the fact that he had failed to answer the appeal published in the newspapers, offering a large reward, was a logical proof that it was not he who had got hold of the famous gem. However, since the missing stone was world-famed and easily recognizable, it was hoped that one day or other it would come to light.

The emigrant, meantime, was on his way home to a country town in Southern Italy after five years' absence and was ignorant of all this stir. He had with him the most unusual collections of odds and ends—even for an emigrant. A suitcase, made of artificial leather which he thought was real, contained his blue overalls, pressed and cleaned, twelve fountain pens which he intended to sell to the people of the district, forgetting that most of them were herdsmen and not more than half a dozen of the inhabitants could put pen to paper. In addition, he had some crested table services, a pair of hair clippers which he had used on his fellow workers, a metal object whose function completely mystified him—it had the form of a pistol, but did not fire— twelve squares of American cloth and some novelties to impress and amuse his wife, son and friends. The heavy part of his luggage was the somewhat battered steel strongbox; the lock was operated by a combination, the six-letter name, *Annina*. By way of ready cash he took a thousand dollars, which included three hundred to be paid back later to those from whom he had borrowed it for the voyage. In his waistcoat pocket he carried a lump of red crystal; it was many-faceted and as large as a walnut. He had come across it by chance in the taxi that had taken him down to the harbor, but he had no idea what it was for. His fingers had felt it behind the seat cushions. He kept it as a lucky charm for the future; perhaps he would have it attached to his watch chain as a pendant. It seemed odd that it had no hole bored through it. It could not, therefore, be one of those large stones which city ladies have on their necklaces.

The various objects one picks up just before leaving a foreign country are apt to acquire an extraordinary souvenir value, giving one, as it were, a foretaste of distance and nostalgia. It was just such an affection that our emigrant felt for this lump of crystal, so cool to the touch, as translucent and clear as sugar candy.

He had established a small trade with all these different acquisitions. The strongbox, now fixed against the wall, the counter for his transactions, fountain pens in a box, crested table services, squares of American cloth on which were depicted the Statue of Liberty and angels in the corners bearing the portraits of the founders of American Independence, each square embroidered with white and blue stars—five long years he had patiently built up his collection against his eventual return; selecting whatever would seem most of a novelty to the folk in a region like his own, though he might have taken his choice from the shabby second hand goods that come from heaven knows where and go the rounds among the emigrant population.

So he who had started life as a day laborer had now become a dealer in various wares. It had been the strongbox that had set him on that train of thought; he had taken to shopkeeping for no other reason. He had felt almost rich because all the money he had in his pockets was in foreign currency and would turn into a larger number of coins when he exchanged them. Mental calculations connected with this engrossed him at all sorts of odd moments. He felt a childish delight every time he fingered the red crystal in his pocket. He began to regard it as a kind of talisman. It became one of those useless objects we cherish all our lives and never have the strength of mind to get rid of, so that in the end they become part of ourselves and even family heirlooms. Whereas important things that we watch over or hide away disappear, objects of the kind referred to never get lost, and our minds hark back to them at intervals. A few days later, for example, the crystal reminded our emigrant of the day when he had embarked for home, the interior of the taxi, the streets which seemed to roll slowly up like a piece of drop scenery at the end of a play and become distant memories.

He set up his shop in the upper part of the country town inhabited by peasants and herdsmen. A fortnight after his arrival he had furnished the ground floor of a peasant's cottage with a long counter and shelves, where the blue packets of flour paste and the blue muslin for housewives found a place, and on one side of the shop stood a cask of wine on a couple of trestles, and an earthenware jar of oil. The strongbox had been fixed against the wall, and he felt a great sense of pride when he opened it in the presence of his customers. In it reposed his account ledger and the notebook containing a list of all the goods sold on tick that were to be paid for at harvest time or after the animal fairs. Gradually his business got to look like any other business; it acquired its own peculiar smell, there were chalkmarks made on the wall by his wife—who could not write—recording goods supplied on credit. His young son, however, who attended school, and was now beginning to be able to write customers' names in the register, sometimes took a turn in the shop and managed it quite expertly on hot afternoons when all trade had ceased except that in iced drinks for gentlemen recovering from their afternoon siesta.

Slowly, his wife's narrow, American-style slippers acquired more and more creases and she herself the complacent, meticulous air of a shopkeeper's wife. The supply of new material which her husband had brought home had finally ended up among the shop-soiled goods, and only the hard hat, looking almost new, was still left in the wardrobe. The squares of American cloth had been distributed as presents among the important customers; as for the fountain pens, no one had wanted them. Someone had handled them roughly and the fragments still lay in the box. The shopkeeper, who was a boy at heart, often imagined that the pen nibs were of pure gold and he cherished them as a small boy cherishes tinfoil-wrapping off chocolates. He also hung on to an old newspaper printed in English. He had refused to part with it even when he was short of wrapping paper. Sometimes he would scrutinize it carefully and the advertisement illustrations would recall to him the people who smoked gold-tipped cigarettes, the street boys, the gramophones, in fact all the life he had seen in the central parts of the city on the rare occasions of his visits there. As for the lump of crystal, he remembered it one day and gave it to his son who was celebrating his birthday with his friends. At that time, boys played a game which consisted in knocking down and conquering castles made of hazelnuts by throwing a heavier one at it; the usual procedure was to select a larger nut, make a small hole in it, patiently scrape out the kernel, then fill it with small lead pellets. The crystal missile was just the thing, it was heavy enough to carry to the mark. Another of the boys used a glass marble of the kind extracted from lemonade bottles,[1] which had the advantage of being round. The shopkeeper's son claimed that his was more beautiful because it came from America and because it was red. He cherished it in the way that boys do who never lose objects of that kind. As his father contemplated this curiosity which had become his child's plaything, his mind would often dwell on the illusions he had once entertained in the days when he traveled about the world, and the world seemed to be filled with valuable things that had been lost which the lucky ones found. That was why he had always felt with his fingers under mattresses of berths on steamers, behind leather cushions on buses and coaches, according to where he happened to be. But he had never found anything. Yes; there had been one occasion. He had found five dollars in the street. It had been raining that day, he remembered.   ✤

---

1. *a glass marble . . . lemonade bottles.* Beverage bottles were formerly stoppered with glass marbles.

Giambattista Basile[1] (1575–1632)

THE CAT CINDERELLA

Translated from the Italian by
Benedetto Croce

IN THE SEA OF MALICE, envy always exchanges ruptures for
bladders, and when she hopes to see others drowned, finds herself under water or dashed to pieces against a rock. This happened to certain envious girls whose story I intend to tell you.

There was once, therefore, a Prince who was a widower, and
he had a daughter so dear to him that he saw with no other eyes
but hers. He gave her an excellent teacher of sewing, who taught
her chain work, openwork, fringes and hems and showed her
more love than was possible to describe. The father, however,
shortly remarried, and his wife was an evil, malicious, bad-
tempered woman who began at once to hate her stepdaughter
and threw sour looks, wry faces and scowling glances on her
enough to make her jump with fright.

From the book THE PENTAMERONE OF GIAMBATTISTA BASILE
edited by N. M. Penzer. Translated by Benedetto Croce. Published 1933 by
E. P. Dutton & Co., Inc. Reprinted with permission of E. P. Dutton & Co.,
Inc. and The Bodley Head.

1. *Basile* (bä zē′ le).

The poor child was always complaining to her governess of her stepmother's ill-treatment, finishing up with "O would to God that you could be my little mother, who are so kind and loving to me," and she so often repeated this song to her that she put a wasp in her ear and, at last, tempted by the devil, her teacher ended by saying, "If you must follow this madcap idea, I will be a mother to you and you shall be the apple of my eye." She was going on with the prologue, when Zezolla (as the girl was called) interrupted her by saying, "Forgive my taking the words out of your mouth. I know you love me well, mum's the word, and *sufficit*[2]; teach me the way, for I am new; you write and I will sign." "Well, then," answered her governess, "listen carefully; keep your ears open and you shall always enjoy the whitest bread from the finest flour. When your father leaves the house, tell your stepmother that you would like one of those old dresses that are kept in the big chest in the closet, to save the one you now have on. As she always wants to see you in rags and tatters, she will open the chest and say, 'Hold the lid.' You must hold it while she is rummaging inside and then suddenly let it fall so that it breaks her neck. After that, you know well that your father would even coin false money to please you, so when he fondles you, beg him to take me for his wife, and then you shall be happy and the mistress even of my life."

When Zezolla had heard the plan, every hour seemed a thousand years until she had carried out her governess's advice in every particular. When the period of mourning for her step-mother was over, she began to sound her father about marrying her governess. At first the Prince took it as a joke, but Zezolla so often struck with the flat that at last she thrust with the point, and he gave away to the persuasive words of his daughter. He therefore married Carmosina, the governess, with great celebrations.

Now, while this couple were enjoying themselves, Zezolla was standing at a balcony of her house, when a dove flew on to the wall and said to her, "If ever you desire anything, send to ask for

---

2. *sufficit*, enough. [*Latin*]

it from the dove of the fairies of the Island of Sardinia, and you will at once have it."

For five or six days the new stepmother lavished every sort of caress on Zezolla, making her take the best seat at table, giving her the best tidbits, and dressing her in the finest clothes. But after a little time the service that Zezolla had done her was forgotten, and banished from her memory (how sorry is the mind that has an evil mistress!) and she began to push forward six daughters of her own that she had kept in hiding till then, and so worked on her husband that they won his good graces and he let his own daughter slip out of his heart. So that, a loser today and a pauper tomorrow, Zezolla was finally brought to such a pass that she fell from the *salon* to the kitchen, from the canopy to the grate, from splendid silks and gold to dishclouts, from scepters to spits; not only did she change her state, but also her name, and was no longer called Zezolla, but "Cat Cinderella."

Now it happened that the Prince was forced to go to Sardinia on important affairs of State, and before he left he asked one by one of his six stepdaughters, Imperia, Colomba, Fiorella, Diamante, Colombina, and Pascarella, what they wanted him to bring back for them on his return. One asked for a splendid gown, another for a headdress, one for cosmetics for the face, and another games to pass the time; one one thing and one another. At last, and almost to make fun of her, he asked his daughter, "And you! what would you like?" and she answered, "Nothing, except commend me to the dove of the fairies and beg them to send me something; and if you forget, may it be impossible for you to go forward or back. Bear in mind what I say: thy intent, thy reward."

The Prince went away, transacted his affairs in Sardinia, and bought the things his stepdaughters had asked for, but Zezolla went quite out of his mind. But when they were embarked with the sails ready unfurled, it was found impossible to make the vessel leave the harbor: it seemed as if it were detained by a sea lamprey. The captain of the ship, who was almost in despair, dropped off to sleep with weariness and in his dreams a fairy appeared to him who said, "Do you know why you cannot leave the harbor? Because the Prince who is with you has broken his promise to his daughter, remembering all the others except his own flesh and blood." As soon as he woke up the captain told his dream to the Prince, who was overcome with confusion at his omission. He went to the grotto of the fairies, and commending his daughter to them, begged that they should send her some gift.

Behold, out of the grotto there came a young girl, beautiful as a gonfalon,[3] who bade him thank his daughter for her kind remembrances and tell her to be of good cheer for love of her. With these words, she gave him a date tree, a spade and a golden can with a silken napkin; the date tree for planting and the other articles to keep and cultivate it.

The Prince, surprised at this present, took leave of the fairy and turned toward his own land. When he arrived, he gave his stepdaughters the things they had asked for, and lastly he handed the fairy's present to his own daughter. Zezolla nearly jumped out of her skin with joy and planted the date tree in a fine pot, watering it every day and then drying it with the silken napkin.

As a result of these attentions, within four days the date tree grew to the size of a woman, and a fairy came out who said to the girl, "What do you want?" Zezolla answered that she would like sometimes to leave the house without the sisters knowing it. The fairy replied, "Whenever you want this, come to the plant and say:

> O my golden date tree,
> With golden spade I've dug thee,
> With golden can I've watered thee,
> With silken napkin dried thee,
> Strip thyself and robe thou me,

Then when you want to undress, change the last line and say: Strip thou me and robe thou thee."

One day it happened to be a feast day, and the governess's daughters went out of the house in a procession all fluttering,

---

3. *gonfalon,* a heraldic flag or ensign.

bedaubed and painted, all ribbons, bells and gewgaws, all flowers and perfumes, roses and posies. Zezolla then ran to the plant and uttered the words the fairy had taught her, and at once she was decked out like a queen, seated on a white horse with twelve smartly attired pages. She too went where the sisters had gone, and though they did not recognize her, they felt their mouths water at the beauty of this lovely dove.

As luck would have it, the King came to this same place and was quite bewitched by the extraordinary loveliness of Zezolla. He ordered his most trusty attendant to find out about this fair creature, who she was and where she lived. The servant at once began to dog her footsteps, but she, noticing the trap, threw down a handful of crowns that she had obtained for that purpose from the date tree. The servant, fired by the desire for these glittering pieces, forgot to follow the palfrey and stopped to pick up the money, whilst she, at a bound, reached the house and quickly undressed in the way the fairy had told her. Those six harpies, her sisters, soon returned, and to vex and mortify her, described at length all the fine things that they had seen at the feast.

The servant in the meantime had returned to the King and had told him about the crowns, whereupon the King was furious, and angrily told him that he had sold his pleasure for a few paltry coins and that at the next feast he was at all costs to discover who this lovely girl was and where nested so fair a bird.

When the next feast day came, the sisters went out, all bedecked and bedizened, leaving the despised Zezolla by the hearth. But she at once ran to the date tree and uttered the same words as before, and behold a band of maidens came out, one with the mirror and one with the flask of pumpkin water, one with the curling tongs and another with the rouge, one with the comb and another with the pins, one with the dresses and one with the necklace and earrings. They all placed themselves round her and made her as beautiful as a sun and then mounted her in a coach with six horses accompanied by footmen and pages in livery. She drove to the same place as before and kindled envy in the hearts of the sisters and flames in the breast of the King.

This time too, when she went away, the servant followed her, but so that he should not catch her up, she threw down a handful of pearls and jewels, which this trusty fellow was unable to resist pecking at, since they were not things to let slip. In this way Zezolla had time to reach home and undress herself as usual. The servant, quite stunned, went back to the King, who said, "By the soul of your departed, if you don't find that girl again, I'll give you a most thorough beating and as many kicks on your seat as you have hairs in your beard."

On the next feast day, when the sisters had already started off, Zezolla went up to the date tree. She repeated the magic spell and was again magnificently dressed and placed in a golden coach with so many attendants around it that it looked as if she were a courtesan arrested in the public promenade and surrounded by police agents. After having excited the envy and wonder of her sisters, she left, followed by the King's servant, who this time fastened himself to the carriage by double thread. Zezolla, seeing that he was always at her side, cried, "Drive on," and the coach set off at such a gallop that in her agitation she let slip from her foot the richest and prettiest patten you could imagine.

The servant, not being able to catch up the carriage, which was now flying along, picked up the patten and carried it to the King, telling him what had happened. The King took it in his hands and broke out into these words: "If the foundation is so fair, what must be the mansion? Oh, lovely candlestick which holds the candle that consumes me! Oh, tripod of the lovely cauldron in which my life is boiling! Oh, beauteous corks attached to the fishing line of Love with which he has caught this soul! Behold, I embrace and enfold you, and if I cannot reach the plant, I worship the roots; if I cannot possess the capitals, I kiss the base: you first imprisoned a white foot, now you have ensnared a stricken heart. Through you, she who sways my life was taller by a span and a half; through you, my life grows by that much in sweetness so long as I keep you in my possession."

The King having said this called a secretary and ordered out the trumpeters and tantarara, and had it proclaimed that all the women in the land were to come to a festival and banquet which he had determined to give. On the appointed day, my goodness, what an eating and feasting there was! Where did all the tarts and cakes come from? Where all the stews and rissoles? all the macaroni and graviuoli which were enough to stuff an entire army? The women were all there, of every kind and quality, of high degree and low degree, the rich and the poor, old and young, the well-favored and the ill-favored. When they had all thoroughly worked their jaws, the King spoke the proficiat and started to try the patten on his guests, one by one, to see whom it fitted to a hair, so that he could find by the shape of the slipper the one whom he was seeking. But he could find no foot to fit it, so that he was on the point of despair.

Nevertheless, he ordered a general silence and said, "Come back tomorrow to feast with me, but as you love me well, do not leave behind a single woman, whoever she may be!" The Prince then said, "I have a daughter, but she always stays to mind the hearth, for she is a sorry, worthless creature, not fit to take her place at the table where you eat." The King answered, "Let her be at the top of the list, for such is my wish."

So they all went away, and came back the next day, and Zezolla came with Carmosina's daughters. As soon as the King saw her, he thought she was the one he wanted, but he hid his thoughts. After the banquet came the trial of the patten. The moment it came near Zezolla's foot, it darted forward of itself to shoe that painted Lover's egg, as the iron flies to the magnet. The King then took Zezolla in his arms and led her to the canopy, where he put a crown on her head and ordered everyone to make obeisance to her as to their queen. The sisters, livid with envy and unable to bear the torment of their breaking hearts, crept quietly home to their mother, confessing in spite of themselves that:

He is mad who would oppose the stars. ✤

Ugo Betti (1892-1953)

CORRUPTION IN

THE PALACE OF JUSTICE

PEOPLE IN THE PLAY

VANAN: President of the Court
ELENA: his daughter
ERZI: Investigating Councillor
CROZ: Chief Justice
CUST: a judge
BATA: a judge
MAVERI: a judge
PERSIUS: a judge
MALGAI: a record clerk
A NURSE
And a number of officials, porters, bystanders.

The time is the present.

The action takes place in a foreign city. The scene is the same throughout: a large severe room in the Palace of Justice.

The room is empty. MALGAI, *the record clerk, enters, pushing a wheeled basket. He goes round the tables, which are piled high with documents; some of these he selects and throws into the basket, after checking their dates against certain papers in his hand. He hums to himself.*

(A STRANGER *appears in the doorway.)*

STRANGER. I wonder if you could tell me where I can find Chief Justice Croz's office?

MALGAI. Will you ask the porter, sir? There's a porter for that purpose.

STRANGER. I'm sorry but I haven't been able to find any porters.

MALGAI. Well, you can't expect them to be here before they have to clock in, can you? Oh, it's no good looking at me; I'm one of the old brigade. What do you want to see Chief Justice Croz for?

STRANGER. I have to speak to him.

MALGAI. Well, that would be fine, sir, only unfortunately poor Mr. Croz is dying. Has been for months. He doesn't come to the office any more. It has to be something very special to bring Mr. Croz here, and even then they almost have to carry him.

STRANGER. All the same I think he will come this morning.

MALGAI *(glancing at him).* Ah. *(Cautiously.)* Is there a judges' meeting perhaps?

STRANGER. I fancy we shall see them all here.

MALGAI. Ah. *(His tone has changed slightly.)* Well . . . If you want to get to Chief Justice Croz's office, you go down the corridor to the end, then to the right, then to the right again. . . . But if you don't mind my saying so, I think you'd do best to wait for him in here.

STRANGER. In here?

MALGAI. Yes, you'll hear his cane. You can always hear him when he comes up the corridor: he has to use a cane nowadays. If there *is* a sitting, they'll all have to come in here: this is the council chamber for the division. *(He points to a seat near the door.)* You can sit down if you wish.

STRANGER. Thank you. *(He sits.)*

MALGAI *(throwing another glance at the visitor, as he goes on with his work).* A huge building, this, isn't it? The place is just one great maze. We even get tourists in looking at it. In admiration. *(He drops his voice slightly.)* At the moment, unfortunately, the smell about the place isn't quite as sweet as it might be. I suppose it must be a dead rat or something, under one of the floorboards. What do you think about it all, sir? I don't know if you saw last night's papers?

STRANGER. Yes.

MALGAI. Well, it's no business of mine, of course, but I think there's something of a storm blowing up. There's thunder in the air.

STRANGER. Are you one of the clerks?

MALGAI. No, sir. I'm what you might call the gravedigger. This *(He smacks the side of the trolley.)* is the hearse; and these *(He waves the papers in his hand.)* are the death certificates; and these *(He taps the bundles of documents.)* are the bodies.

STRANGER. And the graveyard?

MALGAI *(pointing to a door).* Through there. The Archives. A quiet, shady little spot; I take all this stuff in there and see it gets decent burial.

STRANGER. Are you one of the record clerks?

MALGAI. The undertaker I always call myself. When I think of all the sweat, and all the money and tears, that have gone into even the silliest little bundle of these things here! Well, well . . . *(He drops a bundle into the trolley, and takes up another one.)* I stick a great big number on them, and register them in a great big book, so that people can pretend to believe they'll go on being important *per secula et seculorum,*[1] and they can always take the thing up again . . .

STRANGER. While actually the only things really concerned about your graveyard are the mice and the grubs?

MALGAI. No, it's not the mice and the grubs, sir. It's the interested parties themselves: they get bored after a time, and turn their

---

1. *per secula et seculorum,* forever. [*Latin*]

minds to other things. It's surprising how easily people *do* get bored and turn to other things.

(A newcomer has entered, looking very worried. MALGAI *turns to him solicitously.)*

MALGAI. Oh, good morning, Judge Bata.

BATA *(as he enters).* Good morning, my dear fellow, good morning. *(Taking him aside, and whispering.)* Have you heard?

MALGAI *(anxiously).* What?

BATA. You didn't come past the secretary's office this morning?

MALGAI. No, I never go round that way.

BATA *(cautiously).* I came past the door a few moments ago; there's an official posted outside it: rather important-looking.

MALGAI. An official?

BATA. Yes, a sort of policeman. He politely told us we couldn't go in.

MALGAI. Not even the judges?

BATA. He was stopping everyone.

MALGAI. What . . . what for?

BATA. Well, I was wondering if *you* . . .

MALGAI. No, sir, I haven't the foggiest.

BATA. You've no idea . . . what it's all about . . . ?

MALGAI. Good gracious, no! They'd never tell *me.* I expect it's just some new piece of nonsense they've—.

BATA *(trying to pooh-pooh the matter).* Oh yes, yes, of course it is, but I do think they might have mentioned it to the magistrates.

MALGAI. Of course, sir! Naturally. I hear there's a special meeting of the division today.

BATA. Yes, it's all very odd. It's taken us all by surprise rather. *(The other judges are entering:* PERSIUS, MAVERI, *and, shortly after,* CUST.*)*

PERSIUS *(as he approaches).* Well, what is it all about?

BATA *(pointing to the archivist, who backs respectfully away).* **He** doesn't seem to know either.

MAVERI *(cautiously).* I think it's just a mistake; some order must have been misunderstood.

PERSIUS *(unconvinced).* Yes, quite. A mistake.

MAVERI. A misunderstanding. *(A brief silence.)*

BATA *(to* PERSIUS, *suddenly)*. My dear Persius, you yourself can bear me out, can't you? I've been saying it for months; there are a lot of things need clearing up in here, we need more light and air in the place. The air in these courts is becoming too thick to breathe. I've said that again and again, haven't I? Haven't I?

PERSIUS. My dear fellow, you don't think you're the only one, do you?

MAVERI. Lots of people have been saying so.

CUST. We've said so, too: all of us.

MAVERI. A man with a clear conscience has nothing to fear from the light; nothing at all.

BATA. It's important to realize of course that it may have all just blown up out of nothing. People thrive on scandal. The law courts are always a hive of discontented murmuring. Someone starts spreading scandal about the place, someone else joins in, and by the next day there are ten or twenty of them, buzz-buzz-buzzing their heads off. It's like gangrene spreading.

MAVERI. And the newspapers too: you can't trust any of them.

PERSIUS. And the politicians: party intrigues the whole time. I can't help feeling the whole thing is a deliberate plot.

BATA. But it's the city itself, more than anything, surely? This filthy, diseased city. I never thought people could be so evil, so nasty.

PERSIUS. Yes, just listen to them talking: there isn't a word of truth in anything they say.

MAVERI. Not to mention the women.

BATA. Yes, the place is just a dungheap. The odd thing is to find them screaming with indignation because right in the middle of their own stink there should be a building where the atmosphere isn't (shall I say?) quite as fragrant as it might be. In fact, the magistrates' crime . . . is simply that they're a little too like the man in the street.

PERSIUS *(acidly)*. My dear friend and colleague, I never think one ought to generalize too readily. I don't think I personally bear the remotest resemblance to a dungheap.

BATA. Neither do I; the very idea.

PERSIUS. As far as I personally am concerned, I'm in the fortunate position of being able to say that I've never even *met* this man called Ludvi-Pol, never. I've never even seen him.

BATA. You sound rather as if your colleagues were less fortunate —what? As if some of us were in danger of being compromised in some way.

PERSIUS *(diplomatically)*. *Did* I say that? Nonsense. I always aim at saying precisely what I mean. And if any of our colleagues *have* been off their feed lately, and *have* been having bad nights, well, I'm not one of them, that's all. There are times when every man has to look out for himself. This is one of them. Don't *you* think so, Cust?

BATA *(spitefully)*. We all know that, my dear friend, we all know that. Some of our colleagues seem to have been very busy pulling strings and turning wheels these last few weeks. There seems to have been a good deal of angry fist-shaking about the place.

PERSIUS *(sarcastically)*. Maybe, but the impression I have is that a lot of people in danger are trying to cling to one another as hard as they can. One notices that certain of one's colleagues have become very friendly all of a sudden. They keep trying to get into conversation with one the whole time. You find them waiting behind for you, so that you can leave the place together. They are all clutching at each other. Unfortunately, I'm always in a hurry. I'm always going in a different direction. I never know anything. I'm made of stone, dear friend. Oh, incidentally, Cust, I wanted to ask you something . . . *(Rather ostentatiously, he draws* CUST *apart.)*

BATA *(to* MAVERI*)*. Did you hear that? In any case, I don't quite see why it's suddenly become so very important whether people have or haven't known Ludvi-Pol. It rather looks—it rather *looks* now as if Ludvi-Pol had been put out of business. Though up to yesterday . . .

MAVERI. He was better respected than a cabinet minister!

BATA. One knows of course that these men are just like spiders; what keeps them going is precisely the web of relationships they so skilfully spin all round them. It stands to reason that a lot of people come into contact with them. It may be perfectly true that our dear friend Persius there has never met Ludvi-Pol; he still may have met one of his agents. *(He drops his voice.)* And considering what went on just before Persius was last promoted, he'd better not try being too self-righteous.

MAVERI *(dropping his voice).* Persius feels he's in a strong position.

BATA. Oh, does he? Why?

MAVERI. Important contacts.

BATA. Very likely; he's a born toady.

MAVERI. And now he's trying to suck up to Cust; as one might expect.

BATA. Oh. Why?

MAVERI. Cust! Our rising star.

BATA. Cust?

MAVERI. Cust. A very able man; and not overburdened with scruples, I imagine.

BATA. But what about the great Vanan?

MAVERI. Done for. A corpse.

BATA. Are you sure? Oh dear, it's very difficult trying to steer one's way, isn't it? One person's up and another's down, the whole time. You can never be sure what's going on. *(Looking thoughtfully at* CUST.*)* I've always been on very good terms with Cust, myself, of course.

MAVERI. Really? I thought he seemed rather offhand with you, just now.

BATA *(disturbed).* Cust? With me?

MAVERI. I expect it's only his way.

BATA. I've always said that he was really one of the best people in this place . . . *(Seeing that* MAVERI *is also about to join* CUST *and* PERSIUS.*)* Look, my dear Maveri, there's something I've been wanting to say to you for a long time. You *are* related to President Tomisco, aren't you?

MAVERI *(warily).* Well, it's a . . . very *distant* relationship. Why?

BATA *(beaming sunnily).* I was with President Tomisco for a time, you know, just when I was starting my career. A most admirable person. Influential. I'd so much like to meet him again sometime. Perhaps you'll be so good as to give him my kind regards, when next you . . .

MAVERI (*evasively*). I hardly ever see him, you know, hardly ever.

BATA (*amiably*). Dear colleague, please don't think that I'm trying to steal a march on you; please don't think that. On the contrary. If there's any way in which *I* can help *you*. . . . I have the greatest admiration for you, as you know.

MAVERI. So have I. For you, I mean.

BATA. Thank you. Sometimes . . . if two people are willing to stick together, they can . . . well, back each other up, stand by each other, as it were. It would be dreadful to have enemies at a time like this!

MAVERI (*cautiously*). Dreadful! But I hope . . .

BATA. One never knows, dear colleague. One can sometimes be betrayed by the very last person one expects it from. Well, of course, it's not for me to say.

MAVERI. What do you mean . . . ?

BATA. Well, you know how it is: one's colleagues . . . sometimes talk rather inconsiderately; I don't say they mean any harm, but . . .

MAVERI. Have you . . . heard anyone say anything about me?

BATA. Oh no, no. But the other night . . . Oh, it was just nonsense of course. But old Hill was in here, you know . . . (*He breaks off, and listens.*) Croz is coming.

(*A cane is heard in the corridor. This sound produces a rapid change in everyone present. The groups break up. Expressions change.* CROZ *enters, leaning heavily on one side on his cane, and on the other on a manservant. His appearance reveals extreme physical prostration and at the same time a malignant energy: a quiver of the head gives him the appearance of continuously approving or disapproving of something. He advances half way across the room; here he halts for a few moments in order to draw breath, his eyes closed. He turns to the manservant without looking at him.*)

CROZ. Come back and fetch me later. That is, unless I die in the meantime. *(The manservant bows slightly and goes out.* CROZ *takes a few more steps forward.)* Is the great Vanan here yet?

BATA. No.

CROZ. Do any of you know if the old fool intends to come?

BATA. I don't really see why we should know any more than you do. With the wind blowing the way it is, I should think it's pretty unlikely.

CROZ. In that case, since the President is absent, it is my duty, as senior judge of the division, to deputize for him. *(Half-turning to* MALGAI.*)* You: get out. What are you doing here?

MALGAI. I'm just going, sir. *(He points to the* STRANGER, *who has just risen.)* I only wanted to tell your worship that there was a gentleman here waiting to see you. *(He goes out.)*

CROZ *(turning to observe the newcomer).* You wanted . . . to speak to me?

STRANGER. Yes, Justice Croz. I have a private communication for you.

CROZ *(to the other judges).* He said private.

(The other judges, half-curious, half-worried, withdraw to the other half of the room. CROZ *walks a few steps towards the back. The* STRANGER *follows, speaking to him in a very low voice.* CROZ *listens, asking questions from time to time: finally he leads the* STRANGER *with great deference to an imposing armchair; then he once more approaches his colleagues.)*

Dear colleagues. *(He pauses and thinks.)* I have to tell you . . . *(Breaking off.)* Damn it, Persius, you *have* gone green in the face! You look scared to death.

PERSIUS. You can spare me your little jests, Croz. You'd do much better to think about yourself.

CROZ. You mean if anyone ought to be scared to death, it's me, eh? But, my dear Persius, I'm already dying in any case, am I not? *Moribundus.* So obviously—

PERSIUS. *Moribundus,* yes, you've been *moribundus* for a long time. It's an old trick, Croz; we're used to it, by now.

CROZ *(grinning).* Oh, such unkindness! Come, come. Well, dear colleagues, it appears that the Minister and the Lord High President are both very disturbed, very upset, poor dear things.

Because of the lawcourts. The city is full of gossip. *(Satirically.)* Justice! Justice! *Justitia fondamentum regni.*[2] *(He breaks off, coughing and gasping heavily.)*

BATA. Quite, my dear Croz, quite; the city is full, etc. etc. I don't quite see the point in coming here to tell *us* that; *we* can't shut the mouths of several million scandalmongers. The only thing to do is to wait till they are tired of this subject and have found another. I don't see . . . *(He breaks off, under* CROZ'S *stare.)*

CROZ. You very rarely do see. Anything. The Minister and the High President have issued orders for an inquiry.

(A silence.)

BATA *(faintly).* An inquiry?

CROZ. I think that's what I said. *(Teasing.)* But come, come, bless my soul, we mustn't let it frighten us.

MAVERI. We are not frightened, as a matter of fact.

CROZ. Good, good. It's nothing very serious, just a little something among ourselves. A little look round, that's all, a few inquiries, clear things up . . . That's all.

BATA *(warmly).* And naturally we all agree very heartily. We shall all be very glad to put our modest talents at the public disposal in order to . . . to investigate the matter and find out what's wrong.

(Murmurs of assent.)

CROZ. Perhaps I didn't make myself clear. It is not ourselves who have to do the investigating.

BATA. No?

CROZ. No. Others will be doing the investigating.

BATA. But what about us?

CROZ. Well, we, if I might so put it, are the ones who have to be investigated. Which is slightly different. *(A silence.)*

PERSIUS *(bitterly).* I would like to know why respectable magistrates, after years and years of irreproachable service—I myself have been on the bench for twenty years—I'd like to know why we have to submit to—

CROZ. You are an ass, Persius! What about me? I'm on the eve of

---

2. *Justitia fondamentum regni.* Justice is the foundation of the State. [*Latin*]

promotion. I've set great store by the thought of being buried with a President's cap on my head—always supposing of course that dear old brother Cust doesn't pop in ahead of me— eh, Cust? What do *you* think about all this nonsense? It *would* have to happen just now, of course, and endanger my promotion . . . My dear Persius, we are *all* respectable and irreproachable. I thought I'd made it quite, quite clear: all we have to do is to look into the matter, among ourselves. The magistrate who will carry out the inquiry is a friendly colleague of ours . . . *(He points to the* STRANGER, *who has risen.)* Councillor Erzi, from the Upper House; he himself was saying to me only a moment ago . . .

ERZI *(with great courtesy).* Yes, all we need is a certain amount of discussion, in strict confidence, as between friends. My only reason for coming was to exchange a few preliminary words with you . . . and to shake hands with you all.

BATA *(advancing with hand outstretched).* But of course, of course. My dear Erzi, I am so glad to meet you.

PERSIUS *(following suit, together with the others).* Welcome into our midst!

MAVERI. My dear Erzi! I've heard a good deal about you. Surely we've met before somewhere?

BATA. Yes, you can understand, my dear friend, that we're the first people, the very first, to want to see the whole thing . . .

PERSIUS. . . . floodlit!

BATA. In strict confidence—that was your own expression—would you like to know my own humble opinion?

ERZI. That is what I'm here for.

BATA *(pompously, to the others).* We have to be quite frank about all this. The time for circumlocution is over. My dear Erzi, we're far from trying to pretend that there hasn't been a considerable amount of confusion piling up in these courts.

CUST. It's slackness, more than anything else; people have been a bit too easy-going.

PERSIUS. A bit too casual, too broad-minded perhaps. One can be too broad-minded, you know.

BATA. One might go even further, I think, and admit that there's been a certain lack of moral earnestness, a certain tolerance towards rogues.

CUST. The law courts have become almost a rogues' paradise.

MAVERI. There are certain forms of tolerance I'm afraid I've always disapproved of.

PERSIUS. Oh, we all have. We've all disapproved of them.

BATA. One might put it like this, I think: it is as if in this immense ramification of corridors and offices and stairs and—and so forth—it's as if there were odd nooks and corners here and there which have never been properly lit; and piles of dirt and dust and what not have accumulated in them. But who are the people scratching about in the middle of it all? Doormen, clerks, penpushers and other fusty old rubbish—

PERSIUS. The main trouble about this place is that out of every hole—

MAVERI. —an army of gnawing rats comes tumbling . . .

BATA. I'd be inclined to say myself that the whole thing has nothing to do with the magistrates at all.

ERZI. The Minister's opinion is that the staleness and poisonous air you speak of have actually produced something rather more: it might be called a poisonous plant. *(A silence.)*

BATA. I see. But think of ourselves for a moment: there are many hundreds of us here, all flapping our black gowns about the place and groaning out our prayers. It would be a little unnatural if so vast a monastery didn't harbor at least one or two wicked or negligent brethren.

ERZI. It is not about negligent brethren that the Minister is concerned. He is convinced that under one of the flapping gowns you speak of, securely hidden away, there must be somewhere a little red pustule of leprosy. Corruption.

BATA. Corruption?

ERZI. It is a leper we're looking for.

BATA. And why . . . why do you begin looking for your lepers in here, pray?

ERZI. You must regard that as an honor. Isn't this the division reserved for Major Causes?

CROZ. Hahaha! It's been a real pleasure to listen to you. What elegant conceits, what metaphors! I'm crazy about that sort of thing; I even try my hand at it myself sometimes. But the one you should really hear is Cust, he's an absolute artist. He's being very quiet today for some reason. I always think eloquence of expression adds so much to a magistrate—it's the sign of a highly developed brain, I think one can say. Well, perhaps you'll listen to a few of my own little similes? Do you know, my dear Erzi, what we poor devils really are?—we judges, in this division—yes, yes, I know, the division for Major Causes. But each of us, every single one, is a little, lonely, insecure rock on which from every direction tremendous waves keep breaking; frightful; great foaming mountains. And those waves are the implacable interests, the boundless wealth, the iron blocks manipulated by dreadfully powerful men: genuine wild forces, whose blows—unhappily for us—are something savage, irre·sistible, ferocious . . .

ERZI *(completing).* . . . a species of telluric phenomenon.

CROZ. Telluric: exactly. Telluric.

ERZI. And it's very difficult to teach that phenomenon good manners.

CROZ. You take the words right out of my mouth. I'd like to see how the Minister would get on in our place.

ERZI. The pity of it is that amidst these iron blocks a fair number of very fragile shells are also tossed about on the waters; and they very easily get dashed to pieces. Take the case, for example, the day before yesterday, of that prostitute in Panama Street: a little smoke and burnt paper were sufficient to send her to her Maker. Was it not this division that had decided in complete secrecy to raid the house in Panama Street and confiscate certain documents?

CROZ. Yes.

ERZI. But when the police arrived, the place had been blazing for a good ten minutes; so had the documents, and so, unfortunately, had a harmless caretaker. The papers are still scream·ing about it.

CROZ. Do you mean—?

ERZI. I mean that someone from here had warned the interested parties. *(Pause.)* That is only one case among many: but it sums up the situation. *(A silence.)*

CROZ. Someone from here? One of us?

ERZI. One of you.

CROZ *(laughing loudly)*. My dear friends. Just let's all take a close look at each other, shall we? You, for example, Bata: you have a look at me, while I of course have a look at you, eh? Can it be possible that not a tiny bead of sweat, not a single movement of the Adam's apple, not the slightest, smallest sign . . . should betray our ailing comrade? Our leper I mean. It could be myself; it could be you, Maveri; you've gone quite white. Or you, Cust.

CUST. No, no, Croz. That's not quite the way things work. There's an error in psychology there. If it were anybody, it would be the innocent man—if he had any imagination: he'd be the one who started to sweat, etc. Feel.

(He holds out his hand.)

CROZ *(touching it)*. Cold and clammy.

CUST. Yes. Once when I was a boy staying with friends, someone came and said a watch was missing. I . . . fainted.

CROZ. So you're the one with the imagination?

CUST. Obviously. And quite apart from that, I'd like to point out —simply in the interests of accuracy—that it isn't quite exact to say: one of us. It isn't true that *all* the men who took part in the decision you mentioned are here at this moment. Now, I don't want this to be taken as an insinuation, mind you. I am, after all, a referendary judge, and because of that I am always in very close contact with President Vanan; and no one knows better than I how completely above suspicion he is. I'm only saying this in order that we may maintain a certain precision, a certain strictness of method: President Vanan also took part in that decision. And he is not here at the moment.

CROZ *(pointing to CUST, and speaking to ERZI)*. Cust. A very fine brain. My great enemy, my rival as successor to Vanan. A most worthy character; and gnawed by the most infernal ambition. We've hated each other from the minute we met.

CUST. That isn't true as far as I am concerned.

CROZ. Old humbug. He's like one of those iron safes. Absolutely impregnable.

BATA. Well, since Vanan's name's been mentioned—and as colleague Erzi has invited us to make a full and friendly disclosure . . . and also . . . out of a real wish for sincerity, mind you, and since all this will remain strictly among ourselves . . .

PERSIUS *(slightly hysterical).* Get *on!* Don't you see we've all got to defend ourselves!

BATA. I consider it my duty to state . . . at all events, it seems to me an affectation to deny that the responsibility for the disorder here, the . . . uneasiness we were talking of earlier, does, unfortunately, lie largely—well, not largely perhaps but partly —with the great Vanan himself.

CROZ *(to* ERZI*).* You don't know the great Vanan?

ERZI. No.

CROZ. He has been a great man in his time; a very handsome one too. Very fond of the women. Well, well. It's horrible to grow old.

BATA. Like Cust, I would be very ashamed indeed to suggest that the great Vanan . . . had let himself be corrupted or bought up by Ludvi-Pol, or by anyone else for that matter. But he has great weaknesses: that I'm bound to say.

MAVERI. There are certain jobs he is no longer fitted for. He seems somehow . . . finished. That's the word, if the truth must be told. One of those old wooden beams that if you go like that to them, your finger goes in.

BATA. Rotten.

CROZ. And terrific with the women, you understand? He himself must know where his strength's gone to, at any rate.

MAVERI. And it's still the same. Even now! One gathers that's the reason for his rapid disintegration, as you might call it. Poor old thing, it's very sad and terrible. He's been seen in the most frightful places.

BATA. In fact, when you talk to President Vanan, it's difficult to be sure if he really knows what he's saying and doing any longer. A thousand pities. A thousand pities.

MAVERI. These last few months, I almost think you could tell from the way he talks and moves about . . . well, he's in the final stages. It's become pathological by now.

CROZ *(to* MAVERI*)*. It's simply this, my dear fellow: he keeps himself going with drink. *(He laughs and coughs.)*

BATA. Naturally, I must repeat that I'm not saying I . . . believe that Vanan himself is the one . . . the man . . .

PERSIUS *(suddenly and brutally)*. My dear colleagues, does this really seem to you the moment for delicacy? Do you understand or don't you, what a hell of a position we're in?

MAVERI *(supporting him)*. The whole city's waiting. It wants somebody's head.

PERSIUS. It's a matter of life and death. Do we want to ruin ourselves, just for Vanan's sweet sake? Don't you think it's about time we all spoke out?

ERZI. Well?

PERSIUS. Look: if there was one man in this place who was absolutely *made* to be swallowed up by Ludvi-Pol, it was Vanan. If there was one man . . .

CUST *(interrupting)*. One man. And why only one man? There's not the slightest evidence to show that our leper stands alone. We might all be infected. We might all have sold our souls to the devil, that is, to Ludvi-Pol.

CROZ. Perfect. Clever old Cust. *(To* ERZI.*)* Logic goes to old Cust's head at times, like drink. He's gleaming with sweat! *(He breaks off. Someone has knocked on the door leading to the corridor. They all turn. A gloomy-looking stranger, possibly a* POLICE OFFICER, *comes in, and goes and speaks privately to* ERZI. ERZI *listens to him, then signs to him to wait, and stands for a moment, lost in thought.)*

ERZI. It's very unfortunate Vanan isn't here. Do you know where he could be found?

CUST. As a matter of fact, it's been rather difficult lately to know where you will or won't find Vanan. His habits have become rather uncertain.

ERZI. You've been very close to him?

CUST. Yes.

ERZI. Would you say that what we've heard about Vanan in here this morning is more or less the truth?

CUST *(after a silence)*. You put me in rather an embarrassing position; Vanan and I were fond of each other. There has perhaps been a certain amount of exaggeration.

ERZI. Go on.

CUST. The scale of human duties has become a little confused in Vanan's mind. He's been sentencing people far too long. That can be rather dangerous after a time.

ERZI. Is there anything else?

CUST *(after a silence, looking down)*. Yes.

ERZI. Go on.

CUST. Vanan did know Ludvi-Pol. They had dealings. *(A silence.)* It's painful, for me, to speak of it. I think . . . I had the impression that Ludvi-Pol had passed a certain sum of money to President Vanan. *(His voice is low and calm.)* But look, Erzi, if what you said is true, surely Ludvi-Pol himself is the one who could give you the name you're after—or names, as the case may be. Don't you think he'd talk?

ERZI. No. I don't.

BATA. Yes, but surely Ludvi-Pol's papers would talk!

CROZ *(laughing)*. Do you think he's such a fool as to have put these things down on paper?

CUST. No, but perhaps under prolonged expert interrogation—

ERZI. No. We shan't get anything out of Ludvi-Pol.

CUST. Why not?

ERZI. Because he's dead. *(A silence.)* His body was discovered by accident in the early hours of this morning; do any of you know where?

CROZ. Where?

ERZI. Here. In this building, in a place where Ludvi-Pol had no reason whatever to be, least of all at night. He's lying there now.

CUST. So he was another fragile shell.

ERZI. It was suicide.

CUST. Are they sure of that?

ERZI. Yes.

CUST *(almost imperceptibly excited)*. Forgive me, but that too could be a put-up job. The person you're looking for had a great interest in seeing that Ludvi-Pol kept his mouth shut, hadn't he? That person must be feeling very relieved at this moment. In any case, this Ludvi-Pol was a very contemptible creature, his death sentence is hardly likely to arouse much protest in the tribunal of any human soul I can think of. Or . . . look: the very things put there purposely to suggest murder, even those could be the results of a put-up job. For what purpose? To put you off the trail. To implicate some innocent person. There are so many possibilities, one can go on multiplying them as one chooses . . . always supposing we attribute a certain amount of subtlety to the man you're looking for. I advise you not to disregard any of those threads.

ERZI. Suicide. *(Pause.)* Are there many people in the building at night?

CUST. Oh, you can see quite a number of windows lit up till a very late hour. Industrious officials, all anxious to get on, losing their sleep over their papers. I myself, as a matter of fact, was here very late last night. *(As though recalling something.)* In fact . . . *(He breaks off.)*

ERZI. Go on.

CUST *(lower)*. When I leave, I always have to go along the corridor that goes past the great Vanan's door. I may as well tell you the truth. As the corridor was in darkness . . . I saw a line of light under the door. I heard—*(He breaks off.)*

(MALGAI enters excitedly: he clearly realizes what the situation is.)

MALGAI. President Vanan.

(MALGAI withdraws immediately. After a few moments VANAN appears; he is an old man, very tall and erect; his face is angry and inflamed, his hair like a mop of white cotton wool; his tones are slightly stentorian. Sometimes he mutters to himself. He comes in, and looks round him.)

VANAN. Quite. Quite . . . of course. Good morning to you all, my dear . . . friends. Here we are. *(To* BATA, *who is the near-est to him.)* Good morning, Bata; of course, yes . . . Give me a what-is-it, a match. *(His words drop into a great silence; everyone has risen.)*

BATA *(backing away).* I don't think I have any.

VANAN. What's the matter? What's the matter? Sit down. You could . . . surely, surely have waited for me too. Eh? Eh? Cust, I'm talking to you. Absolutely. Good morning, Erzi, I'm glad to see you. *(Shouting.)* Sit down! I'm perfectly aware of what's going on. You are here too, my clever Croz.

CROZ *(shrugging his shoulders).* Of course. What do you expect?

VANAN. Good. All of us. Absolutely. . . .

(They are now all seated; only VANAN *is standing.)*

ERZI *(with great courtesy).* Mr. President, we were just waiting for you. There is a little information we need, if you would be so very kind as to give it to us.

VANAN. Absolutely. I know perfectly well what's going on. Fantastic, isn't it? Absolutely disgraceful.

ERZI. Mr. President, I have no doubt that you are acquainted with a person who has in recent years been at the center of the biggest concerns in the city, and who has consequently also been involved here in a number of very important law suits. I mean Ludvi-Pol. *(A silence.)*

VANAN *(muttering).* No . . . not that man . . . no, certainly not. Never. Listen, Erzi; I never knew him.

ERZI. You have, however, judged many cases in which he was involved.

VANAN. But . . . my dear Erzi, how . . . how can you possibly ask . . . *(suddenly roaring)* me, *me,* questions like this. It's fantastic . . . absolutely fantastic.

ERZI *(with extreme politeness).* There was nothing in my question that could possibly offend you.

VANAN. Eh? What? That man . . .

ERZI. Yes. It would appear that you know him. That has been confirmed by several people here. *(A silence.)*

VANAN. Private. Private. An absolutely private matter. Absolutely. *(Dropping his voice slightly.)* In the lift. In the lift, Erzi, that's all! (*He laughs.*) In the lift in this building, that's all. What happens? A gentleman recognizes me and speaks to me. An acquaintance from long long ago, lost sight of. Boys . . . boys together, the family . . . ages ago, ages ago. In the lift. Ridiculous that I should have to . . . talk about that.

ERZI (*gently*). You received a sum of money from Ludvi-Pol? (*A silence.*)

VANAN (*his voice seems to diminish and he looks round him uncertainly*). Croz . . . but why . . . why am I being asked all this? What's going on? Cust, you, say something. And the rest of you, you all know me, what do you think you're doing? (*A silence.*)

ERZI (*quietly*). Certainly, we all know you, Mr. President. You can speak with perfect frankness.

VANAN. Quite, quite, my dear Erzi, quite. There's no reason for me to hide anything . . . it's simple. The whole thing is absolutely . . . simple. It seems that Ludvi-Pol was slightly in debt to us, to my family I mean . . . nothing important, old liabilities, I'd quite forgotten them. But he . . . he remembered. Perfectly. He was very determined . . . to pay them back. That's the truth, that's the truth, Erzi. Absolutely . . . ridiculous, isn't it? He remembered it all perfectly.

ERZI. And did you remember?

VANAN. Well, actually I . . . yes, vaguely.

ERZI. Was it a large amount? Was it at a time when you happened to be in need?

VANAN (*overcome with a kind of anguish*). I don't . . . I don't . . . why . . . Cust! It's all so unexpected, so sudden. Ludvi-Pol himself will surely explain all this to you, won't he? You'll only have to ask him, won't you? He will tell you everything.

ERZI. Were you in this building last night?

VANAN. I? In this building? (*Roaring.*) But whatever do you . . . what does this mean . . . ?

ERZI. In your office, Mr. President: last night: were you alone?

VANAN. Absolutely. Absolutely. Alone. Absolutely.

ERZI. Cust.

CUST (*slowly approaching*). Yes. (*Affectionately, with regret.*) I had to tell him, Vanan. Last night . . . possibly you don't remember now . . .

VANAN *(with some fury)*. I? I don't remember? Shameful! Ridiculous! Absolutely grotesque! I don't remember, don't I? *(He breaks off; there is a moment of absolute silence; suddenly shouting and almost weeping.)* Do you think I don't understand what . . . what you're all trying to do? You're trying to drag me down . . . trying to accuse me . . . aren't you? I understand perfectly! You blackguards! You filthy little pigmies! I'll crush you! I'll show you! I'll bring . . . I'll bring the whole court down! I'll tell them who's the guilty man, I'll tell them in the minutest detail! They don't know me yet. They don't know who Vanan is! I'll tear them to pieces, the whole lot of them. And after that . . . after . . . *(He stands there for a moment with his arm raised, breathing heavily: and then, as though his memory had suddenly given way, he drops slowly across the table, his face in his hands. A silence.)*

ERZI *(politely, rising)*. Gentlemen, thank you all very much; I shan't need to take up any more of your time today. Though I shall have to ask for a little of yours, Croz, in a short while; and I also hope that you will all help me in the course of this inquiry. At the moment I am being waited for elsewhere. *(Thoughtfully, he turns to the police official who is still waiting.)* You. It's about time they removed Ludvi-Pol's body. I don't suppose they will be able to get it out of the building unnoticed. It's probably too late for that now. All the same, try to keep it covered up, if you possibly can, so that we shan't have to see his face in all the newspapers tomorrow, streaked with blood, with his eyes closed. He was a greatly respected man in his time. The city has all the rest of him to trample on now; let's leave his body for the worms alone—to whom all faces are the same. *(To the others.)* Good morning.

(He goes out, followed by the official. BATA, MAVERI, and PERSIUS, one after another, go out cautiously and almost on tiptoe, so as not to attract the attention of VANAN.)

(CROZ and CUST are standing at some distance from him.)

CROZ *(observing his colleague)*. What's the matter, Cust?

CUST *(looking at him before speaking)*. This is going to require a certain amount of courage.

CROZ. What do you mean?

CUST *(drawing him away from VANAN, with a wan smile, and whispering)*. Croz, have you ever been out hunting?

CROZ. No.

CUST. Neither have I, but I've often been told about it. Do you know what it is the hunter always dreads most?

CROZ. No.

CUST. Finishing off the wounded quarry. Dying animals go on struggling; you have to take pity on them. Everyone'd be so very obliged to them, if only they'd die by themselves. But no, they struggle and fight for life; it's almost a point of honor with them. They almost make the hunter feel angry with them, because they actually in the end force one to . . . *(dropping his voice still lower)* smash their skulls in. It's horrible, isn't it? But it's something that has to be faced.

CROZ *(looking at VANAN)*. Yes, yes, of course. The fool is going to ruin himself completely if he goes on like this. All those infantile lies! We shall have to . . . use a little persuasion.

CUST. It may not be difficult. A man who's just had a heavy blow on the head often behaves strangely docile. We are all of us fragile, but old men are like glass.

VANAN *(has risen: his words are threatening, but his voice has completely changed)*. Croz, Cust. Eh? What do you say about all this? Why don't you say something, you filthy traitors! *(CUST and CROZ look at him in silence.)* What are you thinking? Tell me what to do . . . don't stand there looking at me . . .

CUST *(quietly)*. My dear Vanan, do you know who it is *you* must talk to, now? Yourself.

VANAN. Myself?

CUST. Yes. You must explain to yourself the reason for all the lies you've been telling.

VANAN. Lies?

CUST. Lies, Vanan. What was the reason for them?

VANAN. Because . . . my God, actually . . . Cust, I was so confused . . .

CUST. Why were you confused? M'm? Reflect on that, my dear Vanan, and then you'll see for yourself the best way to go about things. Reflect on it, at great length.

VANAN. But oh, my God, I'm . . . an old man now.

CUST. Why ever did you deny that you talked to Ludvi-Pol last night?

VANAN. Cust, I swear to you . . . that man had come simply to plead with me . . . he thought I could still save him . . . he was a fool, a madman . . .

CUST. But why did he come to you? First he asked something from you; and then he asked something else, from death. You were the last door but one he knocked at. Why?

VANAN *(shouting)*. I don't know, Cust! I don't know!

CUST. And why are you so frightened, even now? *(Very quietly.)* Oh no, Vanan, it's all too evident that your conscience is not untroubled. There is a doubt, in your conscience. They're saying that in this fine building of ours there is something rotten. But if you reflect on what you have been doing in here, yesterday, and every other day of your life, are you certain, quite certain, that you will be saved? What I advise you to do, my dear Vanan, is to make a long and minute examination of your conscience. Explore yourself, scrutinize yourself, go to bed with your doubt, carry it about with you by day. And only when one of the two, either you or it, has won, only then, and not before, must you come back here.

VANAN. Cust, what do you mean?

CUST. But of course, Vanan. You wouldn't want to insist on remaining here, in the courts, struggling, threatening, telling more bungling lies.

VANAN. You mean I ought to go away? Now?

CUST. For a few days.

VANAN. Never, never, never. I won't move from here, I'll defy them.

CUST. Good. And let them be even more vindictive against you in their inquiries, and lay more traps for you to fall into.

VANAN. No, Cust, I can't do it. To go away now would be . . .

CUST. . . . to put the matter in the hands of a very great doctor:

time. Besides, would you really have the strength to face, day after day, the looks of contempt, the rudeness, the innuendoes? The very porters, the very walls are cruel to anyone who has fallen.

VANAN. My God.

CUST. Just be clever; let your enemies have a little rope. The important thing is simply to get through these next few days of suspicion and anger, and noise. Admit to some little thing or other, so as to give the fools, who are shouting so loudly, the illusion of victory. Throw a piece of flesh to the wolves who are following you . . .

VANAN. My God.

CUST. And very soon they'll all be thinking of something else; what you should do now is . . . *(He pauses.)*

VANAN. What?

CUST. My belief is that you ought to send the Investigating Councillor a note today; without saying too much, without giving your hand away; just telling him simply that in view of what has happened you don't feel that you ought, for the present—for the present—to remain in the building. For the present. Instead . . . *(He pauses again.)*

VANAN. . . . instead . . .

CUST. Very quietly, very very quietly, just stay at home and think. Reflect. And in the meantime do you know what you can do as well? On your own account, silently. You can write.

VANAN. Write what?

CUST. A full statement, in which you explain everything. Just pass the time doing that. For the present.

VANAN. For the present. . . .

CUST. The important thing is the little note; and you must hurry: the note must arrive before they can decide anything disagreeable. It will restrain them. Write it now, straight away. *(Pointing to a desk.)* There.

VANAN. Cust, I don't want . . . Croz, what do you think?

CUST. Listen, Vanan, I've given you a piece of advice. I've probably gone too far in doing so.

VANAN *(suddenly pleading).* But, of course, I know, I am grateful, you must forgive me. And you too, Croz. Actually . . . you must understand my . . . *(He is gradually approaching the desk.)* Yes, Cust, there's a good deal of sense in what you say. A full . . . precise statement, absolutely! Absolutely. And now, a note: yes, I must write it now. You know, Cust: you've been the only . . . *(almost weeping)* I've no friends: I've always been too proud. And now they'll all . . . be delighted, they all want to humiliate me. They've all become suddenly . . . wicked, treacherous. . . . *(He is fumbling at the desk; suddenly he breaks off, and listens intently; runs to the door, listens; and turns back to the other two men, his eyes widening in real fear.)* She's talking to the porter! My God! Look; the only person I have in the world will be here in a minute! I beg you by whatever you hold most dear . . . *(Trying to control himself.)* Listen: it's my daughter. You don't know her. There's always been just the two of us; her mother died. She thinks I'm almost a king in here, she wouldn't understand anything of what's happened. I beg you, I beseech you not to let her suspect anything: pretend nothing has happened. It's a great favor. *(Changing his tone, speaking towards the door, which has just opened.)* Yes, Elena. Come in, my dear. I'm glad you stopped in, we can go home together. *(A radiant young girl, and at the moment looking rather surprised, is in the doorway. She comes shyly into the room. Breathlessly, to his two colleagues.)* This is my daughter. Elena. Fancy, she's never been here before. (ELENA *smiles at the two judges. Stammering, and fumbling about on the desk.)* Elena, these are two very clever . . . friends of mine who . . . are very fond of me, in spite of the fact that your father is the most exacting president there could possibly be. Yes, certainly . . . I'm an absolute . . . tyrant. Absolutely, quite, quite. *(Fumbling confusedly on the desk.)* Forgive me, Elena, I'm coming at once, I just have to finish a . . . a note; I'll finish it at once, my dear Cust. Tell me, Elena: I wonder whether you heard me in the corridor? I'm always shouting, I get angry over nothing, because . . . because everything falls on my shoulders, do you understand?

The President. I'm the President. It's an honor, but it's also . . . a terrible responsibility.

(He is already scribbling; there is a silence. ELENA, *like someone in very great awe, smiles again at the two judges, who look at her attentively.)*

*(*VANAN *has finished. He goes over in silence to* CUST, *and places the letter in his hand, and then goes over to his daughter and lifts his hand, vaguely touching her hair, as if he wished to smooth it.* ELENA *takes his hand and kisses it.)*

*(*VANAN *looks at the two judges with a flicker of sudden pride; slips his daughter's arm beneath his own, nods good-by, and goes out, very upright, in silence.)*

*(*CROZ *and* CUST *stand there for a moment as though lost in thought.* CROZ *gives a long glance at his companion, and then goes out, leaning heavily on his cane, without speaking.)*

*(*CUST, *after his departure, goes slowly across to a desk, sits at it, and suddenly seems overcome by a genuine prostration; he remains for a little while thus: with his head in his hands.)*

*(*MALGAI *enters and begins to put the room in order.)*

MALGAI *(at the door)*. Please sir, may I . . . ?

CUST *(without raising his head)*. Yes.

MALGAI *(as he tidies up)*. That was the President's daughter, wasn't it, sir?

CUST *(as before)*. Yes.

MALGAI. A pretty girl. She's quite grown up . . . quite a young lady.

CUST *(as before)*. Yes. *(He looks up.)* She reminded me of something.

MALGAI. Sir, you're not looking very well.

CUST. I'm just tired, that's all. I feel rather upset. *(He pretends to unfold a roll of documents, and begins to hum to himself; thinking, quietly.)* My God, how horrible everything is. What a wasted life. Judge Cust. *(He hums again, and thinks idly.)* Yes, the girl reminded me of something. There was something about her. *(Lost in thought, as he goes on.)* Attilio, do you know who Vanan's daughter looked like? She looked like the figure on a box, a tin box we once had at home when I was a boy; a woman with flowing hair . . . and a crown . . . She was lifting a glass, it was an advertisement for something. I used to be tremendously fond of her. Tremendously. She looked like Vanan's daughter.

MALGAI *(as he goes out).* Ah, Mr. Cust, sir . . . When I was a boy, *I* used to . . . *(He smiles.)* Oh, dear, the things that went through one's mind! Well, well . . . *(He goes.)*

CUST *(almost singing the word).* Tremendously. Tremendously. *(He begins to hum again; then, thinking.)* I might very well have had a daughter like that. "Elena, let's go out for a little shall we? Dear Elena." Judge Cust and his daughter . . . *(Hums.)* Or else my wife. "Come on, Elena, let's go home, shall we?" Judge Cust and his wife . . . *(Hums.)* Or my mother perhaps. I am a tiny little frog. She gives me milk. A young beloved mother, very young. *(He rises slowly to his feet. ERZI and CROZ have come in, and are walking across the room. CUST stares at them fixedly; just as they are about to go out, he calls:)* Councillor Erzi!

(ERZI and CROZ stop.)

CUST. How's it going?

ERZI. What?

CUST. The inquiry.

ERZI. Are you interested in it?

CUST. Can't stop thinking about it.

ERZI *(dropping his voice a little).* Cust, was there something you wanted to say to me?

CUST. I? I only wanted to tell you that . . . if I can help you at all . . . in any humble way . . . I'd of course be very pleased.

ERZI. Have you had any ideas?

CUST. Any ideas? Any ideas. *(He looks at ERZI for a moment, and then hands VANAN's letter to him.)* All the same, it would be a good thing, wouldn't it if President Vanan were innocent, and the leper was somebody else.

ERZI *(has glanced at the letter, and now turns and stares at CUST).* Do you think so?

CUST *(sighs).* I'm just thinking. I wonder if it wouldn't after all be a good thing to abandon the inquiry . . .

ERZI. And who's suggested that we intend to abandon it? No. It will be pursued. Right to the end. And you will help me.

(He shakes CUST'*s hand warmly, and goes out with* CROZ.*)*

*(*CUST *stands looking after him.)*

Curtain

ACT TWO

Several days have passed. On one side of the stage, bored and impersonal, stands the gloomy police officer. BATA *and* PERSIUS, *wearing hats and overcoats, are wandering furtively about, rather as if they were spying. They meet, rapidly whisper something together, and part again with assumed indifference, as the door from the corridor opens.*

CUST *enters slowly.* BATA *and* PERSIUS, *torn between curiosity and the fear of compromising themselves by starting a conversation, make cautious nods of greeting towards him: prudence prevails however; and nodding once more to* CUST, *they both slip towards the door; here they throw a further long glance at him; and disappear.*

CUST *has followed them with his eyes. He hesitates; at last he removes his hat and overcoat, and approaches the police officer.*

CUST. I am Judge Cust. Councillor Erzi has sent for me. I don't know what he wants. Would you mind telling him I'm here?

(The officer nods and goes out. After a few moments a door opens and ERZI *enters.)*

ERZI. Ah thank you, my dear Cust, thank you; how good of you to come. Sit down. Well, now. It's always a pleasure to talk with a colleague like yourself. You've no idea, I suppose, why I asked you if you'd mind coming?

CUST. No.

ERZI *(after a pause).* Did it really never occur to you to wonder?
CUST. No.
ERZI. Well . . . you did, after all, make me a promise. Yes, I asked you to help me in my investigation. I was greatly impressed by the acuteness of some of your observations. So I've always been expecting to see you. But you've been in very seldom, and then only fleetingly. I've been rather surprised at that.
CUST. I never thought you'd seriously need me.
ERZI. I needed someone who'd been breathing the air of this place for a long time. Besides, you're expecting a promotion which will be almost the goal of your whole career. It is in your own interest that this mess should be cleared up.
CUST. I'm not the only one with such an interest.
ERZI. Quite so. But Judge Croz will also be here in a short time. So will some of the others. *(A short pause; he smiles.)* My dear Cust, this evening I am expected to present my conclusions. The whole city is holding its breath. But before I go, as I shall do shortly, up to the office of the Lord High Chancellor, I wanted to call a few friends together again in here, and test the evidence once more.
CUST. I thought that the inquiry had already uncovered a great many facts and implicated a great number of people.
ERZI. Yes. But in the end everything must center on one particular fact. There must have been a beginning somewhere.
CUST. Has the inquiry broken down on that point?
ERZI. I'm not at all satisfied in my mind.
CUST. You had your eye on Vanan, or so I thought?
ERZI. Yes. Everything would seem to point to Vanan . . . if it were not that one authoritative voice had spoken in his favor. *(CUST does not break the silence.)*
ERZI. Yours. It was you who told me that Vanan might in fact be innocent. Your observation showed me two things: first, that you had your own opinions, and secondly, that I must regard you yourself as above suspicion. Though in theory I might have suspected you also.
CUST. Yes.

ERZI. But I rather imagine that a guilty person would take great care not to call an investigator back off a false trail . . . and run the risk of having him at his own heels.

CUST. Unless he did so in order to *make* himself above suspicion.

ERZI. Quite so.

CUST *(slowly)*. You have in fact sent for me in order to know what I really think of this matter.

ERZI. Precisely.

CUST. I think that if your leper really exists, and if it's not Vanan, then you're going to find it difficult to catch him.

ERZI. Not impossible, however. And why should it be difficult?

CUST. Because the thread of facts, which might have led you to him, has been snapped. Ludvi-Pol is dead: the mouth that could have talked has been shut.

ERZI. Then you think that, at this very moment, somewhere in one of the many rooms in this vast building, there is a person in whom by now, all fear has ceased.

CUST *(thoughtfully)*. The rooms in this place are very quiet ones. Unhealthy-looking men sit in them; they have the faces of men who rarely see the sun. Over a period of many years, they have listened in silence to thousands of lies; they have examined human actions of the most extraordinary subtlety and wickedness. Their experience is immense. The people who have faced them across the table have seen merely a few polite, rather tired gentlemen. But in reality, especially among those who achieve very high office, there are wrestlers, dear colleague; despite the fact that their hardened veins burst so easily. As a rule they find it difficult to sleep at night. And as a result of that . . . *(He breaks off.)*

ERZI. Well?

CUST. As a result they have a great deal of time to brood over their thoughts. They're capable of listening very attentively; they're tough; and they are extremely careful.

ERZI. It would be difficult to catch them out, in that case.

CUST. Yes. And one of them is the man you're looking for.

ERZI. The leper.

CUST. Today that man is on the heights. The day you succeed in unmasking him, he will stand for a moment dumbfounded; millions of eyes will be on him; and then he will hurtle down into an abyss of darkness.

ERZI. And then?

CUST. Then he will begin to defend himself, dear colleague. I believe that his situation must give him a strange intoxicating feeling of liberty.

ERZI *(looking hard at him).* I imagine that one evening, at a very late hour, this man, this judge we're looking for, lifted his gaze from his desk. The person who had come in was very polite, the visit was a perfectly legitimate one. Then the conversation drifted, important friendships, secret powers, attractive enticements flickered about it . . . *(CROZ appears at the door of the clerk's office and stands listening, unseen by the others. Continuing without interruption.)* . . . The cautious visitor was trying to grope his way towards something already waiting there in the judge's mind: something called ambition; or greed perhaps; or envy; or hate. And at what exact point did that perfectly legitimate cordiality, those vague promises, become something more? When did that subtle bond between them become a leash, held in a master's hand?

CUST *(sweating slightly).* Yes: I think it's a very likely reconstruction.

ERZI *(with a barely perceptible increase of urgency).* That is how this judge of ours came to place an acute and powerful intelligence at the disposal of a master, and in the service of injustice. He falsified decisions, he betrayed secrets, and he changed human destinies. He spread in here a trouble which rapidly defiled the entire Courts of Justice; he drove the iron wheel of the law over many innocent men and women. Even a murderer can sometimes regard himself as an executioner. But our man was well aware that he was falsifying the sacred scales of justice. For the sake of what? Why?

CROZ *(from the back, interrupting unexpectedly).* Probably because he'd begun to have his doubts.

ERZI *(turning).* About what?

CROZ. Oh, about the sacred scales and so forth. *(He laughs, coughs, and goes on.)* The devil—Ludvi-Pol I mean—had come to get him that night, but that was probably just what our man had wanted, wasn't it, Cust! A judge is just like a priest in these matters: after officiating all his life in front of the holy altar, he conceives a terrible hatred of it and a great wish to see the devil himself appear in front of him for a change.

ERZI *(staring now at* CROZ*).* But hadn't so many years of being there made him wise, so many years of being outside the game?

CROZ *(bursts out laughing).* Outside the game? But one's never outside the game, my dear Erzi! My dear good fellow, just think for a minute of one of those nasty black insects, that sting. You excite one of them: and it stings. You cripple it: and it stings. You cut it in two: and it stings. You transfix it and smash its head in: and its sting goes on stinging, stinging, stinging. Just for nothing. That's what life is.

CUST *(pointing a finger towards* CROZ*).* A spite which amuses even the dying quarry. Doesn't it Croz?

ERZI *(suddenly turning to* CUST*).* But then, Cust, if the thread of facts is broken off, and if the person is so sure of himself, and so determined and cautious, why do you only say it will be *difficult* to find him, and not impossible? After all, that's what you said. What can possibly betray him?

CUST *(speaking first with his eyes lowered, and eventually lifting them towards his questioner).* This: that men are rather fragile; the very things that they themselves construct, their thoughts . . . their laws . . . their crimes . . . lie too heavy on their backs.

ERZI *(slightly urging him on).* You mean that the man who was guilty of this crime doesn't sleep very easily.

CUST. Yes.

ERZI. Why?

CUST. Because he thinks about it too much.

ERZI. Guilt?

CUST. No; he's beyond that.

ERZI. Why then?

CUST *(smiling and staring at him).* Because he doesn't want his little red spot to be discovered.

72   *Betti*

ERZI. Well?

CUST *(a little uneasily)*. Well, with extraordinary subtlety and patience, he calculates; he imagines that the slightest break in his voice, the quickest glance, may have left here and there traces, imperceptible signs . . .

ERZI. . . . which someone may find, and follow up . . .

CUST. Yes, and which he, with supreme caution, takes care to baffle and disperse.

ERZI. In what way?

CUST. He hastens to meet every tiny possible suspicion, even before it's born; sometimes indeed he even prompts the suspicion; and then he stares hard at it, and baffles it, makes it unsure of itself, dazed, destroyed by its own vagueness.

CROZ *(with a loud laugh)*. It's a big job, isn't it, Cust?

CUST. It is. If one's to discover the man, the secret is to *be* him.

ERZI. What do you mean?

CUST. . . . to feel that one *is* the man. *(His breathing thickens slightly.)* To feel the same chill here on the scalp, the same heavy pounding, not quite in the heart, but lower, almost in the belly. Boom . . . boom . . . boom . . . the same trembling at the knees . . . the same weariness. I hope you see what I mean?

ERZI. Perfectly. *(Very quietly.)* Then what exactly are his feelings, when he hears that we are at his heels? Fear, wouldn't you say?

CUST. You're wrong.

ERZI. Doesn't he know he's being pursued?

CUST. He's not a fool.

ERZI. You mean it doesn't alarm him?

CUST. Certainly not.

ERZI. Well?

CUST. He manages to control himself.

ERZI. What does he do?

CUST. We pretend to be him; he pretends to be us. He assumes we have a quite supernatural foresight. He dare not make a mistake.

CROZ *(satirically)*. It really is a big job.

CUST (*pointing a finger at* CROZ, *harshly and aggressively*). Above all, he has to keep beginning over and over again.

ERZI. Why?

CROZ (*staring at* CUST *in his turn*). Because our eyes are always on him, our suspicions are always pursuing him . . .

CUST (*counterattacking*). . . . and he goes on arranging and constructing defenses ever more subtle and ingenious. (*Laughing, rather harshly.*) Today, for example, his hand . . . It occurred to me, watching your hand, Croz, lying idly there on the table . . . What I mean is that his hand, or even one finger of his hand, at the precise moment that someone utters the name of Ludvi-Pol . . . at that moment one finger of his hand . . . (*he is still pointing at* CROZ's *hand*) causes a tiny slackening of control; he is affected: for barely a second . . .

CROZ (*nervously and jestingly moving his hand*). Like that?

CUST. Like that. And what a mistake to make. Just because someone was staring at it . . . as we are staring at yours. And suppose someone had noticed that coincidence? And had thought about it? Was that imperceptible movement a confession? Yes, it's *that* that the guilty man thinks about all night long. And by daybreak: he has made up his mind.

ERZI. What to do?

CUST. An experiment. He will go back and face the other person . . . and name Ludvi-Pol again! And he'll put his hand there again, in the same position . . . just as Croz has done! And he'll repeat that imperceptible movement! But what matters this time is that the color of his cheeks, the sweat of his forehead, the sound of his voice, everything shall be beyond question. His hand will feel itself scorched by our look. He'd love to withdraw it . . .

CROZ. You describe it with great accuracy.

CUST. But he has to hold on. The moment has come . . . his heart turns to marble . . . Like this . . . (*He holds his breath for a moment, and then shakes himself and laughs.*) And then everything's all right, he can breathe again!

CROZ. A bit tired?

CUST (*with a wan smile*). Almost exhausted.

CROZ. Can I move my hand, now? These moments are rather overpowering.

ERZI (*pointing his finger at* CUST). But it would be incautious of him to rest for a moment, you said so yourself. . . .

CROZ (*also urgently*). There's not a moment that may not bring him some fresh danger . . .

CUST (*suddenly, hoarsely, looking down*). I believe the real dangers are inside himself.

ERZI. How?

CUST (*painfully, and as though bewildered*). He is at the end of his tether. He longs to run away . . . To run away . . . To be dead and buried. That's the most complete flight of all. But then . . .

ERZI. Go on.

CUST (*almost to himself*). Who would be left, to keep the thing snug and warm, the crime I mean, the danger, who would watch over it . . . ? Who would *live* it?

CROZ (*bending over him*). Do you know what I think, Cust, really? I believe his real wish, his most terrible need, is to talk about it. The whole thing. To talk about it. Am I right?

CUST (*bewildered and lost in thought*). Perhaps. He is alone. Everyone is a long way away from him. Alone. And so . . .

ERZI (*returning to a previous question, almost cruelly*). Guilt!

CUST (*as before*). No. Astonishment. He is amazed. Amazed to see himself so busy, thinking and doing such strange, wild, ridiculous things . . . but he's forced on to them by the chain of consequences.

ERZI. And doesn't he feel a certain alarm?

CUST (*whispering*). Yes . . . he has the feeling one sometimes has in dreams: when one whispers to oneself: "But this isn't true! It's not true! It's not true! . . . I shall wake up in a minute." (*He breaks off. Someone has knocked at the door leading to the corridor. They all turn. The door opens. The* POLICE OFFICIAL *appears in the doorway; he looks at* ERZI *with a slight lift of the eyebrows and immediately withdraws. Coming up to the surface again, and laughing cheerfully to* ERZI.) There are times when I even fear you suspect him. *(He points to* CROZ.*)* . . . or me!

ERZI *(also laughing).* Oh please, please! I'm just looking for help. Well, Cust, since you've penetrated so well into the psychology of our criminal, what would you say, now, are the moves which he expects us to make? What is the point that worries him, in the circle of his defense.

CUST *(is still looking at the doorway where the* OFFICIAL *appeared; he thinks for a moment; then he turns and points to the archives; almost shouting).* The papers! That's where I advise you to attack him!

ERZI. Explain what you mean exactly.

CUST *(almost mildly).* We're dealing with a judge, aren't we? Very well then; think of the vast number of words he uses to sustain the arguments in his statements, in pronouncing sentence, in discussions. All those words are now slumbering in there. The archives. Everyone of them was a weight thrown into the scales you spoke of: but a weight that had been falsified. The records in there, taken singly, page by page, would tell you nothing. But if you were to consider them all together, however tough and clever he had been, don't you feel there must be something there that is bound to betray him? The insistent recurrence of such and such an ambiguity or quibble: the flavor of corruption. That will be the flavor that will distinguish that judge's words from those of all the others. That is the one single thread. *(He points once more.)* The papers.

ERZI. My dear Cust, did you know that the record clerk was already outside in the corridor? It's just as though you'd been reading my thoughts. But you have gone deep down into them, thrown light on them. We are here to obey you, in a sense. But not only because of that, Cust. Your guilty man hasn't thought of everything.

CROZ *(raising his voice slightly).* Are you there, Malgai? Come in. *(The door from the corridor opens and* MALGAI *appears. He crosses and opens the door of the archives, and goes inside.)*

ERZI. He calls it his graveyard. Well, we shall exhume from it whatever may be needed to put our man into our hands. *(Con-*

fidentially.) It seems, among other things, that Ludvi-Pol himself was in the habit of suggesting certain specific and characteristic arguments in his own favor. We shall discover them all in there, shan't we? But with another signature attached to them. Eh? What do you think, Cust?

CROZ. Do you think our leper will be able to escape us?

CUST. It won't be easy. *(Suddenly, almost frightened, pointing towards the corridor.)* But who's that who's come as well? There was someone else besides the record clerk . . . I thought I heard . . .

ERZI. It's another of the people I needed to have here. *(Turning towards the corridor.)* Come in, come in, Vanan. We were expecting you.

(VANAN enters. They look at him in surprise. He is extraordinarily wasted, and even shrunk in size. His daughter accompanies him, and almost pushes him forward as though he were a naughty child. She makes him advance to the middle of the room.)

CROZ. Compassionate Antigone, gentle Cordelia,[1] your father is among friends now, and doesn't need you any more.

(ELENA is about to speak.)

ERZI *(preventing her)*. You may leave us. You would not be of any help to him.

(ELENA strokes her father's arm, and goes out.)

CROZ *(with cruel gaiety as soon as the door is shut)*. By God, Vanan, I believe you've actually shrunk. What's happened to you? I never thought you were so soft.

VANAN. Eh . . .

CROZ. You've crumpled right up, Vanan. It would be damned funny if you went before I did, wouldn't it? Now, you've got to listen to something. Our colleague Erzi, as you no doubt know, has a number of things to say to you.

ERZI *(in severe tones)*. Mr. President Vanan! The High Council had allowed you a deferment; that deferment is up today. You

---

1. *Antigone . . . Cordelia,* examples of filial devotion. The former was the daughter of Oedipus, the latter of King Lear.

have been summoned here today to make your final statement. You promised to prepare your defense.

VANAN *(uncertainly)*. I . . . yes . . . yes, sir.

ERZI. Have you done so?

(A silence.)

CROZ *(mutters)*. You even seem to have lost the power of speech.

ERZI. A number of very grave charges are being made against you. You declared that you could disprove and demolish them. How? *(A silence.)*

CROZ. He's lost his tongue.

ERZI *(his voice becoming steadily more stern as he speaks)*. Above all, you declared that if you were to reconsider certain remarks made by Ludvi-Pol, you would find yourself in a position to reveal the real criminal. Well? Vanan, who is it? *(A silence.)* Tell us the name, Vanan! *(A silence; he turns away and resumes his seat.)* Either from you, or in some other way, we shall know that name today. *(To the others.)* But perhaps this silence is itself an answer. Vanan, am I to assume that you are acknowledging yourself guilty? Is it true then? Is it you who are responsible for the fraud that has poisoned this bench, this whole building, and the city itself?

CUST *(hoarsely)*. Do speak, Vanan; speak out.

VANAN *(stammering, pleading, and oddly false in tone)*. I must . . . express my thanks.

ERZI *(surprised)*. What?

VANAN *(as before)*. I have to say . . . that actually . . . the Administration has treated me . . . with very great kindness . . . *(agitated)* so that I have nothing to complain of.

ERZI *(surprised)*. What are you talking about, Vanan?

VANAN *(as before)*. As an old . . . magistrate, I feel . . . it's my duty to express my . . . to kiss . . . the generous hand . . .

ERZI *(suddenly shouting)*. What do you mean, Vanan!

VANAN *(rather frightened)*. No, don't do that . . . Of course . . . I'm very old, and . . . sick now, as you know.

ERZI *(quickly)*. Vanan, are you admitting that you are guilty?

VANAN *(looks at him suspiciously; suddenly in a false oratorical voice)*. I am innocent, sir! Innocent and falsely accused. Nailed to the cross . . . like our innocent Savior . . . Gentlemen, these gray hairs have been . . . trampled on . . .

ERZI. Vanan, who is the guilty man?

VANAN *(as before).* Oh, yes, sir, yes. There is, there *is* a guilty man. I swear before . . . before God's throne that someone is guilty! And I . . . and I can unmask him . . . The wicked shall be hurled to the dust . . . *(Suddenly becoming once more pitiful and pleading.)* I am innocent, sir, innocent. . . .

ERZI *(sadly).* Vanan, what has happened to you? You don't seem like the same man.

VANAN *(in the tones of a beggar).* Sir . . . you must intercede . . . for this poor unfortunate judge . . . I don't deserve such . . . severity. *(With sincerity, almost whispering.)* I only want . . . a little quiet. Nothing else.

(A silence.)

ERZI *(thoughtfully).* My dear Croz, although the whole thing is really quite clear, it is rather disturbing when one thinks how fragile and delicate the human organism is. Man is far more perishable than even the most trivial object shaped by his own hands. Our colleague is indeed much changed.

CROZ *(giggling).* He'll be even more changed before long.

ERZI. But those cunning papers which he—and the others— blackened with their hurrying pens, those, we shall now find, though they're dead and buried, will be more alive than he is. *(Raising his voice, to VANAN.)* They will tell us the things which you wouldn't or couldn't tell us. You will wait for us here. *(To the others.)* Shall we go?

(ERZI goes across to the archives and enters. CROZ follows him. CUST and VANAN remain behind.)

VANAN *(uneasily, his voice and attitude changing somewhat).* What are they going to do? Why . . . did they tell me to wait for them? I hate those two, I don't trust them. Cust . . . *(He sees CUST'S face.)* Cust! For God's sake, what's the matter with you?

CUST *(approaching him).* Listen, Vanan. I am here to help you, I want you to trust me! It rather looks to me as if you're not being sincere in all this. Or am I wrong? Eh? *(He wipes his brow.*) Listen, Vanan, is it really true that you . . . have been reconsidering . . . certain remarks made by poor Ludvi-Pol . . . Is it true that you have actually discovered the man . . . we're looking for?

VANAN *(moans).* I don't remember anything any more . . .

CUST *(dropping his voice).* But I remember advising you to write a detailed, exact statement. . . .

VANAN. I . . . I . . . what?

CUST *(harshly).* A statement.

VANAN *(moans).* No, no . . .

CUST *(urgently).* Where is it?

VANAN. But I . . .

CUST. Have you written it?

VANAN. No . . . No . . . I couldn't do it, I only want . . . I don't want them to hurt me.

(A silence.)

CUST *(with sudden fierceness).* My God, it's almost comic to think you can let yourself be buried so willingly. It's unnatural. *(Urgently and whispering.)* What's happened, Vanan? What is it? Tell me.

VANAN *(suddenly whispering).* Cust, I'll tell you the truth. I'm tired.

CUST. What of?

VANAN. The whole thing. You told me to think about it.

CUST. Well?

VANAN. People were cross with me, because I always kept saying the same things.

CUST. Well?

VANAN. Well, actually . . . I began to think about it by myself, at night.

CUST. Good. Well?

VANAN. The trouble was that I was alone; everyone believed that things had happened . . . that other way; and so—Cust, have you ever been bathing in a river, and suddenly seen the water all running the other way? You stand there, still, alone, by yourself, in the middle of the flowing water . . . and you feel a sort of giddiness . . . It was like that; I began to . . .

CUST. Yes?

VANAN. I began to feel weighed down, Cust, disheartened. There were times when I spoke out loud, all by myself, boldly, saying I was innocent . . . but even my own voice hadn't any conviction in it any longer . . . (Suddenly.) Do you know what it was? (Whispering.) I almost stopped believing in it myself.

CUST. In what?

VANAN. I stopped believing in it. I admit there may have been some little things, when I've been taking evidence, that I may have modified a little . . . Perhaps I've been responsible for a certain amount of confusion . . . I don't know: I may even have been a bit at fault myself; they all say so . . . (Suddenly pointing towards the corridor.) You know, Cust. She's my principal torment.

CUST. Who?

VANAN (still pointing). My daughter. It's she who drives me on.

CUST. What do you mean?

VANAN. Oh, yes, yes. She's become so naughty. She never leaves me in peace. Sometimes I pretend to be asleep, or feel unwell. But she has no pity, none at all.

CUST. Your daughter?

VANAN. Yes, yes.

CUST. What does she want you to do?

VANAN. She wants me . . . to . . . to write . . . to accuse somebody. She knows I'm innocent, so she wants me to make them listen to me . . . But I'm old, Cust, I'm tired . . . And now everyone here is so rude and insolent to me the whole time. She can't understand that. She can't see that to insist on speaking out only means getting into worse trouble!

CUST. Was it she who brought you here?

VANAN. It was, yes. (He laughs.) You can't think how furious she must have been when they sent her away. She's out there now, waiting for me. But do you know what I'm going to do? I shall go out that way, through the clerk's office. (Suddenly pushing CUST aside, with a loud cry and a strange unexpected energy.) I hate all this! I hate you too, Cust. I could kill you. (Moving almost solemnly towards the office door.) Let me go away. I don't want to think about these things any more. (ELENA *slips in through the corridor door. She makes a sign to* CUST *not to say anything. In a completely different voice, stopping.*) Listen, Cust, I know I keep going about shouting that I am innocent, like Our Lord on the Cross; but suppose that was just a bit of hypocrisy? and suppose the Lord chastised me? (*Vaguely.*) A man needs peace, he can't stand against the whole world . . . sometimes I tell my daughter that I'm coming to the courts, but I actually go to a little public garden I know in the town, and just sit there a little. That's where I go. Goodbye, my dear Cust. Goodbye.

(*He moves towards the door of the clerk's office: there he nods goodbye to* CUST, *and disappears;* CUST *and* ELENA *remain alone.*)

ELENA. I'm his daughter.

CUST. I know.

ELENA (*in distress*). He hasn't anyone else in the world. Neither have I. Don't you think it's sad he should run away from me like that? And silly that I should run after him?

CUST. It's never easy to understand what goes on inside us.

ELENA. Are you in charge of the inquiry?

CUST. Is there something you want to say?

ELENA. Yes, I came specially.

CUST. Well, you can speak. Is it about the inquiry?

ELENA. Yes. It's important, and private.

CUST. You'll have to be quick then. A decision has to be reached this evening.

ELENA. Sir, what my father told you wasn't the truth. I know he wasn't being sincere.

CUST (*cautiously*). When is a man being truly sincere? It's always difficult to be quite sure.

ELENA. Forgive me, sir. The earliest thing I can remember is when I used to sit on my father's knee. His hair wasn't gray in those days. He used to sit with his eyes closed, and I used to pretend I was drawing his face; I used to touch his eyes with my finger, like that, his nose, his mouth . . . it was one of our games; but we had so many games. I can't describe the happiness and delight we both had in those days! When I hear anyone talking of the people they love, I know that no one can ever be as we were, father and I. Whenever anyone said I looked like him I used to feel my cheeks go scarlet with pride. I would have refused to go to heaven, if my father wasn't to be there too. *(She is silent for a moment; then, without saying anything, she takes from her bag an envelope and shows it to him.)*

CUST. What is that?

ELENA. It's his defense, sir. The statement. They've only to read it, and I know my father will be acquitted. *(A silence.)*

CUST. But only a few moments ago your father said. . . .

ELENA. I know. He refuses to present it. I brought it myself, without telling him.

CUST. But he's definitely denied having written it.

ELENA. But he's spent night after night on it . . . I helped him.

CUST. Then why should he deny it now?

ELENA *(sadly and anxiously)*. Because he's so bewildered and frightened. Someone has put the most dreadful doubts and fears into him; it's almost like an illness . . . He's like someone who has fallen down . . . and doesn't want to get up again; he just wants to shut his eyes.

CUST. Do you know the contents of this statement?

ELENA. Yes, of course. Father has remembered a thousand details . . . his innocence is quite plain. It throws light on everything.

CUST. And does this light help us to find who the other man is? The real culprit, I mean.

ELENA. Yes, sir, of course it does. As you read it, page by page, bit by bit, you can see who the real culprit is, you can guess.

CUST. Can you recall the name? Is it someone called Croz?

ELENA *(uncertainly)*. No, that isn't the name *(She puts the statement into CUST's hand.)*

CUST. Good. *(He fingers the statement for a moment: suddenly he hums for a moment to himself.)* My dear child. Elena your name is, isn't it? Sit down. The friendship that binds me to your father . . . and also something that really shines in you yourself and . . . genuinely moves me . . . *(He breaks off.)*

When I first saw you, I said to myself: this is true innocence; the radiance of justice herself entering into this sad place . . . *(Resuming.)* Well, all that, I was saying, compels me to make a request of you. You don't imagine, do you, that what you feel is really anything more than a mere hope? Or that the investigating magistrate *(holding up the document)* is likely to find anything more than that in here?

ELENA. I am certain, sir.

CUST. You will admit that the opinion of a judge may differ from that of a daughter?

ELENA. When you have read it you will run to my father and embrace him. You'll punish everyone who doubted him. You'll be so indignant; there's not a soul on earth who could be indifferent.

CUST. But your father, who is after all not inexperienced in these matters, must have had a reason for keeping silent about this document.

ELENA. But I've explained . . .

CUST. Yes, but you are probably not aware of all he said in here just now. He expressed a fear that any further light thrown on the facts might damage himself.

ELENA. Yes, exactly, he doesn't understand, it's what I was telling you.

CUST. He declares that the treatment given him by the Administration has been extremely indulgent; and that to insist might provoke great severity. Your father expressed his gratitude to us all.

ELENA. Sir, I have read that even people condemned to death— even when they've been innocent—at the last moment, they've begged forgiveness just as though they were guilty. I know that can happen. My father is a very tired man; but he is innocent.

CUST. Very well. *(He hums for a moment between his teeth, throws the statement down on the table, and goes on.)* Very well. You force me to this, my dear child. You are being very stubborn. Just now, while I was listening to you . . . *(He casts a glance towards the archives.)* I know time is very short and we haven't time to dawdle over all this . . . nevertheless, while

I was listening to you, there were a lot of things I couldn't help thinking: rather silly things. For example: I'm old enough to be your father. Everything desirable that passes near us we would like in some way to make our own. *(Suddenly, in an almost anguished outburst.)* And I made you my daughter, I stole you from Vanan! I would have held my breath so as not to sully you in any way. I tell you that in a way I have known you ever since I was a boy, but that's too long to tell about now. There is a very simple word which to me expresses what you seem like: loyal. Loyal. But everyone of us runs on, tied to the indifferent ribbon of time; and that produces an infinite number of mistaken meetings, wrong relationships. One could have been father, brother, husband, son, receiving and giving . . . something. Instead . . . you don't even realize how absurd it is that I, at such a moment, should waste so much time telling you this. However. I wanted to tell you . . . *(with exaggerated anger, to force himself to stop talking)* . . . a few moments ago, in here, your father explicitly confessed himself guilty.

(A silence.)

ELENA *(almost to herself)*. I can't believe it.

CUST. You mean you don't want to believe it. Didn't you say your father avoided you? What does that mean? It means that it's you in particular he wants to hide something from.

ELENA *(lost in her own thoughts)*. There will have been a reason. I will believe anything, but not that he could have disgraced himself.

(A silence.)

CUST *(rather harshly)*. What a cruel word. Disgraced. Sad that you should use it, since it's your own father we're talking about. An inhuman word. *(Almost pleading.)* Can't you believe that one may make mistakes . . . which one only notices . . . after one's made them, and it's too late to turn back? One mistake is enough: the first one.

ELENA *(after reflecting for a moment)*. If I were to think that at some given moment—and that moment must come sooner or later, mustn't it, to people who commit these evil things—if

I were to think of my father, at some given moment, doing something furtive, and secret, and looking round to see that no one was watching; or sitting there listening to a man whispering secret, wicked orders to him, and my father whispering back, hurriedly consenting . . . My father! My father, doing that! My father! *(She almost laughs.)*

CUST *(agitated, pleading).* Don't you think that everyone in the world, even your father, may at some time or other, need a little pity?

ELENA. But my father couldn't, couldn't possibly do anything he'd have to be ashamed or embarrassed about! You should see my father when he's really angry and outraged! There is nothing in my father but nobility and goodness and pride. People who disgrace themselves in such filthy ways have to be made of very different stuff from my father. You can tell at a glance when people are capable of such treachery: you feel a kind of contempt for them the minute you see them.

CUST. Yes, hideous toads leap from their mouths, and go hopping about these rooms. *(He hums for a moment.)* How cruel you are, my little angel. But it's only your age. The blank blue snow of childhood, smitten by the first incandescent ray of youth. *(With a gust of anger.)* Intoxicating dazzle of light! It leaves one melancholy, humiliated; oh, it's not your fault; you shine, literally, in the midst of this hell of ours. You remind one of the pure crystals of which, as you've perhaps been taught at school, inorganic matter is composed. Do you mean to hand in this statement?

ELENA *(a little disturbed).* Yes.

CUST. Good. *(With a touch of harshness in his voice.)* I was saying that we were all crystals like you, once, my dear child; that's why it makes one sad to look at you. It seems that life comes into existence at a later stage, born on the icy geometric forms of the inorganic, like a kind of rash, a malignant growth . . . yes, a leprosy indeed. And on that day your voice will have lost this resonant light, and you won't talk any more about disgrace.

ELENA. My father . . .

CUST (*interrupting*). Your father. Why not let us be quite frank about him? He's a successful man, he's one of those who have got a great deal out of life. Are we to believe that life simply *gave* him what he got? Did he get it for nothing? Was it a gift from life? A birthday present? Did it cost him nothing? Not even cleverness? Cleverness: a name by which many kinds of villainy get past. It is unlikely that the statement refers to those.

ELENA. But my father . . .

CUST. Is after all rather like the unfortunate rest of us, isn't he? The only consolation is we're all made of the same stuff, my dear. Haven't you ever noticed . . . how shall I put it, haven't you ever caught a look on your father's face . . . something in his voice—yes, his voice would be enough to show you—something that worried you a little? That voice, so familiar to you, so dear to you: but did you never hear that voice talking to one of your father's superiors, someone high up: the Minister perhaps; and being very polite, and excited, and eager? And then suddenly did you never hear the same voice, sharp and impatient, speaking to a beggar? Well? Did that never happen? It happens with all of us. And then again . . . didn't you ever hear him pretending to be kind and gentle, from above, with the old man at the gate . . . well? Look at me: of course you remember. You're already a little tarnished, my fair crystal. Such a daily heap of hypocrisy and wickedness in the inflections of one single voice! After all that, shall we really be so very surprised if these pages (*he waves the document in the air*) turn out to be a skillful selection of things which are true in themselves, but have been cunningly prised out of the whole. But if you really want to present it—

ELENA (*at a loss*). I'd like . . .

CUST. And we haven't even got to the real thing yet, have we? We haven't mentioned the words, have we?—only the voice! Do you believe that these actions, just because no law book condemns them, are any less vile than those that you've called vile? Evil actions, hypocrisies, betrayals. Everywhere! Even here, in our own thoughts, which we falsify—yes, even those! As we formulate them inside us . . . not as they first tremble in our conscience, but as soon as certain cunning poisonous calculations occur to us; even in some of our highest impulses whose mysterious purity we contrive to cheat and twist and sully. *(Greatly agitated, but still with an attempt at sarcasm.)* Think, my dear, of the housewife who has carefully stored away her beautiful jars of jam for the winter: it's like that; one day we also decide to open our nice little boxes of fine ideas, and what do we find inside . . . *(He throws the statement on to the table.)* A swarming heap of maggots! And I can think of nothing, nothing on earth, that escapes that fate! *(He breaks off and turns round, as* MALGAI *enters.)* Have you found anything, Malgai?

MALGAI. Not yet; we're still working. *(He takes up a paper from the table and returns to the archives.)*

CUST *(between his teeth)*. Good, so am I. *(He wipes his brow and goes on.)* No, my dear. I know of nothing that escapes. A single opaque mess asking one thing alone: to live. To live.

ELENA. But my father . . .

CUST *(shouting)*. Your father was a man, and he was a man here in this ditch! And let me tell you that there was nothing on earth a man could do that he didn't know of!

ELENA *(impetuously)*. But I am sure—

CUST. Of what? Sure of what?

ELENA. Whenever there's been any sort of injustice or mistake I've always thought of my father; I used to think of him here, in this building, in his ermine gown, looking very stern; and I used to feel calm again at once.

CUST. Well, you were wrong, my dear! Look at me! You know I'm not lying!

ELENA *(with a cry, and moving forward as though to retrieve the statement)*. You don't know my father! You're not his friend!

CUST *(violently, breathing heavily, and seizing the statement again)*. My God! How stubborn you are! You only want to create havoc here! I want to tell you something. Perhaps it's not even connected with all this; I don't know. But once when I was only a boy, I remember an afternoon of atrocious, suffocating heat. It was during the siesta; everyone was asleep, soaked in sweat, naked. I must have heard a whisper some-where in the house, perhaps that was it; or perhaps it was some vicious instinct calling me. I got up, and crept barefoot, fur-tively, through the shadowy house, towards that whisper, and at last, through a half-open door . . . What a silly disgusting commonplace story! Through the half-open door, that white-faced child saw a man and a woman . . . a man and a woman turned into animals by the stifling heat . . . unrecognizable faces, horrible gestures, choking, appalling words . . . It was my father and mother. My father, and my mother. Quite obvious, after all; what of it? Silly to make a tragedy of it; a door not closed properly, a nervous boy. *(Suddenly.)* But no, they weren't my father and mother any more! They were some-thing confused, black, blind, insane! Before that moment I'd never really known them, never known my father and mother; nor myself; nor anyone else. I was horribly shocked. There always comes a day when a door opens a little way and we look through. And that day has come for you too, now, my dear. Look! Look at your father, for God's sake, look at him for the first time; and look at yourself too, my dear child! What do you think, do you think that this sweet flower of your body will never be sullied, that it too won't one day be filled with desire and frenzy, do you think that you'll never damage it, never contaminate it, your beautiful little body—and your voice as well, your angel's breath, your very mind? *(Still excited, but suddenly quiet.)* And did you really not know that the great Vanan was sick? Sick, sick, poor devil, that was what was mak-ing such a farcical muddle of everything he said. Life is very long, you know, it's very rare that towards the end a venerable white head is much more than to cover over a heap of nasti-ness; and nasty filthy sicknesses too, those are the things that make age weigh so heavily upon us. That wasn't written in the statement, I'm sure of it. Sad matters, aren't they? You know that I'm telling you the truth, the absolute truth, don't you? As a rule you blush very quickly. I've noticed. But now your color is slowly draining away from your cheeks. You are saying goodbye to the enchantment of youth. You are becoming a woman; it's a small disturbance, it has to come; like the first cigarette, we feel discomfort here. Yes, so it was I who didn't know the great Vanan! If you only realized how little *you* knew about him! And about the others! And about yourself. That is why you were unjust. You never even knew . . . *(with a sudden cry)* that your father hates you! He hates you, yes, he said so in here! *(With a change of tone.)* You didn't even know about the slimy love affairs in which poor Vanan has got himself mixed up. The court itself, this very office, has had to look into it. No, that wasn't in the statement either. Slimy intrigues: the loves of old men. It's a sad and terrible thing, my poor angel; the loves of old men, horrible, unspeakable, tormenting! We all come to it. That's how we're made. They are things he never spoke to you about, aren't they? The man you used to kiss when he came back home at night! Suppose *you* look through the open door as well; it's a thing you have to get used to. You know it's the truth I'm telling you, don't you? Very well: you didn't even know that on the day when they first accused him, the great Vanan wrote a letter! And confessed! Yes, he confessed, my dear. He confessed right from the start. Do you want me to repeat the exact words of that letter! *(Striking his forehead.)* They're engraved here. *(Beginning.)* "My dear Lord Chief Justice . . . an aged magistrate writes to beg of you your extreme kindness . . ."

ELENA *(signing to him not to go on)*. No. *(After a few moments, in a whisper.)* Poor father. *(A pause.)* And poor me.
(A silence.)

CUST. Do you want your statement back? *(He holds it out to her.)*

ELENA *(shaking her head)*. It won't be any use now. *(She goes towards the door; and stops.)*

CUST. You'd better be quick, and go; no one has seen you.

ELENA *(takes a few steps forward; whispers)*. I'm embarrassed, because now when I meet my father . . . I shan't know what to say to him. I'm afraid that when he looks at me, he'll see that I know. Poor father. I don't want to meet him. *(She moves still nearer to the door; and repeats, almost to herself.)* I don't want to meet him. *(She goes out.)*

(Perturbed, CUST stands looking at the door through which she has departed; suddenly, he begins feverishly unwrapping the statement; a few pages fall to the floor, quickly he picks them up. He breaks off in order to listen for any noise from the archives. He looks once more at the door through which the girl has disappeared.)

CUST. After all, she was no more than a child. Her gentleness will be enough to . . . She is too gentle almost . . . Tomorrow the color will have returned to her cheeks; and she will have forgotten. *(A pause.)* But I . . . Oh God, how tired I am! Tired to death. *(He covers his face with his hands; suddenly he hears steps approaching; he throws the statement down on the table, turns, and waits. The door of the archives opens, and ERZI comes out, followed by CROZ. Loudly, almost shouting.)* Well, dear friends, has any good come of your labors?

CROZ *(with a loud laugh)*. Haha. You're very cheerful, Cust. You've already guessed.

CUST *(as before)*. Haven't you found anything?

ERZI *(casually laying a hand upon the statement)*. We find that in none of the suits have the documents survived.

CROZ *(grinning)*. Cust! One of us has removed them.

CUST *(excited and suspicious)*. Removed them? And then what?

ERZI *(removing his hand, and moving away)*. Destroyed them.

CUST. Destroyed them? How? *(He laughs and almost shouts, excitedly, harshly.)* How! How! *(He gradually gets nearer the statement, takes it up, gesticulates with it, and then without disguising what he is doing, drops it into a basket.)* But, my dear friends, would it really have been as easy as all that? Do you think the criminal would have found it easy, or even possible, to burn or destroy, here, such a great number of documents?

ERZI. He could have . . .

CUST. . . . taken them away bit by bit, hidden about himself, do you think? That man, who doesn't want, *(almost shouting)* DOES NOT WANT to be found out, do you imagine he'd have gambled his whole position here, with the risk, however remote and theoretical, of being found with the papers on

him in some accident or other, a fall, or a faint . . . ! My
dear friends, you can't have the slightest idea what he must
be really like! Why the very thought of it would have given
him a fit!

ERZI *(interrupting him almost with a cry)*. Cust. Where are those
papers?

CUST *(calmly, pointing to the archives)*. Still in there, in my
opinion. But hidden away under mountains and mountains of
other documents and papers. The man had patience, so we
must have patience too . . . *(He breaks off.)* Did you hear that?

ERZI. What?

CUST. A noise. Not a noise exactly. Down there, somewhere in
the building. It sounded to me like . . . *(Breaking off again.)*
Yes, there must be something wrong. There's someone running
up the corridor.

MALGAI *(comes running out of the archives and hurries out of
the door to the corridor)*. They say there's been an accident.
(He disappears.)

BATA *(comes running in from the corridor, crosses the room
towards the clerk's office)*. There's been an accident! Why are
people always so careless? They go up and down, up and down,
God knows what they're looking for. The gate up at the top
must have been opened. Didn't you hear the shout? Yes, as she
fell. A loud scream. *(He disappears.)*

(ERZI runs out into the corridor.)

CROZ *(following him)*. This building: horrible things happening
the whole time, blood on the ground, accidents. And it's no
worse than they deserve, most of the people who come here. If
you ask me . . . *(He disappears.)*

*(CUST is alone; he has stood perfectly still throughout; hurried
footsteps and voices are heard outside.)*

A VOICE *(outside the room)*. Let's have some light! Put the lights
on!

ANOTHER. Call somebody! Tell somebody to come!

ANOTHER. Where's the porter? Porter!

MALGAI *(re-entering, breathless)*. It was there, down at the bottom of the elevator shaft. It's so dark everywhere in this

damned place, especially the stairs, and the passages. *(He is hastily clearing a divan of the documents on it.)*

CUST *(without turning, almost tonelessly).* Is she dead?

MALGAI. They don't think so, not yet. They say it's the daughter—

CUST *(interrupts him with a gesture, turning round in sudden terror).* What are you doing?

MALGAI. I'm getting this couch ready . . .

CUST *(horrified).* Here? Why . . . No. No. *(He childishly points towards the clerk's office.)* In there . . .

ERZI *(rushing back in: to* MALGAI*).* Yes, in there, that'll be better. We'll take her in there. Call somebody! Do call somebody! Telephone. *(He runs out again.)*

MALGAI. But who am I to call? There's no one there at this hour; everything's shut up. I ought to be at home too . . .

CUST *(stopping him).* Malgai, did you hear her cry out . . . ?

MALGAI. Yes, a loud cry—

CUST *(his teeth almost chattering).* What . . . what do you think?

MALGAI. About what?

CUST. Do you think it's . . . an accident?

MALGAI. I think she must have tripped, people never look where they're going. She tried to dart back, but it was too late. *(He breaks off, and turns toward the corridor.)* Here she is.

(A low murmur of voices is heard, and the scrape of footsteps approaching: finally the door on the corridor is thrown open wide. A big man enters carrying the girl in his arms, apparently unharmed and as though asleep, her hair flowing over her shoulders. A number of people follow. The man crosses the room, and disappears into the clerk's office: the door remains open. The others, except for CUST, *follow him, talking in low tones, as though in church.)*

A VOICE. . . . yes, some strands of hair . . . in the iron work . . .

ANOTHER. . . . there was oil . . . there were traces of oil from the elevator shaft . . . They ought to . . .

ANOTHER. . . . clean it, of course, clean it . . .

ERZI *(crossing the room with* MALGAI*).* Anyway, send for somebody . . . send for a woman. Warn them . . . that they must send a car. And her father. Send for him . . . Make some excuse . . . Don't tell him . . .

CUST *(they have all gone into the clerk's office.* CUST *remains alone; he approaches the door of the office; stares at it: suddenly in a hushed voice, with an extraordinary note of pleading).* Elena *(A pause.)* Elena. Don't die. Try to live. *(A silence.)* Elena . . .

(He breaks off, as MALGAI *hurries back in.)*

CUST. How is she, Malgai?

MALGAI. I don't think there's very much hope for her.

CUST *(with terror, almost with fury).* Do you mean this girl is going to die?

MALGAI. It's a terrible accident, sir.

CUST *(stammering).* But that girl . . . she was in here a few moments ago . . . blushing, at a mere nothing . . . she was so young . . . I want to tell her . . . *(He breaks off.)*

MALGAI *(alarmed).* What's the matter, sir?

CUST *(stands looking at one of his hands in real terror; suddenly with a suffocated cry).* Malgai! I have her blood here on my hands! I've not touched her, Malgai! I've not touched her! *(He rubs his hand hysterically.)*

MALGAI. But . . . but there's nothing odd about that, sir. I touched her myself. You might easily have touched me, you might have brushed by me. Or you might have touched the others, there's nothing strange about that. *(He breaks off.)*

CROZ *(rushes in from the corridor, in great distress).* Oh my God, Cust; her father's here! They sent for him. Who's going to tell him, what shall we do? Oh how dreadful it is, what a terrible mess, the whole thing is . . .

CUST *(with a fierce wild movement, runs to the door, throws it open and cries).* Come in, Vanan! Come in. Quickly!

VANAN *(letting himself be dragged in, suspicious and whimpering).* But what more do you want of me? What is it? Leave me alone! Leave me in peace, why can't you?

CUST *(shouting).* You'll never be at peace any more, Vanan! *(Louder still.)* Never, never at peace, Vanan! You must do something! Something terrible! Your daughter. Your beautiful

. . . dear Elena. *(Almost to himself alone.)* She's dead. She's dead.

Curtain

ACT THREE

Late in the evening; a single lamp is burning. MALGAI *is just coming from out of the archives. He puts on his hat and overcoat in preparation for leaving.* CUST *appears at the corridor door.*

MALGAI *(noticing him)*. Good evening, sir. Did you want something?

(CUST does not reply.)

MALGAI. I'm really off duty now, but . . . never mind. We are always here when anybody wants us.

CUST *(absently)*. No, you go along, Malgai. There's something I want to do, I shall be staying for a little while.

MALGAI. Ah yes, sir! You're another one who wears himself out, sir, working after hours!

CUST. Yes, I'm another. Are the archives open?

MALGAI. Yes sir, they're open. Mr. Justice Croz wanted to—

CUST. I'll see that they're locked up afterwards. Goodnight.

MALGAI *(surprised)*. Then what shall I . . . very well, sir, very well. *(He goes out, hesitatingly.)*

(CUST waits until MALGAI's footsteps have died away; then he goes to the door on tiptoe and turns the key; immediately afterwards he goes into the archives, and returns with an armful of documents which he throws on a table and begins to examine; very soon, however, something seems to distract him, and he stands there lost in thought; suddenly he starts: all the lamps have gone on. CROZ has risen slowly from a large armchair whose back has hidden him from sight; he has switched on the

*lights; now he gives way to a long burst of laughter mingled
with coughing.* CUST *has turned round quickly; then he slowly
returns to his previous attitude.)*

CROZ *(frequently pausing for breath).* Once upon a time there
was a little mouse. And there was a trap. Instead of cheese,
there were certain well-known papers hidden under mountains
and mountains of other papers . . .

CUST *(absently).* What do you mean?

CROZ. You're losing your grip, Cust! For example, you just turned
the key in the door there: excellent, but what about the other
doors? A bit of a surprise, wasn't it, Cust, to find old Croz
here?

CUST *(as before).* We heard bad news about your health.

CROZ. Yes, I hardly managed to get up here, as a matter of fact.
But if I've got to die, I wanted to die here. Besides, I know that
spite is almost as good as oxygen. *(With a change of tone.)*
Cust, it's all fixed for tonight, isn't it? The sentence on the
guilty man; and the naming of the new president. *(He points
towards the ceiling.)* The old men are already taking their seats
up there. Cust, which of us two is going to walk off with it?

CUST *(as before).* Do you think the Upper Council will definitely
eliminate Vanan?

CROZ. Self-possessed, aren't you? You even indulge in the luxury
of thinking about Vanan! . . . *(Sarcastically.)* Oh, he'll be
sentenced all right . . . *(He pauses for breath.)* . . . And you
or I will get the nomination. But you're not looking very well
either, Cust. In fact, quite the opposite.

CUST *(in a monotone).* It's just that my thoughts keep going
over and over things which are already beyond the possibility
of being changed.

CROZ. You must look after yourself.

CUST. I shall have to. Look at my hand: it costs me a great effort
to stop trying to wipe it, though it's perfectly clean already.
Like that, you see? *(He wipes his hand.)* I have done that so
often that just here the skin has changed. I don't do it quite so
much now.

CROZ. Cust, you've always interested me, you know. You've given me the creeps before now, often. You are very tough, aren't you? Stubborn. But now we're on the last lap.

CUST (*in a staccato monotone*). Yes, I'm very stubborn. And Vanan's daughter showed that she too was pretty stubborn. She hasn't spoken since that day. They say she won't last until tomorrow morning.

CROZ. Cust, what are you doing in here?

CUST. Most of all, it was the cry she uttered as she fell which shocked me. I have tried to analyze it, these last few days; tried to reconstruct it.

CROZ (*louder*). Cust, what are you doing here?

CUST (*quietly, and as though lost in thought*). You can see; I am looking for something. It wasn't so much a fall into an elevator shaft—I keep getting the idea of her being sucked down into a funnel. Slowly at first, then quickly, then down, vertically, swallowed up. I think that cry expressed other things, besides fear. But what other things? A kind of reproach. But most of all—incredulity; surprise.

CROZ. Cust, you keep on talking to me about that girl. Has she some connection with our problem?

CUST (*as before*). No real connection. What annoys me most of all is the fact of the interruption. That girl still had little round cheeks, almost like a baby's; and in fact she was very young: when you looked at her, it was like looking at a beautiful fresh leaf moving gently on the branch: one caught a hint of seasons, enchanting hours yet to come, long, long days drenched in sun . . . And where is all that now? Broken off. It's very strange. I don't think any logic in the whole world can explain that.

CROZ. Cust, I don't know if you've understood. This is the epilogue, Cust, the auditing. You've waited for the right moment to take me into your confidence.

CUST. Perhaps I've never really talked to anyone. Sometimes one begins to need to. Perhaps you'd understand me better than anyone else.

CROZ. Undoubtedly. I've always understood you. In a way, you've kept me company. I should have been bored without you. Cust, today you've made your first mistake.

CUST *(still in the same indifferent, slightly surprised tones)*. Possibly. What was it?

CROZ. You were wrong to come here tonight! Those famous papers, eh? A feeling of fright lest they should still exist in there, subtle, slight, evil: they've drawn you here, like a rope. Right at the last moment, when everything was over, when the old men up aloft were actually dipping their pens into the ink, you had to stumble over this little pebble. *(Shouting.)* Cust, what are you doing here? What are you looking for?

CUST *(almost wearily)*. The criminal.

CROZ. Well, help me then, because I'm looking for him too. And what is it that drives you on?

CUST. The idea that from tonight onwards he may begin to be calm again, that his footstep from tonight onwards may once more begin to be assured and authoritative in this place; as may his voice. I feel a sort of revulsion and stupefaction at the thought. It's like that girl's cry: I can't find a place for it anywhere in the world.

CROZ. Cust, you're a liar! You've sent the record clerk away by a trick! You've come here at this time of night, in secret! You've fallen into the trap; I have found you out!

CUST *(in a monotone)*. Croz. You too are here in secret. It's I who've found you out.

CROZ. Oh, is it really? Well, tell me then, *(pointing to the documents)* have you found nothing in those things there?

CUST. Nothing.

CROZ *(gives a long laugh, and finds difficulty in getting his breath back)*. Nothing! Nothing! A fine result after all the risks you've taken. *(Mockingly.)* Do you know what I'm afraid of? That it's useless to go on looking any more; and that even in there *(pointing to the archives)* everything's vanished.

CUST. Nothing left. That too is strange.

CROZ. Why is it strange? Suppose the papers kept on going in through that door there, and never came out; suppose all the scoundrels in the city had to sign a piece of paper for every penny they ever stole, every lie they ever told; and suppose all the papers stayed in there: by this time there'd be nothing else left on the surface of the earth but papers; and the sea of papers would go on growing and growing till it reached the moon. Haha. Fortunately *(pointing towards the door of the archives)* so much goes in, and so much comes out. As in everything else. Here's a graveyard that's even more of a graveyard than that: it's called the pulping mill. *(In satirically mysterious tones.)* Our friend has taken advantage of that. There's nothing left.

CUST *(in a monotone).* Not a single trace. At this moment that girl too is perhaps gone without trace. Nothing. It's that that's strange.

CROZ. Nothing? No trace? *(He taps himself on the forehead.)* What about this? You don't count what's inside here? The papers have gone to the pulping mill, but Croz will have to be sent there as well, because Croz knows who the criminal is. *(Shouting.)* He knows, he knows! Stay where you are, Cust. Don't you dare come near me. I know you're not a man of action, but you've good cause to send me to the pulping mill too, haven't you? *(He goes over and unlocks the door.)* We don't quite know yet how this interview is going to finish. *(He pauses for breath.)* What a comfort it would be, wouldn't it, with me here, *moribundus,* almost at death's door, how very nice, when you come to think of it, if just one little vein, here inside me somewhere, were to burst and take your trouble away, now, here, at once, before Old Croz could get out of here and begin to chatter, eh?

CUST *(in a monotone).* It's you whose real interest is that *I* don't get out of here; because the criminal, and I've known it for some time, is you, Croz. Possibly some of the others as well. But you, quite certainly. Not me.

CROZ. Cust, I've always admired you. That was really why I always hated you: and you have quite seriously shortened my life, did you know? You're made of steel. Good God, you're not tired yet: what are you still frightened of? It's done now; there's nothing left inside there. Even if I wanted to accuse you, now, my words would be no more than words. A rival's spite, to try and undermine you. Your words against me would be the same. You needn't hold your breath, Cust. You can speak. I know how much you want to; you're dying to.

CUST *(rubbing his hand).* But I'm not guilty. It's you.

CROZ *(shouting).* Yes! Yes! I too! I've also been a cheat! Bah. I've never even taken much trouble to hide it. I'd go on being one. Yes, it would have been worth it, wouldn't it, being honest among our dear fellow citizens—a lot of filthy traitors in exactly the same way, but above all stupid, and villainous, all of them. And how they multiply! Not a drop of cleanliness in one of them; how disgusting! You too: you were quite right, Cust. They must be stamped out underfoot. Cust! I've spoken! You speak too!

CUST *(in a monotone).* But I am not the criminal.

CROZ. Bah. *(He spits towards him: and stands there panting.)* What a swine you are. And you're a fool as well. It's stupid to care so much. *(He breathes heavily again.)* Who can tell how many men, century after century, must have stood . . . like us two, glaring at each other, quarrelling . . . their foreheads covered in sweat . . . and what a silly fuss to make of anything. It was all a lot of nonsense . . . because . . . *(He grips the table and sits down slowly in a strange way; and mutters.)* Damnation. *(He stays there gasping for breath.)*

CUST *(without moving).* Do you feel bad?

CROZ *(almost speechless).* Yes.

CUST. You've upset yourself. Do you want a drink of water?

CROZ *(does not answer; after a moment).* That'd be very nice. *(He gasps.)* Cust. You've always had the most outrageous luck. *(He slips to the floor.)*

CUST *(without moving).* Croz! *(Silence.)* Croz! *(Silence.)* Come on! *(Seeing that the other is trying to speak.)* What is it, do you want to tell me something?

CROZ *(in a whisper).* I'm going, Cust.

CUST. Going? *(Calmly.)* Ah, one can never tell that.

CROZ *(as before).* It's all over. *(He collapses onto the floor.)*

CUST *(after observing him for a moment).* By God, Croz, I'm almost afraid you're right. Croz! Can you hear me? Where are you in pain? *(A silence.)* It's been the same with me these last few days: did you know? I've felt as if there were something at my back, I've felt like a boy going along a dark corridor and whistling. Mustn't turn round, must go straight on, Croz, stick it out. *(A silence.)* Is it your heart? I don't want to frighten you, but this time it does really look like it, doesn't it? These have been hard days for me too, Croz. I've tried to sleep as much as I possibly could. Even a man condemned to death is like a free man, when he's asleep. Sleep is the same for everyone. And let us hope death will be the same, Croz. You are going to sleep for a very long time now, I think. *(A silence.)* Listen, if it's really true that you're going, that it's all over, and there's no more danger, then . . . I may tell you . . . it's true, I *have* been a lucky man. Yes, Croz, I was the man we were all looking for, and I really needed, *needed,* to say so to somebody. I couldn't bear it any longer. *I* was the leper. You were looking for me, weren't you? But I'm still hopeful. I think I'm quite safe still. It's been a big job. I'd been frightened that I might not be able to carry it through, frightened I might suddenly begin to shout. We take far too much upon ourselves. Do you know, Croz, I've kept having the same dream over and over again, all these nights. I dreamt about a child, a boy. I've never had any children. And what an ugly child this was of mine! Naked, with an enormous belly, an evil face, and horrible, quick, crooked little legs, leaping about like a frog, yes, just like a frog; I would see it hiding in the record clerk's trolley, or disappearing among the bookshelves and the papers, in the most ridiculous places, and I would be after it . . . always after it . . . trying to grab hold of it; sometimes I managed to cut it, with a knife . . . cut it up in a hundred pieces . . . but every piece began to grow again with those little legs . . . and to leap about with me after it, I couldn't catch it. I was soaked in sweat, I had too many things to look out for, here, there, everywhere; it was too much, yes, it was too much! Nobody else could have borne it, I'm sure of that. *(In wild desperation.)* That girl's cry, Croz! I *studied* it! I pored over it! It's difficult to understand what she meant, one can make all sorts of guesses. "Aaaaah!" Like that, she cried! "Aaaaah!" The idea

I've formed of it . . . is that it had somehow scratched something, made a scratch on a piece of glass. No, not quite, not on a glass . . . it was one of those scratches from which small drops of blood issue. Every now and then, a little drop. It all seems finished; but you look again; and there is another drop of blood. Yes, a scratch. Blood. They all believe it was an accident . . . But I . . . I'm mystified. I can't see . . . *(He breaks off.)*

CROZ *(raises his head, gets up slowly from the floor; in an ordinary voice, quietly).* To see ourselves clearly is a great privilege, Cust. You want to set too many things in order. *(Suddenly, wildly, and harshly, he begins to shout.)* Help! I'm dying! Help me, help me! Porter, porter! Hurry! *(He gasps for a moment.)* Quickly someone! Porter! Porter! *(He begins to beat his stick on the table.)* Help, help, help, help!

MALGAI *(running in).* What's the matter?

CROZ. It's me, I'm feeling bad, I am dying. Send for the Investigator, first . . . Councillor Erzi . . . tell him to come here at once. Then call the judges. All of them. Fetch as many people as you can, and Vanan as well, of course. Warn them . . . that I'm here, at the point of death, in the company of . . . him, my colleague Cust, look at him; tell them to hurry if they want . . . to find me alive. Hurry up, you fool. (MALGAI *runs out.)* *(Worn out by his efforts, speaks more slowly, breathing with difficulty.)* My poor Cust, I wish I could say that all this had only been . . . a charade for your benefit. Unfortunately . . . it's only too true . . . that I'm about to die; what a bloody disgrace. *(He pants slightly.)* My dear friend, the popular superstition about the words of the dying, strengthens . . . my credit. Strengthens it a great deal. I shall tell the truth; they will believe me; and you, at the very last minute, will have slipped up. You've spoken, you've told me. I could save you too, my dear fellow, I've always . . . liked a good joke . . . in that case I'd be the one who nominated you as president, I'd be the one who put the ermine gown on the back of the great leper; this filthy shell would have a snail inside worthy of it. A juicy sight! But I could never bring myself to help *you*, Cust.

I don't like you. You're conceited. I want to punish you. *(He gasps for breath.)* The point of death makes me very powerful. I don't believe I have any duties. *(He gasps.)* I believe that things develop . . . according to a purely vegetable law. And it's not without . . . its comic side. I believe that if we . . . decided to think it was disgraceful to wear gray . . . *(he laughs)* ha-ha, to wear gray stockings . . . anyone who actually had worn gray stockings . . . ha-ha-ha, would feel terrible guilt and shame. That's all it is. I don't believe that anything remains of us. We'd be in a real mess if . . . if anything could really be distilled from such a load of nonsense.

(BATA arrives, in haste, accompanied by MAVERI.)

BATA. Croz, how are you?

CROZ. Much as you'd expect a man to be, who knows he'll be dead . . . in about ten minutes. Just stay over there, my dear fellow, there's something I have to say . . . to my colleague. *(To CUST, privately.)* All these judges . . . they've always turned my stomach. A lot of them are very upright and very worthy . . . and they'll live for a long time . . . They are made of wood. As for the rest . . . come a bit closer, Cust. They administer justice! Ha-ha-ha. *(He laughs.)* Which means they express their opinion that certain actions are just, and certain others are not. Just as one sausage is hung on to another sausage, this opinion is hung on to the law books . . . beautifully bound of course . . . and these law books are hung on to other law books—and statutes and tables . . . older still. The trouble is, my dear fellow . . . *(He breaks off, and says to PERSIUS, who has just arrived.)* What's he doing?

PERSIUS. Who?

CROZ. Erzi. Silly old tortoise.

PERSIUS. They've sent for him. Everybody's on their way here.

CROZ *(turning to CUST).* . . . the trouble is that the main hook is missing, the original clasp . . . and without that . . . the whole string of sausages falls to the ground! But where, and how, and when! Who was it who decided one thing was right and another wasn't? We know perfectly well that things . . . are what they are, all equal. That's why we judges are all hypocrites, all of us stuffed with stale rancid sausage meat. That's what the real corruption in these courts is, the whole place stinks terribly of it; I can't wait to be free of it. *(He breathes with difficulty: he points to the group of judges and winks.)* They all pretend. They don't really believe it, those chaps, they don't really believe in the resurrection after death, nor even in Lord Free-will; don't you see? *(He emits a soft scandalized whistle; suddenly thoughtful.)* And as a matter of fact, what reason on earth is there to expect that at some point in this chain, something autonomous will break out? The soul, I mean. I am speaking of the soul. But anyway, all that . . . is rapidly ceasing . . . to concern me. Naturally. *(He remains for a moment with drooping head.)* What about Erzi?

MALGAI *(coming in)*. He's coming up from the offices.

CROZ. Good. Come here, Malgai. And you, Persius. *(The two men obey.)* Take hold of me firmly. You on that side, like that. You on this. That's right. *(He has made the two men take him firmly by the arms and lift him up.)* Now let's go and meet him. I've a number of disclosures to make to him. *(With a touch of pride.)* I don't want . . . to wait for him and death . . . in here . . . bent double . . . like a rat that . . . somebody's trampled on. *(Supported by the two men, indeed almost carried by them, CROZ slowly crosses the room and goes out. CUST, BATA and MAVERI stand looking at each other.)*

BATA *(excitedly to CUST)*. Poor Croz, the whole of his life, he's been nothing but an old tin of poison. What does he want to talk to Erzi about? Revelations at the point of death! What sort? Against whom?

MAVERI *(distressed)*. Do you know anything about it, Cust? What was he saying to you just now?

CUST *(in a monotone)*. I ought in duty to warn everyone that our poor friend is no longer himself; I'm afraid he's raving . . . *(He breaks off.)*

MALGAI *(appearing at the door, excited and jubilant)*. Croz is talking to Erzi! Big things! He has said—and he is dictating to the secretary also—that he, Croz, in solemn declaration, testifies that President Vanan . . .

BATA (taking the words out of his mouth). . . . is innocent!

MALGAI. . . . and that if he manages to live another five minutes, he intends to reveal . . .

BATA. . . . the name of the real criminal!

MALGAI. Exactly! (He rushes out again.)

CUST (as before). Unfortunately the trust we can put in Croz's words is only relative. This crisis has produced a genuine disorder in him, and . . . (He turns.)

(VANAN is entering, bent and terrified: a NURSE leads him in. BATA rushes up to him, making an overwhelming fuss of him.)

BATA. Vanan! Vanan! Please allow someone who has never had a moment's doubt of you and your . . .

MAVERI (in competition with BATA). . . . your absolute integrity, which now shines again in such a sudden, unexpected, even marvellous . . .

NURSE (stepping between the two judges and VANAN, who has timidly drawn back). Forgive me, he has to be treated and spoken to very gently. I always have to be with him.

CUST (who has stood staring at the NURSE, quietly, but in a voice slightly louder than necessary, almost solemnly). You have left Elena? (Something in his voice makes the others turn and look at him.)

NURSE. Didn't you know, sir? The poor child has no need of me or anyone else now.

CUST (in the same tones). Is she dead?

NURSE. Two days ago, sir. What am I saying? Three. Her sufferings are over.

(A silence.)

CUST (as before). What a very small coffin, she will have needed. They told me she was much changed.

NURSE. Just like a tiny little bird, sir. She weighed nothing at all.

CUST. She didn't say anything further?

NURSE. Nor even heard anything. Nor even looked at anything.

CUST. Did she complain at all?

NURSE. No, poor little thing. Only towards the end, she kept doing this with her poor little hand: as though to try and push something from her, or drive it away, a fly or something.

CUST. Was anyone at her side, when that gesture ceased?

NURSE *(dropping her voice).* You will hardly believe it, sir, but poor Mr. Vanan refused to go and see her again. He made the excuse that he was suffering too much. *(She shakes her head.)* At the end he made even stranger and more childish excuses. It isn't his fault.

CUST *(thoughtfully, while they all look at him in some amazement).* So no one will ever again meet the young girl I saw at that door. She stood there a little out of breath, as though after a race . . . No one ever said anything more to her, she never listened to anyone. *(To the woman almost threateningly.)* You: why didn't you make her listen to you, while there was time? Now no one will ever be able to do that. *(Almost to himself.)* I talked to her, I passed long nights with her, begging her not to die, all night through; but she didn't believe in me anymore.

NURSE. But that's not true, sir; you never once came.

CUST *(in a monotone, quietly, turning to VANAN).* Vanan, I fear your daughter did not attribute enough importance to her own life. She ought to have been persuaded that in her there was . . . *(He pauses with his arm upraised.)*

PERSIUS *(bursting in, greatly agitated).* At this very moment Croz is revealing the criminal's name! They even sent *me* away. It appears it really is one of us!

CUST *(who has listened without turning, goes on after a moment, in a louder voice).* . . . that in her there was something which does not exist and will never again exist at any other point of eternity . . . *(Suddenly, almost with fury.)* Something immenser than the immensest star . . .

VANAN *(retreating a little, to the woman).* Take me away, I don't want to see that man.

CUST *(in amazed tones).* Vanan, her cry split the crystal of the heavens in two, and was heard far, far away. You cannot have forgotten, for you were her father. It is your duty . . .

VANAN *(in a distant, almost childish voice).* But it was all so long ago, and our Lord knows what He does. *(Fervently.)* I hope, hope, hope for heaven, and I don't want to know anything more. *(He makes the sign of the cross several times.)* Our Lord be praised forever. *(He mumbles a prayer; suddenly with a strange obstinacy and almost overbearingly.)* My daughter died when she was a little girl. It was years ago.

CUST *(bewildered).* What do you mean, Vanan?

VANAN *(with the same childish obstinacy and distrust).* Yes, yes, my daughter died when she was a little girl. The Lord willed it so . . .

CUST. Vanan . . . *(He breaks off; they have all turned to the door.)*

MALGAI *(has entered in haste, breathlessly).* We know the criminal's name!

BATA. Come on, out with it, Malgai!

MALGAI *(excitedly, enjoying the delay).* I can imagine the outcry there's going to be!

MAVERI. Come on!

PERSIUS. What about Croz?

BATA. Is he dead?

MALGAI. No one will ever hear that fiendish old voice again. Even *I* couldn't tell you the impudent things the old devil invented before he was willing to give the real name of the criminal! He kept coughing, and winking the whole time. He kept letting out the most dreadful curses; he even pretended in the end to make Councillor Erzi play at guess-who, trying the names of this man and that! And suddenly Croz said: *(imitating him)* "No. It isn't any of them. The criminal's name is . . ."

ERZI *(who has already entered).* His name *was* . . . Croz. *(Advancing with a certain detachment.)* Yes, gentlemen, your colleague Croz has disclosed at the point of death that the person responsible for the corruption in these courts was himself, and no one else; that Vanan is innocent; and that all the other judges are likewise innocent, mainly, he observed, because they hadn't the brains to be anything else; and that the best of the lot and the most deserving of being nominated for the Presidency . . . was you, Cust. He spoke of you in very respectful terms . . . though also, of course, satirically and sharply, as is his wont. He asked me to say to you . . . Wait a moment . . .

(He tries to remember.) "That every man has to scratch his own scabs by himself."

BATA. Very fine. Anything else?

ERZI. He coughed, he blew a little, and he said: *(imitating him)* "Well, well, you've been a hell of a bore, Erzi." And died.

BATA *(violently).* And that filthy blackguard dared to pass judgment on his own colleagues!

MAVERI. Not only that, he still contrived to be smart and impudent right to the end.

BATA. Erzi, I'm not blaming you. But my God, dying or not, Croz ought to have been compelled—*(He points to the great doors at the back which have so far remained closed throughout the play.)*—to go out through there, through those doors; to drag himself at his last gasp up the great staircase and to knock at the door of the Lord High Chancellor, and humble himself there under the forms of law.

PERSIUS. And he could have died after that, if he wanted to!

BATA. And where, where, I should like to know are we to have any restitution for the offense against justice . . . ?

ERZI *(almost smiling, absently).* But it's Time, my dear friends, it is Time that repairs all insults, and obliterates all scars. And besides, in this case, since Nature has looked after Croz already, the only thing that remains for us to do is to compensate Vanan for our unjust suspicions by conferring some high distinction on him . . . and also to nominate a new President. And I have a fancy that at this minute the High Council is nominating . . . you, Cust. The news should be here any minute now. I congratulate you, Vanan. And you, Cust.

CUST *(staring before him with wide-open eyes).* The Council will nominate me President of this Court?

ERZI *(lightly and genially).* It's highly probable. The desk behind which, from now onwards, you will cultivate your penetrating thoughts will be very imposing and monumental.

CUST. Have you finished your inquiries?

ERZI. Their goal has been reached, and besides things are hurrying on, everything is moving forward. The stone drops to the bottom, the water becomes calm once more. Croz is dead,

Ludvi-Pol is dead. And they're not the only ones. The town is already turning to other things. . . .

CUST *(almost to himself, pointing to the archives).* . . . Every trace of the crime gone . . .

ERZI *(good-humoredly, jesting).* . . . Our good Vanan is at peace with God, the tempest calmed . . . in a few moments workmen will lower a number of levers and the lights will be extinguished; and while dawn quickens over life's enchanting lake, now once more blue and peaceful, we shall go home to bed, certain that the affairs of this court . . . *(turning to CUST)* . . . are once more in good hands.

BATA *(precipitating himself towards CUST with hand outstretched).* Let me say, my dear Cust, that we're all proud and honored by this nomination. I am sure there can be no doubt about it! Are you glad?

CUST *(absently, nodding).* Very glad.

BATA. You'll be able to have a holiday now, won't you?

CUST. Yes, I could do with one. A holiday.

BATA. Well, goodbye for the present, my dear fellow. *(He goes out.)*

MAVERI *(promptly).* What is it, are you still a bit worried? No, no, don't worry, the nomination's certain. Well, so long. *(He goes out.)*

PERSIUS *(promptly).* Today you will reach the goal for which you have spent the best years of your life.

CUST. Yes, my whole life has been directed towards this moment.

PERSIUS *(watching him).* You will wait here for the news?

CUST *(absently).* Yes. Yes.

PERSIUS. Goodbye then. Till tomorrow. *(He goes out after colleagues.)*

CUST *(suddenly).* The stone dropping to the bottom . . . the lake becoming calm again . . . My God, Erzi! That image of yours . . .

ERZI. Is it that that's worrying you?

CUST. It's not that I'm worried . . . but I should like . . . *(with sudden anguish)* . . . to be able to understand; otherwise . . .

It's difficult to rest. *(Suddenly pleading.)* And God knows I have need of that . . .

MALGAI *(coming forward in his turn).* You're a bit exhausted, sir. A little rest and you'll be back in your old form again, quite recovered, Mr. . . . President! We can say that now, can't we? *(He goes out.)*

CUST *(in a low voice).* But I *am* recovered. *(He raises his hand, and rubs it with the familiar gesture.)* Look, for some days past I've kept wanting to do this. *I* have. I like it, it keeps me company. But now I'm beginning to forget to. Hours go by and I forget to do it. *(To* ERZI, *breathing heavily.)* No, it's not that I'm worried, but certainly . . . there is something . . . that doesn't . . . *(with a cry)* doesn't fit, do you understand? *(Suddenly turning round.)* Vanan! It's you who frighten me. When I look at you I feel that underneath this building, underneath you and me, a black gulf is opening!

ERZI *(his voice unexpectedly loud and severe).* What's the matter, Cust? What's the matter?

CUST *(frantically).* Vanan, the matter is the blood-stained face of your daughter! I can't find a single explanation on earth for that.

VANAN. My daughter died when she was a little girl . . . my daughter died when she was a little girl . . . it's so very long ago now . . .

CUST *(as before).* Vanan, suppose she . . . wanted to die . . . ? Suppose that was the terrible thing that happened? Suppose she threw herself down?

VANAN *(muttering).* You liar. You reptile. My poor Elena died when she was a little girl.

CUST *(with a cry).* Vanan, I fear . . . that when she shouted . . . she was asking something! Is it possible that no one heard? That no one answered? That that has not been inscribed on any register? That such an enormous question should remain unsolved?

ERZI *(suddenly, with sombre intensity).* Cust, I don't think that a man should be more stubborn than his little powers allow him to be! Administration: that is a human fact, its task is to smooth things out, not to dig things up, and turn them upside down! Nature: she heals her wounds so rapidly that perhaps the real truth is something else: that she is unaware of them. *(Dropping his voice.)* And after all, if we want to talk about God . . .

VANAN *(suddenly interrupting, and then slowly making his way to the door). . . .* God is so good. He forgives. He forgets. And we too shall forget, in His blessedness. *(He goes out, supported by the* NURSE.*)*

ERZI. You are left alone to think about these things, Cust. You alone.

CUST *(almost to himself).* I alone. I alone. I alone. And when I too shall have turned my back and gone away . . .

ERZI. . . . what was done and what was left undone will all be the same.

(The POLICE OFFICIAL *enters and hands* ERZI *a paper.* ERZI *looks at it.)*

(With a cry.) Cust! The Council . . . has nominated you! You've won. *(Approaching him, with sombre pity.)* Poor Cust, you've almost changed in appearance during these last few days. In a short time you will have forgotten, exactly as Vanan has. The season granted to us is so brief, don't disturb it with your cries! Don't be stubborn. *(He points upwards.)* The Lord High Chancellor himself is happy that matters have been mended. He is very old; he is probably napping at the moment on his table. Pointless to go and disturb him. *(Moving towards the door.)* Goodbye, Cust, let the world roll on. That is mankind's job.

(He goes out followed by the OFFICIAL. *A silence.* MALGAI *reappears and begins putting out the lights one by one, preparing to close the place up and go away.)*

MALGAI *(moved by curiosity, and with rough kindliness).* You are all alone, Mr. President. Aren't you going home?

CUST. Yes. I shall go now as well. *(He goes slowly towards the corridor entrance; and suddenly stops. The room is almost dark.)*

MALGAI *(worried).* What's the matter? What are you waiting for?

CUST *(his teeth are chattering slightly: he turns back)*. Because there is no argument on earth that would let me shut my eyes in peace tonight. I shall have to wake the Lord High Chancellor. I must confess the truth to him.

MALGAI. Shall I come with you, Mr. President?

CUST. No. I'm a bit frightened. But I know there is no one who can help me.

(He makes his way to the door which leads to the office of the Lord High Chancellor, and which has hitherto remained unopened. He throws the door open. Beyond it a long staircase is revealed going upwards; CUST begins to make his way up the stairs, very slowly, as

Curtain

THE DECAMERON is a collection of a hundred tales, first published in 1353. Boccaccio compounded the title from two Greek words, *deca,* "ten," and *hemera,* "day." The reference is to the narrative framework which he gave to the collection.

In 1348, while the Black Death is raging in Florence, seven young women and three young men meet in a church and agree to flee the city and retire to a villa in the surrounding hills. There they spend two weeks, devoting Saturdays and Sundays to religious observances, and the remaining ten days to amusements of various kinds. Chief among these is storytelling. Every afternoon they gather and each contributes a tale, amounting in the course of the ten days to a hundred. Many of the stories have become famous, the following among them.

Giovanni Boccaccio [1] (1313–1375)
from THE DECAMERON

FEDERIGO'S FALCON
FIFTH DAY, NINTH TALE

> *Translated from the Italian by*
> *Richard Aldington*

FILOMENA HAD CEASED SPEAKING, and the queen, seeing that nobody was left to speak except Dioneo (who had his privilege) and herself, began cheerfully as follows:

---

1. *Boccaccio* (bô kät′ chō).

It is now my turn to speak, dearest ladies, and I shall gladly do so with a tale similar in part to the one before, not only that you may know the power of your beauty over the gentle heart, but because you may learn yourselves to be givers of rewards when fitting, without allowing Fortune always to dispense them, since Fortune most often bestows them, not discreetly but lavishly.

You must know then that Coppo di Borghese Domenichi, who was and perhaps still is one of our fellow citizens, a man of great and revered authority in our days both from his manners and his virtues (far more than from nobility of blood), a most excellent person worthy of eternal fame, and in the fullness of his years delighted often to speak of past matters with his neighbours and other men. And this he could do better and more orderly and with a better memory and more ornate speech than anyone else.

Among other excellent things, he was wont to say that in the past there was in Florence a young man named Federigo, the son of Messer Filippo Alberighi, renowned above all other young gentlemen of Tuscany for his prowess in arms and his courtesy. Now, as most often happens to gentlemen, he fell in love with a lady named Monna Giovanna, in her time held to be one of the gayest and most beautiful women ever known in Florence. To win her love, he went to jousts and tourneys, made and gave feasts, and spent his money without stint. But she, no less chaste than beautiful, cared nothing for the things he did for her nor for him who did them.

Now as Federigo was spending far beyond his means and getting nothing in, as easily happens, his wealth failed and he remained poor with nothing but a little farm, on whose produce he lived very penuriously, and one falcon which was among the best in the world. More in love than ever, but thinking he would never be able to live in the town anymore as he desired, he went to Campi where his farm was. There he spent his time hawking, asked nothing of anybody, and patiently endured his poverty.

Now while Federigo was in this extremity it happened one day that Monna Giovanna's husband fell ill, and seeing death come upon him, made his will. He was a very rich man and left his estate to a son who was already growing up. And then, since he had greatly loved Monna Giovanna, he made her his heir in case his son should die without legitimate children; and so died.

Monna Giovanna was now a widow, and as is customary with our women, she went with her son to spend the year in a country house she had near Federigo's farm. Now the boy happened to strike up a friendship with Federigo, and delighted in dogs and hawks. He often saw Federigo's falcon fly, and took such great delight in it that he very much wanted to have it, but did not dare ask for it, since he saw how much Federigo prized it.

While matters were in this state, the boy fell ill. His mother was very much grieved, as he was her only child and she loved him extremely. She spent the day beside him, trying to help him, and often asked him if there was anything he wanted, begging him to say so, for if it were possible to have it, she would try to get it for him. After she had many times made this offer, the boy said:

"Mother, if you can get me Federigo's falcon, I think I should soon be better."

The lady paused a little at this, and began to think what she should do. She knew that Federigo had loved her for a long time, and yet had never had one glance from her, and she said to herself:

"How can I send or go and ask for this falcon, which is, from what I hear, the best that ever flew, and moreover his support in life? How can I be so thoughtless as to take this away from a gentleman who has no other pleasure left in life?"

Although she knew she was certain to have the bird for the asking, she remained in embarrassed thought, not knowing what to say, and did not answer her son. But at length love for her child got the upper hand and she determined that to please him in whatever way it might be, she would not send, but go herself for it and bring it back to him. So she replied:

"Be comforted, my child, and try to get better somehow. I promise you that tomorrow morning I will go for it, and bring it to you."

The child was so delighted that he became a little better that same day. And on the morrow the lady took another woman to accompany her, and as if walking for exercise went to Federigo's cottage, and asked for him. Since it was not the weather for it, he had not been hawking for some days, and was in his garden employed in certain work there. When he heard that Monna Giovanna was asking for him at the door, he was greatly astonished, and ran there happily. When she saw him coming, she got up to greet him with womanly charm, and when Federigo had courteously saluted her, she said:

"How do you do, Federigo? I have come here to make amends for the damage you have suffered through me by loving me more than was needed. And in token of this, I intend to dine today familiarly with you and my companion here."

"Madonna," [2] replied Federigo humbly, "I do not remember ever to have suffered any damage through you, but received so much good that if I was ever worth anything it was owing to your worth and the love I bore it. Your generous visit to me is so precious to me that I could spend again all that I have spent; but you have come to a poor host."

So saying, he modestly took her into his house, and from there to his garden. Since there was nobody else to remain in her company, he said:

"Madonna, since there is nobody else, this good woman, the wife of this workman, will keep you company, while I go to set the table."

Now, although his poverty was extreme, he had never before realised what necessity he had fallen into by his foolish extravagance in spending his wealth. But he repented of it that morning when he could find nothing with which to do honour to the lady, for love of whom he had entertained vast numbers of men in the past. In his anguish he cursed himself and his fortune and ran up and down like a man out his senses, unable to find money or anything to pawn. The hour was late and his desire to honour the lady extreme, yet he would not apply to anyone else, even to his own workman; when suddenly his eye fell upon his falcon,

---

2. *Madonna*, my lady. [*Italian*]

perched on a bar in the sitting room. Having no one to whom he could appeal, he took the bird, and finding it plump, decided it would be food worthy such a lady. So, without further thought, he wrung its neck, made his little maid servant quickly pluck and prepare it, and put it on a spit to roast. He spread the table with the whitest napery, of which he had some left, and returned to the lady in the garden with a cheerful face, saying that the meal he had been able to prepare for her was ready.

The lady and her companion arose and went to table, and there together with Federigo, who served it with the greatest devotion, they ate the good falcon, not knowing what it was. They left the table and spent some time in cheerful conversation, and the lady, thinking the time had now come to say what she had come for, spoke fairly to Federigo as follows:

"Federigo, when you remember your former life and my chastity, which no doubt you considered harshness and cruelty, I have no doubt that you will be surprised at my presumption when you hear what I have come here for chiefly. But if you had children, through whom you could know the power of parental love, I am certain that you would to some extent excuse me.

"But, as you have no child, I have one, and I cannot escape the common laws of mothers. Compelled by their power, I have come to ask you—against my will, and against all good manners and duty—for a gift, which I know is something especially dear to you, and reasonably so, because I know your straitened fortune has left you no other pleasure, no other recreation, no other consolation. This gift is your falcon, which has so fascinated my child that if I do not take it to him, I am afraid his present illness will grow so much worse that I may lose him. Therefore I beg you, not by the love you bear me (which holds you to nothing), but by your own nobleness, which has shown itself so much greater in all courteous usage than is wont in other men, that you will be pleased to give it me, so that through this gift I may be able to say that I have saved my child's life, and thus be ever under an obligation to you."

When Federigo heard the lady's request and knew that he could not serve her, because he had given her the bird to eat, he began to weep in her presence, for he could not speak a word. The lady at first thought that his grief came from having to part with his good falcon, rather than from anything else, and she was almost on the point of retraction. But she remained firm and waited for Federigo's reply after his lamentation. And he said:

"Madonna, ever since it has pleased God that I should set my love upon you, I have felt that Fortune has been contrary to me in many things, and have grieved for it. But they are all light in comparison with what she has done to me now, and I shall never be at peace with her again when I reflect that you came to my poor house, which you never deigned to visit when it was rich, and asked me for a little gift, and Fortune has so acted that I cannot give it to you. Why this cannot be, I will briefly tell you.

"When I heard that you in your graciousness desired to dine with me and I thought of your excellence and your worthiness, I thought it right and fitting to honour you with the best food I could obtain; so, remembering the falcon you ask me for and its value, I thought it a meal worthy of you, and today you had it roasted on the dish and set forth as best I could. But now I see that you wanted the bird in another form, it is such a grief to me that I cannot serve you that I think I shall never be at peace again."

And after saying this, he showed her the feathers and the feet and the beak of the bird in proof. When the lady heard and saw all this, she first blamed him for having killed such a falcon to make a meal for a woman; and then she inwardly commended his greatness of soul which no poverty could or would be able to abate. But, having lost all hope of obtaining the falcon, and thus perhaps the health of her son, she departed sadly and returned to the child. Now, either from disappointment at not having the falcon or because his sickness must inevitably have led to it, the child died not many days later, to the mother's extreme grief.

Although she spent some time in tears and bitterness, yet, since she had been left very rich and was still young, her brothers often urged her to marry again. She did not want to do so, but as they kept on pressing her, she remembered the worthiness of

Federigo and his last act of generosity, in killing such a falcon to do her honour.

"I will gladly submit to marriage when you please," she said to her brothers, "but if you want me to take a husband, I will take no man but Federigo degli Alberighi."

At this her brothers laughed at her, saying:

"Why, what are you talking about, you fool? Why do you want a man who hasn't a penny in the world?"

But she replied:

"Brothers, I know it is as you say, but I would rather have a man who needs money than money which needs a man."

Seeing her determination, the brothers, who knew Federigo's good qualities, did as she wanted, and gave her with all her wealth to him, in spite of his poverty. Federigo, finding that he had such a woman, whom he loved so much, with all her wealth to boot, as his wife, was more prudent with his money in the future, and ended his days happily with her. ❖

THE ONE-LEGGED CRANE

SIXTH DAY, FOURTH TALE

Translated from the Italian by
Richard Aldington

LAURETTA WAS SILENT, and they all praised Nonna; whereupon the queen ordered Neifile to follow next. And she said:

"Sixth Day, Fourth Tale" from THE DECAMERON OF GIOVANNI BOCCACCIO, translated by Richard Aldington. Copyright 1930, Doubleday & Company, Inc. Reprinted by permission of Rosica Colin Limited for Madame Catherine Guillaume.

Amorous ladies, although quick wits often provide speakers with useful and witty words, yet Fortune, which sometimes aids the timid, often puts words into their mouths which they would never have thought of in a calm moment. This I intend to show you by my tale.

As everyone of you must have heard and seen, Currado Gianfigliazzi was always a noble citizen of our city, liberal and magnificent, leading a gentleman's life, continually delighting in dogs and hawks, and allowing his more serious affairs to slide. One day near Peretola his falcon brought down a crane, and finding it to be plump and young he sent it to his excellent cook, a Venetian named Chichibio,[1] telling him to roast it for supper and see that it was well done.

Chichibio, who was a bit of a fool, prepared the crane, set it before the fire, and began to cook it carefully. When it was nearly done and giving off a most savoury odour, there came into the kitchen a young peasant woman, named Brunetta, with whom Chichibio was very much in love. Smelling the odour of the bird and seeing it, she begged Chichibio to give her a leg of it. But he replied with a snatch of song:

"You won't get it from me, Donna Brunetta, you won't get it from me."

This made Donna Brunetta angry, and she said:

"God's faith, if you don't give it me, you'll never get anything you want from me."

In short, they had high words together. In the end Chichibio, not wanting to anger his ladylove, took off one of the crane's legs, and gave it to her. A little later the one-legged crane was served before Currado and his guests. Currado was astonished at the sight, sent for Chichibio, and asked him what had happened to the other leg of the crane. The lying Venetian replied:

"Sir, cranes only have one leg and one foot."

"What the devil d'you mean," said Currado angrily, "by saying they have only one leg and foot? Did I never see a crane before?"

---

1. *Chichibio* (kē kē′ byô).

"It's as I say, Sir," Chichibio persisted, "and I'll show it you in living birds whenever you wish."

Currado would not bandy further words from respect to his guests, but said:

"Since you promise to show me in living birds something I never saw or heard of, I shall be glad to see it tomorrow morning. But, by the body of Christ, if it turns out otherwise I'll have you tanned in such a way that you'll remember my name as long as you live."

When day appeared next morning, Currado, who had not been able to sleep for rage all night, got up still furious, and ordered his horses to be brought. He made Chichibio mount a pad, and took him in the direction of a river where cranes could always be seen at that time of day, saying:

"We'll soon see whether you were lying or not last night."

Chichibio, seeing that Currado was still angry and that he must try to prove his lie, which he had not the least idea how to do, rode alongside Currado in a state of consternation, and would willingly have fled if he had known how. But as he couldn't do that, he kept gazing round him and thought everything he saw was a crane with two legs. But when they came to the river, he happened to be the first to see a dozen cranes on the bank, all standing on one leg as they do when they are asleep. He quickly pointed them out to Currado, saying:

"Messer, you can see that what I said last evening is true, that cranes have only one leg and one foot; you have only to look at them over there."

"Wait," said Currado, "I'll show you they have two."

And going up closer to them, he shouted: "Ho! Ho!" And at this the cranes put down their other legs and, after running a few steps, took to flight. Currado then turned to Chichibio, saying:

"Now, you glutton, what of it? D'you think they have two?"

In his dismay Chichibio, not knowing how the words came to him, replied:

"Yes, messer, but you didn't shout 'ho! ho!' to the bird last night. If you had shouted, it would have put out the other leg and foot, as those did."

Currado was so pleased with this answer that all his anger was converted into merriment and laughter, and he said:

"Chichibio, you're right; I ought to have done so."

So with this quick and amusing answer Chichibio escaped punishment, and made his peace with his master.　✦

TORELLO'S HOSPITALITY

TENTH DAY, NINTH TALE

Translated from the Italian by
Richard Aldington

FILOMENA ENDED HER TALE and Titus's munificent gratitude was praised by all, when the king, reserving to Dioneo his right to speak last, began thus:

Fair ladies, Filomena is undoubtedly right in what she says about friendship, and she has every reason to complain, as she did at the end, that friendship is now so little accepted by mankind. If we were here to correct or reprove the world's faults, I could follow up her words with a long speech. But our object is different, and it occurs to me to relate to you in a long but pleasant tale one of Saladin's liberalities.[1] From the things

---

"Tenth Day, Ninth Tale" from THE DECAMERON OF GIOVANNI BOCCACCIO, translated by Richard Aldington. Copyright 1930, Doubleday & Company, Inc. Reprinted by permission of Rosica Colin Limited for Madame Catherine Guillaume.

1. *Saladin's liberalities.* Saladin (1138–1193), the Islamic opponent of the Christian kings in the Third Crusade, was renowned for his generosity to his enemies.

you will hear in my tale you will see that, although our vices prevent us from obtaining anyone's complete friendship, we may at least take delight in rendering service, in the hope that some day it will be rewarded.

I say then that, as some relate, in the time of the Emperor Frederick the First, a general Crusade was undertaken by all Christians for the recovery of the Holy Land. Saladin, the Sultan of Babylon and a most valiant Prince, hearing something of this, determined to go personally and observe the preparations of the Christian Princes, so that he could better resist them. He made all his arrangements in Egypt, pretended he was going on a pilgrimage, and set out with two of his wisest and most important councillors, and only three servants, in the guise of merchants. They passed through many Christian provinces, and as they rode through Lombardy towards the Alps, it happened that one evening on the way from Milan to Pavia they met a gentleman, by name Messer Torello d' Istria da Pavia, who was going with his attendants, hounds and hawks, to stay at a handsome estate he had in the Ticino. When Messer Torello noticed them, he saw they were gentlemen and foreigners, and wished to honour them.

Saladin asked one of the attendants how far it was to Pavia and if they could get there in time to enter the city; but Torello, not giving the attendant time to speak, replied himself:

"Gentlemen, you cannot reach Pavia in time to enter the city today."

"Then," said Saladin, "since we are foreigners, will you be kind enough to tell us the best inn where we can lodge?"

"Gladly," replied Messer Torello. "I was just about to send one of my servants to Pavia on an errand; I will send him with you and he will guide you where you will find the best inn."

He then gave orders to the most intelligent of his servants as to what to do, and sent him off with them. He himself rode straight to his house, and arranged the best supper he could, with tables set out in the garden. That done, he waited for them at the door. The attendant rode along talking of different things with the gentlemen, and led them by side roads to his master's house, without their noticing it. And when Messer Torello saw them, he went to meet them on foot, saying with a laugh:

"Gentlemen, you are very welcome."

Saladin, who was very quick-witted, guessed that the gentleman had doubted whether they would have accepted his invitation, if he had invited them when he met them, and so, artfully, had them brought to his own house, so that they could not refuse to spend the evening with him. He returned his salutation, and said:

"Messer, if a man might ever complain of courteous men, we might do so of you, for you have taken us out of our way, and you force us to accept your hospitality without our having deserved such kindness except by a single greeting."

"Gentlemen," said the knight, who was a wise and well spoken man, "if I may guess from your appearance, what you will receive from me will be but poor entertainment compared with what is befitting you. But indeed there is nowhere outside Pavia where you could be well lodged, and therefore do not regret having gone a little out of your way to be lodged not quite so ill."

When he had said this, the servants surrounded the gentlemen as they dismounted, and led away their horses. Messer Torello conducted the three gentlemen into the rooms prepared for them, had their riding boots taken off and refreshed them with cool wines, and retained them in conversation until suppertime.

Saladin and his companions and servants all knew Latin, so they could all make themselves perfectly well understood. Each of them thought that the knight was the most pleasant, courteous man and the best talker they had ever met. Messer Torello, on the other hand, thought they were far more important and magnificent personages than he had at first supposed, and therefore regretted that he could not entertain them that evening with company and with a more ceremonious banquet. He determined to atone for it next day, and, having told one of his servants what he wanted done, sent him to his wife, a most excellent and high-minded woman, who was at Pavia—which was close at hand, and where none of the gates was ever locked. After this he took the gentlemen into the garden, and courteously asked who they were. Saladin replied:

"We are merchants of Cyprus on our way from Cyprus to Paris about our affairs."

"Would to God," replied Messer Torello, "that our country produced such gentlemen as I see the merchants of Cyprus are!"

After spending a short time in conversation about other things, supper was served. He had them sit at his own table, to do them greater honour, and they were well served, as far as an impromptu supper could provide.

Soon after the tables were removed, Messer Torello saw they were tired, and so took them to excellent beds to sleep; soon after which he went to bed himself.

The servant carried the message to Messer Torello's wife in Pavia. She, whose spirit was rather regal than feminine, immediately called together Messer Torello's friends and servants, prepared everything befitting a great banquet, sent out invitations by torchlight to many of the noblest citizens, hung out carpets and arras and hangings, and arranged everything in accordance with her husband's message.

Next day the gentlemen arose, and Messer Torello went to horse with them and ordered out his hawks. He took them to a neighbouring marsh, and showed them how the birds flew. Saladin asked for someone to lead them to the best inn of Pavia, and Messer Torello said:

"I will take you, for I have to go there."

They believed him, and were glad, and together they set out. About Tierce [2] they came to the city, and, thinking they were going to the best inn, went with Messer Torello to his house, where quite fifty of the noblest inhabitants had gathered to receive the gentlemen, whose bridles and stirrups were immediately held for them. As soon as Saladin and his companions saw this, they saw what had happened, and said:

"Messer Torello, this is not what we asked of you. Last night

---

2. *Tierce* (tirs), the third of the canonical hours, or nine A.M.

you did sufficient and more than we required; therefore you might well let us go on our way."

"Gentlemen," said Messer Torello, "I owe more to Fortune than to you for what happened yesterday, since I met you on the road at the time when you had to come to my little house. But today I shall be indebted to you, as will all these gentlemen; and if you think it courteous to refuse to dine with them, you can do so if you wish."

Vanquished by this, Saladin and his companions dismounted and were gaily conducted by the gentlemen to the rooms which had been richly decorated for them. When they had put off their travelling clothes and rested a little, they came to the great hall which was splendidly arrayed. Water was poured on their hands and they were ceremoniously marshalled to their places and magnificently served with all kinds of dishes, so much so that the Emperor himself could not have been better entertained. Although Saladin and his companions were great Princes and accustomed to see the finest things, yet they greatly marvelled at this, and the more so when they considered the knight's rank, for they knew he was a citizen and not a Prince.

After they had eaten and the tables had been removed and they had talked for a time, the gentlemen of Pavia, at Messer Torello's desire went off to rest, since it was very hot. He remained with his three guests, whom he took to a room, and there sent for his wife so that they might see everything that he held dear. She was tall and handsome and dressed in rich clothes, and came into the room with her two children, who looked like two angels, and saluted the guests. They stood up when they saw her and greeted her respectfully. They had her sit down with them, and made much of the two children. After they had been conversing pleasantly for a short time, Messer Torello went away, and she asked them who they were and where they were going. And they made her the same answer as to Messer Torello. Then the lady said gaily:

"Then I see my woman's idea will be useful, and so I beg you as a special grace that you will not refuse or despise a little gift I shall have brought to you. Remember that women give small gifts, in accordance with their small hearts, and so take them, looking more to the good will of the giver than to the value of the gift."

She then had brought to each of them two pairs of robes, one of cloth and the other of silk, fit for Princes rather than for citizens or merchants, and three taffeta coats and linen garments, saying:

"Take these; I have dressed you in clothes like my husband. Although the other things are not worth much, still, they may be useful to you, since you are far from your wives, and have a long way to go and return, and since merchants are neat and fastidious men."

The gentlemen were amazed and saw that Messer Torello was determined to omit no courtesy to them. From the richness of the clothes, far above the status of a merchant, they began to suspect that Messer Torello had recognised them. But one of them answered the lady:

"These are very great gifts, madonna, and could not be lightly accepted, were it not that we are constrained by your request, which cannot be refused."

Messer Torello then returned and the lady, after commending them to God, departed and made like gifts to the servants, suitable to their rank. Messer Torello besought them to spend the rest of the day with him; so, after their siesta, they put on their new clothes and rode through the city with him. And when suppertime came, they supped magnificently with a large and honourable company. At a fitting time they went to bed, and when they got up next morning, in place of their tired hacks they found three good fat palfreys, and likewise new strong horses for their servants. Seeing this, Saladin turned to his companions, and said:

"I swear to God that there was never a more complete or courteous or shrewd man than this. If the Christian Kings are such Kings as he is a knight, the Sultan of Babylon would not be able to resist one of them, let alone all those we have seen preparing to invade him."

Knowing it would be useless to refuse them, they thanked him courteously, and mounted. Messer Torello, with a large company, went with them a great distance on their way. Although the Sultan was reluctant to part from Messer Torello (so much had he already taken a liking to him), yet, since he was in a hurry to push on, he begged them to return. And, though Messer Torello regretted leaving them, he said:

"Gentlemen, I shall do so since you wish it. But this I must say. I do not know who you are, and do not ask to know more than you wish to tell; but whoever you may be, you will never make me believe that you are merchants. And so I commend you to God."

After taking leave of the rest of the company, the Sultan replied to him: "Messer, perhaps we shall be able one day to show you our merchandise and so convince you. God be with you."

Saladin then departed with his companions, determined if his life lasted and he were not worsted in the coming war that he would honour Messer Torello no less than he had been honoured by him. He spoke much of him and his wife and all his deeds and actions and possessions, praising them all to his companions. And when at the expense of much fatigue he had gone through the whole of the West, he and his companions took ship to return to Alexandria, where with full information they prepared for defence.

Messer Torello returned to Pavia and for a long time wondered who the three could have been, but never came anywhere near the truth.

The time for the Crusade arrived, and there were great preparations on all sides. In spite of his wife's tears and entreaties, Messer Torello determined to go. When everything was ready, and he was about to start, he said to his wife, whom he loved profoundly:

"Lady, as you see, I am going on this Crusade, both for the honour of my body and the salvation of my soul. I leave our goods and our honour in your keeping. Now it is certain that I am going, but a thousand things may happen which make my return uncertain. And so I wish you to grant me a favour.

Whatever happens to me, if you have no certain news of my life, wait a year and a month before you remarry, beginning from this day of my departure."

The lady wept bitterly, and replied:

"Messer Torello, I do not know how I shall bear the grief in which you leave me by going. But if my life proves stronger than grief and it should happen otherwise to you, live and die secure in the knowledge that I shall live and die the wife of Messer Torello."

"Lady," said Messer Torello, "I am most certain that as far as concerns you, what you have promised would be carried out. But you are a young and beautiful woman of noble family, and your great virtue is known to everyone. So I have no doubt that if nothing is heard of me, there will be many gentlemen who will ask for you as wife from your brothers and relatives. And however much you wish, you will not be able to defend yourself from their exhortations, and you will be forced to agree to their wishes. That is why I ask this limit, and not a greater one."

"I will do what I can to carry out what I have said," replied the lady, "and I will certainly obey what you enjoin upon me, although I might want to do otherwise. I pray God that neither you nor I may be brought to such an end within that time."

The lady then embraced Messer Torello with tears, and taking a ring from her finger, gave it to him, saying: "If I should happen to die before you return, remember me when you see this."

He then mounted his horse, said farewell to everyone, and went on his way. Coming to Genoa with his company, he went on board a galley and in a short time came to Acre,[3] where he joined the remainder of the Christian host, wherein almost immediately there began a great plague and mortality. While this sickness still lasted, Saladin, either by good fortune or design, captured almost all the surviving Christians and imprisoned them in many different towns. Among them was Messer Torello, who was taken to Alexandria. He was known to nobody there and

3. *Acre,* a city in northern Palestine on the Mediterranean Sea.

was afraid to reveal his identity, and so was forced by necessity to train hawks—in which he was extremely skilled—and in this way came to the notice of Saladin, who had him brought out of captivity and made him his falconer.

Messer Torello was called Saladin's Christian, and neither recognized the Sultan nor was recognized by him. All his thoughts were turned towards Pavia, and several times he tried without success to make his escape. Certain Genoese came as ambassadors to Saladin to ransom their fellow citizens, and when they were leaving, Messer Torello wrote to his wife that he was alive and would come to her as soon as he could and she should wait for him; and he earnestly asked one of the ambassadors, whom he knew, to convey the letter to his uncle, the abbot of San Pietro in Ciel d'Oro.

About this time Messer Torello was one day talking with Saladin about the hawks, when Messer Torello happened to smile, and made a movement with his mouth which Saladin had noticed in his house at Pavia. This movement made Saladin remember Messer Torello, and so he looked at him more carefully and thought he recognized him. Changing the conversation, he said:

"Tell me, Christian, which is your country in the West?"

"Sire," replied Messer Torello, "I am a Lombard from a city called Pavia, a poor man of humble birth."

When Saladin heard this he felt his suspicions almost certainties, and said to himself:

"God has granted me the opportunity to show this man how much I thought of his courtesy."

Without saying another word, Saladin had all his clothes brought into a room to which he took Messer Torello, and said:

"Look, Christian, and tell me if you ever saw any of these clothes before."

Messer Torello looked about and saw the clothes his wife had given to Saladin. It seemed impossible that they should be there, but still he said:

"Sire, I recognise none of them. But it is true that these two are like the clothes in which I clad three merchants who stayed at my house."

Then Saladin, able to restrain himself no longer, tenderly embraced him, saying:

"You are Messer Torello d' Istria, and I am one of the three merchants to whom your wife gave those clothes, and now the time has come for me to show you my merchandise, as I said might happen when I left you."

Hearing this Messer Torello was both happy and ashamed—happy that he had had such a guest, ashamed because he felt he had entertained him but poorly. Then said Saladin:

"Messer Torello, since God has sent you here, you must feel that not I but you are the master."

They rejoiced greatly together, and Saladin had him clothed in royal garments, and led him forth in the sight of all his great barons, speaking much praise of him and commanding that all who valued his favour should honour Messer Torello as if he were the Sultan himself. And this each of them immediately did, but especially the two lords who had been with Saladin in his house. The height of this sudden glory in which Messer Torello found himself to some extent withdrew his thoughts from Lombardy, especially since he had every hope that his letters had reached his uncle.

In the camp or army of the Christians on the day when Saladin captured them, there died and was buried a knight of Provence, of small importance, named Messer Torello of Dignes. Now, since Messer Torello d' Istria was known to the whole army through his nobility, everyone who heard the news "Messer Torello is dead" thought this meant Torello d' Istria and not Torello of Dignes. And the subsequent event of their being captured prevented them from learning the truth. Thus many Italians returned with this piece of news, and some of them were so reckless as to say that they had seen him dead and had been present at his burial. When his wife and relatives heard it, the news gave them inexpressible grief, as it also did to all who had known him.

It would be a long task to relate the lady's grief and sadness and woe; but when after some months of continual mourning her grief had begun to subside, she was courted by the most eminent men in Lombardy, while her brothers and other relatives urged her to marry again. At first she refused many times and with great lamentations, but being constrained she finally agreed to do what her relatives asked, on condition that she should be allowed to remain unmarried for the period she had promised Messer Torello.

While the lady's affairs in Pavia were in this state and only about a week remained before she was to marry again, Messer Torello in Alexandria happened to meet a man whom he had seen go on board the galley which was to take the Genoese ambassadors to Genoa. He therefore called to him, and asked what sort of a voyage they had had, and when they had reached Genoa.

"My lord," said the man, "the galley had an ill voyage, as we heard in Crete, where I remained on shore. When it was near Sicily a dangerous gale arose and drove it on the shores of Barbary, and not one man escaped; two of my own brothers perished in it."

Messer Torello believed what he said (and indeed it was perfectly true), and, remembering that the period of time he had asked his wife to give him would expire in a few days, that no news of him could have come to Pavia, he felt certain that his wife would be on the point of remarrying. Consequently he fell into such distress that he lost his appetite and took to his bed, determined to die.

The news of this came to Saladin, who had the greatest affection for him, and went to see him, and thus after many entreaties and questionings discovered the reason of his grief and sickness. Saladin reproached him for not having spoken of it sooner, and then told him to cheer up, saying that he would manage things in such a way that Messer Torello would be in Pavia on the appointed day, and told him how. Messer Torello believed Saladin, and, since he had often heard that this was possible and had been done, he was comforted and begged Saladin to carry it out.

Saladin ordered one of his magicians, whose skill he often proved, to discover some means whereby Messer Torello could be carried to Pavia in his bed in a single night. The magician replied that it could be done, but that for his own good Messer Torello should be conveyed in his sleep.

Having arranged this, Saladin returned to Messer Torello. Seeing that he was determined either to be in Pavia on the given day if he could or to die if he could not, Saladin said:

"Messer Torello, God knows that you are in no wise to be reproved for loving your wife affectionately and for suspecting that she may be married to another, for among all the ladies I ever saw I think her behaviour, her manners, her garb, apart from her beauty which is but a perishable flower, are most to be commended. Since Fortune has brought you here, it would have greatly delighted me for us to live together as equal princes in the government of my kingdom for as long as we lived together. God has not granted me this, for it has come into your mind either to die or to return to Pavia at the appointed date; but I should greatly have liked to know it in time so that I could have sped you to your home with the honour, grandeur and the company your virtues deserve. This too has not been granted me. You desire to be there at once, and so I shall send you there, as I can, in the way I have told you."

"Sire," replied Messer Torello, "your words show me the effects of your kindness, which I never deserved to this supreme degree; but even if you had not spoken I should have lived and died most certain of it. But since I have made this determination, I beg that what you tell me may be done quickly, because tomorrow is the last day she will still await me."

Saladin said that it should be accomplished without fail. Next day, with the intention of sending him that night, Saladin ordered that in a great hall there should be prepared a rich and handsome bed of cushions, all of which were made of velvet and cloth of gold, in accordance with their customs. Over the bed was a coverlet worked in designs of very large pearls and most precious stones, and two pillows befitting such a bed. This done, he ordered that Messer Torello (who was already recovered) should be clothed in Saracen clothes of the richest and most beautiful kind ever seen, while about his head was wound one of his longest turbans.

It was now late, and Saladin with many of his barons went to Messer Torello's room, sat down beside him, and said, almost in tears:

"Messer Torello, the hour which must separate us draws near; and since I cannot go with you or send anyone along with you because the manner of your travelling forbids it, I must take leave of you in this room, and have therefore come here. Before I commend you to God, I beg you by the love and friendship between us that you will remember me. Then, if possible, before our lives end, I beg that when you have arranged your affairs in Lombardy you will come at least once to see me, to make up for the loss of pleasure in seeing you which your haste to be gone imposes on me. To make this easier, do not shrink from visiting me with letters and from asking what you please of me, for I will certainly do it more gladly for you than for any other man living."

Messer Torello could not restrain his tears, and being hindered by them replied in a few words that it was impossible Saladin's benefits and virtue should ever leave his memory, and that he would indeed do what the Sultan commanded, if life were granted him. Saladin then tenderly embraced and kissed him with many tears, and said:

"Go, in God's care."

He then left the room. After this, all the barons took their leave, and went with Saladin to the room where the bed had been prepared. Since it was now late and the magician was waiting and in haste to despatch him, there came a doctor with a certain drink, telling him that it would strengthen him. This Messer Torello drank, and in a short time fell asleep. By Saladin's command he was carried in his sleep to the handsome bed, and beside him was laid a large beautiful crown of great value, which was marked in a way to show plainly that it was sent by Saladin to Messer Torello's wife.

After this he placed on Messer Torello's finger a ring, set with a carbuncle of such brilliance that it seemed like a torch, while its value could scarcely be estimated. He was girt with a sword, whose ornaments could not easily be valued. On his chest was fastened a clasp, set with pearls whose like was never seen, and other precious stones. Then, on either side of him was set a large gold bowl filled with double ducats, and many strings of pearls and rings and girdles and other things, which would take long to describe. This done, he kissed Messer Torello once again, and told the magician to hurry; and immediately in Saladin's presence the bed and Messer Torello disappeared, and Saladin remained talking of him with his barons.

Messer Torello, with all the above-mentioned gems and ornaments, had reached the church of San Pietro in Ciel d'Oro, as he had asked, and was still asleep when the sacristan, having rung the angelus, entered the church with a light in his hand. Suddenly he saw the rich bed, and was not only surprised but terrified, so that he fled. When the Abbot and the monks saw him fly, they were amazed and asked him the reason; and the monk told them.

"Oh," said the Abbot, "you're not such a child now or so new to this church that you should be frightened so easily. Let us go and see what has scared you so much."

They lit more torches, and the Abbot with all his monks entered the church, where they saw the marvellous rich bed, and the knight sleeping on it. While they were doubtfully and timidly looking at the noble gems, without going too near the bed, the effect of the potion came to an end and Messer Torello awoke and heaved a deep sigh. The Abbot and monks saw this and fled in terror, shrieking "Lord help us!"

Messer Torello opened his eyes and looked about him, and saw he was in the place where he had asked Saladin to send him, which gave him great joy. He sat up and looked at some of the things about him; although he already knew Saladin's munificence, he now thought it greater than ever and knew it better. Nevertheless, when he heard the monks run away and knew the reason, he did not move but called to the Abbot by name, and begged him to have no fear, since it was Torello his nephew. At this the Abbot was still more frightened, since for several months he had believed Torello was dead. But in a little time, feeling reassured by good reasons and finding himself still called, he made the sign of the holy cross, and went up to Messer Torello, who said:

"Why are you suspicious, father? I am alive, thank God, and returned here from beyond the seas."

Although Torello had a long beard and was dressed in Arab clothes, the Abbot soon recognised him, and being completely reassured took him by the hand, saying:

"My son, you are welcome." And then proceeded: "You must not be surprised at our fear, because there is not a man in this place but thinks you are dead; so much so that I must tell you Madonna Adalieta, your wife, overcome by the entreaties and threats of her relatives, has agreed to marry again, and this morning is to go to her new husband—the marriage feast and everything connected with it are all prepared."

Messer Torello arose from the rich bed and greeted the Abbot and the monks with marvellous cheer. He begged every one of them to say nothing about his return, until he had done what he had to do. After this, he had the rich gems placed in safe keeping, and told the Abbot all that had happened to him until that moment. The Abbot, delighted at his good fortune, returned thanks with him to God. Messer Torello then asked the Abbot who was his wife's new husband; and the Abbot told him.

"Before my return is known," said Messer Torello, "I want to see how my wife behaves at this wedding feast. I know it is not customary for churchmen to go to such banquets, but out of love for me I should like you to arrange for us to go there together."

The Abbot replied that he would gladly do so. It was now full day, and he sent to the bridegroom to say that he would like to come to the wedding feast with a friend. And the gentleman replied that he would be happy for them to come.

At the appointed hour, Messer Torello, still in the same clothes, went to the bridegroom's house with the Abbot, gazed at by everyone he met but recognised by no one. And the Abbot told everyone he was a Saracen, sent as ambassador by the Sultan to the King of France.

Messer Torello was placed at a table opposite the lady, whom he beheld with the greatest joy, while he thought from her face that she looked discontented with her new marriage. She also looked several times at him, but she did not recognise him on account of his long beard and foreign clothes, and her firm belief that he was dead.

When Messer Torello thought the time had come to find out whether she remembered him, he took from his finger the ring she had given him when he set out, and called to a boy who was serving at his table, saying:

"Say to the bride from me that in my country the custom is when a stranger, as I am here, eats at a bride's feast, that to show her pleasure at his coming to eat with her she sends him her own wine-cup filled with wine, and when the stranger has drunk, the cup is covered, and the bride drinks the wine that is left."

The boy took the message to the lady. She thought the stranger was a great personage, and, being a well-bred woman, wished to show that she was pleased at his coming; so she ordered them to wash a large gold cup which stood before her, to fill it with wine and take it to the gentleman.

Messer Torello put the ring in his mouth, and while drinking managed to let it fall in the cup without anyone noticing. Leaving only a little wine, he covered up the cup, and sent it back to his wife. To carry out the custom, she took the cup, uncovered it, carried it to her mouth, saw the ring, and gazed at it without saying anything. She saw that it was the ring she had given Messer Torello at his departure, took it in her hand and looked closely at the man she had thought a foreigner. She recognised her husband, and overthrew the table in front of her, as if she had gone mad, screaming:

"There is my husband! It is Messer Torello!"

She ran to the table where he was sitting, and without caring for her clothes or what was on the table, threw herself across it and closely embraced him; and nobody there could get her to loose him, until Messer Torello told her to restrain herself a little since there would soon be plenty of time for them to embrace. Whereupon she stood up. The banquet was in confusion, but in part happier at the return of such a knight. At his request every man was silent, and then Messer Torello related all that had happened to him from the day of his departure until that moment, ending up by saying his being there alive must not displease the gentleman who, thinking him dead, had married his wife.

Although the gentleman was a little irate, he replied freely and like a friend that Messer Torello should dispose of what was his as he wished. The lady took off the new husband's ring and crown, and put on the ring she had taken from the cup and the crown sent her by the Sultan. They then left the house and with all the wedding pomp returned to Messer Torello's house, where he rejoiced with his relatives and friends and all the citizens, who looked upon him almost as a miracle.

Messer Torello gave some of the gems to the man who had paid for the wedding banquet, and some to the Abbot and many others. He sent several letters to the Sultan to announce his happy return, declaring himself Saladin's friend and servant; and then lived many years with his virtuous wife, with more chivalrous courtesy than ever.

Thus ended the trials of Messer Torello and his beloved wife, and such was the reward of their ready and cheerful courtesy. Many attempt to do the same, but do it with so ill a grace that they make their guests pay more for it beforehand than it is worth; and thus if no reward follows, neither they nor anyone else should be surprised. ❖

PATIENT GRISELDA
TENTH DAY, TENTH TALE

Translated from the Italian by
Richard Aldington

WHEN THE KING had ended his long tale, which, to judge by their looks, had greatly pleased everyone, Dioneo said, laughing:

"The good man who was waiting to bring down the ghost's stiff tail that night would not have given two cents for all the praise you give Messer Torello!"

Then, knowing that he was the only one left to tell a tale, he began:

Gracious ladies, as far as I can see, today has been given up to Kings, Sultans and such like persons; so, not to wander away too far from you, I shall tell you about a Marquess, but not of his munificence. It will be about his silly brutality, although good came of it in the end. I do not advise anyone to imitate him, for it was a great pity that good did come to him.

A long time ago the eldest son of the Marquess of Saluzzo was a young man named Gualtieri. He was wifeless and childless, spent his time hunting and hawking, and never thought about marrying or having children, wherein he was probably very wise. This displeased his subjects, who several times begged him to take a wife, so that he might not die without an heir and leave them without a ruler, offering to find him a wife born of such a father and mother as would give him good hopes of her and content him. To which Gualtieri replied:

"Tenth Day, Tenth Tale" from THE DECAMERON OF GIOVANNI BOCCACCIO, translated by Richard Aldington. Copyright 1930, Doubleday & Company, Inc. Reprinted by permission of Rosica Colin Limited for Madame Catherine Guillaume.

"My friends, you urge me to do something I was determined never to do, seeing how hard it is to find a woman of suitable character, and how many of the opposite sort there are, and how wretched is the life of a man who takes a wife unsuitable to him. It is foolishness of you to think you can judge a girl by the characters of her father and mother (from which you argue that you can find me one to please me), for I do not see how you can really know the fathers' or the mothers' secrets. And even if you did know them, daughters are often quite different from their fathers and mothers.

"But you want me to take these chains, and I am content to do so. If it turns out badly I want to have no one to complain of but myself, and so I shall choose for myself. And I tell you that if you do not honour the wife I choose as your lady you will find out to your cost how serious a thing it is to have compelled me by your entreaties to take a wife against my will."

They replied that they were content, if only he would take a wife.

For some time Gualtieri had been pleased by the character of a poor girl in a hamlet near his house. He thought her beautiful, and that he might live comfortably enough with her. So he decided that he would marry her without seeking any further, and, having sent for her father, who was a very poor man, he arranged to marry her. Having done this, Gualtieri called together all his friends from the surrounding country, and said:

"My friends, it has pleased you to desire that I should marry, and I am ready to do so, more to please you than from any desire I have of taking a wife. You know you promised me that you would honour anyone I chose as your lady. The time has now come for me to keep my promise to you and you to keep yours to me. I have found a girl after my heart quite near here; I intend to marry her and to bring her home in a few days. So take thought to make a handsome marriage feast and how you can honourably receive her, so that I may consider myself content with your promise as you may be with mine."

The good men cheerfully replied that they were glad of it, and that they would consider her their lady and honour her as their lady in all things. After which, they all set about preparing a great and handsome wedding feast, and so did Gualtieri. He prepared a great and fine banquet, and invited many friends and relatives and noblemen and others. Moreover, he had rich and beautiful dresses cut out and fitted on a girl, who seemed to him about the same build as the girl he proposed to marry. And he also purchased girdles and rings and a rich and beautiful crown, and everything necessary to a bride.

When the day appointed for the wedding arrived, Gualtieri about the middle of Tierce [1] mounted his horse, and so did those who had come to honour him. Everything being arranged, he said:

"Gentlemen, it is time to go for the bride."

Setting out with all his company he came to the hamlet and the house of the girl's father, where he found her drawing water in great haste, so that she could go with the other women to see Gualtieri's bride. And when Gualtieri saw her, he called her by her name, Griselda, and asked where her father was. She blushed and said:

"He is in the house, my lord."

Gualtieri dismounted, told everyone to wait for him, entered the poor little house where he found the girl's father (who was named Giannucole), and said to him:

"I have come to marry Griselda, but first I want to ask her a few things in your presence."

He then asked her whether, if he married her, she would try to please him, and never be angry at anything he said or did, and if she would be obedient, and several other things, to all of which she said "Yes." Gualtieri then took her by the hand and led her forth. In the presence of all his company he had her stripped naked, and then the clothes he had prepared were brought, and she was immediately dressed and shod, and he had a crown put on her hair, all unkempt as it was. Everyone marvelled at this, and he said:

---

1. *Tierce* (tirs), the third of the canonical hours, or nine A.M.

"Gentlemen, I intend to take this girl as my wife, if she will take me as her husband."

He then turned to her, as she stood blushing and irresolute, and said:

"Griselda, will you take me as your husband?"

"Yes, my lord," she replied.

"And I will take you as my wife," said he.

Then in the presence of them all he pledged his faith to her; and they set her on a palfrey and honourably conducted her to his house. The wedding feast was great and handsome, and the rejoicing no less than if he had married the daughter of the King of France.

The girl seemed to have changed her soul and manners with her clothes. As I said, she was beautiful of face and body, and she became so agreeable, so pleasant, so well-behaved that she seemed like the daughter of a nobleman, and not Giannucole's child and a cattle herder; which surprised everyone who had known her before. Moreover, she was so obedient and so ready to serve her husband that he felt himself to be the happiest and best matched man in the world. And she was so gracious and kindly to her husband's subjects that there was not one of them but loved her and gladly honoured her, while all prayed for her good and prosperity and advancement. Whereas they had said that Gualtieri had showed little wisdom in marrying her, they now said that he was the wisest and shrewdest man in the world, because no one else would have known the lofty virtue hidden under her poor clothes and village garb.

In short, before long she acted so well that not only in the marquisate but everywhere people were talking of her virtues and good actions; and whatever had been said against her husband for having married her was now turned to the opposite. She had not long been with Gualtieri when she became pregnant, and in due time gave birth to a daughter, at which Gualtieri rejoiced greatly.

Soon after this the idea came to him to test her patience with a long trial and intolerable things. He said unkind things to her, seemed to be angry, and said that his subjects were most discontented with her on account of her low birth, and especially when they saw that she bore children. He said they were very angry at the birth of a daughter and did nothing but murmur. When the lady heard these words, she did not change countenance or cheerfulness, but said to him:

"My lord, you may do with me what you think most to your honour and satisfaction. I shall be content, for I know that I am less than they and unworthy of the honour to which you have raised me by your courtesy."

Gualtieri liked this reply and saw that no pride had risen up in her from the honour done her by him and others.

Soon after, he informed his wife in general terms that his subjects could not endure the daughter she had borne. He then gave orders to one of his servants whom he sent to her. The man, with a dolourous visage, said:

"Madonna, if I am to avoid death I must do what my lord bids me. He tells me I am to take your daughter and . . ."

He said no more, but the lady, hearing these words and seeing the servant's face, and remembering what had been said to her, guessed that he had been ordered to kill the child. She went straight to the cradle, kissed and blessed the child, and although she felt great anguish in her heart, put the child in the servant's arms without changing her countenance, and said:

"Do what my lord and yours has ordered you to do. But do not leave her for the birds and animals to devour her body, unless you were ordered to do so."

The servant took the child and told Gualtieri what the lady had said. He marvelled at her constancy, and sent the servant with the child to a relative at Bologna, begging her to bring her up and educate her carefully, but without ever saying whose daughter she was.

After this the lady again became pregnant, and in due time brought forth a male child, which delighted Gualtieri. But what he had already done was not enough for him. He pierced the lady with a worse wound, and one day said to her in pretended anger:

"Since you have borne this male child, I cannot live at peace with my subjects, who complain bitterly that a grandson of Giannucole must be their lord after me. If I am not to be driven out, I fear I must do now as I did before, and in the end abandon you and take another wife."

The lady listened to him patiently, and her only reply was:

"My lord, content yourself and do what is pleasing to you. Do not think about me, for nothing pleases me except as it pleases you."

Not many days afterwards Gualtieri sent for his son in the same way that he had sent for his daughter, and while pretending in the same way to kill the child, sent it to be brought up in Bologna, as he had sent the girl. And his wife said no more and looked no worse than she had done about the daughter. Gualtieri marvelled at this and said to himself that no other woman could have done what she did; and if he had not seen that she loved her children while she had them, he would have thought she did it to get rid of them whereas he saw it was from obedience to him.

His subjects thought he had killed his children, blamed him severely and thought him a cruel man, while they felt great pity for his wife. And when the women condoled with her on the death of her children, she never said anything except that it was not her wish but the wish of him who begot them.

Several years after his daughter's birth, Gualtieri thought the time had come for the last test of his wife's patience. He kept saying that he could no longer endure to have Griselda as his wife, that he knew he had acted childishly and wrongly when he married her, that he therefore meant to solicit the Pope for a dispensation to marry another woman and abandon Griselda; for all of which he was reproved by many good men. But his only reply was that it was fitting this should be done.

Hearing of these things, the lady felt she must expect to return to her father's house and perhaps watch cattle as she had done in the past, and see another woman take the man she loved; at which she grieved deeply. But she prepared herself to endure this with a firm countenance, as she had endured the other wrongs of Fortune.

Not long afterwards Gualtieri received forged letters from

Rome, which he showed to his subjects, pretending that the Pope by these letters gave him a dispensation to take another wife and leave Griselda.

So, calling her before him, he said to her in the presence of many of his subjects:

"Wife, the Pope has granted me a dispensation to leave you and to take another wife. Now, since my ancestors were great gentlemen and lords of this country while yours were always labourers, I intend that you shall no longer be my wife, but return to Giannucole's house with the dowry you brought me, while I shall bring home another wife I have found more suitable for me."

At these words the lady could only restrain her tears by a great effort, beyond that of women's nature, and replied:

"My lord, I always knew that my lowly rank was in no wise suitable to your nobility; and the rank I have had with you I always recognised as coming from God and you, and never looked upon it as given to me, but only lent. You are pleased to take it back, and it must and does please me to return it to you. Here is the ring with which you wedded me; take it. You tell me to take the dowry I brought you; to do this there is no need for you to pay anything nor shall I need a purse or a sumpter horse, for I have not forgotten that I came to you naked. If you think it right that the body which has borne your children should be seen by everyone, I will go away naked. But in exchange for my virginity, which I brought here and cannot carry away, I beg you will at least be pleased to let me take away one shift over and above my dowry."

Gualtieri, who was nearer to tears than anyone else present, managed to keep his countenance stern, and said:

"You shall have a shift."

Those who were present urged him to give her a dress, so that she who had been his wife for thirteen years should not be seen to leave his house so poorly and insultingly as it would be for her to leave it in a shift. But their entreaties were vain. So the lady, clad only in her shift, unshod and with nothing on her head, commended him to God, left his house, and returned to her father accompanied by the tears and lamentation of all who saw her.

Giannucole (who had never believed it was true that Gualtieri would keep his daughter as a wife and had always expected this event) had kept the clothes she had taken off on the morning when Gualtieri married her. So she took them and put them on, and devoted herself to drudgery in her father's house, enduring the assaults of hostile Fortune with a brave spirit.

After Gualtieri had done this, he told his subjects that he was to marry the daughter of one of the Counts of Panago. He therefore made great preparations for the wedding, and sent for Griselda to come to him; and when she came, he said:

"I am bringing home the lady I have just married, and I intend to do her honour at her arrival. You know there is not a woman in the house who can prepare the rooms and do many other things needed for such a feast. You know everything connected with the house better than anyone, so you must arrange everything that is to be done, and invite all the women you think fit and receive them as if you were mistress of the house. Then, when the marriage feast is over, you can return home."

These words were a dagger in Griselda's heart, for she had not been able to dispense with the love she felt for him as she had her good fortune, but she said:

"My lord, I am ready."

So, in her coarse peasant dress, she entered the house she had left a little before in her shift, and had the rooms cleaned and arranged, put out hangings and carpets in the halls, looked to the kitchen, and set her hand to everything as if she had been a scullery wench of the house. And she never paused until everything was ready and properly arranged.

After this she invited all the ladies of the surrounding country in Gualtieri's name, and then awaited the feast. On the wedding day, dressed in her poor clothes, she received all the ladies with a cheerful visage and a womanly manner.

Gualtieri had had his children carefully brought up in Bologna by his relative, who was married into the family of the Counts of Panago. The daughter was now twelve years old, the most beautiful thing ever seen, and the boy was seven. He sent to her and asked her to come to Saluzzo with his son and daughter, to bring an honourable company with her, and to tell everyone that she was bringing the girl as his wife, and never to let anyone know that the girl was anything else. Her husband did what the Marquess asked, and set out. In a few days he reached Saluzzo about dinner-time, with the girl and boy and his noble company; and all the peasants of the country were there to see Gualtieri's new wife.

The girl was received by the ladies and taken to the hall where the tables were spread, and Griselda went cheerfully to meet her, saying:

"Lady, you are welcome."

The ladies had begged Gualtieri, but in vain, to allow Griselda to stay in her room or to lend her one of her own dresses, so that she might not have to meet strangers in such a guise. They all sat down to table and began the meal. Every man looked at the girl and said that Gualtieri had made a good exchange, and Griselda above all praised her and her little brother.

Gualtieri now felt that he had tested his wife's patience as far as he desired. He saw that the strangeness of all this did not alter her and he was certain it was not the result of stupidity, for he knew her to be an intelligent woman. He thought it now time to take her from the bitterness which he felt she must be hiding behind a smiling face. So he called her to him, and in everyone's presence said to her smilingly:

"What do you think of my new wife?"

"My lord," replied Griselda, "I see nothing but good in her. If she is as virtuous as she is beautiful, as I well believe, I have no doubt that you will live with her the happiest lord in the world. But I beg you as earnestly as I can not to give her the wounds you gave the other woman who was your wife. I think she could hardly endure them, because she is younger and because she has been brought up delicately, whereas the other laboured continually from her childhood."

Gualtieri saw that she really believed he was to marry the

other, and yet spoke nothing but good of her. He made her sit down beside him, and said:

"Griselda, it is now time that you should reap the reward of your long patience, and that those who have thought me cruel and wicked and brutal should know that what I have done was directed towards a pre-determined end, which was to teach you to be a wife, then how to choose and keep a wife, and to procure me perpetual peace so long as I live with you. When I came and took you to wife, I greatly feared that this would not happen to me; and so, to test you, I have given you the trials and sufferings you know. I have never perceived that you thwarted my wishes by word or deed, and I think that in you I have the comfort I desire. I mean to give you back now what I deprived you of for a long time, and to heal the wounds I gave you with the greatest delight. Therefore, with a glad spirit, take her whom you think to be my wife and her brother as your children and mine. They are the children whom you and many others have long thought that I had cruelly murdered. And I am your husband, who loves you above all things, believing I can boast that no man exists who can so rejoice in his wife as I in you."

He then embraced and kissed her. She was weeping with happiness. They both arose and went to where their daughter was sitting, quite stupefied by what she had heard, and tenderly embraced her and her brother, thus undeceiving them and many of those present.

The ladies arose merrily from table and went with Griselda to her room. With better hopes they took off her old clothes and dressed her in one of her noble robes, and brought her back to the hall a lady, which she had looked even in her rags.

They rejoiced over their children, and everyone was glad at what had happened. The feasting and merrymaking were prolonged for several days, and Gualtieri was held to be a wise man, although they thought the testing of his wife harsh and intolerable. But above all they esteemed the virtue of Griselda.

The Count of Panago soon afterwards returned to Bologna. Gualtieri took Giannucole away from his labour and installed him as his father-in-law, so that he ended his days honourably and in great content. He afterwards married off his daughter to a nobleman of great wealth and distinction, and lived long and happily with Griselda, always honouring her as much as he could.

What more is to be said, save that divine souls are sometimes rained down from Heaven into poor houses, while in royal palaces are born those who are better fitted to herd swine than to rule over men? Who but Griselda could have endured with a face not only tearless but cheerful, the stern and unheard-of tests imposed on her by Gualtieri? It would perhaps not have been such a bad thing if he had chosen one of those women who, if she had been driven out of her home in a shift, would have let another man so shake her fur that a new dress would have come from it. ❖

Massimo Bontempelli (1878–1960)

MIRRORS

Translated from the Italian by
Eduardo Corsi

TALKING OF MIRRORS it is necessary that I relate another experience. I know that I shall be accused of abusing this theme, but patience, my friend. Rather I would prefer not to have some malicious person think that I spend most of my life before a mirror. On the contrary it is because I so seldom use this baffling contrivance that it still deigns to create for me the strange illusions it denies to those who make of it as constant and ordinary an article of use.

About eight days ago, on a morning toward noon, my landlady woke me up with a telegram. After a few willing efforts I managed to put myself in a condition to read it. It was a telegram from Vienna. It was addressed to me, to me alone, and it was correctly addressed. This is what it said:

"Leave for Rome day after to-morrow stop *arrivederci* stop Massimo."

I was in Vienna two months ago, for fifteen days. I tried to

---

recall all the persons I had met there during those fifteen days. There was an old Hungarian friend of mine called Tibor, and some others named Fritz, Richard and John. I thought and thought again, but I could think of no other Massimo in Vienna but myself.

There was just one conclusion and it was a clear one. Since I was the only Massimo I could think of in Vienna, the Massimo who sent me that telegram was myself.

It was my telegram therefore.

I understand!—I shouted.

But the reader, on the other hand, cannot as yet have understood.

I shall explain. But before I do so it is necessary that I tell my reader of some of the other experiences I have had in this matter of telegrams. A single example will suffice. I was arranging my belongings in my room one day when, as luck would have it, I noticed that my umbrella was gone. I looked for it everywhere. More than once (as we are in the habit of doing in such cases, as if once were not enough) I looked for it in the corner where I usually kept it, but in vain. I finally resigned myself to the loss and went about my business: we lose greater things in life than an umbrella.

I had almost forgotten it when, two days later, I received the following telegram: "Shall arrive to-night Umbrella." I gave it little thought, and at night I retired peacefully. The following morning the first thing to attract my attention was my umbrella. Sure enough there it was, in the very corner where I had looked for it many times.

Of course, I know perfectly well that it is not an uncommon thing (even if science has not as yet explained it) to find a lost article in the very place where one has looked for it many times before. And there is really no use in talking about it. But to have a lost article announce its return by telegram, that is not so common.

With this example in mind, the thing that struck me intuitively in reading that telegram from Vienna, and which I am about to explain, ought to seem quite natural even to the most materialistic of my readers.

But here we have got to go back a bit.

Two months ago in Vienna I was standing before a mirror fixing my tie. I was getting ready to take my train back to Rome. There were political demonstrations going on throughout the city at the time.

As I have said, I was standing before a mirror fixing my tie. Suddenly a tremendous explosion shook the house and smashed my mirror into bits.

I realised it was a bomb, and I went on fixing my tie without a mirror. When I was through, I took my bag, drove to the station, and left. A few days later I was in Rome. It was late at night, so I immediately undressed and went to bed.

The next morning I stood before the mirror with my shaving brush in one hand and a towel in the other, when to my great surprise I saw nothing there. To be more precise, there was everything there but me. I could see a soap-soaked brush dangling to and fro, and a towel equally agitated, as if it had suddenly gone mad in the empty space. But I, I was not to be seen. Neither my face nor my image was there.

Realising at once what had happened, I broke into laughter.

All those who use a mirror, the women especially, must have noticed, I believe, that the moment they pull themselves away from it, from the mirror into which they are looking, they feel a slight sense of discomfort. There is a little jerk in the parting. Well, this results from the very light, imperceptible effort we all make when tearing ourselves away, when withdrawing the image that is there.

Now this is exactly what happened to me on that day in Vienna. My mirror broke so instantly, it was smashed and destroyed so suddenly, that I was not quick enough to withdraw my image, to pull it back before it vanished.

Naturally, hurried as I was to get away, I paid little attention to the incident at the time. I first realised what had happened when I found myself facing a mirror here in Rome, or two days later, as I have said.

152 *Bontempelli*

And so for these past two months I have been without my image. It was somewhat of a nuisance at first, especially for my tie and beard. But I learned to get on without it. I learned to make my tie by memory, and as to my beard I shaved it by ear with a Gillette.

I took the mirror down from its accustomed place and put it away in my trunk.

The only thing I had to be very careful about was not to have anyone see me standing before any of the mirrors along the streets, in the cafés, or in the homes of others. People are easily surprised, you know. They would want to know why and how, and then I should have to explain. I should have to discuss metaphysics and other such annoyances.

For this reason, though the loss itself may have been anything but serious, I was happy to receive that telegram eight days ago. I understood at once (and by this time I presume that even the densest of my readers has understood) that that telegram had been sent to me by my own image so that I might be informed of its homecoming.

Naturally, I did not hasten to look at myself in the mirror. Not at all. I did not want to give my image the satisfaction of knowing that I care very much about it, that I have been waiting for it impatiently, that I cannot do without it. Since it left Vienna eight days ago, even admitting that it travelled on a very fast train, it should have reached here at least four days ago. But I did not show myself until yesterday. It was only yesterday that I went after the mirror in my trunk, whistling an air from Aida as I did so. I restored it to its place in the bathroom without even looking at it. Then with the utmost tranquillity and indifference I adjusted my collar and tie and took a glimpse at myself. There I was: there was my image, not a whit changed. I had had a vague fear that I might find it a little disturbed, somewhat resentful of my indifference, and probably tired from the long trip and its many experiences. Instead it seemed to be in the finest condition, and as indifferent and tranquil as its owner.   ✤

Dino Buzzati (1906–1972)

SEVEN STORIES

Translated from the Italian by
Ben Johnson

ONE MARCH MORNING, at the end of a day's journey by train, Giuseppe Corte arrived in the city where the famous nursing home was located. He had a slight fever, but chose nonetheless to walk from the station to the hospital, carrying his overnight bag himself.

Detected in an early stage and negligible though his infection was, Giuseppe Corte had been counseled to seek treatment at the renowned sanatorium, to which sufferers from his disease were the only ones admitted. This thereby guaranteed exceptional competence on the part of the doctors and the soundest disposition of facilities within the hospital itself.

As he caught sight of it from a distance—recognizable from a photograph he had once seen in a prospectus—Giuseppe Corte was most favorably impressed. With a façade of projecting wings, the white seven-storied structure bore a vague resemblance to a hotel. It was surrounded by a border of tall trees.

After a brief physical examination, with promise of a more careful, more thorough one to follow, Giuseppe Corte was assigned to a cheerful room on the seventh and uppermost floor. His furniture there, like the wallpaper, was bright and clean, and the armchairs were of wood with cushions of a polychrome material. His view dominated one of the loveliest quarters of the city. All was tranquil, hospitable, and reassuring.

Giuseppe Corte slipped into bed at once and, turning on the light above the bolster, began to read a book he had brought with him. Presently a nurse entered to ask if there was anything he desired.

No, nothing at all; but he quickly seized upon the opportunity to engage the girl in conversation, to question her about the nursing home. It was thus that he came to hear of its unique arrangement. The patients were distributed on various floors depending on the gravity of their cases. On the seventh—that is, on the top floor—were those whose infections were very slight. The sixth handled cases which, if not grave, could by no means be neglected. Cases treated on the fifth floor were serious; and so on, all the way down, floor by floor. The condition of patients on the second, for instance, was extremely critical. And the first was reserved for those for whom there could be no hope.

This singular stratification, apart from greatly accelerating the hospital service, insured mildly infected patients against being disturbed by neighbors in agony, and guaranteed in each ward a homogeneous atmosphere. Moreover, it lent itself to a perfect graduation of treatment, the achievement of optimum results.

It followed, then, that the patients were divided into seven progressive castes. Each floor was like a little world in itself, with its own rules and special traditions which were meaningless on other floors. And since each section was under the direction of a different doctor, there had developed, though on a very minor scale, subtle differences in the method of treatment, despite the fact that the director general had established in the institution one fundamental procedure.

When the nurse left, Giuseppe Corte, feeling that his temperature had subsided to normal, went to the window and looked out, not so much to view the city, new though it was to him, as in hopes of catching a glimpse of other patients through the windows on the floors below. The structure of the building, with its projecting wings and recesses, lent itself to this sort of observation. Mostly Giuseppe Corte's attention was focused on the windows of the first floor, which looked to him to be very far away and were seen only slantwise. But there was nothing of interest. Nearly all the windows were shuttered tight with gray sliding blinds.

Corte then noticed that a man had appeared at a window next to his. The two men looked at each other for some time with a growing sense of fellow feeling, but neither knew just how to break the silence.

At length Giuseppe Corte summoned courage enough to ask: "Have you just arrived yourself?"

"Oh, no," answered the other. "I've been here for two months now. . . ." He was silent for a moment or so, and then, uncertain how to continue, added: "I was looking at my brother."

"Your brother?"

"Yes," explained the stranger. "We entered together—quite an exceptional case, ours; but he got worse. Just think, he's already on the fourth!"

"The fourth?"

"Yes, the fourth floor," explained the man, enunciating these words with accents of such commiseration and horror as to evoke in Giuseppe Corte a feeling almost of terror.

"Is it really so serious on the fourth floor?" he ventured cautiously.

"Goodness," said the other, slowly shaking his head, "they're not desperate, those cases, but there's precious little to rejoice about."

"But then," pursued Corte with the playfully detached manner of one who alludes to tragic events of no concern to him, "well, if they're that serious on the fourth floor, whom do they put on the first?"

"Oh," said the other, "the first is for patients who are dying—actually dying. In fact, down there the doctors don't have a thing to do. The only person who's kept busy is the priest. Naturally —"

"But there's hardly anybody there, anyway," interrupted Corte, as if eager for confirmation; "nearly all the rooms are closed."

"True, there aren't many at the moment, but they had a number this morning," replied the stranger, with a subtle smile. "Wherever you see that the blinds are drawn, it means that someone has just died. Anyway, you can see, can't you, that the shutters on the other floors are all open? . . . But you'll excuse me now," he said, slowly withdrawing. "It's growing a bit chilly, I feel. I'm going back to bed. I wish you luck . . . the best of luck!"

The man disappeared from the sill and the window was closed energetically; a light came on in his room. Giuseppe Corte remained at his window, motionless, his eyes fixed on the drawn blinds of the first floor; he stared at them with morbid intensity, trying to imagine the funereal secrets of that dreadful floor where patients were assigned to die; and a sense of relief pervaded him, knowing that he was so far away. Evening settled over the city. One by one, lights appeared at the thousand windows of the sanatorium; from a distance one might have mistaken it for a hotel party. Only on the first floor, at the foot of the precipice, were there windows, scores of them, that remained blind and dark.

The results of his thorough physical examination reassured Giuseppe Corte. Inclined as a rule to expect the worst, he was already inwardly prepared for a harsh verdict, and would not, indeed, have been surprised if they had declared that he would have to be sent to the floor below. In fact, his fever, though his general condition continued good, had shown no signs of subsiding. The doctor, however, chose to speak to him in terms that were amicable and encouraging. There was certainly, he said, an incipient trace of the disease, but it was very slight and would no doubt clear up in two or three weeks.

"Then I'm to remain on the seventh?" Giuseppe Corte had asked, anxious, at this juncture.

"Why, of course!" the doctor had replied, patting him in a friendly fashion on the shoulder. "Where did you expect to go?

Certainly not to the fourth?" he laughed, as if this were the worst, the most absurd of possibilities.

Giuseppe Corte, in fact, remained in the room to which he had originally been assigned. He came to know some of his fellow patients in the hospital on those rare occasions, in the afternoon, when he was permitted out of bed. He attended scrupulously to his treatment, doing his very utmost to hasten recovery; yet, despite his efforts, his condition seemed to remain unchanged.

About ten days had elapsed when the chief attendant of the seventh floor introduced himself to Giuseppe Corte. He wanted to know if Corte would grant him a favor, a purely personal favor: a lady with two children was scheduled to arrive the following day; they happened to have two free rooms on either side of Corte's, but they needed a third. Would Signor Corte mind moving to another, but equally comfortable, room?

Giuseppe Corte had, naturally, no objections; one room or another was quite the same to him, and there was a chance that he might find himself with a new and prettier nurse.

"Thanks ever so much," said the chief attendant, bowing lightly. "But from a person like you, I admit, so kind and gentlemanly a gesture scarcely surprises me. In an hour, then, if that is suitable to you, we'll proceed with the transfer. You realize that you'll have to go down to the next floor," he added offhand, as if this were a detail hardly worth mentioning. "Unfortunately, we do not have any other vacant rooms on this floor. But this is a temporary arrangement," he went on quickly, observing that Corte, suddenly sitting up in bed, was about to protest. "An absolutely temporary arrangement. Just as soon as we have a free room, and I believe we shall within two or three days, you'll be able to come back up."

"I must say," said Giuseppe Corte, smiling, to make it quite clear that he was no child, "I must say that a transfer of this sort does not please me in the least."

"But it is not being made on any medical grounds whatever; I understand perfectly what you mean, but this is no more than a gesture of courtesy toward a lady who does not wish to be separated from her children. . . . Really," he added, laughing aloud, "you mustn't even think that there are other reasons."

"Very well," said Giuseppe Corte. "Only it looks to me like a bad sign."

Thus Signor Corte went to the sixth floor. And although convinced that his transfer was in no way due to a worsening of his condition, he felt uneasy at the thought that between him and the world at large, the world of healthy people, an obstacle had been interposed. On the seventh floor, at the port of arrival, one still had contact somehow with the society of man; it might even be considered a kind of annex to the everyday world. But on the sixth, one had then entered the hospital proper: the mentality of the doctors, of the nurses, and of the patients themselves was already a little different. Here, it was admitted, was a ward for real, genuinely ill patients, slight though their infections were. In fact, from his first discussions there, with patients in the neighboring rooms, with attendants and doctors, Giuseppe Corte remarked the way the seventh floor was dismissed as a joke, as a place reserved for amateur patients suffering largely from imaginary complaints; only on the sixth did the hospital, so to speak, really begin.

And Giuseppe Corte understood that before returning upstairs to his rightful level, according with the characteristics of his particular case, he would encounter, certainly, some difficulties; to return to the seventh floor, he would have to set in motion a complicated organism, however slight was the effort required of it; doubtless, had he not spoken up, no one would have dreamed of returning him to the floor of the "amateurs."

He was determined therefore not to yield on any of his rights, and not to let himself fall a prey to habit. He was fond of pointing out to his ward mates that he would be with them for only a few days, that it had been merely his desire to accommodate a lady that accounted for his presence there, and that as soon as they had an empty room upstairs he was leaving them. His listeners would nod assent, but skeptically.

Giuseppe Corte's convictions were bolstered, however, by the opinion of his new doctor. The doctor himself admitted that Corte could perfectly well be assigned to the seventh floor; his infection was ab-so-lute-ly neg-li-gi-ble—syllabizing the words to give them due importance; fundamentally, though, he believed that Signor Corte stood to benefit more from the treatment on the sixth—

"I don't care to hear such talk as that," interrupted the patient determinedly at this point. "You said that the seventh floor is where I belong, and I want to go back!"

"No one has suggested anything but," the doctor returned. "Mine was purely and simply the advice not of your doc-tor, but of a gen-u-ine friend! Your infection, may I repeat, is very slight —it would not be an exaggeration to say that you're not even ill; in my judgment, however, yours is distinguished from analogous cases by the rather sizable area infected. Let me explain: the intensity of your infection is hardly worth mention, but the affected area is considerable; the destructive process in the cells" —it was Giuseppe Corte's first occasion to hear this sinister expression in the hospital—"the destructive process in your cells is absolutely in its initial stage; perhaps it has not even begun, but it may—mind you, only *may*—it may attack simultaneously over a vast area of the organism. It is for this reason alone that, in my opinion, you can be treated more effectively here, on the sixth floor, where the therapeutic methods are of a more specific and intensive nature than upstairs."

One day it was reported that, after prolonged discussion with his colleagues, the director general of the institution had decided to alter the subdivisional status of the patients. The grade, so to speak, of each patient was to be lowered a half point. If, say, the patients on each floor were divided, according to the gravity of their cases, into two categories (this subdivision was actually made by the respective ward doctors, but for their own guid-ance), the lower half was automatically to be transferred to the floor below. For instance, half the patients on the sixth floor, those cases that were somewhat more advanced than the others, would proceed to the fifth; and the more slightly infected patients on the seventh would go to the sixth. Giuseppe Corte was delighted: in such a complete shake-up, his return to the seventh floor would be more easily effected.

Upon mentioning this hope of his to the nurse, he received, however, a rude surprise. He was certainly scheduled for transfer, he learned, but not to the seventh; rather, to the floor below. For reasons which were beyond the nurse to explain, he had been included in the more serious half of the inmates on the sixth floor, and he would, therefore, have to proceed to the fifth.

Once recovered from the first shock, Giuseppe Corte gave vent to his fury. They had played a low trick on him! he screamed; he wanted to hear no further talk of a transfer downstairs! he was going home! he stood on his rights! and the hospital was not permitted to ignore so blatantly the doctors' diagnoses!

He was still raging when the doctor came puffing in to calm him. He advised Corte not to excite himself, unless he wanted his temperature to rise, and he explained that there had been a misunderstanding, or in any case a partial one. He again admitted that Giuseppe Corte's rightful place was on the seventh floor, but added that his opinion of Corte's case—a purely personal opinion, naturally—was a little at variance with this judgment. Actually, Corte's infection might in a certain sense, of course, be classified in grade six, considering the magnitude of morbid manifestation. He himself, however, was utterly at a loss to explain why Corte had been included in the lower half of the sixth floor. Except, perhaps the administrative secretary, who had just that morning telephoned to ask about Corte's exact position—perhaps the secretary had made an error. Or more likely, the administration itself had "stepped down" his own recommendations, for, though an expert doctor, he was felt to be too lenient. In conclusion, the doctor counseled Corte not to let himself become overwrought, and to submit to the transfer with good grace; after all, it was not the floor to which a patient was assigned that mattered, but the actual status of his disease.

And, added the doctor, as regarded his treatment, Giuseppe Corte would have no cause for regret; the doctor on the floor below was certainly more experienced: it was almost dogmatic that the ability of the doctors gradually increased—at least that's what the directors thought—as one descended. His room would be no less comfortable and elegant. The view was equally spacious: only from the third floor was it obstructed by the girdle of trees.

Gripped by an evening fever, Giuseppe Corte listened carefully, but with a growing sense of weariness, to the various points the doctor raised by way of justifying the transfer. Eventually, Corte realized that he simply lacked strength and, still more, the will to oppose this unjust action. And he let himself be carried to the floor below.

Giuseppe Corte's sole comfort—a cold one, however—once he was installed on the fifth floor, lay in his knowledge that there was universal agreement, among the doctors, nurses, and patients alike, that his was the least serious case in the entire ward. Within the confines of the fifth floor, in any case, he could consider himself by far the most fortunate inmate. Yet on the other hand, rankling in his brain was the thought that, interposed between him and the normal world, there were now *two* barriers.

Spring advanced and the air grew warmer, but Giuseppe Corte had ceased to enjoy, as in the early days, lounging at the window; perfectly ridiculous though his fears were, a peculiar shudder convulsed him whenever he looked at the windows of the first floor—most of them always closed—now that they were considerably nearer.

His condition appeared to be unchanged. But after he had spent three days on the fifth floor a rash broke out on his right leg, which, in the days that followed, showed no signs of healing. It was an infection, the doctors informed him—in no way related to his principal one: something, in fact, that could befall the healthiest person in the world. And it would require, that he might be rid of it in a few days, intensive digamma-ray treatments.

"But that can be done here, can't it?" asked Giuseppe Corte.

"Certainly," replied the doctor with pride. "Our hospital is equipped to handle any eventuality. There's only one inconvenience."

"An inconvenience?" said Giuseppe Corte with a vague presentiment.

"An inconvenience only in a manner of speaking," said the doctor, correcting himself. "I mean that this particular apparatus is located on the fourth floor. And I certainly wouldn't advise your making such a trek three times a day."

"Then there's nothing to be done, is there?"

"Well, I would recommend that you agree to move to the fourth floor until the rash clears up."

"No!" Giuseppe Corte exploded. "I'm fed up with forever going downstairs. I'd die first!"

"Suit yourself," said the doctor, conciliatory, not wishing to irritate the patient; "but as your attending doctor, please note that I shall not permit you to climb the stairs three times a day."

And the worst of it was that his eczema, instead of healing, slowly began to spread. Constantly tossing in bed, unable to rest, Giuseppe Corte endured it, furious, for three days before finally having to yield. Then, voluntarily, he requested that the doctor have them proceed with the digamma-ray treatments, that he be transferred to the floor below.

Down there, Corte noted with unconfessed delight that he stood out as an exception. The other patients, their cases decidedly more serious than his, were not allowed up for a minute, whereas he was able to indulge in the luxury of strolling from his bed to the digamma-ray room, to the compliments and marvel even of the nurses.

He was careful to explain to his new doctor the highly specialized nature of his case, of a patient, that is, who actually belonged on the seventh floor but found himself on the fourth. And as soon as his rash was cured, he had every intention of returning upstairs. He would accept absolutely no more excuses. He, whose proper place was still on the seventh!

"The seventh, the *seventh!*" exclaimed the doctor, smiling; he had just finished examining Corte. "You patients are eternally exaggerating! May I be the first to state that you ought to be pleased with your condition. By your progress chart, I see there has been no marked worsening. Still, between this and talk of the seventh floor—you'll pardon me if I am brutally frank—there's a considerable difference! You *are* one of our least critical cases; this I quite admit, but you are a sick man all the same."

"Well," said Giuseppe Corte, his face reddening, "well, you—on what floor would you put me?"

"Heavens, it's not that easy to say. I've given you only a cursory examination. I should have to watch your progress for a week or more before hazarding an opinion."

"Agreed. But you know more or less," persisted Corte.

The doctor pretended for a moment to lose himself in thought, allowing Corte time to compose himself; then, nodding his head, he said deliberately, "Heavens. All right, to satisfy you, we might actually put you on the sixth. Yes . . . yes," he added, as if persuading himself, "the sixth might do very well."

This, the doctor believed, would please his patient; instead, a look of dismay darkened Giuseppe Corte's face: it was apparent now that the doctors had deceived him; for here, this new one, obviously more competent and honest than the others, would *really* put him—it was perfectly clear—not on the seventh, but on the fifth, and perhaps in the *lower* fifth! His temperature that evening was high.

Giuseppe Corte's residence on the fourth floor marked his most tranquil period since his arrival at the hospital. The doctor was a particularly likable person, friendly and attentive, and on numerous occasions spent entire hours discussing a wide range of subjects with his patient. Giuseppe Corte enjoyed their sessions together, during which he sought topics relating to his accustomed life as an attorney and man of the world; he sought to convince himself that he still fitted into the company of healthy men, that he still had ties with the world of business, that he was still concerned with current happenings. All this he sought—but without success. And, unfailingly, their discussions would eventually return to his disease.

Meanwhile, his desire for improvement, any improvement whatever, had become obsessive. Although the digamma rays had arrested the spread of his eczema, they had not, unfortunately, succeeded in removing it entirely. Each day Giuseppe

Corte would dwell at length on this with the doctor, making at the same time an effort to appear strong, even ironical—again without success.

"Tell me, doctor," he asked one day, "how is the destructive process in my cells getting along?"

"My word, what an ugly expression!" said the doctor, gently chiding him. "Where did you ever pick that up? It is not at all seemly—not at all!—especially from a patient. Please, I don't wish to hear such talk as that again from you."

"Very well, but you haven't given me an answer yet," objected Corte.

"Oh, I shall give you an answer at once," said the doctor civilly. "The destructive process in your cells, to repeat your horrible expression, remains in your case at a minimum—at an absolute minimum. Although I might be tempted to call it obstinate."

"Obstinate—do you mean chronic?"

"You mustn't try to put words into my mouth. I mean simply obstinate. But anyway, this applies to most cases. Even the mildest of infections may often require long and vigorous treatment."

"But tell me, doctor, when may I look for some improvement?"

"When? . . . Really, predictions in these cases are somewhat difficult to make. . . . But look," he added after a reflective pause, "I notice that you have a real mania to recover . . . and if I were not afraid of making you angry I would offer you a little advice—"

"Please, doctor, don't hesitate . . ."

"Very well, then. I shall put it in the clearest possible terms. If I had this disease of yours—even the very mildest form of it—and found myself in this sanatorium, which is perhaps the best anywhere, I would ask on the very first day—on the very first day, mind you—to be assigned to one of the lower floors. I would see to it that I was sent directly to the—"

"First?" suggested Corte with a forced smile.

"Oh, no, not to the first!" replied the doctor, gently ironic, "my word, no. But to the third or even, certainly, to the second. I guarantee you that the treatment down there is vastly superior, the facilities are more complete, more efficacious, the personnel more competent. You're aware, of course, who the guiding spirit of the hospital is?"

"Professor Dati, isn't it?"

"Quite true, Professor Dati. It was he who devised the method that is practiced here, he who designed the entire hospital. . . . Well, Professor Dati, the master himself, is located, so to speak, between the first and second floors. His force as director radiates from that point. But I assure you, his influence does not extend up beyond the third floor; above the third, one might say that even his orders diminish, lose consistency, go astray. The heart of the hospital is downstairs, and downstairs is where one must be to receive the best treatment."

"In other words," said Giuseppe Corte, his voice quavering, "you recommend—"

"Consider one other thing," the doctor ran on dauntlessly, "consider that in your particular case there is your eczema that would need attention. A matter of no importance, I assure you, but rather irksome, and something which, in time, could weaken your morale; and you, of course, recognize that serenity of mind is essential to recovery. The digamma-ray treatments which I have been giving you have been only partially successful. Now why? It may be pure chance; however, it may be that the rays have not been sufficiently intense. Well, then, the apparatus down on the third floor is considerably more powerful. The likelihood of getting rid of your eczema would be vastly increased. Then, once recovery has begun, you see, you have already cleared the most difficult hurdle. Once you have started up, it's quite unlikely that you'll slip back again. When you really feel better, there is nothing to prevent your rising back to us or still higher, according to your 'merits,' to the fifth, sixth—even, I daresay, to the seventh—"

"And you believe that this would really hasten the cure?"

"Why, there can be no doubt of it! I have already told you what I should do if *I* were in your shoes."

The doctor presented arguments of this nature daily. And the moment ultimately came when the patient, no longer able to endure the eczema, and notwithstanding an instinctive reluctance to descend to the realm of even more serious cases, decided to act upon the doctor's advice and was transferred to the floor below.

As soon as he arrived, he detected in the ward a special note of gaiety, in both the nurses and the attending doctor, despite the fact that there, on the third floor, cause for concern about the patients under treatment was a good deal greater. In fact, with each passing day he remarked that the gaiety increased: his curiosity aroused, he waited a while, until he had gained a degree of confidence in the nurse, and then asked her why it was that they were all so gay.

"Oh, don't you know?" answered the nurse. "In three days we're going on vacation."

"Vacation?"

"Yes. For fifteen days the third floor will be closed down and the staff is to be let off. Each floor takes its turn."

"But the patients, what about them?"

"There are relatively few, so two floors will be combined."

"You mean they'll put the patients of the third and fourth floors together?"

"No, no," said the nurse, correcting him: "the third and second. The patients up here will all be sent downstairs."

"Downstairs?" said Corte, pale as clay. "You mean, then, that I'll have to go down to the second?"

"Of course. Is there anything so unusual about that? When we come back, in a fortnight's time, you'll all return to your rooms up here. It doesn't seem such a dreadful thing to me."

Yet Giuseppe Corte—some mysterious instinct gave him notice—was assailed by fear. But since he could scarcely prevent the staff from taking its vacation, and convinced that the new digamma-ray treatments were proving beneficial—his eczema had almost completely cleared up—he did not dare object to the new transfer. However, when he reached the second floor he insisted, despite the nurses' banter, on having a notice tacked to the door that read: GIUSEPPE CORTE OF THE THIRD FLOOR—TRANSIENT.

This delusion of his was without precedent in the history of the sanatorium, but the doctors said nothing, fully aware that in a nervous temperament such as Corte's the slightest annoyance was liable to produce shock.

It was a question now merely of waiting for fifteen days—not one day more or one day less. Giuseppe Corte set to counting them with dogged avidity as he lay abed, motionless for hours on end, his eyes focused on the furniture which, on that floor, was not modern and gay as in the upper wards, but was heavier, more solemn and severe in style. And occasionally he pricked up his ears, for he seemed to hear from the floor below—from the floor of the dying, the "death cells"—the indistinct rattle of death throes.

All this, naturally, had a tendency to depress him. And his increased uneasiness seemed to aggravate his illness: his temperature rose, his debility sank to new depths. From the window—it was now midsummer and the window was nearly always open—neither the rooftops nor any of the houses of the city were visible: only the green wall of trees surrounding the hospital.

Seven days passed. One afternoon around two, the chief attendant and three nurses pushing a stretcher suddenly entered. "Well, are we ready for the transfer?" asked the attendant in a tone of good-natured jest.

"What transfer?" asked Corte in a pinched voice. "What sort of joke is this? Don't those of us of the third floor still have a week before being sent back?"

"The third floor?" said the chief attendant, as if not quite understanding. "I have instructions to take you to the first. Look." And he held out a printed form ordering the patient's transfer to the floor below. It was signed by no less a personage than Professor Dati himself.

All Giuseppe Corte's terror and uncontainable fury erupted into a long outburst that echoed down through the ward. "Calm yourself. For goodness' sake, calm yourself!" the nurses entreated. "There are other patients here who are not well." But that alone could hardly have been expected to quiet him.

Finally he noticed the doctor in charge of the ward, a very kind and well-mannered person. Informed of the transfer, he looked at the form and asked Corte what was happening. Then he turned angrily to the chief attendant and declared that there was some mistake, that he had not given any order to this effect, that for some time there had been an insufferable amount of confusion, and that he was kept completely in the dark about everything. . . . Having thus taken his subordinate to task, he turned politely to Corte, begging him to accept his deepest apologies.

"Unfortunately, however," added the doctor, "unfortunately, Professor Dati left only an hour ago on a short holiday and will not be back for a couple of days. I am very, very sorry about this, but the Professor's orders cannot be countermanded. I assure you, though, he will be the first to deplore such an error! I can't understand how it could have happened!"

By now Giuseppe Corte was in the throes of a pitiable fit of trembling. He had lost complete control of himself. He was like a child, terror had so overwhelmed him. His sobs filled the room.

And thus, by virtue of a monstrous error, he arrived at the last station. In the ward of the dying, he who actually, in light of his condition, according even to the diagnoses of the most uncompromising doctors, ought to have been assigned to the sixth, if not the seventh floor! The situation was so grotesque, really, that he felt at times a desire to roar with laughter.

The heat of the summer's afternoon crept slowly across the city. Lying abed, he gazed at the green of the trees through the window, with the sensation of having arrived in an unreal world, a world created of absurd sterilized-tile walls, of cold mortuary passages, of white soulless figures. He had even a notion that the trees, which he thought he discerned through the window, were also unreal: he became finally convinced of it, in fact, after noticing that the leaves did not move.

This idea so upset him that he rang for the nurse and asked to be given his glasses, which he did not normally wear in bed; only then was he able to set his mind a little at rest: aided by his glasses, he was able to establish that the trees, after all, were real, and that the leaves, if ever so slightly, occasionally did flutter a little in the thin breeze.

After the nurse left, a quarter-hour of deep silence ensued. Six floors, six terrible walls, although the result simply of a clerical error, lay upon Giuseppe Corte with their implacable weight. How many years—yes, now he must really think in terms of years—how many years would it take to regain the heights of that precipice?

But why now had the room suddenly begun to darken? It was still midafternoon. With great effort for he felt himself to be paralyzed by a curious languor Giuseppe Corte looked at his watch which lay on the night table beside the bed. It was three-thirty. Then he turned, facing the other way. He saw that the blinds, obedient to some mysterious command, were slowly drawing to, shutting off the light.   ❖

Giosué Carducci[1] (1835–1907)

THE OX

Translated from the Italian by
Frank Sewall

I love thee, pious ox; a gentle feeling
Of vigour and of peace thou giv'st my heart.
How solemn, like a monument, thou art!
Over wide fertile fields thy calm gaze stealing,

5 Unto the yoke with grave contentment kneeling,
To man's quick work thou dost thy strength impart.
He shouts and goads, and answering thy smart,
Thou turn'st on him thy patient eyes appealing.

From thy broad nostrils, black and wet, arise
10 Thy breath's soft fumes; and on the still air swells,
Like happy hymn, thy lowing's mellow strain.

In the grave sweetness of thy tranquil eyes
Of emerald, broad and still reflected dwells
All the divine green silence of the plain.

"The Ox" by Giosué Carducci, translated by Frank Sewall from SELECTIONS FROM ITALIAN POETRY by A. Michael de Luca and William Giuliano. Copyright © 1966 by Harvey House, Inc. Reprinted by permission of Evelyn Singer Agency.

1. *Carducci* (cär düt′ chē).

ANCIENT LAMENT

Translated from the Italian by
A. Michael de Luca

The tree toward which you'd stretch
Your little child's hand,
The green pomegranate
With the pretty scarlet flowers,

5 In the silent, lonely garden
Has just burst into bloom again,
And June is restoring it
With its light and warmth.

You, blossom of my tree,
10 Smitten and withered,
You of my now useless life
Last and only flower,

Are in the cold earth,
Are in the black earth;
15 No more will the sun cheer you,
Nor will you be awakened by love.

"Ancient Lament" by Giosué Carducci, translated by A. Michael de Luca from SELECTIONS FROM ITALIAN POETRY by A. Michael de Luca and William Giuliano. Copyright © 1966 by Harvey House, Inc. Reprinted by permission of Evelyn Singer Agency.

ALPINE AFTERNOON

Translated from the Italian by
A. Michael de Luca

In the great circle of the Alps, over granite
Bleak and drab, over glaciers brightly glowing,
Rules serene, intense and infinite
In its immense silence the noon of day.

5 Pines and firs, not a gust of wind blowing,
Stand erect in the penetrating sunlight;
One hears the lyre-like prattle only, ever so slight,
Of water that among stones thinly made its way.

Benvenuto Cellini[1] (1500–1571)

from THE AUTOBIOGRAPHY

Translated from the Italian by
Robert Hobart Cust

AT THAT TIME there came to Florence a sculptor who was named Piero Torrigiani.[2] He came from England, where he had resided many years, and, since he was a great friend of my master's,[3] he came every day to (see) him. And when he saw my drawings and my work, he said: "I have come to Florence to engage as many young men as I can: for having a great work to execute for my king [4] I want the aid of my Florentine fellow citizens; and since your style of execution and your designs are more those of a sculptor than of a goldsmith, and as I have vast works in bronze to carry out, I will make you at one and the same time both skillful and wealthy." This man was of the most handsome presence, and most bold looking; he had more the air of a great soldier than of a sculptor, especially in his magnificent gestures and his sonorous voice, together with a trick of contracting his brows enough to terrify most men. And every day he talked of his bold doings among those beasts of Englishmen. In this

---

From THE AUTOBIOGRAPHY OF BENVENUTO CELLINI, translated by Robert Hobart Cust. Reprinted by permission of Dodd, Mead & Company, Inc. Copyright © 1961 by Dodd, Mead & Company, Inc.

1. *Cellini* (chel lē′ nē) **2.** *Piero Torrigiani* (tôr′ rē jä′ nē), (1472–1528). **3.** *my master,* the goldsmith Andrea Marcone. **4.** *my king,* Henry VIII of England.

connection he chanced to speak of Michelagniolo Buonarroti,[5] which was caused by a drawing that I had made, a copy of a cartoon by that most divine Michelagniolo. This cartoon was the first fine work wherein Michelagniolo displayed his marvellous talents, and he executed it in competition with one made by another artist, namely, Lionardo da Vinci, which were to adorn the Sala del Consiglio in the Palace of the Signoria.[6] They represented events when Pisa was taken by the Florentines[7]; and the admirable Lionardo da Vinci had chosen to illustrate a battle of cavalry, together with the capture of certain standards, as divinely composed as it is possible to imagine. Michelagniolo Buonarroti in his painting depicted a number of foot soldiers who, since it was summertime, were in the act of bathing in the Arno; and in that instant he shows that an alarm has been given, and those naked infantry are rushing to arms with such fine gestures that there has never among ancient or other modern artists been seen a work that attained to so high a pitch of greatness; and as I have said, the work of the great Lionardo was most beautiful and wonderful. These two cartoons stood, one in the Palace of the Medici, and the other in the Sala del Papa. Whilst they continued in existence they formed a school of Art for the world. Although the divine Michelagniolo subsequently painted the Great Chapel for Pope Julio,[8] he never by half

5. *Michelagniolo Buonarroti* (me′ kel ä nyô′ lô bwô′ när rô′ tē), Michelangelo. **6.** *the Palace of the Signoria.* During the period 1503–1504, Michelangelo and Leonardo were both commissioned by the Florentine government to paint frescoes on the wall of the large council hall of the Palace of the Signoria, or Palazzo Vecchio. Michelangelo's work never progressed beyond the stage of the *cartoon,* or preliminary drawing, which has itself been lost. Leonardo's fresco suffered serious damage through being hurriedly dried and was ultimately lost when the hall was redecorated by Georgio Vasari (1511–1574), though it still exists in copies made by other artists, notably one by Peter Paul Rubens. **7.** *They represented . . . by the Florentines.* Actually only Michelangelo's subject—the Battle of Cascina—was an engagement between the Florentines and the Pisans. Leonardo depicted the Battle of Anghiari, fought between the Florentines and the Milanese in 1440. **8.** *Pope Julio,* Julius II (1443?–1513) for whom Michelangelo painted the ceiling of the Sistine Chapel.

reached this point; his talents never again arrived at the power of these early efforts.

. . . . .

WE NOW RETURN to Piero Torrigiani, who with my drawing in his hand, spake thus: "This Buonaaroti *(sic)* and I from boyhood used to go to study in Masaccio's [9] chapel in the Church of the Carmine; and because Buonaaroti was accustomed to make fun of all those who were drawing there, one day when the said youth was annoying me among the rest, he aroused in me more anger than usual, and clenching my fist I gave him so violent a blow upon the nose, that I felt the bone and the cartilage of the nose break under the stroke, as if it had been a wafer; and thus marked by me he will remain as long as he lives." These words begat in me so great a hatred, since I saw continually the works of the divine Michelagniolo, that, notwithstanding that I had conceived a desire to go with him to England, I could not bear even to see him.

I applied myself continually in Florence to study after the fine style of Michelagniolo, and from that I have never deviated. At that period I commenced an intercourse and a very close friendship with a charming youth of my own age, who was also working in the goldsmith's trade. He bore the name of Francesco, son of Filippo, the son of that most excellent painter, Fra Filippo.[10] In our relations with one another there arose so great an affection that we never passed either day or night apart; and, moreover, since his home was full of those beautiful studies that his brilliant father had made, which consisted of a number of books of drawings by his own hand, representations of the fine antiquities of Rome: the which when I saw them enchanted me very much, and for about two years we kept company together. At this time I executed a work in silver in low relief as large as

---

9. *Masaccio* (mä sät′ chô), (1401–1428?), a Florentine painter. 10. *Fi-lippo, the son of . . . Fra Filippo.* Filippo, or Fillipino Lippi (1457–1504), was the son of Fra Filippo Lippi (1406?–1469), and both were celebrated Florentine painters.

the hand of a small boy. This article served for the clasp of a man's girdle, for they then wore them so big. There was carved upon it a group of leaves, arranged after the ancient manner, together with many small cherubs and other very fine masks. This work I executed in the workshop of a man named Francesco Salinbene. When this work was seen by the Goldsmiths' Guild, I acquired the reputation of being the most promising young man in that trade. And perchance a certain youth, Giovanbatista, surnamed Tasso, a wood-carver, a youth of precisely my own age, began saying that if I would like to go to Rome, he would willingly accompany me (this conversation that we had together took place immediately after dinner); and since I was enraged with my father over the usual subject of music, I said to Tasso, "You are a man of words and not of deeds." Tasso then replied to me: "I also am in a rage with my mother, and if I had money enough to take me to Rome I would not turn back even to close up that wretched little shop that I possess (at present)." To these words I replied that if it was on that account that he remained I was possessed of sufficient funds to take us both to Rome. Conversing thus together, as we walked along we found ourselves at the Gate at Sanpiero Gattolini without noticing it. Upon which I said to him: "Tasso mine, we are at this gate where neither you nor I expected to be; now since I am here it seems to me as though I had completed half the journey." Being thus in agreement, he and I said as we continued our journey, "What will our old folks say this evening?" Having said this we entered into a compact together not to think of them any more until we should have arrived in Rome. So we bound our aprons upon our backs, and proceeded almost in silence as far as Siena. When we were in Siena, Tasso said that he was footsore, so that he did not want to come any further, and he begged me to lend him the money to return home. To which I replied that there would not be enough left for me to go forward: "You should have thought of this ere leaving Florence; and if it be only on account of your feet that you do not want to come further we will find a horse returning to Rome, and then you will have no excuse for not coming." Having therefore hired a horse, when I saw that he did not answer me, I took the road towards the gate that leads to Rome. He, when he saw that I was determined, not ceasing to grumble, limping along to the best of his ability, came slowly at a good distance behind me. When I reached the gate, pitying my poor companion, I waited for him and took him up behind me, saying to him, "What would our friends say of us tomorrow, if when we had set out to go to Rome, we had not sufficient courage to go beyond Siena?" Whereupon the excellent Tasso admitted that I spoke the truth, and being a lively creature he began to laugh and sing; and thus continuing to sing and laugh we took our way to Rome. My age was then exactly nineteen, in correspondence with the century. When we had arrived in Rome I immediately engaged myself with a master craftsman, whom they called Firenzuola. This man bore the name of Giovanni, and was from Firenzuola in Lombardy; and he was a most skilful workman in the fashioning of plate and articles of large size. When I showed him a small idea of the model of that buckle which I had executed in Florence with Salinbene, he was wondrously pleased and spake these words to me, turning to a youth whom he employed, who was a Florentine, and was called Giannotto Giannotti,—who had, moreover, been with him some years—he spake as follows: "This is one of those Florentines who know their business, but you are one of those who know it not." Thereupon recognizing Giannotto I turned to accost him. For before he went to Rome, we often set to work together to draw, and had been very intimate comrades. But taking great offence at the words which his master had spoken, he said that he did not recognize me, nor did he know who I was. Upon which I being indignant at such statements, said to him: "Oh! Giannotto, once my intimate friend, for we were often to be found in such and such places, and used to draw, eat, drink and sleep at your country house, I do not need you to go bail for me to this worthy man your master, because I hope that my own hands may suffice to testify without your aid what sort of workman I am." When I had finished these words, Firenzuola, who was very excitable and violent, turned to the said Giannotto and said to him: "Oh! you vile rascal! Are you not ashamed to use such treatment and conduct towards one who has been so intimate a companion of yours?" And turning to me in the same excited manner he said: "Come into the shop and do as you have said; so that your hands may prove of what you are capable"; and he set me to carry out a most beautiful commission in silver for a cardinal. It was a casket copied from that in porphyry which stands before the door of the Rotonda. Besides copying it I enriched it with so many beautiful grotesques that my master went about eulogizing it and exhibiting it throughout the trade, because so well-executed an object should have issued from his workshop. It was about half a *braccio* [11] in size; and was arranged to serve as a saltcellar, to be kept upon the table. This was the first fruits of the earnings that I tasted in Rome: and one portion of these same earnings I forwarded to the assistance of my good father. The other portion I reserved to live upon myself: and with it I went about studying the remains of antiquity until my funds came to an end when it suited me to return to the shop to work. My comrade, Batista del Tasso, did not stay long in Rome, but returned to Florence. Having taken up again fresh work, the desire came upon me, when I had completed what I had on hand, to change my employer, being seduced thereto by a certain Milanese, who was called Master Pagholo Arsago. My former master Firenzuola raised a great disturbance with this Arsago, uttering in my presence certain insulting expressions: whereat I took up my parable in defence of my new master. I told him that I had been born a free man, and thus free I meant to live; and that he had no reason to complain of his conduct, still less of me, for there remained in his hands a few *scudi* [12] due upon our contract: and that as a free journeyman I wished to go where I liked: knowing that I did wrong to no man. My new master also made a few remarks, stating that he had not summoned me, and that I should oblige him by returning with Firenzuola. To this I rejoined that I was not aware that I had done wrong in any way, and since I had finished the work that I

---

11. *half a braccio* (brat' chō). The braccio has varied from around 15 to around 39 inches. 12. *a few scudi.* A scudo was an Italian coin, either gold or silver.

had begun, I wished to be at my own disposal and not at that of anyone else, and whoever wanted my services might ask me for them. To this Firenzuola replied: "I have no wish to ask anything further of you, and never upon any account do you come into my presence." I reminded him of the money due to me. He began to jeer at me; upon which I replied, that just as I could manipulate my tools upon the jobs that he had seen, was I not less skilful with my sword for the recovery of my dues. At these words there stopped by chance an elderly man, who was called Master Antonio da Sanmarino. This man was by far the most able goldsmith in Rome and had been Firenzuola's master. Having listened to my argument, which I uttered in such a manner that he could very easily understand it, he immediately undertook my cause, and said that Firenzuola should pay me. The disputes were violent, because this Firenzuola was marvellously skilled in arms, very much more indeed than in the art of the goldsmith. But reason turned the situation, and I assisted it with the same spirit, to such purpose that I was paid; and in course of time the said Firenzuola and I were reconciled, and I stood godfather at his request to one of his sons.

Continuing to work with Master Pagholo Arsago I earned a great deal, always sending the greater part to my good father. At the end of two years, at the prayers of my good father, I returned to Florence and set myself to work once more with Francesco Salinbene, with whom I made very good earnings and took great pains to learn. Having renewed my relations with Francesco di Filippo, although I was much given up to certain diversions on account of that accursed music, I never omitted to devote certain hours of the day or of the night to my studies. I made at that time a silver Heart's-Key *(chiavaquore);* for so they were called in those days. It was a girdle the width of three fingers, which they were accustomed to make for newly wedded brides; and it was made in low relief with some small figures besides upon it in full relief. I made it for a man named Raffaello Lapaccini. Although I was very badly paid for it, I acquired from it such reputation as was of more advantage to me than the price that I ought justly to have received. Having at this period worked for many divers employers in Florence, where I was acquainted with some men of worth among the goldsmiths, such as was Marchone, my first master, there were others who bore the name of very good men, but who, by overreaching me in my work, robbed me shamefully as far as they were able. Upon seeing this I avoided them, and reckoned them as evil fellows and thieves. One goldsmith amongst the rest, named Giovanbatista Sogliani, courteously accommodated me with a part of his shop, which was in a corner of the Merchato Nuovo, beside the bank kept by the Landi. Here I executed many beautiful little works and earned a good deal: I was able to assist my family very much. I aroused the envy of those evil masters whom I had formerly served, who were called Salvadore and Michele Guasconti (they owned three large shops for the carrying on of the goldsmith's trade, and executed many commissions): to such an extent, that when I saw that they were injuring me, I complained to a certain worthy man, saying that those knaveries ought to have sufficed, which they exhibited towards me under the cloak of the treacherous good will displayed by them. When this remark reached their ears they boasted that they would make me greatly repent such a speech; to which I who knew not the color of fear paid little or no attention. One day it chanced that as I was leaning against the shop of one of them, he called out to me, partly rebuking, and partly defying me. To which I replied that if they had done their duty by me I should have spoken those things of them that one says of good and worthy persons: but since they had done the opposite the fault lay with them and not with me. Whilst I stood arguing, one of them, who was called Gherardo Guasconti, their cousin, instigated perhaps by their common consent, spied a beast of burden that was passing. (It was a beast laden with bricks.) When the said load came up to me, Gherardo pushed it on to me in such a way that it hurt me very much. Turning myself round suddenly and seeing him laughing, I struck him such a blow on one of his temples that he fell down insensible as though dead. Then I turned to his cousins and said: "Thus do they treat cowardly thieves like you." And upon their wishing to make some attack upon me, because there were many of them, I being infuriated, drew a little knife that I carried, saying thus: "If any one of you issues from your shop, another had better run for a confessor, for the doctor will have naught to do." My words struck such terror into them that no one ventured to the assistance of their cousin.

As soon as I had departed, the fathers and the sons hurried to the Eight (Judges), and there stated that I had with force of arms assaulted them in their shops; an event that had never occurred in Florence.

The Eight caused me to be summoned; whereupon I appeared: and administering to me a severe reprimand they rebuked me because they saw me in my cloak only whilst the others were in civil dress of mantle and hood; and moreover, because my adversaries had been to speak with all the judges at home in private, whilst I having no personal acquaintance with any of those judges, had not spoken with them, trusting to the great justification that I had; and I told them that on account of the great injury and insult that Gherardo had shown me, provoked to very great anger, I had given him nothing more than a *buffet,* which did not seem to me sufficient to deserve so severe a censure.

Scarcely would Prinzivalle della Stufa, who was one of the Eight, allow me to finish the word *buffet,* before he said: "You gave him a violent blow and not a buffet."

When the bell had been rung and we all had been put outside, Prinzivalle spoke to his colleagues in my defence: "Consider, sirs, the simple-mindedness of this poor young man, who accuses himself of having struck a buffet only, thinking that to be a minor fault than to give a violent blow: whereas the penalty for a buffet administered in the Mercato Nuovo is twenty-five *scudi,* whilst that for a violent blow is little or nothing. He is a very virtuous youth, and supports his indigent family by his very strenuous exertions; and would to God our city had an abundance of his kind, for there is a great need of them." There were among them some of those twisted-hooded fellows *(arronzinati cappuccetti),* who, influenced by the prayers and false witness of my adversaries (because they were of the faction of Fra Girolamo [13]), would have had me put in prison and condemned to (a fine of) a measure of charcoal; but in this matter the excellent Prinzivalle wholly prevailed. So they condemned me to a small fine of four bushels of flour, to be bestowed in alms upon the convent of the Murate. Calling us back they immediately commanded me not to say another word under pain of their displeasure and to obey that punishment to which I had been condemned. So administering to me a severe reprimand they sent us to the chancellor. But I kept on murmuring: "It was a buffet and not a violent blow": in such a way that the Eight burst out laughing. The chancellor in the name of the judges ordered us both to give securities; and they condemned me only to pay those four bushels of flour. It seemed to me that I had been shamefully treated, nevertheless I sent for one of my cousins, who was called Master Anniballe, the surgeon, the father of Messer Librodoro Librodori, desiring that he would go surety for me. This man, however, did not choose to come, at which I was very indignant; fuming I became like an adder, and took a desperate resolution. (It is well known how much the planets do not only guide, but even coerce us.) Recollecting what great obligation this Anniballe owed to my family, my fury so much the more increased that it turned everything to evil, and being besides by nature somewhat hot-tempered, I composed myself to wait in that office until the Eight had adjourned for dinner. And whilst I remained there alone, observing that none of the attendants of the Eight were watching me any longer, bursting with rage, I issued from the palace, ran to my workshop, where, having found a small poniard, I sprang into the dwelling of my adversaries, who were both in their shop and their house. I found them at table, and the young Gherardo, who had been the original cause of the trouble, threw himself upon me; to whom I struck a blow with my poniard in the

---

13. *the faction of Fra Girolamo,* followers of Fra Girolamo Savonarola (1452–1498), Florentine religious reformer executed by the Medici. Savonarola had urged the Florentines to forgo wearing jewelry and ornaments, and so his followers were antagonistic to the goldsmith Cellini.

breast, so that it passed right through his frock *(saio)* and jerkin *(colletto)* to his shirt, without touching his flesh or doing him any sort of harm. Since it appeared to me from the disappearance of my hand and the sound made by his clothes that I had wounded him very seriously, and he fell terrified to the ground, I cried out: "Traitors! Today is the opportunity for me to kill you all." The father, mother and sisters believing that it was the Day of Judgement, immediately flung themselves on their knees upon the ground, and with a loud voice and in no measured terms begged for mercy. And when I saw that they offered no defence to me, and that he lay extended upon the ground as one dead, it seemed to me too vile a thing to touch them; but I ran madly down the stairs; and when I reached the street, I found all the rest of the tribe, who were more than twelve in number. One of them had an iron shovel, another a big piece of iron piping, some hammers and anvils, and others sticks. When I came among them like a maddened bull, I threw four or five of them to the ground, and I fell with them, always plying my poniard now on this one, now on that. Those who had kept their feet joined in as far as they were able, showering blows upon me with both hands, with hammers, sticks and anvils. But because God sometimes mercifully intervenes they did me not the least injury in the world, nor I them. My cap only was left, which my adversaries secured, and though they kept themselves at a distance from it, every one of them struck at it with his weapon. Then looking round among themselves for the dead and wounded there was no one who had received any hurt. I departed towards Santa Maria Novella, and immediately met Brother Alesso Strozi, with whom I was unacquainted. To this good friar I commended myself for the Love of God, that he would save my life, for I had committed a great fault. The good friar told me that I need fear nothing; for though I had committed all the crimes in the world, I should be most safe in his little cell. In the space of about an hour the Eight, having summoned an extraordinary meeting, directed the publication of one of the most terrifying of bans that was ever heard against me, placing under the severest penalties whoever should harbor or know me, regarding neither the place nor the quality of any one who should protect me. My poor afflicted and excellent father going in to the Eight, threw himself upon his knees on the ground, imploring mercy for his poor young son: whereupon one of those democrats tossing back the crest of his twisted-up hood, and rising to his feet, with some insulting words said to my poor father: "Get up and go away instantly, lest we send you to-morrow to the gallows." My poor father, nevertheless, boldly answered them, saying, "What God shall have ordained such will be done and no more." Upon which the same man replied that for certain God has ordained it thus. And my father said to him: "I take comfort to myself that you certainly don't know that"; and having gone out of their presence, he came to see me in company with a certain youth of my own age, who was called Piero di Giovanni Landi: (we loved each other more than if we had been brothers). This young man carried under his mantle a splendid sword and a very handsome coat of mail. And when they came to me my brave father told me what had occurred and what the Eight Judges had said. Then he kissed me on the forehead and both eyes; blessed me heartily and spake thus: "May the Grace of God assist you." And taking up the sword and the armor, with his own hands he helped me to put them on. Then he said: "My good son! With these in your possession you must either live or die." Pier Landi, who was there present, never ceased weeping; and when he handed me ten gold *scudi,* I asked him to remove for me a few hairs of my beard, which were the first down. Friar Alesso robed me after the fashion of a monk and provided me with a lay-brother to accompany me. Leaving the convent and issuing by the Porta al Prato, I went along the town wall as far as the Piazza di San Gallo; and mounting the slope of Montui, at one of the first houses I found a man who was called Grassuccio, own brother to Messer Benedetto da Montevarchi. I immediately unfrocked, and becoming a layman again we mounted two horses which were there for us, and under cover of night proceeded to Siena. The said Grassuccio, being sent back to Florence, visited my father and told him that I had reached safety. My father was greatly overjoyed and it seemed a thousand years ere he met again that member of the Eight who had insulted him. And when he found him he spake thus to him: "Do you see, Antonio, that it was God who knew what should happen to my son, and not you?" To which he replied: "Let us but catch him another time." My father said: "I shall give my attention to thanking God that he has escaped this time."

· · · · ·

ARRIVING AT SIENA, I awaited the post to Rome and joined company with him. When we had crossed the Paglia [14] we met the courier who was bringing news of the newly elected pope, who was Pope Clemente.[15] Having reached Rome I set myself to work in the shop of master Santi the goldsmith. For although he himself was dead, his son still carried on the business. He, however, did no work himself, but committed all the shop orders to a young man who was called Luca Agniolo da Jesi. This man was a peasant, who as a very small boy had come to work with master Santi. He was small of stature but well-proportioned. This youth did his work better than any man that I had ever seen up to that time, with greatest dexterity and much beauty of design; and he labored solely upon large pieces of plate (grosseria), that is to say, very handsome vases, bowls, and suchlike articles. Setting myself to work in that shop, I undertook to make certain candlesticks for the Spanish Bishop (of) Salamanca. These same candlesticks were richly ornamented, as far as is suitable to such work. A pupil [16] of Raffaello da Urbino,[17] named Gianfran, surnamed il Fattore (i.e. the Artisan), he was a very brilliant painter; and since he was a friend of the said bishop, he set me high in his favor, to such purpose that I received a great many commissions from this bishop, and earned a great deal of money. At that period I went to draw sometimes in the Chapel of Michelagniolo, and sometimes at the house of Agostino Chigi, the Sienese, in which house there were many very beautiful works of painting by the hand of the most excel-

14. *the Paglia* (pä′ lyä), a river of central Italy. **15.** *Pope Clemente,* Clement VII (1478–1534). **16.** *pupil,* Giovanni Francesco Penni (1488?–1528). **17.** *Raffaello da Urbino,* the painter Raphael (1483–1520).

lent Raffaello da Urbino. But this was on feast days, because in the said house there was residing Messer Gismondo Chigi, brother of the said Messer Agostino. They (the family of Chigi) took much pride in seeing young men like myself going to study within their walls. The wife of the said Messer Gismondo saw me often in this house of hers; this lady who was as charming as possible and unusually handsome, coming up to me one day and regarding my drawings, asked me if I was a sculptor or a painter. I replied to the lady that I was a goldsmith. Said she, that I drew too well for a goldsmith; and causing one of her maids to bring a lily of most beautiful diamonds set in gold, showing it to me she desired me to value it. I valued it at eight hundred *scudi*. Then she said that I had valued it very excellently. After that she asked me if I had sufficient spirit to reset it handsomely; I replied that I would do so very willingly, and in her presence I made a rough sketch; and I executed it so much the better, inasmuch as I took pleasure in dealing with this so very beautiful and agreeable a gentlewoman. When I had finished the sketch, there joined us another very beautiful Roman gentlewoman who was upstairs and who on coming down asked the said Madonna [18] Portia what she was doing there. She answered smiling: "I take great pleasure in watching this honest youth draw, for he is clever and handsome." I, having acquired a little confidence, mingled nevertheless with a small amount of honest bashfulness, blushed and said: "Whatever I may be, Madonna, I shall always be most ready to serve you." The gentlewoman, also blushing a little, replied: "You know very well that I want you to serve me"; and handing me the lily she told me to take it with me. And she gave me besides twenty gold *scudi* that she had in her pocket and said: "Set it after this fashion that you have designed for me, and preserve for me the old gold in which it is set at present." The Roman gentlewoman then said: "If I were that young man, I would gladly run away (with what I'd got)." Madonna Portia rejoined, that virtues rarely stand alongside vices, and that if I did such a thing, I should very greatly belie that open look of an

---

18. *Madonna,* my lady. [*Italian*]

honest man that I exhibited; and turning away, taking the hand
of the Roman gentlewoman, with a most charming smile she said
to me: "Adieu, Benvenuto." I stayed on a while longer, engaged
upon the drawing that I was making, copying a certain figure of
Jove by the hand of the said Raffaello da Urbino. When I had
finished I went away and set myself to the fashioning of a little
model in wax, whereby to show how the finished work ought
subsequently to turn out; and having carried this to the said
Madonna Portia to see, that same Roman gentlewoman, of
whom I spoke before, being also present, being greatly satisfied
both of them with my labors, they paid me so many compliments
that, impelled by some small amount of boldness, I promised
them that the completed work should be half as good again as
the model. So I set to it and in twelve days I finished the said
jewel in the form of a lily, as I have said above, adorned with
little masks, cupids, animals, etc., and very beautifully enameled,
in such a manner that the diamonds of which the lily was
composed were improved in appearance by more than half.
While I was laboring upon this work, that clever man Lucagniolo, of whom I have spoken above, showed that he was much
displeased, saying to me many times over that it would be far
more useful and creditable to me to help him in his work on
large silver vases, as I had begun to do. To which I replied that I
should be able, whensoever I wished, to fashion large silver vases;
but that those works upon which I was now engaged did not
come my way to do every day; and that in these same commissions there was no less credit to be obtained than in large silver
vases, but even much more profit. This Lucagniolo laughed at me
saying: "You will see, Benvenuto; for by the time that you have
finished that work of yours, I shall hasten to get this vase
finished, which I commenced when you (began) your jewel, and
by experience I will demonstrate the profit that I shall derive
from my vase, and that which you will gain from your jewel." To
which I replied that I should willingly enjoy making such a trial
with so able a man as he was, because at the completion of such
works we should see which of us was in error. So both of us with
a slightly scornful smile bent our heads somewhat fiercely, each

of us desirous of bringing to a completion the works that we had begun; to such purpose that at the end of about ten days each of us had completed his work with much finish and skill. That of the said Lucagniolo was a very large vase to be used at the table of Pope Clemente, wherein he threw whilst he was at table, meat-bones and the rinds of various fruits; an article made rather more for display than for necessity. This vase was adorned with two fine handles, with many masks, both large and small, with very beautiful foliage, of as fine a grace and design as it is possible to imagine: wherefore I told him that it was the most beautiful vase that I had ever seen. Upon this, Lucagniolo, fancying that he had proved his point, said to me: "Your work appears to me no less beautiful, but we shall soon see the difference between the two." So, taking up his vase, and carrying it to the Pope, the latter expressed himself very greatly satisfied, and immediately caused him to be paid according to the usual custom of the trade for such large works. Meanwhile I carried my work to the said gentlewoman Madonna Portia, who told me with profoundest surprise, that I had far and away exceeded the promise that I had made to her; and then she added, telling me that I must ask for my labors everything that might please me, because it seemed to her that I deserved so much that even in giving me a fortress it would seem scarcely sufficient satisfaction for me; but since she was unable to do this, she smilingly told me to ask whatever she was able to accomplish. To which I replied that the greatest reward desired for my exertions, was that I should have satisfied her ladyship. So smiling also and making a bow, I was withdrawing, saying that I desired no other recompense than that. Then the said Madonna Portia turned to that Roman gentlewoman, and said: "Do you see how great are the company of the virtues that we reckoned to be in him, and that they are not vices?" Whilst both stood surprised, Madonna Portia said: "Benvenuto mine, have you ever heard it said, that when the poor give to the rich, the Devil laughs?" Upon which I replied: "And since he has so many disappointments, this time I would like to see him laugh"; but as I was departing she said that she did not wish on this occasion to do him such a favor. When I returned to my shop Lucagniolo had the money which he had received for his vase in a paper packet; and when I appeared he said: "Let us make here a small comparison between the recompense paid for your jewel beside that given for my vase." To which I replied that he might keep the matter in that state until the following day; because I hoped that, inasmuch as my work in its kind was not less beautiful than his, so I expected to make him see the recompense for it. When the next day arrived Madonna Portia sent one of her stewards to my shop, who called me outside, and having placed in my hand a paper packet full of money on behalf of that lady, said to me, that she did not want the Devil to laugh on any consideration; explaining that what she sent me was not the entire payment that my labors deserved, with many other courteous words, worthy of such a lady. Lucagniolo, to whom it seemed a thousand years ere he could compare his packet with mine, immediately upon my return to his shop, in the presence of his twelve workmen and some other neighbors warned beforehand, who wished to see the result of such a contest, took his packet, and laughing mockingly and saying "Ho, ho" three or four times he emptied the money on to the counter with a great noise. They were twenty-five *scudi di giuli,* whereas he thought that mine might be four or five *scudi di moneta.* Whereupon I,—overpowered by his clamor, and by the glances and smiles of the bystanders,—looking thus a little into my package, and perceiving that it was all gold, from one side of the counter, keeping my eyes lowered, and without the least noise, raised my package high in the air firmly with both hands, which caused the contents to pour out after the fashion of a mill hopper. My money amounted to half as much again as his; so that all those eyes, which were gazing upon me with some mockery, turning immediately towards him, said: "Lucagniolo, this money of Benvenuto's, inasmuch as it is gold and half as much again, produces a much finer effect than yours." I would certainly have believed that out of envy together with the shame that that Lucagniolo felt, he would have immediately dropped down dead; and that although a third part of that money of mine must come to him, since I was but a workman, for that is the custom: the workman receives two-thirds, and the other third part goes to the masters of the shop—unbridled envy prevailed more than avarice within him, whereas it should have worked in exactly the opposite direction, since this Lucagniolo had been born of a peasant from Jesi. He cursed his trade and those who had taught it to him, declaring that from thenceforward he had no more desire to practise that art of making plate, he only wished to devote his attention to making those little trumperies, since they were so well paid for. Not less indignantly did I retort that every bird sang its own strain; that he was talking after the fashion of the hovels whence he had issued, but that I declared for certain that I could succeed most excellently in fashioning his monstrosities, but that he would never succeed in making that sort of trumperies. So leaving him in a rage, I told him that he would soon be made to see this. Those who were present vociferously declared him to be in the wrong, reckoning him in the character of the clown that he was, and me in that of a man of worth as I had shown myself to be. ❖

Gabriele D'Annunzio[1] (1864-1938)

THE END OF CANDIA

Translated from the Italian by
Frederick Taber Cooper

I

THREE days after the Easter banquet, which was traditionally a
great occasion in the Lamonica household, both in its lavishness
and in the number of its guests, Donna Cristina Lamonica was
counting the table linen and silver service, and replacing them
one by one, methodically, in drawer and cupboard, in readiness
for future banquets.

As usual, she had with her, to help in the task, the chamber-
maid, Maria Bisaccia, and the laundress, Candida Marcanda,
familiarly known as Candia. The huge hampers, filled with fine
linen, stood in a row upon the floor. The silver platters and other
table service gleamed brightly from the sideboard—massive
vessels, somewhat crudely wrought by rustic silversmiths, and of
more or less liturgical design, like all the plate which rich
provincial families hand down from generation to generation. A
fresh fragrance of soapy water pervaded the room.

From the hampers Candia took tablecloths, napkins, and
towels; she made the mistress take note that each piece was

1. *D'Annunzio* (dän nün′ tsyô).

intact, and then passed them over to Maria, who laid them away in the drawers, while the mistress sprinkled lavender between them and entered the numbers in a book. Candia was a tall, lean, angular woman of fifty, with back somewhat bent from the habitual attitude of her calling, with arms of unusual length, and the head of a bird of prey mounted on a turtle's neck. Maria Bisaccia was a native of Ortona, a trifle stout, with a fresh complexion and the clearest of eyes; she had a soft fashion of speech, and the light, leisurely touch of one whose hands were almost always busy over cakes and sirups, pastry and preserves. Donna Cristina, also an Ortonese, and educated in a Benedictine convent, was of small stature, with a somewhat too generous expanse of bosom, a face overstrewn with freckles, a large, long nose, poor teeth, and handsome eyes cast downward in a way that made one think of a priest in woman's clothing.

The three women were performing their task with the utmost care, giving up to it the greater part of the afternoon. All at once, just as Candia was leaving with the empty baskets, Donna Cristina, in the course of counting the small silver, found that a spoon was missing.

"Maria! Maria!" she cried, in utter dismay, "count these! There's a spoon missing! Count them yourself!"

"But how could it? That's impossible, Signora!" replied Maria, "let me have a look." And she in turn began to count the small pieces, telling off the numbers aloud, while Donna Cristina looked on, shaking her head. The silver gave forth a clear, ringing sound.

"Well, it's a fact!" Maria exclaimed at last, with a gesture of despair; "what's to be done about it!"

She herself was safe from all suspicion. For fifteen years she had given proofs of her fidelity and honesty in this very household. She had come from Ortona together with Donna Cristina at the time of the wedding, almost as though she were a part of the marriage settlement; and from the first she had acquired a certain authority in the house, through the indulgence of her mistress. She was full of religious superstitions, devoted to the saint and the belfry of her birthplace, and possessed of great shrewdness. She and her mistress had formed a sort of offensive alliance against Pescara and all pertaining to it, and more particularly against the saint of the Pescarese. She never missed a chance to talk of her native town, to vaunt its beauty and its riches, the splendor of its basilica, the treasures of San Tommaso, the magnificence of its religious ceremonies, as compared with the poverty of San Cetteo, that possessed only one single little silver cross.

Donna Cristina said:

"Take a good look in there."

Maria left the room to extend the search. She explored every nook and corner of the kitchen and the balcony, but in vain. She came back empty-handed.

"It isn't there! It isn't there!"

Then the two together tried to think, to make conjectures, to ransack their memories. They went out upon the balcony that communicated with the court, the balcony back of the laundry, to make one last research. As they talked together in loud tones, women's heads began to appear at the windows of the surrounding houses.

"What has happened, Donna Cristina? Tell us about it."

Donna Cristina and Maria related the occurrence with many words and many gestures.

"Lord, Lord! Then there have been thieves here?"

In a moment the report of the theft had spread through the neighborhood, through all Pescara. Men and women fell to discussing, to imagining who could have been the thief. By the time the news had reached the most distant houses of Sant' Agostino, it had gathered volume; it was no longer a question of a mere spoon, but of all the silver plate in the house of Lamonica.

Now, since the weather was fine and roses were beginning to bloom upon the balcony, and a pair of linnets were singing in their cage, the women lingered at their windows, for the pleasure of gossiping across the grateful warmth of the outdoor air. Female heads continued to appear from behind the pots of sweet basil, and a chatter arose that must have rejoiced the cats upon the housetops.

Clasping her hands, Donna Cristina asked: "Who could it have been?"

Donna Isabella Sertale, nicknamed the Polecat, who had the lithe and stealthy movements of a beast of prey, asked in a strident voice:

"Who did you have with you, Donna Cristina? It seems to me that I saw Candia on her way—"

"Ahah!" exclaimed Donna Felicetta Margasanta, nicknamed the Magpie because of her continuous garrulity. "Ahah!" repeated the other gossips.—"And you hadn't thought of it?"—"And you never noticed?"—"And you don't know about Candia?"—"We can tell you about Candia!"—"Indeed we can!"—"Oh, yes, we can tell you about her!"

"She washes clothes well, there is no denying it. She is the best laundress in Pescara, there's no question about it. But the trouble with her is that she is too light-fingered—didn't you know that, my dear?"

"She got a couple of towels from me once."—"And a napkin from me."—"And a nightgown from me."—"And three pairs of stockings from me."—"And a new petticoat from me."—"And I never got them back again."—"Nor I."—"Nor I."

"But I didn't discharge her. Whom could I get? Silvestra?"

"Oh! oh!"

"Angelantonia? The African?"

"Each one worse than the other!"

"We must put up with it."

"But it's a spoon this time!"

"That's a little too much!"

"Don't you let it pass, Donna Cristina, don't you let it pass!"

"Let it pass, or not let it pass!" burst forth Maria Bisaccia, who, in spite of her placid and benign appearance, never let an opportunity pass for displaying her superiority over her fellow servants. "That is for us to decide, Donna Isabella, that is for us to decide!"

And the chatter continued to flow back and forth from windows to balcony. And the accusation spread from lip to lip throughout the whole countryside.

THE FOLLOWING MORNING, Candia Marcanda already had her arms in a tubful of clothes, when the village constable, Biagio Pesce, nicknamed the Little Corporal, appeared at her door.

"His Honor, the mayor, wants you up at his office right away," he told the laundress.

"What's that?" demanded Candia, wrinkling her brows into a frown, yet without interrupting the task before her.

"His Honor, the mayor, wants you up at his office, right away."

"Wants me? What does he want me for?" Candia demanded rather sharply, for she was at a loss to understand this unexpected summons, and it turned her as stubborn as a horse balking at a shadow.

"I can't tell you what for," replied the Little Corporal, "those were my orders."

"What were your orders?" From an obstinacy that was natural to her, she would not cease from asking questions. She could not convince herself that it was a reality. "The mayor wants me? What for? What have I done, I should like to know? I'm not going. I haven't done anything."

The Little Corporal, losing his temper, answered: "Oh, you won't go, won't you? We'll see about that!" and he went off, muttering, with his hand upon the hilt of the ancient sword he wore.

Meanwhile there were others along the narrow street who had overheard the conversation and came out upon their doorsteps, where they could watch Candia vigorously working her arms up and down in the tubful of clothes. And since they knew about the silver spoon, they laughed meaningly and interchanged ambiguous phrases, which Candia could not understand. But this laughter and these phrases awoke a vague forboding in the woman's mind. And this forboding gathered strength when the Little Corporal reappeared, accompanied by another officer.

"Step lively," said the Little Corporal peremptorily.

Candia wiped her arms, without replying, and went with them.

In the public square, people stopped to look. One of her enemies, Rosa Panura, called out from the door of her shop, with a hateful laugh:

"Drop your stolen bone!"

The laundress, dazed by this persecution for which she could find no reason, was at a loss for a reply.

Before the mayor's office a group of curious idlers had gathered to watch her as she went in. Candia, in an access of anger, mounted the steps in a rush and burst into the mayor's presence, breathlessly demanding: "Well, what is it you want of me?"

Don Silla, a man of peaceful proclivities, was for the moment perturbed by the laundress's strident tones, and cast a glance at the two faithful custodians of his official dignity. Then, taking a pinch of tobacco from his horn snuff box, he said to her: "My daughter, be seated."

But Candia remained standing. Her beaklike nose was inflated with anger, and her wrinkled cheeks quivered curiously. "Tell me, Don Silla."

"You went yesterday to take back the wash to Donna Cristina Lamonica?"

"Well, and what of it? What of it? Was there anything missing? All of it counted, piece by piece—and not a thing missing. What's the matter with it now?"

"Wait a moment, my daughter! In the same room there was the table silver—"

Candia, comprehending, turned like an angry hawk, about to swoop upon its prey. Her thin lips twitched convulsively.

"The silver was in the room, and Donna Cristina found that a spoon was missing. Do you understand, my daughter? Could you have taken it—by mistake?"

Candia jumped like a grasshopper before the injustice of this accusation. As a matter of fact she had stolen nothing.

"Oh, it was I, was it? I? Who says so? Who saw me? I am astonished at you, Don Silla! I am astonished at you! I, a thief? I? I?"

And there was no end to her indignation. She was all the more keenly stung by the unjust charge, because she knew herself to be capable of the action they attributed to her.

"Then it was you who took it?" interrupted Don Silla, prudently sinking back into the depths of his spacious judicial chair.

"I am astonished at you!" snarled the woman once more, waving her long arms around as though they had been two sticks.

"Very well, you may go. We will see about it."

Candia went out without a salutation, blindly bumping into the doorpost. She had turned fairly green; she was beside herself. As she set foot in the street and saw the crowd which had gathered, she realized that already public opinion was against her; that no one was going to believe in her innocence. Nevertheless, she began to utter a vociferous denial. The crowd continued to laugh as it dispersed. Full of fury, she returned home, and hopelessly began to weep upon her doorstep.

Don Donato Brandimarte, who lived next door, said mockingly: "Cry louder, cry louder! There are people passing by!"

Since there were heaps of clothing still waiting for the suds, she finally calmed herself, bared her arms, and resumed her task. As she worked, she thought out her denials, elaborated a whole system of defense, sought out in her shrewd woman's brain an ingenious method of establishing her innocence; racking her brain for specious subtleties, she had recourse to every trick of rustic dialectic to construct a line of reasoning that would convince the most incredulous.

Then, when her day's work was ended, she went out, deciding to go first to see Donna Cristina.

Donna Cristina was not to be seen. It was Maria Bisaccia who listened to Candia's flood of words, shaking her head but answering nothing, and withdrawing in dignified silence.

Next, Candia made the circuit of all her clients. To each in turn she related the occurrence, to each she unfolded her defense, continually adding some new argument, amplifying her words, growing constantly more excited, more desperate, in the face of incredulity and distrust. And all in vain; she felt that from now on there was no further defense possible. A sort of blind hope-

lessness took possession of her—what more was there to do?
What more was there to say?

III

MEANWHILE Donna Cristina Lamonica gave orders to send for
Cinigia, a woman of the people, who practised magic and em-
pirical medicine with considerable success. Cinigia had several
times before discovered stolen goods; and it was said that she
was secretly in league with the thieves.

"Find that spoon for me," Donna Cristina told her, "and you
shall have a big reward."

"Very well," Cinigia replied, "twenty-four hours are all I
need."

And twenty-four hours later she brought back her answer;
the spoon was to be found in a hole in the courtyard, near the
well.

Donna Cristina and Maria descended to the courtyard, made
search, and, to their great amazement, found the spoon.

Swiftly the news spread throughout Pescara.

Then triumphantly Candia Marcanda went the rounds of all
the streets. She seemed to have grown taller; she held her head
erect; she smiled, looking every one straight in the eye, as if to
say, "I told you so! I told you so!"

The people in the shops, seeing her pass by, would murmur
something and then break forth into a significantly sneering
laugh. Filippo La Selvi, who sat drinking a glass of liqueur
brandy in the Café d'Ange, called Candia in.

"Another glass for Candia, the same as mine!"

The woman, who was fond of strong spirits, pursed up her
lips covetously.

"You certainly deserve it, there's no denying that!" added
Filippo La Selvi.

An idle crowd had gathered in front of the café. They all had
the spirit of mischief in their faces. While the woman drank,
Filippo La Selvi turned and addressed his audience:

"Say, she knew how to work it, didn't she? Isn't she the foxy one?" and he slapped the laundress familiarly upon her bony shoulder.

The crowd laughed. A little dwarf, called Magnafave, or "Big Beans," weak-minded and stuttering, joined the forefinger of his right hand to that of his left, and striking a grotesque attitude and dwelling upon each syllable, said:

"Ca—ca—ca—Candia—Ci—ci—Cinigia!" and he continued to make gestures and to stammer forth vulgar witticisms, all implying that Candia and Cinigia were in league together. His spectators indulged in contortions of merriment.

For a moment Candia sat there bewildered, with the glass still in her hand. Then in a flash she understood—they did not believe in her innocence. They accused her of having brought back the silver spoon secretly, by agreement with the sorceress, to save herself further trouble.

An access of blind anger came upon her. Speechless with passion, she flung herself upon the weakest of them, upon the little hunchback, in a hurricane of blows and scratches. And the crowd, at the sight of this struggle, formed a circle and jeered at them in cruel glee, as at a fight between two animals, and egged on the two combatants with voice and gesture.

Big Beans, badly scared by her unexpected violence, tried to escape, hopping about like a little ape; and held fast by the laundress's terrible arms, whirled round and round with increasing velocity, like a stone in a sling, until at last he fell violently upon his face.

Some of the men hastened to pick him up. Candia withdrew in the midst of hisses, shut herself within her house, and flung herself across her bed, sobbing and gnawing her fingers, in the keenness of her suffering. The new accusation cut her deeper than the first, and all the more that she knew herself capable of such a subterfuge. How was she to clear herself now? How was she to establish the truth? She grew hopeless as she realized that she could not allege in defense any material difficulties that might have interfered with carrying out the deception. Access to the courtyard was perfectly simple; a door, that was never fastened, opened from the ground floor of the main stairway; people came and went freely through that door, to remove the garbage, or for other causes. So it was impossible for her to close the lips of her accusers by saying, "How could I have got in?" The means of successfully carrying out such a plan were many and easy.

Candia proceeded to conjure up new arguments to convince them; she sharpened up her wits; she invented three, four, five different cases to prove that the spoon never could have been found in that hole in the courtyard; she split hairs with marvelous ingenuity. Next she took to making the rounds of the shops and the houses, seeking in every possible way to overcome the people's incredulity. They listened to her, greatly entertained by her captious reasoning; and they would end by saying, "Oh, it's all right!"

But there was a certain tone in their voice that left Candia annihilated. So, then, all her trouble was for nothing! No one would believe her! Yet with marvelous persistence she would return to the attack, spending whole nights in thinking out new arguments. And little by little, under this continued strain, her mind gave way; she could no longer follow any sustained thought but that of the silver spoon.

Neglecting her work, she had sunk to a state of actual want. When she went down to the river bank, under the iron bridge, where the other washwomen congregated, she would sometimes let slip from between her fingers the garments that the current swept away forever. And she would talk continually, unweariedly, of the one single subject. In order not to hear her, the young laundresses would begin to sing, and would mock her with the improvised rimes of their songs. And she meanwhile would shout and gesticulate like a crazy woman.

No one could give her work any longer. Out of pity, some of her former employers would send her food. Little by little she fell into the habit of begging, and wandered through the streets, bowed over, unkempt, and all in rags. The street urchins would tag behind her, shouting: "Tell us the story of the spoon, 'cause we never heard it, Auntie Candia!"

She would stop strangers sometimes as they passed by, to tell them the story and to argue out her defense. Young fellows would sometimes send for her, and pay her a copper to tell it all over, two, three, or four times; they would raise up difficulties against her arguments; they would hear her all the way through, and then at last stab her with a final word. She would shake her head, and go on her way; she found companionship among other beggars and would reason with them endlessly, indefatigably, invincibly. Her chosen friend was a deaf woman, whose skin was a mass of angry blotches, and who limped on one leg.

In the winter of 1874 she was at last stricken with serious illness. The woman with the blotches cared for her. Donna Cristina Lamonica sent her a cordial and a scuttle of coals.

The sick woman, lying on her pallet, still raved of the silver spoon. She would raise herself on her elbow and struggle to wave her arm, to give emphasis to her fevered arguments.

And at the last, when her staring eyes already seemed overspread with a veil of troubled waters that rose from within, Candia gasped forth:

"It wasn't I, madam—because you see—the spoon—"

THE RAIN IN THE PINE GROVE

Translated from the Italian by
William Giuliano

You keep silent. On the threshold
of the forest I don't hear
the words you say,
human words, but I do hear
5 new words
which raindrops and leaves utter
far away.
Listen. Rain falls
from the scattered clouds.
10 It falls on the tamarisks
salt-laden and parched,
it falls on the pines
scaly and straight,
it falls on the myrtle
15 sacred to Venus,
on the broom plant, refulgent
with clusters of flowers,

---

on the juniper thick
with fragrant berries,
20 it falls on our faces
sylvan faces,
it falls on our hands
naked hands,
on our clothing
25 light clothing,
on the fresh thoughts
our souls unfold
new souls,
on the beautiful tale
30 that yesterday
beguiled you, that today beguiles me,
Oh Hermione.[1]
You hear? The rain falls
on the lonely
35 verdure
with a patter that endures
and varies in the air
according to the leaves,
some thick, some thin.
40 Listen. An answer
to the weeping is the singing
of the cicada
whom the southern lament
does not terrify,
45 nor the ashen sky.
And the pine
has one sound, and the myrtle
another sound, and the juniper
yet another, instruments
50 diverse
under innumerable fingers.
And immersed

---

1. *Hermione* (hẻr mī′ ə nē).

are we in the spirit
of the wood-land,
55 pulsating with arboreal life:
and your inebriated face
is moist with rain
like a leaf,
and your tresses
60 are fragrant like
the bright broom plant,
oh terrestrial creature
by name
Hermione.

Grazia Deledda[1] (1875–1936)

THE SARDINIAN FOX

Translated from the Italian by
William Fence Weaver

THE LONG, WARM MAY days had come back, and Ziu[2] Tomas
again sat as he had the year before—ten years before—in the
open courtyard in front of his house, which was the last in a
bunch of little, black buildings huddled against the gray slope of
a mountain. But in vain spring sent its breath of wild voluptuous-
ness up there: the decrepit old man, motionless between his old
black dog and his old yellow cat, seemed as stony and insensible
as everything around him.

Only, at night, the smell of the grass reminded him of the
pastures where he had spent most of his life; and when the moon
rose out of the sea, far off, as huge and golden as the sun, and
the coastal mountains, black beneath a silver sky, and all the
huge valley and the fantastic semicircle of hills before and to the
right of the horizon were covered with shimmering veils and
areas of light and shadow, then the old man used to think of
childish things, of Lusbé, the devil who leads damned souls to the

1. *Deledda* (de led′ dä). 2. *Ziu,* "uncle," used loosely. *Zia* is "aunt."

pasture, after they have been changed into wild boars; and if the moon hid behind a cloud, he thought seriously of the seven calving cows which the planet, at that moment going to supper, devoured calmly in its hiding place.

He almost never spoke; but one evening his granddaughter Zana, when she shook him to tell him it was bedtime, found him so stubbornly silent, erect, and rigid on his stool that she thought he was dead. Frightened, she called Zia Lenarda, her neighbor, and both women succeeded in moving the old man, helping him into the house where he stretched out on the mat in front of the hearth.

"Zia Lenarda, we have to call a doctor. Grandfather is as cold as a corpse," the girl said, touching the old man.

"Our doctor's gone away. He went to the mainland for two months to study ear diseases, because he says they're all deaf around here when he asks them to pay the rent on his pastures . . . as if he hadn't bought all that land with the people's money, may justice find him! And now, instead of him, we have that foolish snob of a city doctor, who thinks he's the court physician of the king of Spain. Who knows if he'll come or not?"

"Zia Lenarda, he has to come. He charges twenty lire a visit!" Zana said haughtily.

And the woman went off.

The substitute was living in the regular doctor's house, the only habitable one in the whole village. Surrounded by gardens, with terraces and arbors, with a great courtyard covered with grapevines and wistaria, the house was a comfort even to this substitute, who came from a town that, though small, had all the necessities, vices, murderers, loose women, and gambling houses that the larger cities have.

Zia Lenarda found him reading a yellow-backed book in the dining room, which opened onto the courtyard; no doubt a medical work, she thought, judging by the intensity with which he consumed it, his nearsighted eyes stuck to the page, his white fists supporting his dark, rather soft cheeks, his thick lips parted to show his protruding teeth.

The maid had to call him twice before he noticed the woman's presence. He closed the book sharply and, slack and distracted, followed Zia Lenarda. She didn't dare to speak, and went before him as if to show him the way, leaping, agile and silent, down from rock to rock over the rough lanes, struck by the moon.

Below, in the valley's depth, in front of the woman's darkened window, the doctor looked up and saw the mountains' silver peaks. The pure smell of the valley was mixed with the sheepfold odor that came from the hovels, from the forms of shepherds crouched here and there on the steps before their doors: all was sad and magnificent. But in the courtyard of Ziu Tomas the smell of hay and sage dominated; and in front of the low wall by the embankment, with the huge moon and a star almost scraping her head, the doctor saw a woman's form so slender, especially from the waist down, so shrouded, without outlines, that she gave him the impression of a bust set on a narrow pedestal.

Seeing him, she went back to the kitchen, got a light, and knelt down beside her grandfather's mat, while Zia Lenarda ran into the other room to fetch a painted chair for the doctor.

Then the girl raised her head and looked into his eyes, and he felt a sensation that he would never forget. He thought he had never seen a woman's face more lovely and more enigmatic: a broad forehead covered almost to the eyebrows (one higher than the other) by two bands of black, shiny hair; a narrow, prominent chin; smooth cheekbones that cast a little shadow on her cheeks; and white, straight teeth, which gave a suggestion of cruelty to her proud mouth; while her great black eyes were full of sadness and a deep languor.

Seeing herself examined in this way, Zana lowered her eyes and didn't raise them again; but when her grandfather didn't answer the doctor's questions, she murmured: "He's been deaf for twenty years or more."

"You don't say? Well, at least you might prepare a foot bath for him; his feet are frozen."

"A foot bath? Won't that hurt him?" Zia Lenarda asked, consulting Zana. "He hasn't taken his shoes off for eight months."

"Well, then, are you going to leave him here now?"

"Where else can I put him? He's always slept here."

The doctor got up, and after he had written out a prescription, he gave it to Zana and looked around him.

The place was black as a cave; he could make out a passage at the back, with a wooden ladder; everything indicated the direst poverty. He looked with pity at Zana, so white and thin that she reminded him of an asphodel blooming at the mouth of a cavern.

"The old man is undernourished," he said hesitantly, "and you are, too, I believe. You'd both need a more plentiful diet. If you can . . ."

She understood at once. "We can do anything."

Her expression was so full of scorn that he went away almost intimidated.

Up, from stone to stone, along the sandstone path he went back to his oasis; the moon silvered the arbor, and the wistaria blooms hung like bunches of fantastic grapes whose very perfume was intoxicating. The old maidservant was spinning in the doorway, and with Zana's strange face still before his eyes, he asked: "Do you know Ziu Tomas Acchittu?"

Who didn't know the Acchittu family?

"They're known even in Nuoro, my prize! More than one learned man wants to marry Zana."

"Yes, she's beautiful. I had never seen her before."

"She never goes out. There's no need of that, to be sure. The rose smells sweet even indoors. Foreigners come from everywhere, even from Nuoro, and pass by just to see her."

"What? Has the town crier gone around to announce her beauty?"

"That's not it, my soul! The old man is so rich he doesn't know how much he has. Land as big as all of Spain, and they say he has more than twenty thousand *scudi* [3] in a hole somewhere. Only Zana knows the place. That's why she doesn't want even Don Juacchinu, who's noble but not so rich."

"And may I ask where these riches come from?"

"Where do the things of this world come from? They say the

---

3. *twenty thousand scudi,* nearly twenty thousand dollars.

old man (on my life, I can't say yes or no about it, myself) had a hand in more than one bandit raid in the good old days when the dragoons weren't as quick as the *carabinieri*[4] are nowadays. Then, in those days, more than one shepherd came home with one sack full of cheese and the other of gold coins and silver plate . . ."

The old woman began to relate all this, and it seemed that she drew the stories from her memory like the thread from her distaff; the man listened, in the shadow of the arbor, sprinkled with gold pieces, and now he understood Zana's laugh and her words: "We can do anything!"

The day after the first visit he was back at the house: the old man was sitting on the mat, calmly gumming his barley bread soaked in cold water, the dog on one side of him, the cat on the other. The sun slanted in through the low door, and the May wind bore away the wild, leathery smell of the old man.

"How's it going?"

"Well, as you can see," Zana said, with a hint of scorn in her voice.

"Yes, I can see. How old are you, Ziu Tomas?"

"Yes, I still can," the old man said, showing the few, blackened teeth he had left.

"He thought you said *chew*. Grandfather—" Zana said, bending over the old man, showing him her hands with all the fingers sticking out except the right thumb, "—like this, isn't that right?"

"Yes, ninety, may God preserve me."

"Good for you. I hope you live to be a hundred—more than a hundred! And you, Zana, you've stayed here with him, alone?"

She told him how all her relatives were dead, her aunts, uncles, cousins, the old, the children; and she spoke calmly of death as of a simple event without importance; but when the doctor turned to the old man, shouting: "Change your way of living! Cleanliness! Roast meat! Good wine! and make Zana enjoy herself a little, Ziu Tomas."

Then the old man asked: "When's he coming back?"

---

4. *carabinieri,* policemen.

"Who?"

"Oh," Zana said, "it's just that he's waiting for our regular doctor to come back and cure his ears."

"Wonderful! Our doctor's fame is assured then."

The old man, who went on understanding everything in his own way, touched the sleeve of his torn jacket, which was shiny with grease. "Dirty? It's the custom. People who are well off don't have to make a show of it."

As a matter of fact, the doctor observed that the cleanest people in town were the poor; the rich paid no attention to their clothes, scorning appearances, and also finding it convenient perhaps. Here, one day, was Zia Lenarda, waiting for the doctor in the courtyard, dressed like a servant, though she too was a woman of means, with property and flocks, so rich that in spite of her forty-three years she had married a handsome boy of twenty.

"Good morning, doctor, your honor. I'd like to ask a favor of you. My husband Jacu is off on military service: now it's shearing time and I want him to come home on leave. Your honor doesn't know anyone at the Court?"

"No, unfortunately, my good woman."

"I asked our regular doctor about it. Take care of it, I said, if you pass through Rome. But he always says yes, then he forgets. My Jacu is a handsome boy (I'm not boasting just because I'm his wife) and just as good as honey . . . with a little pushing he could get everything. . . ."

She made a gesture of pushing with her spindle, but the doctor went off, sighing.

"It's not enough to be handsome and good in this world to get what we want, my dear lady."

And he went back to his oasis, thinking of Zana and of many things in his past. He was thinking that in his youth he had been handsome and good and yet he had got nothing, not love, or wealth, or even pleasure. True, he had not hunted for them; perhaps he had been waiting for them to offer themselves spontaneously; and as he had waited and waited, time had passed in futility. But in the past few years he had been seized sometimes by fits of mad rebellion; he sold his property and went off to search urgently for love, wealth, pleasure. But one day he realized that these cannot be bought, and when his wallet was empty, he went back to his few patients, joked with them good-naturedly, took long, absent-minded walks, and read yellow-backed French novels.

Zia Lenarda, on her side, convinced that good looks can obtain everything, seeing that the doctor went to the Acchittu's every day even though the old man was well, turned to Zana.

"You tell him, treasure! Everyone's getting ready for the shearing. What can I do, with everything turned over to the hired hands? The doctor looks at you with eyes as big as doorknobs. . . . How can he help it, dear heart? If you tell him to ask for Jacu's leave, he can't say no."

But Zana didn't promise; and when, after the tedium of those long days when the warm wind, the empty blue sky, the bright sun created an ineffable sadness, the doctor went at evening to the courtyard of Ziu Tomas, where he sat astride the painted chair in front of the hedge, full of fireflies and stars, she joked with him and asked him what causes certain diseases, how poisons are made, and she spoke calmly of many things, but she didn't ask the favor her neighbor wanted.

Sometimes Zia Lenarda herself, seated on the low wall, spun in the dark and joined in the conversation. This annoyed the doctor, who wanted to be alone with Zana after he had convinced the old man to go to bed early because the night air was bad for the deaf. The older woman spoke of nothing but the shearing.

"If you could just see the celebration, your honor! Nothing is more fun, not even the feast of San Michele and San Constantino. I'd invite you if Jacu came, but without him the feast would be like a funeral for me."

"Well, my good woman, do you want to know the truth? They'd give Jacu leave only if you were ill, and you're as healthy as a goat."

Then she began to complain; she had had so many aches since Jacu left, and now that shearing time approached, she really was suffering mortally. To convince the doctor more readily, she took to her bed. He was touched. He wrote out the certificate and ordered some medicine. Zana waited on her neighbor, poured out the dosage, looking at it in the reddish light of the oil lantern, and murmured: "It's not poison, is it?"

Then she went back to the courtyard, where the doctor was sitting on the painted chair. It was an evening in early June, warm already and scented. Night of love and memories! And the memories came, sweet and bitter, from the doctor's dark, tortuous past, as from the dark and tortuous valley came the sweet and bitter odor of the oleander. He drew his chair closer to the low wall where Zana was sitting, and they began their usual conversation. Occasionally a shepherd passed in the lane, without too much surprise at hearing the doctor's voice in the courtyard of Ziu Tomas. By now everybody believed that the doctor was regularly courting Zana, and they were sure that Zana would accept him, otherwise she would have kept him at a distance. But the two of them spoke of matters apparently innocent, of grasses, poisonous plants, medicaments.

"Oleander? No, that isn't poisonous, but hemlock is. Do you know what it looks like?"

"Who doesn't?"

"It's called the sardonic plant. It makes people die laughing . . . like you!"

"Let go of my wrist, doctor. I don't have the fever like Zia Lenarda."

"I have the fever, Zana."

"Well, take some quinine. Or is that poison, too?"

"Why do you keep talking about poisons tonight? Are you planning to kill somebody? If you are, I'll kill him for you at once . . . but . . ."

"But?"

"But . . ."

He took her wrist again, and she allowed it. It was dark anyway, and nobody could see from the lane.

"Yes, I do want some poison. For the fox."

"What? She comes this close?"

"She certainly does! Let go of me," she added in a whisper, twisting threateningly, but he took her other hand and held her fast, as if she were a thief.

"Give me a kiss, Zana. Just one."

"You can go and kiss a firebrand. Well, all right, if you give me the poison. That fox even comes and steals our newborn lambs . . ."

When Jacu's application for leave had been mailed off, along with the doctor's certificate, Zia Lenarda recovered and went back to minding her neighbors' business. And without any surprise she realized that the doctor was aflame like a field of stubble. He went back and forth in the lane like a boy, and even twice in a day he visited Ziu Tomas, claiming he would cure the old man's deafness before his colleague came back from the mainland. Zana seemed impassive; often she wouldn't make an appearance, but stayed shut in her room, like a spider in its hole.

On Sundays, the only day she went out—to go to mass—the doctor waited for her in front of the church.

One after another, the women came up the winding lane, stiff in their holiday clothes, their hands folded on their embroidered aprons, or carrying their babies on their arms, in red cloaks marked with a blue cross. When they reached a certain spot they turned toward Mount Nuoro, guarded by a statue of the Redeemer, and blessed themselves. The sun gleamed on the gold of their sashes and illuminated their fine Greek profiles. But the doctor, as if bewitched, looked only at Zana, and the old gossips thought: "The daughter of Tomas Acchittu has given him mandrake to drink. . . ."

One day, among the few men who took part in the women's procession, there was Jacu, home on leave. He was really handsome, no two ways about it: tall, ruddy, clean-shaven, with green eyes so bright that the women lowered theirs when they went by him, even if he were paying no attention to them. Military life had given him the air of a conqueror, but of things far more serious than mere women. As soon as he arrived, he had gone up to the doctor's to thank him, bringing him a young kid and an invitation to the famous shearing. The doctor spoke to him in dialect; he answered in proper Italian. And when the doctor asked, rather pointedly: "Are you inviting many people?" he answered: "Yes, because it's a big family, and a man like me—well, I may have many enemies, but I also have many friends. Besides, I'm broad-minded, and I'm inviting even the relatives of Lenarda's first husband. They can kill me, if I'm lying. And if she had had three husbands, I'd invite the relatives of them all."

"You're a man of the world, I see. Good for you. I suppose you'll invite your neighbors, too."

Being a man of the world, Jacu pretended to know nothing of the doctor's madness over Zana.

"Of course, a neighbor is more than a relative."

The day of the shearing came, and Zana, Zia Lenarda, and the other women took seats in the cart that Jacu drove.

The sheepfold was on the plateau, and the heavy vehicle, drawn by two black steers, scarcely broken, bounced up along the rocky path; but the women weren't afraid, and Zana, her hands clasping her knees, was calmly crouched down as if in front of her own hearth. She seemed sad, but her eyes gleamed with a kind of hidden lightning, like a far-off blaze, shining on a dark night in the heart of a forest.

"Neighbor," Jacu said, good-humoredly, "hang me, but you have a face like a funeral. He'll come, he'll come. He's coming later, with the priest, as soon as mass is over. . . ."

"Cheer up, Zana," the women said then, joking a little maliciously, "I hear a horse now, trotting like the devil himself."

"What a chair that is! How much would that chain cost? Nine *reali?*" [5]

Then Zana grew angry. "Evil take you all. Leave me alone. I can't bear him. The crows can pluck out my eyes if I even look at that man's face today. . . ."

The doctor and the priest arrived a little before noon, welcomed with shouts of joy. In the shade of a cork tree Jacu, the

5. *nine reali,* slightly over a dollar.

servant, and his friends sheared the sheep, laying them out, carefully bound, on a broad stone that looked like a sacrificial altar. The dogs chased one another through the grass, birds chirped in the oak, an old man who looked like the prophet Elijah gathered the wool into a sack, and all around the asphodel and the wild lilies, bent by the scent-laden wind, seemed to lean forward, curious to see what was happening in the midst of that group of men who stooped down, the shears in their hands. Once they were sheared and released, the sheep jumped up from the heap of wool, as from a foaming wave, and bounded off, shrunken, the muzzles rubbing the earth.

For a while the doctor stood watching, his hands clasped behind him, then he turned to the hut, where the women were cooking, assisted by Jacu's old father, who reserved for himself the honor of roasting a whole kid on the spit. Farther on, the priest, stretched out on the grass in the shade of another cork tree, was telling a Boccaccian tale to a select group of youths. The women nudged Zana and pointed to the doctor; and all at once, with a change of mood, she began to joke with him, asking him to make himself useful at least, by going to get some water at the spring. He went along with her jokes and, taking a cork pail, walked off in the bright sunlight that scorched the grass and the sage and made a perfume that was enough to intoxicate a man.

The group around the priest sent whistles and shouts after the doctor, and the old man roasting the kid caught his thumb in his fingers as a gesture of contempt. A learned man, a grown man, letting himself be made a fool of like this by the women! Then Zana cursed and ran off, holding her kerchief to her head, until she caught up with the doctor and took the pail out of his hand. From a distance, the women saw the man follow her along the path that led to the spring, and Jacu's old father began to spit furiously on the fire, as if he wanted to put it out.

"The granddaughter of Tomas Acchittu—you see her? She wanted to be alone with the man. If she was my daughter, I'd put my foot on her neck."

"Let her be, father-in-law," Zia Lenarda said kindly. Ah, she knew what love was, how it made you mad, like drinking bewitched water.

The doctor, in fact, dazed by the bright sun, followed Zana into the thicket around the spring, and again he tried to take her in his arms. She looked at him with those eyes of hers, like the Queen of Sheba's; but she pushed him away, threatening to pour the pail full of water on his head. Always the same, since the first evening there by the low wall of the courtyard; she led him on and repulsed him, half ingenuous, half treacherous, and asked him always for the same thing: some poison.

"All right, then, Zana, I'll make you happy. Tonight I'll come to your house, and I'll bring one of those little bottles with a skull on it. But be careful you don't end in jail."

"It's for the fox, I tell you. All right, but leave me now. You hear? Someone's coming."

In fact, the thicket around the fountain shook as if a boar were crashing through, then Jacu appeared. His face was overwrought, although he pretended that finding the two of them was a joke.

"Hey! What are you doing there in the dark? It's time to eat, not to be courting. . . ."

"You're not so hungry; you're thirsty," Zana said sarcastically, lifting the pail, "have a drink, handsome. . . ."

But Jacu threw himself full-length on the ground and drank, panting, from the spring.

During the banquet the doctor laughed, while the priest threw bread crumbs at him and hinted maliciously. He laughed, but from time to time he was distracted, struck by a new idea. After the banquet was over he went off to lie down in the shade among the rocks behind the hut; from there he could see without being seen, and he commanded a view of the area down to the oak in whose shade the shepherd went on shearing. The priest and the others, nearer by, had begun a singing contest, and the women were listening, seated in a row, their hands in their laps.

In the intense silence, the voices, the songs, the laughter were dispelled like the thin white clouds in the blue vastness; and the doctor could hear a horse cropping the grass beyond the rocks, a dog gnawing a bone inside the hut, where Jacu came every so often to empty the sheared wool.

All at once Zana, as the song contest grew more lively, got up and came into the hut. The doctor was smoking; he observed the blue thread that rose from his cigar, and a kind of grin raised his upper lip, showing the gold fillings of his teeth.

Finally Jacu arrived, and Zana's choked voice came like a moan through the cracks in the hut.

"I swear . . . May I be eaten by the hawks . . . if he's even touched my hand. I have my own reasons for smiling at him. . . . It's all for our own good. . . . But this suffering will end . . . end. . . ."

The man, intent perhaps on emptying the wool, was silent. She went on, exasperated, her voice filled with hate: "What about me? Am I ever jealous of your wife? The old crow, the fox. But it's going to end . . . soon. . . ."

Then Jacu laughed; and again there was heard the laughter, the singing, the grazing horse.

But the doctor wanted to enjoy himself a little. He leaped to his feet and began to shout: "Hey! A fox! a fox!"

And the two lovers ran out of the hut, amazed, while below, the group stopped their singing, the women looked all around them, and the dogs started to bark as if a fox had really gone past.   ✜

Luciano Erba (1922–   )

THE INATTENTIVE

Translated from the Italian by
Robert Fitzgerald

But when and how will they arrive?
and who will send them among us?
you find them, one day, near at hand
in visored cap, red scarf around the neck,
5 hands pushed forward in trouser pockets—
new companions for our games,
mute but smiling playmates
smaller than ourselves, and paler,
tired out after a short run, clumsy
10 at wrestling and jumping, weightless.
I remember one on an October morning
climbed with me up to Horse Mountain,
his cheeks were red with pain around the heart,
he smiled, running to keep up with us.

"The Inattentive" by Luciano Erba, translated by Robert Fitzgerald from POETRY (August, 1959). Reprinted by permission of the Editor of *Poetry* and Robert Fitzgerald.

15 And another, or perhaps the same, I can't say,
knowing that way they all have of walking and
the blue sweaters they wear:
he followed me through vineyards to the valley
of trout streams—where the river
20 branches in bright channels.
Till evening we stayed in the water
and he never once asked me to try
fishing; then he disappeared
by a path I could never find now.
25 And a third—or again the same one,
going by that big knot in the woolen scarf
and the way he stood beside me, silent,
in the yellow meadows outside town—
imaginary Africa—
80 one motionless long day.
                And a fourth . . .
All gone. Destroyed by pitiless fevers,
consumed by an unknown ill, and far away.
I don't know. Nor do I know
if they will come again, nor when, nor how—
85 the friends, the days, the bright season,
if life lost by inattention
will come again.

Giacomo Leopardi (1798–1837)

THE INFINITE

Translated from the Italian by
John Heath-Stubbs

This lonely hill was always dear to me,
And this hedgerow, that hides so large a part
Of the far sky-line from my view. Sitting and gazing
I fashion in my mind what lie beyond—
5 Unearthly silences, and endless space,
And very deepest quiet; until almost
My heart becomes afraid. And when I hear
The wind come blustering among the trees
I set that voice against this infinite silence:
10 And then I call to mind Eternity,
The ages that are dead, and the living present
And all the noise of it. And thus it is
In that immensity my thought is drowned:
And sweet to me the foundering in that sea.

"The Infinite" by Giacomo Leopardi, translated by John Heath-Stubbs from SELECTED POEMS. Reprinted by permission of David Higham Associates, Ltd.

THE EVENING AFTER THE HOLY DAY

Translated from the Italian by
John Heath-Stubbs

The night is soft and clear, and no wind blows;
The quiet moon stands over roofs and orchards
Revealing from afar each peaceful hill.
Sweetheart, now every field-path is silent;
5 At intervals along the balconies
The night-long lantern gleams: you are asleep,
And gentle slumber now gathers about
Your quiet chamber, and no single care
Gnaws at your heart; you do not know at all,
10 Nor think that you have opened in my breast
A very grievous wound. You are asleep:
And I have come abroad to reverence
This sky whose aspect seems to be so gentle,
And ancient Nature powerful over all,
15 Who has fashioned me for trouble. "I deny
All hope to you," she has said, "Yea, even hope;
Your eyes shall not be bright for any cause,
Except with weeping." This was a festal day:
And you are resting after its amusements;
20 And maybe in your dreams you still remember
How many eyes took pleasure in your beauty,
How many, too, pleased you: I find no place—
Not that I hoped it now—among your thoughts.
Meantime I ask how many years of life

25 Remain to me, and then it is I cast
Myself upon the ground, and cry, and rage.
Oh terrible days, even of our green youth!
Alas, I hear not far along the road
The lonely singing of a workman, coming
30 Back to his poor home so late at night,
After the sports; and fiercely my heart aches
Thinking how all this world passes away
And leaves no trace. For look, the festival
Is over now, an ordinary day
35 Succeeds tomorrow; all things our race has known
Time likewise bears away. Where now is the voice
Of the ancient peoples, the clamour of our ancestors
Who were renowned, and that great Empire of Rome,
The arms, and the clash they made by land and sea?
40 All is silence and peace; the world is still;
There are no tidings now remain of them.
Once in my boyhood, when so eagerly
We would look forward to the holiday,
Finding it over, I lay upon my bed,
45 Wakeful and very unhappy; late that night
A singing heard along the field-paths
Little by little dying into the distance,
Even as this does now, pierced through my heart.

The Evening After the Holy Day   223

TO THE MOON

Translated from the Italian by
John Heath-Stubbs

O gracious Moon, I call to mind again
It was a year ago I climbed this hill
To gaze upon you in my agony;
And you were hanging then above the woods,
5 Filling them all with light, as you do now.
But dim and tremulous your face appeared,
Seen through the tears that rose beneath my
        eyelids,
My life being full of travail; as it is still—
It does not change, O my sweet Moon. And now
10 I would remember it, and reckon up
The cycles of my sorrow. How sweet the thought
That brings to mind things past, when we are young—
When long's the road for Hope, for Memory brief—
Though they were sad, and though our pain endures.

"To the Moon" by Giacomo Leopardi, translated by John Heath-Stubbs from SELECTED POEMS. Reprinted by permission of David Higham Associates, Ltd.

Niccolò Machiavelli[1] (1469–1527)

THE DEVIL TAKES A WIFE

Translated from the Italian by
J. R. Hale

TRADITION, supported by the old chronicles of Florence, relates that an aged and most holy man whose life was an object of admiration to his contemporaries, being rapt in his prayers, saw through their means how all, or nearly all of the souls of those unhappy beings who die out of grace with God and go to Hell, complained that it was marriage that led them to such a miserable fate. Minos and Radamanthus[2] and the other judges of the infernal region were much amazed by this, and finding it hard to believe that all these calumnies against the female sex were true, and as the complaints grew day by day, they reported the matter to Pluto[3] and he decided that with all the princes of the underworld he would carefully examine the question and take the course that was thought best to prove it or expose it as a fallacy. After calling them together, then, Pluto spoke as follows:

"Since, my beloved friends, by heavenly decree and dread,

From THE LITERARY WORKS OF MACHIAVELLI translated by J. R. Hale, published Oxford University Press.

1. *Machiavelli* (mä′ kyä vel′ lē). 2. *Minos and Radamanthus,* brothers, sons of Zeus and Europa. They were kings and lawgivers of Crete who were renowned for their justice while on earth, and after death were made judges in the Underworld. 3. *Pluto,* the ruler of the Underworld in the mythology of the Romans; here the reference is to Satan.

irrevocable destiny I rule this kingdom, I thus cannot be made to submit to any judgment, either of heaven or earth. All the same, as the greatest proof of wisdom on the part of those who have most power is to submit to the law and esteem the opinions of others, I have decided to seek your advice as to how I should act in a matter that could bring such shame to our rule. For as all the souls of men who come into our kingdom claim women to have been the cause, and as this would seem to be impossible, I fear that if we admit their testimony we run the risk of being blamed as overcredulous, and if we do not, as insufficiently severe and but faint friends of justice. And as one is the vice of the frivolous while the other is that of the unjust man, and anxious to avoid being accused of either, but not knowing the means, we have summoned you to aid us with your counsel and ensure that this realm, which has always lived free from scandal in the past, may so continue in the future."

Each of the princes found the matter of great weight and importance; all agreed that the truth must be discovered, but not how this should be done. For while some considered sending one, and others several of their number into the world in human shape to investigate the truth of the matter in person, many of the others thought it could be managed more simply by forcing a number of souls to reveal it under various sorts of torture. As the majority were in favour of sending someone, however, it was this course that was decided on. And as no one could be found to volunteer to take up the enterprise it was resolved to choose by casting lots. The lot fell on Belfagor, once, before his fall from Heaven, an archangel, now an archdevil. While reluctant to accept the commission, nevertheless, compelled by Pluto's authority, he prepared to do whatever the council determined and bound himself to observe the conditions which they had solemnly discussed. These were: that a hundred thousand ducats should at once be given to whoever was chosen for the mission, that he should proceed with it into the world and, in human shape, take a wife and live with her for ten years. Then, pretending to die, he should return and report to his superiors on the strength of his experience what the burdens and inconveniences of marriage were. It was further laid down that during this period he was to be subject to all the troubles and ills that men are subject to, and which bring with them poverty, imprisonment, sickness and every other misfortune that men incur, unless he could, by ingenuity or wit, escape them. So Belfagor took the money, and a human shape, and went into the world, and accompanied by his band of horsemen and attendants, made a brilliant entry into Florence—which city he chose above all others to live in because it offered the best opportunities for anyone who wanted to get a high interest on his money.

He gave himself out to be Roderigo of Castile and rented a house in the Ognisanti district, and as he could not reveal his true origin he said he had left Spain and gone as a child to Syria where he had made his fortune at Aleppo, whence he had come to find a wife in a country more humane, civilised and sympathetic. Roderigo looked about thirty years old and was exceedingly handsome, and when he had shown in the course of a few days the extent of his wealth and that he was a generous and warm-hearted man, many noble citizens, who had more daughters than money, offered them to him. From all these Roderigo chose a most lovely girl called Onesta, the daughter of Amerigo Donati, who had three others who were almost of marriageable age as well as three grown sons, and though his family was among the noblest, and his reputation in Florence stood high, he was, considering his rank and the size of his family, very poor. Roderigo arranged a brilliant and magnificent wedding. He omitted nothing suitable to such a festivity. And as he was subject, under the terms of his leaving Hell, to all the passions of humankind, he had begun at once to relish worldly prestige and ceremony and the good opinion of other men, and this involved him in no little expense. Besides this, he had not been living long with his Onesta before he was up to the ears in love with her and could not bear to see her looking sad or in any way discontented.

Onesta had brought with her to Roderigo not only her noble blood and her beauty but as much pride as Lucifer ever had, and Roderigo, who had tasted both, judged his wife's to be the greater; and it increased more than ever when she realised how much her husband loved her. When she saw that her rule could be absolute in every way she began to order him about without sympathy or moderation, nor did she hesitate, when he denied her anything, to bait him with curses and reproaches. This caused Roderigo untold misery. However, his consideration for her father, her brothers and the rest of her family, his respect for the marriage tie, and, above all, the depth of his love for her, made him keep his patience. I will say nothing of the great sums he spent to give her the pleasure of wearing the latest fashions and enjoying all the novelties which our city, in her accustomed vein, produces. What is more, to keep the peace with her, he was forced to help his father-in-law marry off the other daughters, which forced him to spend large sums of money. To stay in her good books after that, he fitted out one of her brothers with cloth for the Levant,[4] another with silks for the western trade and set up the other as a goldsmith in Florence. On all this he spent the greater part of his fortune. Furthermore, at carnival time, and on St. John's day,[5] when by ancient custom the whole city makes festival, and many of the noble and wealthy citizens entertain one another with splendid banquets, Onesta was determined that Roderigo's should outshine the rest, so that she would not feel inferior to the other women. All these things he bore for the reasons already given, and despite their oppression he would have put up with them if, as a result, his household had been at peace, and if he had been able to wait for ruin in tranquillity. But it happened quite otherwise, for on top of these crushing expenses her arrogant nature led to one crisis after another. There was not a servant, who could bear to stay in the house more than a day or two, and having no faithful servant to entrust with his affairs was a source of grave inconvenience to Roderigo; even the devils he had brought with him to serve in his household preferred to return to the fires of Hell rather than stay in the world under her authority.

---

4. *the Levant,* the countries of the eastern Mediterranean, or the East in general. 5. *St. John's day,* June 24. St. John the Baptist was the patron of Florence.

In this worrying and distracted life, and with all his ready money swallowed up by these immoderate expenses, Roderigo began to live on the hope of profits which he expected from his western and Levantine enterprises, and as his credit was still good, maintained his standard of living by raising loans. As this led to his notes-of-hand circulating widely, however, this was soon noticed by those who engage in this sort of business. And while his position was already delicate, news arrived suddenly from the west and from the Levant to the effect that one of Onesta's brothers had gambled away all Roderigo's goods, and that the other, returning on a ship loaded with his merchandise, which he had not insured, had been drowned together with it.

The news was scarcely abroad when Roderigo's creditors banded together; they suspected him to be bankrupt, but not being able to show their hand until their notes became due, decided that it would be wise to keep a close eye on him so that he could not suddenly spirit himself away. Roderigo, for his part, seeing no way out of his difficulty, and knowing how his powers were circumscribed by the Infernal edict, decided, come what may, to flee, and one morning he mounted his horse and left through the Prato gate, which was near his house. As soon as his flight was known his creditors raised the alarm, notified the magistrates and not only sent the police runners after him but a mob of the people as well.

When the hue and cry was raised, Roderigo was no more than a mile from the city, so seeing the situation was a hazardous one, he decided to flee more secretly by leaving the road and trusting his luck across the fields. The many ditches which crossed the countryside impeded him, and as they prevented him from going on horseback, he left the horse on the road and continued his flight on foot, going from field to field—planted, as is common in that part of the country, with vines and reeds—till he came out near Peretola at the house of Gianmatteo del Brica, a man who worked for Giovanni del Bene. By chance he found Gianmatteo, who had come home to feed his oxen, and explained his position, promising that if he would save him from the hands of his enemies, who were pursuing him in order to imprison him till he died, he would make his fortune, and that before he left he would produce proof of this, or, if he did not, would willingly yield himself into his enemies' hands. Gianmatteo, although a peasant, had his wits about him, and reckoning that he had nothing to lose by helping, agreed, and hurried him on to a dung heap in front of his house, concealing him with old reeds and other refuse he had got ready to burn.

Roderigo was no sooner hidden than his pursuers appeared; for all their threats, they were unable to make Gianmatteo say that he had seen him, and so went on until, after searching in vain for the rest of that day and the next, they returned exhausted to Florence.

When the noise had died away, Gianmatteo let him come out and asked him to make good his promise.

"My brother," Roderigo said to him, "I am deeply obliged to you and fully intend to reward you; and so that you will not doubt that I can, I will tell you who I am."

Then he told him what sort of being he was and the conditions on which he had left Hell, and about the wife he had taken, and he went on to describe the way he was going to make him rich, which was, in brief: if Gianmatteo heard of any woman becoming possessed, he could assume that the spirit responsible was himself, and that he would refuse to leave her unless he came to exorcise her; so he would have the chance of getting what he liked by way of payment from the woman's family. And when that had been arranged, he vanished.

Not many days passed before the news was spread through the whole of Florence that a daughter of Ambruogio Amidei, whom he had married to Bonaiuto Tebalducci, was possessed by a devil; her family tried all the remedies usual in such a situation, touching the girl's head with the mantle of San Giovanni Gualberto and with the head of San Zenobi,[6] all of which Roderigo merely laughed at. And to make it clear to everyone the girl was

---

6. *San Giovanni Gualberto . . . San Zenobi.* St. John Gualbert (d. 1073) was the Florentine founder of a religious order. St. Zenobius was a fourth-century Bishop of Florence.

really possessed, and not suffering from some other mental disturbance, he spoke Latin, argued points of philosophy and discovered a number of people's sins, revealing, for instance, those of a monk who had kept a woman dressed in his order's habit in his cell for more than four years. All this aroused a general amazement, and made Ambruogio's life a misery. He had tried every remedy in vain and had lost all hope of her recovery when Gianmatteo came to him and promised to restore his daughter's health if he would give him five hundred ducats with which to buy a farm at Peretola. Ambruogio agreed, whereupon Gianmatteo, after having masses said and dressing up the occasion in a certain amount of ceremony, bent down to the girl's ear and said:

"Roderigo, I have come to hold you to your promise." To which Roderigo replied, "I am willing. But this is not enough to make you rich. So when I have left here I will go into the daughter of Charles, King of Naples, and I will leave her for no one but you. You can then make whatever sum you like. But after that, do not trouble me again."

And after saying this he left the girl, to the joy and wonder of all Florence.

It was not long after that when all Italy heard of the misfortune which had befallen the daughter of King Charles. As in this case, too, no remedy could be found, the King, hearing about Gianmatteo, sent to Florence for him, and after some bogus ceremony he cured her. Before he left the girl, however, Roderigo said:

"You see, Gianmatteo, I have kept my word and made you rich. Now we are quits and I am not bound to you any more. So you would be wise to keep out of my way, for I will hurt you in the future just as I have helped you now."

Gianmatteo went back to Florence a wealthy man (he had received more than fifty thousand ducats from the King) and expected to enjoy his riches in peace and quiet, not imagining, in fact, that Roderigo had any intention of harming him. But his peace was suddenly shattered by the arrival of news that a daughter of Louis the Seventh, King of France, had become possessed. This news thoroughly disturbed Gianmatteo when he considered both the authority of the King and the declaration of Roderigo. The King, indeed, unable to find any remedy for his daughter and hearing of Gianmatteo's powers, sent for him by means, in the first place, simply of a messenger. But when Gianmatteo pleaded illness the King was forced to have recourse to the city government, which compelled him to obey.

So he went, with despair in his heart, to Paris, and explained at once to the King that while it was true that in the past he had cured the possessed, this did not mean that he knew how to, or would be able to cure them all, because some of them were possessed by spirits of so evil a nature that they feared neither threats nor exorcisms nor anything that religion could do. For all this, he would do his duty, and begged forgiveness and pardon if he should fail. To which the King roundly answered that if he failed to cure her he would have him hanged. These words filled Gianmatteo with despair. However, he put a bold face on it and had the possessed girl brought to him. Then, leaning close to her ear, he humbly commended himself to Roderigo, reminding him of the service he had done him, and what an example of ingratitude he would become if he deserted him when his need was so great.

"What, treacherous boor," Roderigo replied, "do you dare come before me? Did you think you would be able to boast that you became rich through my means? I intend to show you and everyone else that I know how to give and to take away as I choose, and before you get away from here I will make sure you are hanged."

Since there was no escape in this way Gianmatteo thought he would try his luck in another. He had the possessed girl taken away and said to the King:

"Sire, as I have told you, there are many spirits so evil that no impression can be made on them, and this is one of that sort. However, I would like to try a last resort; if it succeeds, then our aim will have been achieved, if not, I will be in your hands, and you will give me what mercy my innocence deserves. Meanwhile, have a large scaffold built in the square before Notre Dame, big enough to hold all your nobles and the clergy of the city, have it covered with silks and cloth of gold, and set up an altar in the middle. Next Sunday morning I want you, and the clergy, and all your princes and nobles to assemble on it with royal pomp and dressed in magnificent robes, and after celebrating a solemn mass, have the possessed girl brought there. I want there to be besides in one corner of the square at least twenty men with trumpets, horns, drums, bagpipes, flutes, cymbals and any other loud instruments who, when I raise my hat, are to sound their instruments and march towards the scaffold playing them. All this, and certain other secret methods will, I believe, put this spirit to flight."

The King at once ordered it all to be done, and when Sunday morning had come and the scaffold was crowded with dignitaries and the square with the populace, mass was celebrated and the possessed girl was led on to the scaffold by two bishops and many noblemen. When Roderigo saw such a crowd gathered and such elaborate preparations he was greatly taken aback and said to himself.

"What does this miserable peasant think he is up to? Does he think he will frighten me with all this show? Doesn't he realise that I am used to seeing the marvels of heaven and the terrors of Hell? I will punish him, come what may."

And when Gianmatteo went up close and begged him to depart, he answered:

"Oh, you have had a fine idea! What do you expect to do with all your apparatus here? Do you think that will help you escape from the King's wrath and from my power? Vile peasant, I will get you hanged for sure."

And what with renewed pleas and repeated insults, Gianmatteo thought he had better lose no more time. He made the signal with his hat and all those who had been entrusted with making the noise struck up their instruments and came towards the scaffold with a din which reached the skies. At the noise, Roderigo pricked up his ears, and not knowing what it was, in his astonishment and bewilderment, asked Gianmatteo what was happening, and Gianmatteo, in great excitement, replied:

"Alas, my poor Roderigo! It is your wife coming to fetch you back!"

It was marvellous what a revolution the bare mention of his wife produced in Roderigo's mind. It was such that without thinking whether it was possible or likely for her to be there, and without another word, he fled in panic, leaving the girl cured; preferring to return to Hell to give an account of his actions than to subject himself again to the troubles, humiliations and hazard of the matrimonial yoke. And so Belfagor witnessed, on this return to Hell, to the evils which women bring with them into the home. And Gianmatteo, who had kept his wits about him better than the devil himself, went home full of joy. ✤

THE PRINCE is a treatise on the art of ruling. Machiavelli completed it in 1517, while in exile from Florence, and dedicated it to one of the Medici, the city's ruling family, in the hope of being recalled, but was disappointed. The topics covered range from philosophical speculation on the origin of states to practical advice on the conduct of war. To support his arguments Machiavelli drew on his wide reading of classical writers and intimate knowledge of contemporary affairs.

from THE PRINCE

Translated from the Italian by
W. K. Marriott

THAT WHICH CONCERNS A PRINCE ON THE SUBJECT OF THE ART OF WAR

A PRINCE OUGHT to have no other aim or thought, nor select anything else for his study, than war and its rules and discipline; for this is the sole art that belongs to him who rules, and it is of such force that it not only upholds those who are born princes, but it often enables men to rise from a private station to that rank. And, on the contrary, it is seen that when princes have thought more of ease than of arms they have lost their states. And the first cause of your losing it is to neglect this art; and what enables you to acquire a state is to be master of the art.

From the book THE PRINCE by Nicolo Machiavelli. Translated by W. K. Marriott. Everyman's Library Edition. Reprinted by permission of E. P. Dutton & Co., Inc. and J. M. Dent & Sons Ltd.

Francesco Sforza,[1] through being martial, from a private person became Duke of Milan; and the sons, through avoiding the hardships and troubles of arms, from dukes became private persons. For among other evils which being unarmed brings you, it causes you to be despised, and this is one of those ignominies against which a prince ought to guard himself, as is shown later on. Because there is nothing proportionate between the armed and the unarmed; and it is not reasonable that he who is armed should yield obedience willingly to him who is unarmed, or that the unarmed man should be secure among armed servants. Because, there being in the one disdain and in the other suspicion, it is not possible for them to work well together. And therefore a prince who does not understand the art of war, over and above the other misfortunes already mentioned, cannot be respected by his soldiers, nor can he rely on them. He ought never, therefore, to have out of his thoughts this subject of war, and in peace he should addict himself more to its exercise than in war; this he can do in two ways, the one by action, the other by study.

As regards action, he ought above all things to keep his men well organized and drilled, to follow incessantly the chase, by which he accustoms his body to hardships, and learns something of the nature of localities, and gets to find out how the mountains rise, how the valleys open out, how the plains lie, and to understand the nature of rivers and marshes, and in all this to take the greatest care. Which knowledge is useful in two ways. Firstly, he learns to know his country, and is better able to undertake its defence; afterwards, by means of the knowledge and observation of that locality, he understands with ease any other which it may be necessary for him to study hereafter; because the hills, valleys, and plains, and rivers and marshes that are, for instance, in Tuscany, have a certain resemblance to those of other countries, so that with a knowledge of the aspect of one country one can easily arrive at a knowledge of others. And the prince that lacks this skill lacks the essential which it is desirable

1, *Francesco Sforza* (sfôrt′ tsä) (1401–1466).

that a captain should possess, for it teaches him to surprise his enemy, to select quarters, to lead armies, to array the battle, to besiege towns to advantage.

Philopoemen,[2] Prince of the Achaeans, among other praises which writers have bestowed on him, is commended because in time of peace he never had anything in his mind but the rules of war; and when he was in the country with friends, he often stopped and reasoned with them: "If the enemy should be upon that hill, and we should find ourselves here with our army, with whom would be the advantage? How should one best advance to meet him, keeping the ranks? If we should wish to retreat, how ought we to set about it? If they should retreat, how ought we to pursue?" And he would set forth to them, as he went, all the chances that could befall an army; he would listen to their opinion and state his, confirming it with reasons, so that by these continual discussions there could never arise, in time of war, any unexpected circumstances that he could not deal with.

But to exercise the intellect the prince should read histories, and study there the actions of illustrious men, to see how they have borne themselves in war, to examine the causes of their victories and defeat, so as to avoid the latter and imitate the former; and above all do as an illustrious man did, who took as an exemplar one who had been praised and famous before him, and whose achievements and deeds he always kept in his mind, as it is said Alexander the Great imitated Achilles, Caesar Alexander, Scipio Cyrus.[3] And whoever reads the life of Cyrus, written by Xenophon,[4] will recognize afterwards in the life of Scipio how that imitation was his glory, and how in chastity, affability, humanity, and liberality Scipio conformed to those things which have been written of Cyrus by Xenophon. A wise prince ought to observe some such rules, and never in peaceful

2. *Philopoemen* (fil′ ō pē′ men), (252?–183 B.C.), Greek general and statesman. **3.** *Scipio Cyrus*. Scipio (237–183? B.C.) was a Roman general who defeated Hannibal at Zama in 202 B.C. Cyrus (d. 529 B.C.) was the founder of the Persian Empire. **4.** *Xenophon* (zen′ ə fən), (434?–355? B.C.), Athenian general and historian.

times stand idle, but increase his resources with industry in such a way that they may be available to him in adversity, so that if fortune changes it may find him prepared to resist her blows. . . .

COMMENCING THEN with the first of the above-named characteristics, I say that it would be well to be reputed liberal. Nevertheless, liberality exercised in a way that does not bring you the reputation for it, injures you; for if one exercises it honestly and as it should be exercised it may not become known, and you will not avoid the reproach of its opposite. Therefore, any one wishing to maintain among men the name of liberal is obliged to avoid no attribute of magnificence; so that a prince thus inclined will consume in such acts all his property, and will be compelled in the end, if he wish to maintain the name of liberal, to unduly weigh down his people, and tax them, and do everything he can to get money. This will soon make him odious to his subjects, and becoming poor he will be little valued by any one; thus, with his liberality, having offended many and rewarded few, he is affected by the very first trouble and imperilled by whatever may be the first danger; recognizing this himself, and wishing to draw back from it, he runs at once into the reproach of being miserly.

Therefore, a prince, not being able to exercise this virtue of liberality in such a way that it is recognized, except to his cost, if he is wise he ought not to fear the reputation of being mean, for in time he will come to be more considered than if liberal, seeing that with his economy his revenues are enough, that he can defend himself against all attacks, and is able to engage in enterprises without burdening his people; thus it comes to pass that he exercises liberality towards all from whom he does not take, who are numberless, and meanness towards those to whom he does not give, who are few.

We have not seen great things done in our time except by

those who have been considered mean; the rest have failed. Pope Julius the Second [5] was assisted in reaching the papacy by a reputation for liberality, yet he did not strive afterwards to keep it up, when he made war on the King of France; and he made many wars without imposing any extraordinary tax on his subjects, for he supplied his additional expenses out of his long thriftiness. The present King of Spain [6] would not have undertaken or conquered in so many enterprises if he had been reputed liberal. A prince, therefore, provided that he has not to rob his subjects, that he can defend himself, that he does not become poor and abject, that he is not forced to become rapacious, ought to hold of little account a reputation for being mean, for it is one of those vices which will enable him to govern.

And if any one should say: Caesar obtained empire by liberality, and many others have reached the highest positions by having been liberal, and by being considered so, I answer: Either you are a prince in fact, or in a way to become one. In the first case this liberality is dangerous, in the second it is very necessary to be considered liberal; and Caesar was one of those who wished to become pre-eminent in Rome; but if he had survived after becoming so, and had not moderated his expenses, he would have destroyed his government. And if any one should reply: Many have been princes, and have done great things with armies, who have been considered very liberal, I reply: Either a prince spends that which is his own or his subjects' or else that of others. In the first case he ought to be sparing, in the second he ought not to neglect any opportunity for liberality. And to the prince who goes forth with his army, supporting it by pillage, sack, and extortion, handling that which belongs to others, this liberality is necessary, otherwise he would not be followed by soldiers. And of that which is neither yours nor your subjects' you can be a ready giver, as were Cyrus, Caesar, and Alexander; because it does not take away your reputation if you squander

---

5. *Pope Julius the Second* (1443?–1513). 6. *the present King of Spain*, Ferdinand of Aragon (1452–1516), founder of the Spanish monarchy.

that of others, but adds to it; it is only squandering your own that injures you.

And there is nothing wastes so rapidly as liberality, for even whilst you exercise it you lose the power to do so, and so become either poor or despised, or else, in avoiding poverty, rapacious and hated. And a prince should guard himself, above all things, against being despised and hated; and liberality leads you to both. Therefore it is wiser to have a reputation for meanness which brings reproach without hatred, than to be compelled through seeking a reputation for liberality to incur a name for rapacity which begets reproach with hatred.

CONCERNING CRUELTY AND CLEMENCY, AND WHETHER IT IS BETTER TO BE LOVED THAN FEARED

COMING NOW to the other qualities mentioned above, I say that every prince ought to desire to be considered clement and not cruel. Nevertheless he ought to take care not to misuse this clemency. Cesare Borgia [7] was considered cruel; notwithstanding, his cruelty reconciled the Romagna, unified it, and restored it to peace and loyalty. And if this be rightly considered, he will be seen to have been much more merciful than the Florentine people, who, to avoid a reputation for cruelty, permitted Pistoia to be destroyed. Therefore a prince, so long as he keeps his subjects united and loyal, ought not to mind the reproach of cruelty; because with a few examples he will be more merciful than those who, through too much mercy, allow disorders to arise, from which follow murders or robberies; for these are wont to injure the whole people, whilst those executions which originate with a prince offend the individual only.

And of all princes, it is impossible for the new prince to avoid the imputation of cruelty, owing to new states being full of

---

7. *Cesare Borgia* (1476–1507), Italian cardinal and military leader.

dangers. Hence Virgil, through the mouth of Dido, excuses the inhumanity of her reign owing to its being new, saying:

> *Res dura, et regni novitas me talia cogunt*
> *Moliri, et late fines custode tueri.*[8]

Nevertheless he ought to be slow to believe and to act, nor should he himself show fear, but proceed in a temperate manner with prudence and humanity, so that too much confidence may not make him incautious and too much distrust render him intolerable.

Upon this a question arises: whether it be better to be loved than feared or feared than loved? It may be answered that one should wish to be both, but, because it is difficult to unite them in one person, it is much safer to be feared than loved, when, of the two, either must be dispensed with. Because this is to be asserted in general of men, that they are ungrateful, fickle, false, cowardly, covetous, and as long as you succeed they are yours entirely; they will offer you their blood, property, life, and children, as is said above, when the need is far distant; but when it approaches they turn against you. And that prince who, relying entirely on their promises, has neglected other precautions, is ruined; because friendships that are obtained by payments, and not by greatness or nobility of mind, may indeed be earned, but they are not secured, and in time of need cannot be relied upon; and men have less scruple in offending one who is beloved than one who is feared, for love is preserved by the link of obligation which, owing to the baseness of men, is broken at every opportunity for their advantage; but fear preserves you by a dread of punishment which never fails.

Nevertheless a prince ought to inspire fear in such a way that, if he does not win love, he avoids hatred; because he can endure very well being feared whilst he is not hated, which will always be as long as he abstains from the property of his citizens and

---

8. *Res dura . . . tueri.* Hard times and the newness of the state force me to undertake such measures, and guard my borders with outposts.

subjects and from their women. But when it is necessary for him to proceed against the life of someone, he must do it on proper justification and for manifest cause, but above all things he must keep his hands off the property of others, because men more quickly forget the death of their father than the loss of their patrimony. Besides, pretexts for taking away the property are never wanting; for he who has once begun to live by robbery will always find pretexts for seizing what belongs to others; but reasons for taking life, on the contrary, are more difficult to find and sooner lapse. But when a prince is with his army, and has under control a multitude of soldiers, then it is quite necessary for him to disregard the reputation of cruelty, for without it he would never hold his army united or disposed to its duties.

Among the wonderful deeds of Hannibal this one is enumerated: that having led an enormous army, composed of many various races of men, to fight in foreign lands, no dissensions arose either among them or against the prince, whether in his bad or in his good fortune. This arose from nothing else than his inhuman cruelty, which, with his boundless valour, made him revered and terrible in the sight of his soldiers, but without that cruelty, his other virtues were not sufficient to produce this effect. And shortsighted writers admire his deeds from one point of view and from another condemn the principal cause of them. That it is true his other virtues would not have been sufficient for him may be proved by the case of Scipio, that most excellent man, not only of his own times but within the memory of man, against whom, nevertheless, his army rebelled in Spain; this arose from nothing but his too great forbearance, which gave his soldiers more licence than is consistent with military discipline. For this he was upbraided in the Senate by Fabius Maximus,[9] and called the corrupter of the Roman soldiery. The Locrians were laid waste by a legate of Scipio, yet they were not avenged by him, nor was the insolence of the legate punished, owing entirely to his easy nature. Insomuch that someone in the Senate,

---

9. *Fabius Maximus* (fl. 210 B.C.), Roman general and statesman. He opposed Hannibal in Italy.

wishing to excuse him, said there were many men who knew much better how not to err than to correct the errors of others. This disposition, if he had been continued in the command, would have destroyed in time the fame and glory of Scipio; but, he being under the control of the Senate, this injurious characteristic not only concealed itself, but contributed to his glory.

Returning to the question of being feared or loved, I come to the conclusion that, men loving according to their own will and fearing according to that of the prince, a wise prince should establish himself on that which is in his own control and not in that of others; he must endeavour only to avoid hatred, as is noted.

CONCERNING THE WAY IN WHICH PRINCES SHOULD KEEP FAITH

EVERY ONE ADMITS how praiseworthy it is in a prince to keep faith, and to live with integrity and not with craft. Nevertheless our experience has been that those princes who have done great things have held good faith of little account, and have known how to circumvent the intellect of men by craft, and in the end have overcome those who have relied on their word. You must know there are two ways of contesting, the one by the law, the other by force; the first method is proper to men, the second to beasts; but because the first is frequently not sufficient, it is necessary to have recourse to the second. Therefore it is necessary for a prince to understand how to avail himself of the beast and the man. This has been figuratively taught to princes by ancient writers, who describe how Achilles and many other princes of old were given to the Centaur Chiron to nurse, who brought them up in his discipline; which means solely that, as they had for a teacher one who was half beast and half man, so it is necessary for a prince to know how to make use of both natures, and that one without the other is not durable. A prince, therefore, being compelled knowingly to adopt the beast, ought to choose the fox and the lion; because the lion cannot defend himself against snares and the fox cannot defend himself against wolves. Therefore, it is necessary to be a fox to discover the snares and a lion to terrify the wolves. Those who rely simply on the lion do not understand what they are about. Therefore a wise lord cannot, nor ought he to, keep faith when such observance may be turned against him, and when the reasons that caused him to pledge it exist no longer. If men were entirely good this precept would not hold, but because they are bad, and will not keep faith with you, you too are not bound to observe it with them. Nor will there ever be wanting to a prince legitimate reasons to excuse this nonobservance. Of this, endless modern examples could be given, showing how many treaties and engagements have been made void and of no effect through the faithlessness of princes; and he who has known best how to employ the fox has succeeded best.

But it is necessary to know well how to disguise this characteristic, and to be a great pretender and dissembler; and men are so simple, and so subject to present necessities, that he who seeks to deceive will always find someone who will allow himself to be deceived. One recent example I cannot pass over in silence. Alexander VI [10] did nothing else but deceive men, nor ever thought of doing otherwise, and he always found victims; for there never was a man who had greater power in asserting, or who with greater oaths would affirm a thing, yet would observe it less; nevertheless his deceits always succeeded according to his wishes, because he well understood this side of mankind.

Therefore it is unnecessary for a prince to have all the good qualities I have enumerated, but it is very necessary to appear to have them. And I shall dare to say this also, that to have them and always to observe them is injurious, and that to appear to have them is useful; to appear merciful, faithful, humane, religious, upright, and to be so, but with a mind so framed that should you require not to be so, you may be able and know how to change to the opposite.

And you have to understand this, that a prince, especially a

---

10. *Alexander VI* (1431–1503), Italian ecclesiastic: pope 1492–1503.

new one, cannot observe all those things for which men are esteemed, being often forced, in order to maintain the state, to act contrary to faith, friendship, humanity, and religion. Therefore it is necessary for him to have a mind ready to turn itself accordingly as the winds and variations of fortune force it, yet, as I have said above, not to diverge from the good if he can avoid doing so, but, if compelled, then to know how to set about it.

For this reason a prince ought to take care that he never lets anything slip from his lips that is not replete with the above-named five qualities, that he may appear to him who sees and hears him altogether merciful, faithful, humane, upright, and religious. There is nothing more necessary to appear to have than this last quality, inasmuch as men judge generally more by the eye than by the hand, because it belongs to everybody to see you, to few to come in touch with you. Everyone sees what you appear to be, few really know what you are, and those few dare not oppose themselves to the opinion of the many, who have the majesty of the state to defend them; and in the actions of all men, and especially of princes, which it is not prudent to challenge, one judges by the result.

For that reason, let a prince have the credit of conquering and holding his state, the means will always be considered honest, and he will be praised by everybody; because the vulgar are always taken by what a thing seems to be and by what comes of it; and in the world there are only the vulgar, for the few find a place there only when the many have no ground to rest on.

One prince [11] of the present time, whom it is not well to name, never preaches anything else but peace and good faith, and to both he is most hostile, and either, if he had kept it, would have deprived him of reputation and kingdom many a time. ✤

---

11. *prince,* Maximilian I (1459–1519), Holy Roman Emperor.

Alberto Moravia (1907–)

THE SECRET

Translated from the Italian by
Hélène Cantarella

I

DON'T TALK TO ME about secrets! I had one—and it was the kind that weighs on your conscience like a nightmare.

I am a truck driver. One beautiful spring morning, while hauling a load of lava rock from a quarry near Campagnano to Rome, I ran square into a man who was coming in the opposite direction on a motor bike. It was right at the 25 Kilometer marker on the old Cassia road. Through no fault of his, either. I had kept going on the wrong side of the road long after having passed a car, and I was speeding; he was on the right, where he belonged, and going slow. The truck hit him so hard that I barely had time to see something black fly through the blue air and then fall and lie still and black against the soft whiteness of a daisy field. The motor bike lay on the other side of the road, its wheels in the air, like a dead bug.

Lowering my head, I stepped down hard on the gas. I tore down the road to Rome and dropped my load at the yard.

The next day the papers carried the news: So-and-so, forty-three years old, a jobber by trade, leaving a wife and several children, had been run down at Kilometer 25 of the Cassia road and instantly killed. Nobody knew who had struck him. The hit-and-run driver had fled the scene of the accident like a coward. That's exactly what the paper said: *like a coward.* Except for those three little words that burned a hole in my brain, it didn't take more than four lines to report on what was, after all, only the death of a man.

During the next couple of days, I could think of nothing else. I know that I am only a truck driver, but who can claim that truck drivers have no conscience? A truck driver has a lot of time to mull over his own private business, during the long hours behind the wheel or lying in the truck's sleeping berth. And when, as in my case, that private business is not all it ought to be, thinking can get to be really pretty tough.

One thing in particular kept nagging at me. I just couldn't understand why I hadn't stopped, why I hadn't tried to help the poor guy. I lived the scene over and over again. I would be gauging the distances again before passing that car; I would feel my foot pressing down hard on the accelerator. Then the man's body would come flying up in front of my windshield . . . and at this point I would deliberately block out the picture, as you do at the movies, and I would think, "Now, jam on your brakes, jump down, run into the field, pick him up, put him in the bed of the truck and rush him to Santo Spirito Hospital. . . ."

But, you poor fool, you're just dreaming again. I had *not* stopped, I had driven straight on, with head lowered like a bull after a goring.

To make a long story short, the more I thought about that split second when I had stepped on the gas instead of jamming on the brakes, the less I could make it out. Cowardice—that was the word for it all right. But why does a man who has, or at least thinks he has guts, turn into a coward without a moment's warning? That stumped me. Yet the cold hard facts were there: the dead man was really dead; that split second when I might have stopped had passed and was now sinking farther and farther away and no one would ever be able to bring it back. I was no longer the Gino who had passed that car but another Gino who had killed a man and then had run away.

I lay awake nights over it. I grew gloomy and silent and after a while everybody shied away from me at the yard and after work: nobody wants to pass the time with a kill-joy. So I carried my secret around as if it were a hot diamond that you can't entrust to anyone or plant anywhere.

Then, after a while, I began thinking about it less and less and I can even say that there came a time when I didn't think about it at all. But the secret was still stowed away deep down inside me and it weighed on my conscience and kept me from enjoying life. I often thought that I would have felt better if I could have told somebody about it. I wasn't exactly looking for approval—I realized there was no pardon for what I had done—but if I could have told this secret of mine I would have thrown off part of its dead weight onto somebody else who would have helped me carry it. But who could I tell it to? To my friends at the yard? They had other things to worry about. To my family? I had none, being a foundling. My girl friend? She would have been the logical person because, as everybody knows, women are good at understanding you and giving you sympathy when you need it, but unfortunately, I had no girl friend.

II

ONE SUNDAY IN MAY I went walking outside the Rome city gates with a girl I had met some time before when I had given her and one of her friends a lift in my truck. She had told me her name and address, and I had seen her again a couple of times. We had enjoyed each other's company, and she had made it clear that she liked me and would be willing to go out with me.

Her name was Iris. She was a lady's maid in the house of some wealthy woman who had lots of servants. I had fallen from the start for her serious little oval face and those great big sad gray eyes of hers. In short, here was just the girl for me in the present circumstances. After we had had a cup of coffee at the Exposition Grounds, with all those columns around us, she finally agreed in her shy, silent, and gentle way to go and sit with me in a meadow not far from St. Paul's Gate, where you get a good view of the Tiber and of the new apartment houses lined up on the opposite bank. She had spread out a handkerchief on the grass to keep her skirt from getting dirty and she sat quietly, her legs tucked under her, her hands in her lap, gazing across at the big white buildings on the other side of the river.

I noticed that there were lots of daisies in the grass around us; and like a flash I remembered the soft whiteness of those other daisies among which, just a month earlier, I had seen lying still and dead the man I had struck down. I don't know what got into me but suddenly I couldn't hold back the urge to tell her my secret. If I tell her, I thought, I'll get rid of the load on my chest. She wasn't one of those dizzy, empty-headed girls who, after you've told them a secret, make you feel so much worse than you did before, that you could kick yourself hard for having spilled all you know. She was a nice, understanding person who had doubtless had her share of knocks in life—and they must have been pretty rough knocks if the sad little look on her face meant anything. Just to break the ice, I said to her, in an offhand way: "What are you thinking about, Iris?"

She was just raising her hand to choke back a yawn. Perhaps she was tired. She said: "Nothing."

I didn't let that answer get me down but quickly went on. "Iris, you know that I like you a lot, don't you? That's why I feel that I shouldn't hide anything from you. You've got to know everything about me. Iris, I've got a secret."

She kept on looking at the tall buildings on the other side of the river, all the while fingering a little red lump on her chin, a tiny spring pimple.

"What secret?" she asked.

With an effort I got it out: "I've killed a man."

She didn't move but kept on poking gently at her chin. Then she shivered all over, as though she had finally understood. "You've killed a man? And you tell me about it just like that?"

"And how else do you expect me to tell you?"

She said nothing. She seemed to be looking for something on

the ground. I went on. "Let's get this thing straight. I didn't mean to kill him."

Suddenly she found what she wanted: picking a long blade of grass, she put it into her mouth and began chewing on it, thoughtfully. Then, hurriedly, but without hiding anything, I told her about the accident, bringing out the part about my cowardice. I got pretty wrought up in spite of myself, but already I was beginning to feel relieved. I concluded:

"Now tell me what you think about all this."

She kept munching on her blade of grass and didn't say a word.

I insisted. "I'll bet that now you can't stand the sight of me."

I saw her shrug her shoulders, lightly. "And why shouldn't I be able to stand the sight of you?"

"Well, I don't know. After all, it was my fault that poor guy got killed."

"And it bothers you?"

"Yes. Terribly." Suddenly, my throat closed tight as if over a hard knot of tears. "I feel as if I can't go on living. No man can go on living if he thinks he's a coward."

"Was it in the papers?"

"Yes. They gave it four lines. Just to say he had been killed and that nobody knew who had hit him."

Suddenly she asked, "What time is it?"

"Five-fifteen."

Another silence. "Listen, Iris, what does a man have to do to find out what's going on in that mind of yours?"

She shifted the blade of grass from one corner of her mouth to the other and said frankly, "Well, if you must know, there's nothing on my mind. I feel good and I'm not thinking about anything."

I couldn't believe my ears. I protested. "It can't be! You must have been thinking something about something. I'm sure of it."

I saw her smile, faintly. "Well, as a matter of fact, I was thinking about something. But if I tell you, you'll never believe it."

Hopefully, I asked, "Was it about me?"

"Good heavens, no! It had absolutely nothing to do with you!"

"What was it, then?"

She said slowly, "It was just one of those things that only women think about. I was looking at my shoes and seeing that they have holes in them. I was thinking that there is a big clearance sale on in Via Cola di Rienzo and that I've got to go there tomorrow and buy myself a pair of new shoes. There . . . are you satisfied?"

This time I shut up like a clam, my face dark and brooding. She noticed it and exclaimed: "Oh, dear! You're not mad, are you?"

I couldn't help blurting out: "Sure, I'm mad. Damn mad. Here I tell you the secret of my life, and it makes so little impression on you I wonder why I didn't keep it to myself!"

This bothered her a bit. "No," she said, "I'm glad you told me about it. It really did make an impression on me."

"Well, what kind of an impression?"

She thought it over and then said, scrupulously, "Well, I'm sorry that such a thing had to happen to you. It must have been awful!"

"Is that all you've got to say?"

"I also think," she added, fingering the pimple on her chin, "that it's only right it should bother you."

"Why?"

"Well, you said so yourself. You ought to have stopped to help him but you didn't."

"Then you think I am a coward?"

"A coward? Well, yes . . . and then no. After all, a thing like that could happen to anybody."

"But you just said that I ought to have stopped!"

"You should have; but you didn't . . ."

At this point I saw her glance down at something in the daisies. "Oh, look! How pretty!"

It was an insect, a green and gold beetle, resting on the white petals of a daisy. Suddenly I felt as if I were emptied out—almost as if that secret over which I had agonized so long had vanished in the spring air, carried away, lightly, like the white butterflies that were flitting around in pairs in the sunlight.

Yet with one dogged last hope, I asked: "But tell me, Iris, in your opinion, was I right or wrong not to stop?"

"You were right and you were wrong. Of course, you ought to have stopped. After all, you had run into him. But, on the other hand, what good would it have done if you had? He was dead by that time anyway and you would probably have got into a terrible mess. You were both right and wrong."

After these words, a thought flashed through my mind. "This is the end of Iris. I'll never take her out again. I thought she was a bright, understanding girl. Instead, she is really nothing but a half-wit. Enough is enough." I jumped to my feet.

"Come on, let's go," I said. "Otherwise, we'll be late for the movies."

Once inside the theater, in the dark, she slipped her hand into mine, forcing her fingers through mine. I didn't budge. The film was a love story, a real tear-jerker. When the lights went on at the end I saw that her big gray eyes were filled with tears and that her cheeks were wet. "I just can't help it," she said, patting her face dry with a handkerchief. "Pictures like this always make me want to cry."

Afterwards we went into a bar and ordered coffee. She pressed so close to me that our bodies touched. Just as the *espresso* machine let off a loud stream of steam, she said softly, "You know that I really like you, don't you?" staring at me with those great big beautiful eyes of hers.

I felt like answering: "Fine. You really like me, but you'll let me carry the whole weight of my secret alone!" Instead, I said nothing.

Now I understood that from her, as from everybody else, I could ask only for affection, nothing more than that.

I answered with a sigh, "I like you a lot, too."

But already she had stopped listening to me. She was peering at herself in the mirror behind the bar, absorbed and concerned as she fingered the little red lump on her chin. ❖

Anna Maria Ortese[1] (1914–   )

A PAIR OF GLASSES

Translated from the Italian by
Frances Frenaye

"It's sunny, oh, it's sunny . . ." Don Peppino Quaglia was humming at the door of the *basso*.[2]

"All right, all right," answered his wife, Rosa, in a subdued but vaguely cheerful voice, from the bed where a combination of heart trouble and rheumatic pains had for some time confined her. And she added to her sister-in-law, who was sitting in the hole-in-the-wall of a lavatory, "Do you know what, Nunziata? I've a mind to get up and wring out the wash!"

"Whatever you say," answered Nunziata in her usual dry and melancholy manner, "but I think you'd be crazy. After the pain you've had, another day in bed won't hurt you." And after a moment of silence, "We'll have to sprinkle some more insect powder. A cockroach was crawling up my sleeve this morning."

From a crib wedged into a recess with a low, cobwebby ceiling, at the back of the room, came the frail voice of Eugenia: "Today I'm getting my glasses!"

1. *Ortese* (ôr te′ ze). 2. *the basso*, ground-floor apartment.

In these words there was a note of secret joy. Eugenia was the third child. Her elder sisters, Carmela and Luisella, were boarded out at a convent and were already so resigned to the miseries of this life that they intended to take the veil. There were also two younger children, Pasqualino and Teresella, at this moment curled up fast asleep in their mother's bed.

"And be sure you'll break them, first thing!" her aunt called out, in a voice still loaded with irritation, from the lavatory. She vented the disappointments of a lifetime upon other people; the first of all being, naturally, the fact that she had never married and was dependent upon her sister's charity. Such at least was her complaint, which she always followed by stating that she offered up all her humiliation to the Lord. Actually, however, she had a little money of her own tucked away, and was fundamentally kindhearted. She had offered, for instance, to buy glasses for Eugenia when the family became aware of the fact that the child could not see.

"With prices what they are today!" she went on. "Eight thousand lire,[3] hard cash!"

After that she turned on the tap and they could hear her splashing water over her face with one hand while she held the other over her eyes to keep the soap out of them. Eugenia knew that it was no use to answer. And anyhow, nothing could mar her happiness on this day.

Just a week ago she had gone with her aunt to the oculist's in Via Roma. There, in a very handsome shop, with shiny tables and a curtain at one end that shed a marvelous green light, the "doctor" had tested her sight by making her read, through various lenses, long rows of letters of the alphabet, some of them as big as boxes, others no more than tiny black spots against a white background.

"She's almost entirely blind," the doctor said to her aunt with something like compassion. "She'll never be able to see without glasses."

A moment later, while Eugenia perched trembling on the

---

3. *Eight thousand lire,* around thirteen dollars.

stool, he slipped another pair of lenses into the steel frame and said, "Look outside into the street."

Eugenia got up, her knees knocking together with emotion, and let out a stifled cry of joy. On the pavement she saw, very distinctly and at a size slightly smaller than normal, people dressed in the most beautiful clothes. There were women in silk dresses with make-up on their faces, young men in bright sweaters, graybeards with their rosy fingers entwined about the silver handle of a cane. On the street beyond she could see fine cars, painted red and petroleum green, like so many shiny toys; trackless trolleys as large as houses with well-dressed passengers sitting behind the open windows; and across the way fashionable shops, with overpoweringly luxurious displays spread out behind panes of glass which were being polished up by black-aproned boys. She could also see an open-air café, where golden-haired girls sat with their legs crossed under red and yellow tables, drinking out of big, colored glasses. Above the café, balcony windows were open and curtains fluttered in the spring breeze, revealing fragments of blue and gold walls and glittering crystal chandeliers hanging like fruit baskets. What a wonderful sight! Eugenia was so carried away that she failed to hear the conversation between her aunt and the oculist. Her aunt in her brown Sunday dress, hovering with unusual timidity at some distance from the glass counter, had brought up the question of price.

"Don't charge us too much, will you, Doctor?" she said. "We're simple people. . . ." And when she heard "eight thousand lire," she almost fainted away.

"For two little pieces of glass! Lord help us!"

"There you are, you see, you know nothing about it!" said the oculist, putting away the discarded lenses after he had polished them with a special cloth. "You aren't taking costs into account. Just try holding up two pieces of ordinary glass to her eyes and see if her sight is improved. She needs nine diopters on one side and ten on the other, if you want to know. She's practically blind, that's all."

While the oculist was taking down the child's name and address—Eugenia Quaglia, Vicolo della Cupa, near Santa Maria in Portico—Nunziata went over to the door, where she stood, holding up the trial glasses in her dirty hands and staring tirelessly through them.

"Listen to this, my girl! Eight thousand lire! That's what it costs to fix you up! Eight thousand lire, hard cash! Did you hear me?"

She choked over the figure, and Eugenia turned crimson, not so much on account of the mute reproach in these words as because the cashier was staring at her, apparently measuring the degree of poverty of the family. Finally she took off the glasses.

"How can she be so nearsighted when she's still so very young?" the cashier asked, as she signed a receipt for the deposit. "She's a skinny little thing, too."

"All the rest of us have good eyes," the aunt answered, "but we have plenty of troubles, too; this is just one of them. God had to rub salt into our wounds."

"Come back a week from today," said the oculist. "And the glasses will be ready."

Eugenia stumbled on a step as they went out.

"Thank you, Zia [4] Nunziata," she said as they walked down the street. "I'm rude to you and answer you back, and then you go and get me glasses. . . ." Her voice quavered.

"As far as this world's concerned, you're better off without seeing it," Nunziata observed with sudden melancholy.

Once more Eugenia did not answer. Zia Nunziata was often strange; she lost her temper or cried at the least provocation, and used all sorts of bad language. But, on the other hand, she was always going to church, and whenever anyone was in trouble she came to the rescue. No use taking her moods too seriously.

From that day on, while she waited for the glasses which would enable her to see everyone and everything as they really were, Eugenia lived in a sort of happy daze. Up to this time, there had always been a sort of mist around her. The room where they all lived, the courtyard full of clothes hung out to

---

4. *Zia,* aunt. [*Italian*]

dry, and the noisy, colorful alley were all hidden under the mist. Only the faces of the family, especially those of her mother and the younger children, were familiar to her, because often they all slept in the same bed, and when she woke up in the middle of the night, she would examine them by the glare of the kerosene lamp. Her mother slept with her mouth wide open, exposing a set of jagged yellow teeth, and the faces of the two little ones were dirty and covered with pimples. Their noses were perpetually stuffy and they made queer noises, as if little animals were shut up inside. Sometimes Eugenia caught herself staring at them, without being aware that she was lost in her imagination. She had a confused feeling that beyond this room with its tubs of soaking clothes, its broken chairs and smelly lavatory, there was a world of light and beauty. And the moment in which she tried on the glasses brought her a real revelation. The world outside was even more beautiful than she had imagined.

"My respects to you, Marchesa. . . ."

Her father was speaking. His back, covered by a torn shirt, had ceased to fill the doorway, and passed out of Eugenia's sight.

In a quiet, indifferent voice the marchesa proceeded to say, "I came to ask you a favor, Don Peppino. . . ."

"At your service, Marchesa. . . . Anything you say . . ."

Eugenia glided noiselessly out of bed, slipped a dress over her head, and went over, barefoot, to the door. The early morning sun, which streamed through a slit in the houses and into the ugly courtyard, fell in all its marvelous purity upon her precociously wizened little face, her tangled hair and rough hands with their dirty, overgrown fingernails. Oh, if only she could have had her glasses already, to see the marchesa in her black silk dress with a touch of white lace at the neck, her bejeweled white fingers and the benevolently majestic air which made her so enchanting! Eugenia could not make out the expression on the marchesa's face; it was only a vaguely outlined white oval, with a mass of purple feathers above it.

"I must get you to stuff a mattress for my grandchild's crib. Can you come up at about half past ten?"

"Of course, but if you don't mind, Marchesa, I'd rather come in the afternoon."

"No, Don Peppino. I need you in the morning. This afternoon I'm expecting guests. Now you can work out on the terrace. Surely you won't refuse me. . . . The bell is just ringing for Mass. . . . At half past ten you can call me. . . ."

And without waiting for an answer she went away, stepping nimbly around a puddle of yellow water, which had dripped off a balcony onto the ground.

"Isn't the marchesa good, though, Father?" said Eugenia, tagging after Don Peppino as he came back into the house. "She treats you with such consideration! God will reward her for that, I'm sure."

"She's a good Christian, all right," mumbled Don Peppino, with an intonation which gave the phrase a meaning quite different from that understood by his daughter. On the grounds of being the owner of the house, Marchesa D'Avanzo was always demanding petty services of the tenants of the courtyard. She gave Don Peppino only the most miserable pay for doing odd jobs, and called upon Rosa, his wife, to wash and mend sheets continually. No matter how Rosa's bones ached, she had to be ready to serve the marchesa. True, the marchesa had arranged for the two elder girls' admission to the convent and thus saved them from the many temptations to which the poor are exposed. On the other hand, for this *basso*, where all of them had caught some sickness or other, she demanded three thousand lire a month rent. "I've got a good heart," she was always saying, "but I simply haven't enough money. . . . You people are the real ladies and gentlemen of today. My dear Don Peppino," she would add, "you have none of our worries. You can thank the Lord for the state of life to which it has pleased Him to call you. It means the salvation of your souls!"

Donna Rosa had a feeling of something close to veneration for the marchesa, because of her well-known piety. Whenever the two women saw each other they talked about the next life. The marchesa didn't really believe in it so very deeply, but she thought this mother of a large family needed some future consolation on which to pin her hopes.

Now Donna Rosa called out from her bed, "What did the marchesa have to say?"

"She wants me to stuff a mattress for her grandson's bed," said Don Peppino wearily. He took out the portable gas ring, which the convent nuns had given the family, and drew enough water to make some coffee. "I won't do it for less than five hundred lire," he added.

"That's fair enough."

"Then who's going to get Eugenia's glasses?" asked Zia Nunziata, coming out of the lavatory. She was wearing her bedroom slippers, a skirt with the hem coming out and a blouse which outlined her sharp, stone-gray shoulders. She added out of a towel, with which she was drying her face, "I can't go, and Rosa here is sick. . . ."

Without anyone's taking notice, tears welled up in Eugenia's nearly blind eyes. Perhaps another day would go by without her having the glasses. She went over to her mother's bed and threw herself down in pitiful fashion. Donna Rosa stretched out a hand to caress her.

"I'll go, Nunziata, don't get excited. . . . It will do me good to get out. . . ."

Eugenia kissed her mother's hand.

At eight o'clock the courtyard became alive. Rosa came out of the door, a gaunt figure in a drooping, spotty black coat, so short that her legs stuck out like matchsticks below, with a big bag over one arm so that on the way back from the oculist's she could do her marketing. Don Peppino, with a long broom in his hand, was sweeping water out of the center of the courtyard, a completely futile task, since more continued to ooze from the ground, like a bleeding vein. Overhead hung two family washes: one belonging to the Greborio sisters on the second floor; and the other to Signora Amodio, who had had a baby just two days before. Lina Tarallo, the Greborios' maidservant, was noisily beating rugs on a balcony just above. Dust, mingled with out-

and-out trash, floated down like a cloud, but no one paid any attention. In the background there were shouts and crying, the shouts from Zia Nunziata, who insisted upon telling the world of her misfortune, which was presently caused by her small nephew, Pasqualino, who wanted to go with his mother.

"Look at him, the little jailbird, will you? Holy Mother of God, strike me dead, if You're really up there in heaven! As far as I can see, no one has any luck in this life except sluts and pickpockets."

Teresella, who was smaller than her brother, having been born the year the king went away,[5] smiled goodhumoredly on the doorstep, nibbling a piece of bread which she had picked up underneath a chair.

Eugenia sat on the doorstep of another *basso,* which belonged to the concierge, Mariuccia, looking at part of a children's weekly which had fallen from the fourth floor. She held her nose to the paper in order to make out some of the printed words. There was a blue river, flowing endlessly through a meadow, and a red boat sailing, sailing into . . . the unknown. The text was in regular Italian, instead of Neapolitan dialect, and although she couldn't follow it very exactly, she burst into intermittent laughter.

"So you're getting your glasses today," said Mariuccia, peering over her shoulder. Everyone in the courtyard knew all about it. Eugenia hadn't been able to resist spreading the news, and Nunziata, too, wanted to have it known that she was spending her money on the family.

"They're a present from your aunt, is that it?" said Mariuccia with a kindly smile. She was a tiny, almost dwarflike woman with a wispy sort of mustachio on her upper lip. Just now she was combing her long black hair which came down to her knees and furnished one of the few proofs that she was a woman. She combed it very slowly, smiling out of her benevolent, crafty, mouselike eyes.

---

5. *the year the king went away.* In 1946 Umberto II, having succeeded to the throne upon the abdication of his father Victor Emmanuel III, reigned for a month and then himself abdicated and went into exile.

"Mother's just gone to Via Roma to get them," said Eugenia, throwing her a grateful look. "They cost eight thousand lire, you know. Eight thousand lire, hard cash! My aunt is—" and she was about to say "terribly kind," when all of a sudden Zia Nunziata called ill-naturedly from the entrance of the *basso,* "Eugenia!"

"Here I am, Auntie!" she answered, running faithfully to the door.

Pasqualino was standing behind his aunt, with flushed cheeks and an expression on his face of mingled scorn and surprise.

"Go and buy two three-lira candies from Don Vincenzo, the tobacconist. And bring them back right away!"

"Yes, Auntie."

She grasped the money in her little fist, forgetful of the paper in which she had been absorbed a few minutes before. By a sheer miracle she avoided running into a towering cart of vegetables, drawn by a team of horses, which was just coming to a halt in front of the door. The driver, with a whip in his hand, was calling his wares in a singsong, *"Fre-e-sh fruit and vegetables . . ."* dragging out the words as if they belonged to a love song. When the cart was behind her, Eugenia raised her protruding eyes and somehow perceived the warm, blue glow of the sky and the animation that filled the scene around her. There were loaded wagons, one after another, big trucks crammed with khaki-clad American soldiers, and bicycles that seemed to be freewheeling down the street. The balconies above were crowded with flower boxes and over the railings, like flags or horse blankets, hung red and yellow bed covers, sheets, newly shaken mattresses and baby clothes in pastel colors, while baskets traveled up and down on ropes, carrying the fish and vegetables sold by itinerant vendors in the street below. Although the sun beat only on the top-floor balconies, because the street was no more than a narrow slit along a chaotic pile of houses, and the shadowy pavement was piled high with filth of every description, Eugenia could guess at the rich unfolding of the Neapolitan spring. Drab little creature as she was, imprisoned like a mouse in the mud of her courtyard, she unconsciously breathed faster, as if she too participated in the lightness and brightness of the air and the pervasive feeling of festivity. As she went into the tobacconist's, the basket of Signora Amodio's maidservant, Rosaria Buonincontri, brushed against her side. Rosaria was a stout woman, dressed in black, with very white legs and a placid red face.

"Ask your mother to come upstairs for a minute," she said to the child. "Signora Amodio has something to tell her."

"Mother's not at home. She's gone to Via Roma to get my glasses."

"I need glasses myself, but my fiancé won't hear of my wearing them."

Eugenia couldn't fathom the reason for this unwillingness, and she answered ingenuously, "They cost an awful lot of money. You have to look after them very carefully."

They went on into the shop, which was crowded with people, so that Eugenia found herself pushed back to the rear.

"Go on and fight for your place," said Rosaria, good-naturedly. "You must be nearly blind, just as they say."

"But her aunt's getting glasses for her," Don Vincenzo, the tobacconist, interrupted, winking at the two of them. He wore glasses himself, for that matter. "At your age," he went on, as he handed her the candies, "I had eyes as sharp as a cat's. I could thread a needle in the dark, and my grandmother was always after me to help her. But now I'm an old man . . ."

Eugenia nodded her head vaguely. "That's right. None of my friends has glasses. I'm the only one. I need nine diopters on one side and ten on the other. I'm almost blind," she pointed out sweetly.

"Then you're lucky to be taken care of," said Don Vincenzo with a hearty laugh. "And how about you?" he added to Rosaria. "How much coarse salt do you want?"

"Poor little girl!" sighed Rosaria, with an air of satisfaction, as Eugenia went out of the shop. "It's all on account of the dampness of the *basso,* that's what I say. Donna Rosa is full of rheumatic pains. . . . Give me a kilo of rock salt and a box of refined. . . ."

"Here you are!"

"A fine morning, isn't it, Don Vincenzo? It seems like summer."

Eugenia walked back more slowly than she had come, unconsciously unwrapping one of the candies and slipping it into her mouth. The candy had a lemon flavor.

"I'll tell Zia Nunziata I lost it along the way," she said to herself. She was so happy that she couldn't worry too much over the prospect of her kind aunt's anger. Suddenly someone took her hand and she realized that it must be Luigino.

"You *are* blind, aren't you?" said the boy, laughing. "What about those glasses?"

"Mother has gone to Via Roma to pick them up."

"I stayed away from school today, because of the fine weather. What do you say we go for a walk?"

"You must be crazy! Today I have to be on my best behavior."

Luigino stared at her and laughed scornfully, his mouth open like a piggy bank, from ear to ear.

"Your hair's a mess," he told her.

Instinctively, Eugenia raised a hand to her head.

"I can't see it, and Mother doesn't have time," she answered humbly.

"What are the glasses like?" Luigino asked her. "Have they got gold rims?"

"They're all gold," lied Eugenia, "and very shiny."

"Glasses are for old women," said Luigino.

"Fashionable ladies wear them, too," Eugenia retorted. "I saw them myself in Via Roma."

"Those are dark glasses for the beach," Luigino insisted.

"You're jealous, that's all. They cost eight thousand lire!"

"Well, show them to me when they come. I want to see if they're really gold-rimmed. . . . You're such a little liar!" And he walked away, whistling.

As she came back to the big main door of the house, Eugenia wondered anxiously whether or not the glasses were really rimmed with gold. In case they weren't, what else could she say about them to convince Luigino of their value? . . . It *was* a wonderful day, though! Perhaps her mother was on the way back already, with the glasses wrapped up in paper. . . . Soon she would have them on. . . . But just then a rain of blows fell upon her head. She thought she was going to fall down and tried in vain to defend herself with her two hands. It was Zia Nunziata, of course, infuriated by the delay of her return. Behind her, Pasqualino was screaming because he thought his aunt had never meant to give him the candy.

"Just look at her!" raged Nunziata. "I'll make you spit blood, you little blind wretch! . . . Take this! . . . I've sacrificed my whole life in return for this ingratitude! You'll come to a bad end, my girl. Eight thousand lire, hard cash! I'm the one that's bled to death by these jailbirds. . . ." She let her upraised hands fall to her sides and burst into tears. "Holy Mother of God! For the sake of Your Son and all He suffered, let me die! . . ."

Now Eugenia was weeping too. "Auntie . . . forgive me! . . ."

"Waah!" bawled Pasqualino, with his mouth wide open.

"Poor little girl!" said Donna Mariuccia, going over to Eugenia, who didn't know where to hide her red, tear-streaked face. "She didn't do it on purpose, Nunziata. Don't take it so hard. . . . Eugenia, where is the candy?"

Eugenia held out a dirty hand.

"I ate one of them," she said despairingly. "I was hungry."

Before her aunt could raise her hand to strike Eugenia again, the marchesa's voice floated down from the sunny fourth floor:

"Nunziata!"

Nunziata looked up with a face as ravaged as that of the figure of Our Lady of Sorrows, which hung at the head of her bed.

"This is the first Friday of the month," said the marchesa. "Offer your troubles to God!"

"Oh, Marchesa, how very good you are! These children make me sin so often that I'll lose my soul!" And she buried her face in a pair of dark, wrinkled hands.

"Is your brother there?"

"Your poor auntie!" Mariuccia was saying to the trembling

Eugenia. "She's buying your glasses, and that's the way you thank her!"

"Here I am, Marchesa!" called up Don Peppino, who had been all this time behind the door to his apartment, waving a piece of cardboard over the gas ring on which some beans were cooking for lunch.

"Can't you come up now?" called down the marchesa.

"My wife's gone to get Eugenia's glasses, and I've got to keep an eye on the lunch. Can you wait a few minutes longer?"

"Very well. But send up your little girl. I have a dress she can take down to Nunziata."

"God reward you for your kindness!" said Don Peppino with a sigh of relief, knowing that this was one of the rare things that might calm his sister down. But when he looked over at her, he saw that she did not seem to be in the least appeased. She was weeping uninterruptedly, and the flow of her tears so amazed Pasqualino that he had quieted down and was calmly licking the drippings from his own nose.

"Did you hear that, Eugenia?" asked Don Peppino. "You must go up to the marchesa's and bring down the dress she has for your aunt."

Eugenia was staring into the distance with vacant, gaping eyes. She started, and rose obediently to her feet.

"Say, 'God reward you for your kindness!' and wait just outside the door."

"Yes, Father."

"You've got to believe me, Mariuccia," said Zia Nunziata, after the girl had gone away. "I love the poor little thing, and I'm sorry, God help me, the minute after I've hit her. My head whirls when I have to struggle with those children. I'm not so young any more, you can see that. . . ." And she held a finger up to her hollow cheeks. "Sometimes I feel as if I were going mad. . . ."

"They can't help a little mischief," said Donna Mariuccia. "After all, they're only children. They'll have plenty of time to cry. When I stop to think that some day they'll be the way we are now . . ." She went to fetch a broom and swept a cabbage leaf out of the doorway. "I wonder what God's really up to. . . ."

"Why, you're giving us something brand new!" exclaimed Eugenia, plunging her face into the green dress hanging over the back of a kitchen chair, while the marchesa looked for a newspaper in which to wrap it.

The marchesa reflected that the child must indeed be blind as a bat, for the dress had belonged to her dead sister and had been mended and patched all over. But she waited for a moment until she had actually found the paper before saying, "Have you got those glasses yet? Did your aunt buy them new?"

"Yes, they're gold-rimmed ones, they cost eight thousand lire," said Eugenia all in one breath, feeling overpowered once more by the privilege conferred upon her by such a possession. "I'm nearly blind, you know," she added naïvely.

"It seems to me your aunt could have spent less money," said the marchesa, partially undoing the newspaper wrapping in order to tuck in a sleeve which hung out of the parcel. "I saw some perfectly good glasses for two thousand in a shop in Via dell'Ascensione."

Eugenia turned crimson, aware of the marchesa's displeasure. "Every state of life has its limitations," she had so often heard the marchesa say, when her mother brought up the laundry and would linger to complain of her poverty.

"They might not have been strong enough," she said timidly. "You know, I need nine diopters on one side and ten on the other."

The marchesa raised an eyebrow, but fortunately Eugenia could not see.

"They would have been perfectly good," the marchesa insisted, with a note of hardness in her voice. But then she felt sorry. "Never mind," she added. "I spoke of them only because I know something about your family's troubles. With the six thousand lire's difference, you could have bought enough bread for ten days for the lot of you. . . . And I don't know what good it will do you to see . . . in those surroundings! . . ." And after a brief pause: "You don't care about reading, do you?"

"No, Marchesa."

"That's not true! I've seen you with your nose in a book. You're a little liar, you know. . . . That's very bad. . . ."

Eugenia did not answer. She was utterly cast down as she stared out of her almost colorless eyes at the half-wrapped dress.

"Is it silk?" she asked dully.

The marchesa looked at her pensively.

"You don't deserve it, but I'm going to give you a present," she said abruptly, going over toward a cabinet made of pale-colored wood.

Just then the telephone rang in the hall, and instead of opening the cabinet, the marchesa went to answer it. Eugenia had not heard her last words, because she was totally absorbed in the discomfiture brought upon her by what had been said. Now she raised her feeble eyes and looked around, as well as she could, at the room. What beautiful things! Just like the oculist's shop in Via Roma! And just before her there was an open balcony, with flower boxes on either side. What a wealth of blue sky! A pale blue haze hung over the houses, and the narrow street below was like a dark well, with ants scurrying to and fro, ants that might belong to her own family. They ran in and out of their holes, carrying big crumbs of bread, just as they had done every day for centuries past and would do for centuries to come. There were so many of them. And beyond, almost invisible in the bright light, lay the great world of God's creation, with the sun and the wind and the clean, wide, blue sea. . . . She stood in a mood of unaccustomed thoughtfulness, leaning her chin on the railing with a look of sorrowful bewilderment which did not make her any the prettier. The marchesa spoke in a deliberate, reverent voice. In her smooth, ivory-white hand she held a little black book with gold-leaf letters on the cover.

"Meditations of the saints, my dear. Young people don't read anything worth while today, and that's why the world has taken such an ugly turn. It's a present to you. But you must promise to read a little of it every evening before you go to bed, now that you have your glasses."

"Yes, Signora Marchesa," Eugenia said hurriedly, blushing again because the marchesa had caught her out on the balcony. The marchesa looked at her with satisfaction as she took the book.

"God wants you to save your soul, my dear," she said, going to get the dress and laying it in her arms. "You're not much to look at, and you're old for your years. It's a sign of God's favor that He should preserve you from temptation."

Although these words did not really wound her, because for years Eugenia had unconsciously been preparing herself for a life without joy, they were to some degree perturbing. For a second, it seemed as if the sun were shining less brightly and even the prospect of the glasses failed to please. She stared vaguely, with all the light gone out of her eyes, at a point across the distant water, where the outline of Posillipo [6] lay, like a dull green lizard, against the sky.

"And tell your father not to bother about the mattress, after all," the marchesa continued. "My cousin just called up, and I must spend the day at Posillipo."

"I went there once . . ." Eugenia said hesitantly, roused by this familiar name, and staring spellbound in its direction.

"Really?" said the marchesa, absently, untouched by any peculiar significance in the name. Majestically, she led Eugenia away from the vision of light and out onto the landing, where she slowly closed the door behind her.

Only when she reached the bottom of the stairs and came out into the courtyard did the shadowy frown disappear from Eugenia's face, for she saw the familiar, gaunt figure of her mother coming toward her. She threw the dress down and started to run.

"Mother! The glasses!"

"Watch out! You nearly knocked me down!"

A small crowd gathered around: Donna Mariuccia, Don Peppino, one of the Greborio sisters, who had sat down to rest on a

---

6. *Posillipo,* a volcanic ridge extending southwest from Naples, the site of many villas.

chair in the courtyard before climbing the stairs, the maidservant of the Amodios, who was on her way home, and, needless to say, Pasqualino and Teresella, emitting loud squeals and holding out their hands. Meanwhile, Nunziata was looking disappointedly at the dress, which she had just taken out of the newspaper.

"See here, Mariuccia, it looks terribly old, doesn't it? It's badly worn under the arms."

But no one paid any attention. Donna Rosa had just extricated the box containing the glasses from an inside pocket and carefully begun to open it. A sort of shiny insect, with two big eyes and curved antennae, glistened in the sun falling upon her bony, red hand, surrounded by general admiration.

"Just think! Eight thousand lire!" exclaimed Donna Rosa, staring with a mixture of awe and reproach at the precious object she was holding. Silently she placed the glasses on Eugenia's face, and the little girl ecstatically fitted the antennae over her ears. "Can you see now?" her mother whispered intensely.

Holding the glasses with both hands, as if she were afraid someone might take them away, her eyes half-closed and mouth half-open in a dazed smile, Eugenia stepped backward and stumbled over a chair.

"Good luck!" said Rosaria.

"Good luck!" echoed Signorina Greborio.

"Doesn't she look like a little schoolteacher, though?" observed Don Peppino proudly.

"And she hasn't even thanked me!" said Zia Nunziata, still looking back regretfully at the dress. "But I wish her good luck, too, just the same."

"She's afraid, that's all," said Donna Rosa, going over to the door of the *basso* in order to lay her packages down. "This is the first time she's worn her glasses," she added, in the direction of a balcony above, where the other Greborio sister was looking down.

"Everything seems so small," said Eugenia, in a voice so weak that it seemed to come from underneath a chair. "And all black."

"Naturally, it's a double lens," said Don Peppino. "But do you see clearly? That's all that matters." And he repeated for the benefit of Cavaliere Amodio, who had just come into the courtyard with an open newspaper in his hand, "This is the first time she's worn her glasses."

Cavaliere Amodio looked at Eugenia as if she were a stray cat and said to Mariuccia, "I have to tell you that the stairs aren't swept the way they should be. I found some fish bones in front of the door." And he walked away, with his head bent over the newspaper, where there was news of some projected legislation in regard to pensions, which held a particular interest for him.

Still holding the glasses up with her hands, Eugenia walked over to the front door to look at Vicolo della Cupa outside. Her legs trembled, her head spun, and all her joy was gone. Her pale lips were trying to smile, but the result was only a stupid grimace. There seemed to be a thousand, ten thousand balconies hanging over her, and vegetable carts rushing at her from every side; the shouting voices and cracking whips that filled the air beat upon her brain as if she were delirious, and when she staggered back into the courtyard, this impression was all the more overwhelming. The courtyard was like a sticky funnel pointed toward the sky, peeling walls and thickly clustered balconies around it. On the ground there was a circle of low arches and at one point a statue of the Madonna surrounded by votive lights. The paving stones were marked with streaks of soapy water and littered with scraps of paper, cabbage leaves, and other bits of garbage. And in the middle of the scene there stood a little group of sickly, ragged individuals, with the pockmarks of poverty and despair on their faces, staring at her with adoring expectation. As she looked at them through the magic glasses, their bodies seemed to twist about and mingle together; then, as they bore down noisily upon her, they suddenly seemed to grow twice their normal size. Mariuccia was the first one to realize that the child was unwell and to snatch the glasses away. For Eugenia was bent over double and vomiting upon the ground.

"They've upset her stomach," she called out, holding her hand against Eugenia's forehead. "Bring me a coffee bean, Nunziata!"

"Eight thousand lire, hard cash!" groaned Zia Nunziata, running to fetch a coffee bean from a jar in the cupboard and holding up the glasses in one hand as if to ask God for an explanation. "And they're made all wrong!"

"That's always the effect when you put on a pair of glasses for the first time," Rosaria explained to Donna Rosa. "Don't let it bother you. She'll get used to them in due time."

"It doesn't matter, little girl; don't worry," said Donna Rosa reassuringly. But there was a twinge in her heart as she thought of the bad luck which seemed to overhang them all.

Zia Nunziata was still crying out when she came back, "Eight thousand lire, hard cash!"

As for Eugenia, she was pale as death, and retching spasmodically, with nothing left in her stomach. Her protruding eyes seemed to be contorted by pain and her little old face was flooded with tears. She leaned trembling against her mother.

"Mother, where am I?"

"You're in the courtyard, dear," Donna Rosa answered patiently, and the delicate smile, half amazed and half compassionate, which lit up her face, suddenly restored the rest of those present to their normal humor.

"She's half-blind, after all, poor creature!"

"I say she's simple-minded!"

"Let the poor thing alone," said Donna Mariuccia. "She's been taken by surprise, that's all." Her face was dark with pity as she went back into her own *basso,* which suddenly seemed to her more sordid than ever before.

Zia Nunziata stood alone, wringing her hands.

"Eight thousand lire, hard cash, I tell you!"

Aldo Palazzeschi[1] (1885–1974)

BISTINO AND THE MARQUIS

Translated from the Italian by
Robert A. Hall, Jr.

"NUNZIA . . . YOU KNOW, Nunzia . . . I saw the Marquis."

"Ah!" Nunzia would reply, without turning away from the fireplace where she was bending to put the last touches on the lunch or the dinner; and all the while a little white table, neat and shining, set in front of the window facing the little garden, was waiting with open arms for the two table companions. The woman showed no curiosity about that meeting, but sometimes she would add, more condescendingly: "What did he say to you? What is he doing?" dragging out the words in such a tone as not to desire certain news too much, nor to spend much time in listening to it.

At other times, Bistino, arriving at the kitchen door frightened and upset, as if he lacked the courage to enter, would say hurriedly: "You know, I saw him, I met him, I spoke to him." As if there were in the world only one person who could be seen, met, or spoken a word to; and as if all others did not hold for

1. *Palazzeschi* (pä′ lät ses′kē).

him the slightest interest. "So glad," Nunzia would answer dryly, scuttling between the fireplace and the cupboard.

It was charming to see that big man who was almost as tall as the door (to get under it he would bow his head instinctively in anticipation of the lintel) in an astonished attitude of waiting, and like a giant child following the movements which his wife made in front of the fireplace (than which she was only slightly taller, so that she had to stand on tiptoe to look inside the kettle).

When they were side by side, Nunzia with her saucy pile of hair did not come up to Bistino's shoulder: a well assorted couple, and perhaps for that reason perfect and happy.

"Did he ask you for anything?" she would add after a cold silence which made her husband stand still and open-mouthed.

And he, incapable of lying to his wife, would answer cautiously:

"I treated him to coffee . . . coffee . . . and a pastry."

"He was hungry, eh?"

After pronouncing these words with an edge of cruelty, the woman would heave a long sigh.

"That's the profit you get from certain meetings. You can be sure that he won't return your courtesy." She understood that her husband must have done something more.

Bistino felt disarmed, discouraged, wounded.

"You see . . . what do you expect . . . what is one to do . . ." he would stammer, trying to hide and excuse the impulse of his heart, and to excuse at the same time the Marquis who had drunk the coffee and eaten the pastry. And perhaps put in his pocket a few lire that the worthy man had offered him as a friendly loan.

And sometimes Nunzia, who loved her Bistino very dearly, would say a word that would uncork the flow of narration and he, like rivers when they overflow their banks, would overwhelm her.

"If you could see . . . if you could see . . ."

She would uncork his narration, but she would only interrupt him and block his way.

"He who has caused his own woe, let him weep for himself."
She would announce sententious sayings as if she were reading
from the tables of sacred and universal law; with these, she
would act as a brake on her husband after giving him rein. And
he, a true big boy, rosy and fresh despite his fifty-five years, with
blue eyes that smiled kindly and childlike, would stop with his
mouth open. Even though he dominated the woman physically,
he felt himself dominated in spirit. That harshness which was
evident only when the Marquis was under discussion, proclaimed
loudly and clearly her principles of life, the strength of virtue
with which there is no joking. Only in this case did he see her
leap in front of him like a little viper; in every other, there was
no wife more docile, affectionate and tender, but above all proud
of having, at sixty, that fine husband with the jovial appearance,
still strong and attractive.

Bistino could not persuade himself that she did not feel any
compassion for a person towards whom he felt so much; that
pity which good Christians should feel for all creatures, none
excepted, and which he, on the other hand, felt for only one. The
objects of his affection were two: his wife, and the Marquis,
whom he was unable to forget. But the fact is that his wife was
too shrewd and intelligent not to be aware of the disadvantages
of allowing expression to that affection and that compassion
which, in his simple mind, he had not succeeded in overcoming,
and which, on the contrary, from day to day he felt growing.

So that in the retired servants' little home there were two
divinities: one black, the Marquis, who had become infernal; and
the Countess, who had become celestial. Twice celestial, we
might add, since after being for eighty-six years an angel on
earth, she had been in Paradise for five, and had left a foretaste
of Paradise to her faithful maid: that neat and respectable house,
an allowance of ten lire per day, and so many other little things.
It was understandable that she could give vent to her stories, and
at all times too, and Bistino would listen to her as children listen
to their mother when she tells stories; as for him, basically, he
cared nothing at all about the Countess, whom, nevertheless, he

had served for ten years; as a matter of fact, way down in his heart he disliked her, a little bit through jealousy of his wife, but more because it was she who made his Marquis be cast down into the nether regions. He found her boring with all her virtues, a real bore, but he would have been very careful not to let it filter through to Nunzia that he rarely, quite rarely and in moments of tenderness, paid any attention to her stories. And he, for that matter, would not have found anyone to consider him right. How could one compare a woman who had been for eighty-six years an example of nobility and wisdom, of austerity and modesty, of charity, with a man who had become little by little a sink of all iniquities; who, having inherited it as a very young man, had squandered his own fortune, and had dissipated in the twinkling of an eye several little inheritances which Providence had let fall his way to hold him back on the edge of the abyss. And now, seventy-ish, he was reduced to beggary, living on the niggardly bounty of some distant relative or friend among those who had not rejected him and turned their backs on him and who were still willing to listen to him for a few moments in the street or to read his plaintive requests. He was reduced to asking for fifty or a hundred lire as a loan, to see himself given, with tolerance, ten or five, and, by means of most humiliating petitions, subsidies which never came or which came only in very small part. And if he dared to go to the doors of his former friends, he found them inescapably blocked, and, going downstairs empty-handed, holding onto the rich supports, supporting himself on the monumental balustrades, finding again in those surroundings a scrap of his lost pride and dignity, he would mutter ironically: "Either they are tired . . . or they are indisposed . . . or they are sick. One must really say that the race is declining." And even if a lucky chance caused him to meet some charitable old friend who would tactfully slip fifty lire into his waistcoat pocket, he did not think of setting it aside or of giving it on account to his landlord for the debt which was always hanging over him, but he would call a taxi, and after stopping and having the taxi wait while he had an apéritif, he would give the address of one of the best restaurants, where, affecting indifference, he would skilfully avoid the greeting of some old acquaintance, who would, in his turn, wonder: "Has he come into another inheritance?" And when he went back to his infamous hotel, of the lowest class, on getting out of the taxi (which would infuriate the landlord, who would remind him immediately and rudely of his outstanding bill), he would say to himself, giving the last lire to the driver: "My [mode of] life is expensive, but worthy."

How could Bistino talk about such a character to Nunzia, who kept in her heart the memory of a holy woman, and, like a relic, her picture in the beautiful silver frame above the chest of drawers? Bistino, too, had the picture of the Marquis when he was young, and what a handsome young man he was, what a fine gentleman! He had more than one, but he kept them hidden in the bottom of a trunk, together with so much useless trash, so that his wife would not find them. Those pictures he had to keep in the bottom of the trunk, and for himself alone.

When Bistino had decided, finally, to leave the Marquis, who no longer had a house and was living from hand to mouth, he had eighteen months' salary due him and was penniless. He was hired by the Countess as coachman. The Countess had kept her horse until the end of her days, tenaciously, saying that there was no need of being in such a hurry to arrive at death; and Bistino, in recent times, although he had an inborn adoration for horses, was almost ashamed to take that old lady out riding in a horsedrawn carriage among the automobiles. She set great store by her servants' appearance, and wanted her coachman and butler to cut a decorative and imposing figure. And the handsome coachman, who at forty still seemed a young man because he was so fresh and vigorous and because his appearance was so serene and manly, struck the heart of Nunzia, who had thought that she was by then protected against certain surprises.

With this girl, who up to that day had not known what love meant, love took a strange turn: she began to weep. Without any apparent reason, she would hide her face and she would weep copiously, as if it were a shame to love, as if she were ashamed to be alive. First of all on account of her age, but above all what gave her a sense of discomfort and shame, was that she, who was so little and thin, was in love with a man who was too handsome and was a meter and eighty-six centimeters [2] tall, in love with that big man who seemed to be a cuirassier.[3] It seemed to her to be something unfitting and dishonorable. She would have fits of weeping which she was not able to overcome.

When the Countess noticed that the woman's mind was upset, she called her to her side in a loving way, and with a smile full of indulgence she received her confession. The heart cannot be commanded, and even at forty-five, even if one is little and thin, one can fall in love with a cuirassier.

She spoke frankly to Bistino, and the upshot was that the wedding was set without delay. In her house, only legal ways were permitted. Bistino did not have to be asked twice; he could not believe that he was marrying that little woman, who was indeed homely and of an indefinable age, but who he felt had a secure position in the heart of the Countess.

It was the Countess's doing that they had as their property that little house of four rooms, all free, with a little garden surrounded by climbing roses, and in which Bistino amused himself growing lettuce, tomatoes, fruit and green vegetables: "a prize," those who came to see it would say, "a little jewel, a tidbit." Four rooms full of furniture, a fine bedroom, the living room, the kitchen, and another little room which Nunzia kept in readiness to be rented to a student or to a young lady, in case their income was insufficient to live on. But their income was enough, quite enough without having to go without anything, for the Countess had left her ten lire per day as pension, and before dying, every day she used to pull something out of the drawer of her night table, or had her look for it in the bureau drawers: an envelope, another envelope, a piece of clothing, a valuable object: "Take it, take it, Nunzia, carry it away, don't let them see you," so that her children should not become aware that she was leaving too many things to her loving and faithful maid. And Nunzia had, in

---

2. *a meter and eighty-six centimeters,* slightly over six feet, one inch.
3. *a cuirassier* (kwir′ ə sir′), a member of a unit of heavy cavalry.

her savings bank books, the savings of twenty-five years, all the money she had earned; she had not spent a penny on clothing, for all the Countess's things fitted her well; she was a woman of the same build, and her dresses and linen, even her shoes and stockings fitted her well, and she had a supply sufficient to last her a hundred years if the Lord should let her live that long. The little room was ready to be rented to a young lady or a student, but for the time being it did not represent a necessity, quite the opposite; their income was sufficient and having their own house to themselves was worth more than what a young lady or a student might bring in; they were keeping this extra resource for possible need.

"If you could see . . . if you could see what shoes . . . what shoes!" The old servant recalled in his mind's eye the wardrobe in which forty pairs of shoes had been arranged in rows— "greasy, threadbare, without buttons on his coat and with his stockings mended badly; he must have mended them by himself."

He recalled in his mind's eye, in the cloak-room, the four huge wardrobes, two on each side, chock full of his master's suits and overcoats, for all seasons and all places, for all the occasions of his life as a worldly, elegant man: a hundred-odd shirts, two hundred ties. "If you could only see his collar and his shirt . . . and his cuffs, they are so frayed they seem to have fringes, and with an inch of dirt on the seams."

The woman nodded with her head and smiled bitterly, answering every report or letting it be understood: "Good, good, good, I'm glad of it . . ."

"And do you know where he goes to sleep? In a hotel where they house those women of easy virtue . . ."

Nunzia, who kept on nodding: "Good, good, good, that's the place for him, I'm glad of it," would suddenly flash forth: "You wouldn't be getting the notion of going to see him?"

"No, of course not! Do you think . . ." the man would answer, feeling as if attacked by such a question. "You understand, of course, they send him away from all the houses; he hasn't the money to pay his rent. At the hotel, he ought to pay three lire per night, but the hotelkeeper gives him an advance of three hundred lire, puts him in a tiny room without any window, and at night he has to undress by the light of a piece of candle, when he has it, and sometimes without anything, in the dark. The proprietor has taken away his electric light bulb because he is afraid that he will stay awake in his bed reading the paper."

Forgetting those women of easy virtue for a minute, Nunzia started to nod again: "Good, good!" Good that he should have ended up in filth with evildoers, good that he had to live in darkness day and night: "Good, good!"

Bistino's youth had been entirely linked with the life of the Marquis. He had been a peasant of his, and he had taken him at fifteen years of age as a stable boy. Then, as the Marquis had become more and more aware of the kind of man he was, he had become at the same time his stableman and valet, confidant, administrator and secretary, in private and amatory matters. In his master's life he knew how to put everything straight, take care of everything, provide everything on time, foresee and manage everything, remedy everything. He had been all over Europe with him, but in the last analysis he had seen nothing except his master himself in all the nations of Europe. Of the world, he knew a reflection through him, his tastes, his habits, his ideas, his mode of life, as if it had been the only one and the most reasonable: his clothes, his shoes, his things. His master and his horses. The horses were the thing that had held them firmly together; in the world, with his eyes he had seen only the horses, on elegant promenades, at meets, at famous races. He had lived in so many hotels in so many cities, he could see them all at the same time in a dizzying merry-go-round without being able to fix anything or grasp anything, or of which he would remember a particular which might have struck the imagination of himself alone, which he alone had been able to perceive. And he would talk about their character in such a perceptive and original way that you had to wonder how his head was built to supply him with comparisons of that kind. This was what he had seen. And the maids; in twenty-five years, how many maids? He would not have been able to remember them all. Of course, he had finally married one of them, not the most beautiful but certainly the most sensible; he could have come to no other end, and he could not have ended up any better.

If Nunzia had only known! She understood, in fact she understood only too well, but she didn't want to admit it, and above all she didn't want to hear anything said about it; woe to him if he spoke to her about it, for if he had even hinted at it, she, jealous as she was, would have turned against him in a rage. The Marquis had been a woman's man from the word go, very renowned, a real Don Juan. He too had been a handsome young fellow, and, preserving the freshness and the serenity of a man of the country, he had become an elegant, irreproachable servant, who knew how to ride and drive his master's horses. He took a cold-water bath every morning. Between master and man there seemed to be an understanding, and, basically, a mutually shared pride, and a mutually shared satisfaction of men in making, each of them from his own vantage-point, certain observations which a sly and discreet smile, or a little pat on the shoulder was enough to emphasize. And in that smile, as in the contact of the hand, were hidden these words: "How inexhaustible life is, and how good it is to be alive!" Could Bistino forget these things?

"If you could only see him, dried up, gaunt, as yellow as a melon, bent over . . . he no longer has the breath to speak; I say that he is sick, he seems reduced to half his size, he is no longer recognizable, he hasn't even got one of his old ideas."

And there had been the Marquis' ill humors, the messes, the things that went wrong: the moneylenders, the promissory notes, the mortgages, the debts to be paid, the adventures which were difficult or went wrong, his expressions of impatience, his tremendous rages. And as he always had Bistino at his heels and no one but him, Bistino stood for his domestic staff and everything ended up on his shoulders. Bistino was happy to offer them, broad as they were. If the clothes had not been kept in proper condition, or the shoes had been poorly shined, or the horses had not been inspected before setting out, or errands had been carried out clumsily, there were yells and shouts from the Marquis until, bang! went a shoe or a boot on Bistino's back. He, instead of complaining, loved those intimate outbursts, those rages, those furies; he felt in that moment, more than in any other, what he symbolized for his master, what he was; he felt that he was joined to him and indispensable, considerably more so than when he [his master] was happy and everything was going ahead full sail. In the last analysis, he felt that he was the only one who loved him, and the only one whom his master really loved. His anger and rows symbolized affection, even the shoes in the small of his back. In fact, as soon as he calmed down—and the Marquis, who underneath his indolence had a generous and noble spirit, calmed down quickly—he became genial and cordial and was cheerful and witty again, and felt the need of showing Bistino that he was sorry and of begging his pardon; he would give him money, a box of cigarettes, a couple of ties, or whatever happened to be within reach at the moment, and he would put a hand on his shoulder in a friendly, confidential manner. His rages would intensify their mutual attachment; the simple heart could not be wrong.

Seated in the kitchen where his wife was preparing lunch or supper, the man would see again, as if on a screen, all these things together, and would speak to himself, finding no adequate expression for his feelings: "Poor man . . . he had absolutely all of them!" He meant that all the human passions had possessed him, devoured him, consumed him: horses, gaming, women, riotous living. He would on occasion get so drunk that he would fall into Bistino's arms in a coma, limp, and he would have to put him to bed like a baby: "Poor man . . . he had them all . . . he had them all, all . . ." he would repeat as in a trance. "Poor man, my eye!" the woman would answer to bring him to his senses. "He had them all and now he is paying for them all; in this world, you have to pay, the day of reckoning always comes, don't doubt it." She would dish out the steaming soup and Bistino would come to the table, thoughtful and worried. "Sooner or later it comes, it comes, it certainly does come, and some people pay and some people collect what is due them," she would mutter as she put the pot back away under the fireplace again, "and one is enough so that you have to pay for a lot of them."

One day Nunzia let fall a sentence which Bistino did not have the strength to answer, because he felt so overcome with happiness. He could not even believe his ears, and he touched himself to make sure that he was still himself and was not dreaming.

"One of these Sundays we must invite your Marquis to dinner. For that day he'll be relieved of his hunger, and he must have his share of that."

As soon as he came to himself he took her up and carried her around throughout the whole house as if she had been a child, a cat or a dog; he even carried her out into the garden, where the inhabitants of the upper floors looked out of the windows to see, while she was struggling and floundering, kicking her legs and laughing convulsively:

"Let me go! Let me go!" she yelled, "Let me go, you're hurting me! Leave me alone!"

But instead of setting her down he kept on running and saying:

"He will accept, you'll see, he'll come, I know, I'm sure that he'll come, he'll be overjoyed to come, I know . . ."

She knew that she was giving him so great a consolation that she could not resist: "We'll just see what will happen," she thought, "the world won't come to an end just because we invite him once to lunch." And when Bistino had set her down, she said: "I too say that he'll come, with that little mouth to be fed . . ."

The Marquis showed that he appreciated the invitation, but without a smile; his mouth was no longer capable of smiling. And that Sunday, at the hour set, he went to his former servant's, where there was waiting for him a little meal of which he partook frugally. His constitution had been shaken to its depths; he was no longer anything but a sick and defeated man, an empty shell. With great naturalness he showed that he was grateful and, even in his present sad condition, still a gentleman, so much so that his hosts experienced during the meal a marked disappointment rather than the instinctive embarrassment of two old servants in the presence of the man who had been the master.

Bistino looked at him in ecstasy, not believing his own eyes, forgetting to eat and continually waiting for what could not come—a sign of happiness on the pale, wearied and suffering face of the old man—and coming out of his absorption only to offer the Marquis something further, which, on being invited, he would refuse with grace but without smiling. Was he not happy to be there? Was he not comfortable? "My lord Marquis, my lord Marquis," Bistino kept repeating, half enraptured and half frightened. The woman was observing. The Marquis would have preferred not to hear pronounced too often that title which was so discordantly at variance with his present condition, but he did not dare to show his vexation, whereas on the other hand he indeed showed uneasiness over his garb, after the fashion of a person who, out of innate modesty, covers with a sense of shame the bareness of his body which he would not like to expose to view. Deeply curious concerning this interplay, whose aim she could not fathom, the woman kept looking at both of them. Now she would look at the Marquis and think "How your lack of sense has ruined you!"; then she would look at her husband and think: "What must we see! What is it that pleases this big scatterbrain!" And gradually she felt herself overcome by a vague pity for her guest and by a strong feeling of tenderness for her husband, which, however, was immediately broken off and wiped out by bitter resentment, and almost by repentance for having felt tenderness and pity.

After dinner the two men went out together; Nunzia remained at home because she had been tired out by the preparations that the invitation had made necessary, and then because she had to put things back in shape again; the lunch had been served in the living room, with solemnity.

Once he was alone with him, Bistino would have liked for his former master to come to life again, to cheer up; he gazed at him, offering him his soul, but he could not succeed in enlivening him and cheering him up. The poor fellow, both outdoors and at home during the meal, remained gloomily laconic. Above all, Bistino would have liked to bring the conversation around to the past, and sought every pretext to do so: he recalled twenty-five years of life in common, the trips, the adventures, the horses, the women, the sprees . . . But it was clear that the other man was not of the same opinion; the things which had formerly excited him so much were just the ones which he did not wish to remember, as if they had not even existed; and he lit up only when he talked about the present, about his miserable way of life, the meanness of the low-class hotelkeeper, his shameful lodging, his cousin in Siena who was always supposed to send him a remittance and who remitted either nothing or too little. When the Marquis had threatened to get himself committed to the old people's home, the cousin had promised him a hundred and fifty lire per month to save the family honor, and then he sent him fifty, or (very rarely) a hundred, with the excuse that the harvests had been poor. A friend of his in Milan, too, who was very rich, would send him something from time to time as a subvention, but he had to write at length and repeatedly. The others turned a deaf ear and were discourteous to him; no one had any intention of receiving him and listening to him: "Either they are tired . . . or they are indisposed . . . or they are sick. The race is declining." Or they would reply with offers that were out of proportion to the demands of living. These were the topics over which the old man could still get excited, and about these Bistino cared nothing.

Once more the husband and wife invited the Marquis to dinner on Sunday; then a third time and a fourth, until, when they perceived that they could invite him without disturbing their domestic habits, and setting the table in the kitchen as usual, it was decided to invite him every Sunday. A good soup, with the broth well drawn—Nunzia made an excellent soup—was what he enjoyed most, for which he felt a deep need and for which he showed true satisfaction and gratitude; afterwards, he appeared relieved and well-fed. All he needed was a few mouthfuls of anything whatsoever, which he would consume slowly, without the voracity characteristic of uninhabited stomachs. "This will embrace your stomach," Nunzia would say, with a dash of irony which she could not succeed in overcoming, while the poor man in truth felt it embraced. Or otherwise, on inviting him to eat more, she would display a curious figure of speech: "The mouth carries the legs," proud of saying something witty and paradoxical.

Finally one Sunday, to the unprecedented surprise and joy of Bistino, the Marquis, no one knows how, all of a sudden began to laugh: "Ha, ha, ha! You swine!" he said to his old servant. "Where does that laughter come from? Is he going crazy?" thought Nunzia, who had grown accustomed to seeing him gloomy: "This is the end of him, we shall have to call someone in to have him tied up." "Ha, ha, ha! You swine!" repeated the Marquis, making as if to punch Bistino in his stomach, which he was holding for laughter.

His unexpected hilarity was not madness, but downright shrewdness, and, since Bistino was laughing fit to burst, the woman thought: "They are both going crazy, we'll have to have the cage from the madhouse and tie them both up at the same time."

After which, recovering from that leaden depression, he began to talk, and to talk about everything, about all things, important and unimportant, but especially about the past, the horses, the women, yes, even about the women. And growing continually more and more hilarious, he would repeat: "Ha, ha! You swine!" to his old valet. And the woman kept repeating to herself: "I told you so, it took my soup to bring this starved man back to life."

Bistino was beside himself with happiness. And he kept prompting the Marquis and reminding him with the eagerness of one who wants to hear the whole story. At a certain point he looked at him in a fright, fearing that, along with his own doings, the Marquis might let the cat out of the bag concerning some of Bistino's, and Nunzia would jump at him and scratch his eyes out. But the Marquis was clever, really clever; he knew what was what, and although he was utterly ruined he had not forgotten the art of living, so that the woman, when she was alone with her husband, had to admit finally: "After all, these good-for-nothings are amusing; when he's going strong, your Marquis is not unpleasant." For this reason he was invited on Thursdays, too: then every day, and finally, after a very difficult discussion, in which the woman eventually had to give in, seeing that the room was available and was not being used by anyone, and seeing that the Marquis ate so little that he cost no more than a dog, one fine day he was awaited at Bistino's on a permanent basis. "We'll try it out . . . we'll see . . ." said Nunzia, in concluding.

He arrived wearing everything he owned, and of what a kind it was! Not a single handkerchief, not a shirt, not a collar, not a pair of socks. Either because the stuff was in such shape that it would not have survived the move, or because, so as not to arouse the suspicions of the hotelkeeper, he had brought nothing with him; probably he had absconded under the very eyes of the hotelkeeper, to whom he owed four hundred lire. They had to start over again from scratch, and with a lot of Bistino's things, to put him in a tolerable condition again.

Once he had been installed in the bright and respectable room, the unfortunate man seemed to be born again, just as he had on that Sunday at the first spoonfuls of that health-restoring soup; and he devised every way possible not to risk lightly this new well-being which nothing in the world could have led him to hope for. His upbringing and the logic of life would have suggested to him that he behave with such delicacy and such a refinement of tact in these painful circumstances as to cause his weight to be felt as little as possible, as if he were not there; at the same time, this was the only way to save, with his two benefactors who were also former servants, the last remaining shred of his dignity. But logic is not always the law of our life; on the contrary, on most occasions it doesn't even come in through the keyhole, since our life is characterized by the most absurd illogicality.

Bistino, for his part, was grieved that the Marquis accepted everything without a word, and that, with the good manners of a wellborn person who has come down in the world, he found that everything was good and well done, and never uttered an opinion, a request, an order: "I'm at your service, I'm at your service, don't be hesitant, don't be shy; I have nothing else to do," Bistino would say, offering his services with all his heart: "I'm at your service, my lord Marquis," he would repeat, shamed and offended that the other would not give him orders. He could not convince himself that the person whom he had obeyed for twenty-five years had forgotten how to give orders and to rule with an iron rod as his custom had been, without delay or reticence; Bistino thought that the Marquis must suffer from this more than everything else, and looked at him with disappointment as he had done at table on the first Sundays when the Marquis had been unwilling to laugh and to re-live with him all those beautiful memories and to talk about a time and a kind of life which now caused him sorrow. From time to time he would go up to the door and listen, and then say softly, smothering his voice: "My lord Marquis, don't you need anything?"

Like the connoisseur of the world and of life that he was, even in total ruin, the Marquis understood that he had to do something in reply, and one morning there came from his room a hoarse and angry voice, and a name repeated unceasingly: "Bistino! Bistino! Bistino!" Bistino tumbled out of bed and ran half naked to find what his old master wanted, while Nunzia jerked upright and, rubbing her eyes, wondered impatiently: "What's gotten into him? What does he want? Is he having a fit? Is he feeling bad? What manner of calling is this?"

"Bistino!" the Marquis yelled, and Bistino answered as he ran along, all excited, buttoning his underwear: "Here I am, I'm coming right away, at your service, my lord Marquis."

"What did he want?" his wife asked afterwards, taking sides: "What did he want, may one ask?"

"Nothing, his suit and shoes, this morning he's going out early, it's a good idea on a day like this; there's a sun . . ."

"Oh! . . . his suit and shoes . . . just listen to that . . . and he calls you with such arrogance! Is that why he waked us up and made you get up?"

"You see . . . after all, he's still a marquis, no matter what you say, he's accustomed to giving orders, poor man, it's not his fault, he does it without realizing, he doesn't realize," Bistino said, radiant.

"He doesn't realize . . . because he's still a marquis . . ." Nunzia rose up, swelling with threats: "When all's said and done, I'll see to making him realize, and then I'll tell him what he is. And I'll tell him also what you are when you answer. A marquis . . . A fine fellow, yes, a fine fellow, this marquis of yours; I'll chuck him out today, I'll tell him to get out of here."

Bistino cast himself at the knees of his wife, who was unable to analyze the feeling that animated him, when she saw him apparently confused but perceived that he was inwardly happy; he begged her to pardon him and not to send him away. But from that day on, in the unassuming, quiet room was heard, louder and louder, the voice of a master: "Bistino! Hurry up, for Heaven's sake! What are you doing, you loafer? You slow-poke! You lazy-bones! Are you standing there scratching your rear? Hurry up, you oaf, you snail!" Shouts, orders, scoldings, insults, threats. Nunzia observed what was going on and tried to understand, but said nothing. "I'll fire you! Get out of here!" the Marquis would shout. As they travelled around Europe, Bistino had not learned a single word in any language, but when his master shouted he understood them all.

"Get out? . . . Where to?" the woman thought in her confusion: "Here, if anybody is to get out, it ought to be you, only you, my dear Marquis, and with all the luggage you brought with you when you came." She did not intend to stand for a merry-go-round of that kind in her house; she would have taken it on herself to send him packing without delay. But her husband's face left her in perplexity, and made her restrain that cry of revolt which her face announced as imminent. She had never seen him so satisfied, so cheerful, so happy. She wanted to wait and see a little while longer how the game would go, then she was going to see about saying a word or two to their guest. It would be quite useless for that lunkhead Bistino to beg and whimper.

But with Nunzia the Marquis was a totally different man. The orders and scoldings and bad language were restricted to his room with mathematical precision, and this caused her to wonder still more. With her he was considerate, kind, full of praise and compliments, bows and smiles, expressions of refinement and delicacy, like a true gentleman. The food was exquisite, marvelous, excellent; he would compare it to that prepared by the famous cooks who had been with the great families whom even she knew by name, or in person because she had seen their members at the Countess's: duchesses, princesses, marquises, even to that very famous cook of Victor Emanuel II,[4] who had left to posterity a highly esteemed cooking manual. He would pay his respects to her as if he were the guest of a lady of high station. But when he was in his room with Bistino, there would be shouts, rows, insults, and in their midst there would be outcries of joy and Homeric laughter. "But, after all, what sort of world is this we are living in?" Nunzia would think, torn between rebellion and flattery. And when she talked with her husband, she would make this difference clear: "He does it to you because he knows he can do it, but with me, you may be sure, he wouldn't do it; with me, my lord the Marquis walks a chalk line. He knows he can do it, of course, he knows you by now, he knows you even too well and is profiting by it; just look how he behaves with me."

This put Bistino in seventh heaven, since, if he was happy that the Marquis was treating him with his old confidence and intimacy, on the other hand he was happy that he was behaving like a gentleman to his wife, that he was respecting her and being considerate in every way, also because this served to quiet her resentment. "I told you so; do you see what a real gentleman he is, how considerate he is towards you, eh? What good breeding!" Bistino kept repeating to her incessantly. "Everyone receives the treatment he deserves," she would conclude, holding her head high, beginning to be sensitive to this state of affairs and to be proud of it, striking an attitude of dignity, an attitude which was

---

4. *Victor Emanuel II* (1820–1878), proclaimed king of united Italy in 1861.

easy for her because she had lived for forty years in contact with high society by the side of an irreproachable lady. To conclude certain disagreements, her husband would answer her:

"Listen, Nunzia, if all of a sudden you were to hear the Countess's voice calling you, you'd even jump down from the window to answer more quickly."

"You can say that out loud, and I would only be doing my duty." She would look at him threateningly: "And would you compare the Countess with this beggar?"

"No, you see, money doesn't matter, in these things what matters is the heart. If the Countess, too, were dying of hunger wouldn't you feed her?"

"I'd take the food out of my own mouth to give it to her." She would rise to her full height: ". . . but would you compare the Countess to this chimpanzee? And then, when the Countess called me, she would do so in a kindly fashion, like a well-brought-up person, she certainly wouldn't call me a swine or a slattern or a slut . . ."

"Yes, but between men it's different, you can't understand."

"Get out!" the Marquis would shout in his room: "I'll fire you! Get out!" Bistino would take refuge in the garden, without daring to go near his wife, until a new order would call him back to restore peace. Then the Marquis would put a hand on his shoulder and they would start to laugh.

"He was acting the fool in order to get himself taken in, this sly rascal; now that he has gotten established he makes demands; he feels the desire to give orders, this grand nobleman. What a nerve! That was all we needed, his dose of effrontery. If he tried it on me he'd get given tit for tat."

But the twofold behavior of the guest, in addition to making her reflect, flattered her deeply.

"What do you expect, he's still a marquis, there's no use talking, they're all alike, I must have known a thousand of them, that's the way they're built, they're accustomed to giving orders, he doesn't realize it."

One morning the Marquis said flatly that he didn't intend to go on living without a bell in his room. He wanted them to get it in a hurry; he wasn't accustomed to ruining his vocal cords so as to call the servant.

"The bell? A bell?" . . . Nunzia kept repeating, running through the house at the height of fury: "The bell?" Stopping, she became more tall and rigid, as if she were of wood: "A bell?" She bent like a sling ready to shoot: "The bell to call whom?" While Bistino, all radiant, had hurried to the electrician's to have it put in: "A bell? What sort of world is this we're living in, may one ask?"

"What do you expect, he doesn't realize it, what do you think, otherwise he wouldn't do it." He was laughing, Bistino was, overjoyed at this novelty: "He does it without realizing." ("He doesn't realize that he isn't a master any more," Bistino meant, "he doesn't remember any more.") "They're all like that, that's the way they're made, do you think he could stand it? A gentleman without a bell . . . it isn't possible! They're the sort of people who, from waking in the morning until going to sleep at night, have the bell in their hands all the time. I'm surprised that he didn't ask for it before, that he went without it for so long, that he was able to go without it. How can he have managed? Who knows how much he must have suffered? A gentleman without a bell doesn't exist; gentlemen have bells in their blood."

And once the bell had been installed, the little room worked perfectly.

"What are you waiting for, you oaf? Hurry up, you loafer? How long are you going to take to answer? Don't you hear the bell, you dullard? Have you got peas in your ears?"

Bistino would run, swelled up with laughter: "He doesn't realize, poor man, he doesn't remember any more," and he would laugh in the fullness of his bliss.

The Marquis had brought life back into that house where an excessively secure and even happiness had made it stagnant.

And with Nunzia at table, how much gallantry! It was an endless crescendo, a running fire of blandishments. What flattering comparisons, what aristocratic topics of conversation: obeisances and bows. The cooks of history and the ladies of high society. The poor kitchen became a dazzling salon. The duchesses, the marquises and the countesses, whom Nunzia had known at her mistress's, or about whom she had heard—he knew their stories and anecdotes, secrets, scandals, quarrels: an inexhaustible repertory. And if she did not know them, she made believe she knew, in order to keep pace with the Marquis like a person in the know, showing that she was up to the situation. All the uproar was restricted to the room, to which Bistino, in the morning, waking up with a start at the sound of the bell, would run to put himself at the orders of the Marquis, who, from time to time, would give him a scolding and fly into a rage. Nunzia would turn over and go back to sleep, grumbling: "Stupid blockhead, he'd even let himself be beaten to a pulp." She paid less and less attention to what went on between the two, to the shouts and scoldings, and also to the uproar and laughter, as if they were two boys playing off to one side without disturbing anyone. And one morning, "bam!" Bistino got a shoe in his back; finally! She had been expecting it for so long.

"Good! Hit him hard! Even harder! That too, but it's too little," Bistino's wife kept repeating, without turning her attention away from the fireplace where she was going about her business.

Once this way of life had become normal, and Nunzia had gotten accustomed to it, the strange situation made her mind take another tack, in exactly the opposite direction. She began to want to go out with the two of them, and, very gracefully, to strut between them; to haunt a café in the center of Florence, the "Grande Italia" in Piazza Vittorio Emanuele, where she made some friendships: a retired guardsman and his wife, a postman with his wife and their daughter who was engaged to a sergeant-major—the poor children were going to have to wait ten years before they could get married; two ladies who rented rooms to big shots, high-ranking employees, top-echelon officers, rich foreigners—and who had learned and could tell about many things; a streetcar conductor, with his wife and four daughters, who, partly through distrust and partly through exercising too much patience, were still waiting for that match which was never going to come along again. And presenting the Marquis to their new friends: "This is the Marquis; he lives with us, we are together," seeming to say: "Watch out, because we folks are very, very high up in the scale." And those who did not know the Almanach de Gotha,[5] who didn't even know it existed, would at first look askance at him, with mistrust, stroking their noses and looking at each other: "Can he really be a marquis? A real marquis?" Shouldn't they say, as of gems: "Just a piece of glass?" Even though they had put him back in good shape again, the appearance of the old man was not such as to make such a thing certain. But later, because of the splendor that was reflected from him onto all of them, impressed by a double name, and even more because of certain bits of information circulating in the café, they all ended up believing and aspiring to that aristocratic company. "Isn't it so, Marquis? Did you hear, Marquis? Marquis, what do you think about it? What do you say to that?" Nunzia would repeat, with unfailing amiability, and with every few words.

And, starting with the Marquis, gradually, growing in affectation and in brazenness, she would hint in passing, or let people think something about herself too, so as to start the rumor that even if she wasn't actually a titled lady, she was certainly noble, or that at least her mother or her grandmother must have been. Both of those ladies, to tell the truth, had known only one coat-of-arms: the sickle to cut hay for the animals and the hoe to get the field ready for the potatoes; instruments which, in their own kind, are very noble. But now that she was on the high road, she wasn't referring to this. She would boast of her aristocratic acquaintances, she would tell anecdotes and adventures in which there entered duchesses and countesses, as though they were of her own sphere: "Do you remember, Marquis?" It was understood, in short, that they were dealing with a lofty world for

5. *Almanach de Gotha,* a periodical containing information concerning the noble families of Europe.

which they insisted on continually making a greater place, and giving higher and higher homage.

Bistino was happy, and did nothing but laugh. Like the perfect servant that he was, he would make bows that might be mistaken for expressions of a thousand-year-old aristocracy by people who were not in the know regarding these matters.

As for the Marquis, who every morning in his room had to ring the bell like an aristocrat and, from time to time, go into highly aristocratic rages, which he would have been very glad to get along without (without knowing that he was enjoying such luxury, Bistino was getting a master at bankruptcy clearance-sale rates), he showed no astonishment at the woman's effrontery; nothing could astonish him any more, and he understood her too and entered into the game with promptness, displaying the remnant of his real and unfortunate aristocracy among the ladies of the café.

By now, there was no choice; from Siena there came a bare fifty lire per month, the harvests were going from bad to worse, and from Milan there came nothing because he didn't want to be bothered writing his well-known letters; for a plate of good soup and a decent lodging, he had to make the other man into the Marquis. ✤

Petrarch began a collection of his Italian poetry in 1342. In its final form it contained three hundred sixty-six compositions, principally sonnets, with other verse forms interspersed. The main theme of his lyrics is his love for the woman he called "Laura."

Francis Petrarch (1304–1374)

SONNET 3: IT WAS THE MORNING

Translated from the Italian by
Joseph Auslander

It was the morning of that blessèd day [1]
Whereon the Sun in pity veiled his glare
For the Lord's agony, that, unaware,
I fell a captive, Lady, to the sway

5 Of your swift eyes: that seemed no time to stay
The strokes of Love: I stepped into the snare
Secure, with no suspicion: then and there
I found my cue in man's most tragic play.

Love caught me naked to his shaft, his sheaf,
10 The entrance for his ambush and surprise
Against the heart wide open through the eyes,

The constant gate and fountain of my grief:
How craven so to strike me stricken so,
Yet from you fully armed conceal his bow!

---

1. *that blessèd day,* Good Friday.

SONNET 36

Translated from the Italian by
Morris Bishop

If I believed that death could make an end
to love's long torture that has laid me low,
my hand would long ere this have dealt the blow
to summon up oblivion, my friend.
5 But since I fear that I would but descend
from tears to tears, from woe to a worse woe,
on the gulf's edge, with half a step to go,
irresolute, above the black I bend.

Oh, it were time the pitiless bow were drawn,
10 the cord pulled taut, aim taken carefully,
time that the shaft into my heart were gone!
Thus I pray Love, and that deaf deity,
Death, whose pale colors I have now put on.
Why is she silent? She has forgotten me.

From PETRARCH AND HIS WORLD, translations and text by Morris
Bishop. Copyright © 1963 by Indiana University Press. Reprinted by permission.

SONNET 47: BLEST BE THE DAY

Translated from the Italian by
Joseph Auslander

Blest be the day, and blest the month and year,
Season and hour and very moment blest,
The lovely land and place where first possessed
By two pure eyes I found me prisoner;

5 And blest the first sweet pain, the first most dear,
Which burnt my heart when Love came in as guest;
And blest the bow, the shafts which shook my breast,
And even the wounds which Love delivered there.

Blest be the words and voices which filled grove
10 And glen with echoes of my Lady's name;
The sighs, the tears, the fierce despair of love;

And blest the sonnet-sources of my fame;
And blest that thought of thoughts which is her own,
Of her, her only, of herself alone!

"Blest Be the Day" by Francis Petrarch, translated by Joseph Auslander from THE CONTINENTAL EDITION OF WORLD MASTERPIECES, Vol. 1, Maynard Mack, General Editor. Copyright © 1956, 1962, 1965, and 1966 by W. W. Norton & Company, Inc.

SONNET 90

Translated from the Italian by
Morris Bishop

She used to let her golden hair fly free
for the wind to toy and tangle and molest.
Her eyes were brighter than the radiant west.
(Seldom they shine so now.) I used to see
5 pity look out of those deep eyes on me.
("It was false pity," you would now protest.)
I had love's tinder heaped within my breast;
what wonder that the flame burned furiously?

She did not walk in any mortal way,
10 but with angelic progress. When she spoke,
unearthly voices sang in unison.
She seemed divine among the dreary folk
of earth. You say she is not so today?
Well, though the bow's unbent, the wound bleeds on.

SONNET 112

Translated from the Italian by
Morris Bishop

Sennuccio,[1] would you have me, then, confide
my way of life, the tale of my duress?
I burn, I melt, with all the old grievousness,
and Laura rules me still, for woe betide,
5 here she was humble, there she walked in pride,
now harsh, now gentle; pitiful, pitiless;
now she was gay; now in her sober dress;
now scornful; now demure; now angry-eyed.

Here she sang sweetly; here she sat awhile;
10 and here she turned; and here she held her ground;
her eyes here stabbed my heart with a fatal ray.
And here she spoke; and here I saw her smile;
'twas here she blushed-oh, in this helpless round
our master, Love, pursues me night and day.

From PETRARCH AND HIS WORLD, translations and text by Morris
Bishop. Copyright © 1963 by Indiana University Press. Reprinted by permission.

1. *Sennuccio* (sen nüt′ chô).

SONNET 134

Translated from the Italian by
Morris Bishop

There is no peace; I am too weak for war.
I fear and hope; a burning brand, I freeze.
I fly o'er heaven, and lie upon earth's floor.
I grasp the void; the whole world's on my knees.
5 I'm jailed without a sentence; at the door
pauses my captor, balancing her keys.
Love will not let me live unprisoned nor
will he let death bring me its blessed ease.

Eyeless, I see; tongueless, I shout and cry;
10 I beg my doom and succor with one breath.
Loathing myself, another I'd be wooing.
I feed on grief; I laugh with streaming eye;
and equally I hate both life and death.
This is my state, my lady. It's your doing.

SONNET 181

Translated from the Italian by
Morris Bishop

Love made a snare, a beautiful device
woven of gold and pearls, and this he laid
twined in the grass, under the sorrowful shade
of the laurel tree to which I sacrifice.
5 Sweetmeats were strown thereon, of greatest price,
though bitter at core. I took them unafraid
Ever unearthly-lovely music played,
unheard since Adam's hour in Paradise.

The radiance of her eyes outdid the sun,
10 transfiguring the earth in a holy blaze.
Then with her ivory hand she twitched the rope!
And so I fell in the net, and was undone
by her angelic words, her darling ways;
also by pleasure; by desire; by hope.

From PETRARCH AND HIS WORLD, translations and text by Morris
Bishop. Copyright © 1963 by Indiana University Press. Reprinted by permission.

SONNET 267

Translated from the Italian by
Morris Bishop

Alas, that gentle look and that fair face!
Alas for the body's beauty when you wended
your gracious way! Alas, your words that mended
the brutal, and taught honor to the base!
5 Alas, that smile of yours, whose wounding grace
has come to death, and all my hope is ended!
You'd have been queen of earth, had you descended
to a younger world, to a less evil race!

Still I must burn in you, in you respire.
10 I was yours utterly; my stricken heart
can feel no other hurt, after today.
You showered hope upon me and desire
in our last moment, ere we came to part.
And then the wind blew all your words away.

From PETRARCH AND HIS WORLD, translations and text by Morris Bishop. Copyright © 1963 by Indiana University Press. Reprinted by permission.

SONNET 272

Translated from the Italian by
Morris Bishop

Life hurries on, a frantic refugee,
and death, with great forced marches, follows fast,
and all the present leagues with all the past
and all the future to make war on me.
5 Anticipation joins with memory
tearing my soul in torment; and at last,
did not damnation set me so aghast,
I'd put an end to thinking, and be free.

The few glad moments that my heart has known
10 return to me; and now I watch in dread
the winds upgathering against my ways,
storm in the harbor, and the pilot prone,
the mast and rigging down; and dark and dead
the lovely lights whereon I used to gaze.

IT IS THE EVENING HOUR

Translated from the Italian by
Morris Bishop

It is the evening hour. The rapid sky
bends westward; and the hasty daylight flees
to some new land, some strange expectant race.
An old and weary pilgrim-woman sees
5 the lonely foreign desert-dark draw nigh.
Fearful, she urges on her stumbling pace,
and to her resting-place
at last she comes, and knows
the sweetness of repose.
10 The pains of pilgrimage, the road's duress
fade in enveloping forgetfulness.
But oh alas, my hurts that ache by day
are but more pitiless
when the light sinks into the west away.

15 When the sun's burning wheels have sped along,
and night pursues, rolling his deepest black
from highest peaks into the sheltered plain,
the hardfist yokel slings upon his back
his tools, and sings his artless mountain-song,
20 discharging on the air his load of pain.
And yet his only gain
is, on his humble board,

From PETRARCH AND HIS WORLD, translations and text by Morris
Bishop. Copyright © 1963 by Indiana University Press. Reprinted by permission.

rude fare, which poets honor, yet abjure.
Let him be happy, let him sleep secure,
25 though I no happiness have ever won,
     no rest, no ease, no cure,
     with all the turning of the stars and sun.

And when the shepherd sees the evening shade
rising and graying o'er the eastward land,
30 and the sun dropping to its nightly nest,
he rises; takes his well-worn crook in hand;
and leaves the grass, the spring, the beechen glade,
and quietly leads the tired flock to its rest.
He finds a cave, recessed
35 in crags, wherein to spread
     green branches for his bed,
and there he sleeps, untroubled, solitary.
But then, O cruel Love, the more you harry
my breaking strength to that most hopeless chase
40 of her who flees apace;
and Love will never aid to noose the quarry.

In the sea's bays the sailors on their bark
throw down their limbs on the hard boards to sleep,
when the sun dips beneath the western main.
45 Oh, though he hide within the farthest deep,
and leave Morocco's mountains to the dark,
Granada and the Pillars and all Spain,
     and though the worldwide pain
     of suffering man and beast
50 in the first night have ceased,
there comes no night with mercy to conclude
my ardor, ever in suffering renewed.
My love grows old; soon will my captor see me
     ten years in servitude.
55 And still no rescuer comes with strength to free me!

And as I seek with words my wounds to numb,

I watch at eve the unyoked oxen turning
in from the fields, down from the furrowed hill.
The heavy yoke is never lifted from
60 my shoulders, and my hurts are ever burning,
and in my eyes the tears are springing still.
Alas, it was my will
to carve the unearthly grace
of her most lovely face
65 in the immutable matter of my heart.
Now it is carved so deep that strength nor art
may rub it thence until that final day
when soul and body part.
Even then, perhaps, it will not pass away.

70 O my unhappy song,
my grief has made you grieve.
You will not dare to leave
my heart, to show your sorrows anywhere.
And yet, for others' praise you shall not care,
75 for all your burden is the weight of pain
left by the flames that flare
from the cold rock to which I cling, in vain.

Guido Piovene[1] (1907–1974)

THE DRESSMAKER'S DAUGHTER

Translated from the Italian by
Michael Bullock

PERHAPS IT IS TRUE that we and food have offended one another.
A memory comes to my mind, and it's not for the first time. It
has returned to distress me several times lately. Perhaps I am
beginning to suffer hunger.

It is a very distant memory. My father worked in a furniture
factory outside the city. He used to go out of the house at dawn,
leaving us alone, my mother and me, until late in the evening. I
had finished with the junior classes at primary school, and my
memory begins with the holiday between two school years. I used
to spend a great deal of the day with my mother, who earned
money as a dressmaker and enjoyed a certain authority in the
family as a result. We used to sit together by the window with
the curtains drawn back. I helped her if I could, and if I couldn't,
I let my gaze wander slowly from her hands to the street below.
In this way, I grew accustomed to remaining silent.

I used to watch the customers ordering and trying on clothes
as though it were a theatrical performance. My mother's most
important customer was a society woman, the wife of an indus-

"The Dressmaker's Daughter" by Guido Piovene, translated by Michael
Bullock from NEW WORLD WRITING. Reprinted by permission of
Michael Bullock.

1. *Piovene* (pyō ve' ne).

trialist, who bought her wardrobe from the big fashion houses, but came to my mother to have last season's clothes altered and also to have copies made of models which my mother pirated from the most celebrated dressmakers with the aid of some employee.

This lady possessed a large wardrobe comprising a whole hierarchy of clothes. She had reached middle age, but her figure was still firm and her complexion fresh; she radiated warmth and vitality. Her face was full, her eyes were heavy-lidded, and she had curly hair and very white teeth—more than the usual number, it seemed to me, so that, sitting in my corner, I often used to count them as she spoke. But her whole body seemed somehow "fruitful," impetuously bearing flesh, words, and expressions of emotion. When she stripped for fittings, she did so in a triumphant manner, standing proudly in the center of the room as though in a position she had taken by storm. The transparent underclothing revealed her milk-white body on which were distributed large red patches, as though someone had slapped her with the palm of his hand.

She knew all about literature, paintings, feeding infants and bringing up children, and love affairs. She moved in high society and was passionately devoted to charity. Occasionally she brought her husband with her, a little fat man, who sat silently in the corner during the fittings. He and I ended by staring at one another from our seats without exchanging a word, like two shy animals.

Now this lady, noticing how attentively I used to watch her, wide-eyed and speechless, discovered that I was very aristocratic in appearance, quite out of keeping with my environment. She began, as though to test me, by inviting me to her house to play with her children, of whom she had five. She appeared amongst them, pink and white and triumphant, in a house like herself, full of well-upholstered furniture, crowded with flowers and leafy with potted plants. She led me with the children to a table on which stood a row of big plates of sweets. Then she took me aside and questioned me about my education. She thought it very regrettable that I attended the state school, where I could only pick up common ways and vulgar expressions.

From that day on, she visited my mother even more frequently than before. Sometimes she used to make me rise from my seat and then examine me as I stood before her in the shadow cast by her body, scarcely veiled by the transparent underclothes. Finally she shook her head as though in doubt about something. She inquired tactfully of my mother whether I might not be the fruit of some youthful love affair with a person of distinction. "Because," she added, "pretty girls are to be found in every milieu, but their hands and feet reveal their humble origins. This child, on the other hand, though one couldn't call her pretty, has hands and feet, wrists and ankles, that a lady might envy."

Then someone she met in society told her that hands and feet were nothing to judge by, because aristocratic hands and feet were to be met with amongst the common people, as could be seen in actresses. An infallible indication of breeding was the line of the neck, but this test was not decisive until maturity, when all the lines of the body had grown heavier. After this she scrutinized the line of my neck, which was long and thin. "It looks beautiful to me," she said, "but you are too young. We shan't know until you are grown up." Then she left me, apparently upset by not having any dependable guarantee as to the excellence of my pedigree.

One day she suggested to my mother that she send me to a boarding school at her own expense. My mother refused her offer, saying that she needed me and that my father would be against it. Thenceforth my benefactress, incited by this opposition, started to talk about me as though I were not merely an aristocratic being, but a miracle, a violation of the laws of nature, which had intended me to be beautiful, but common (as she spoke she turned her gaze on my mother, as though confirming the contrast between us). Nature, she said, would re-establish her supremacy, if I were not snatched once and for all from her fatal influence. She pointed out to my mother the crime she would be committing if she failed to take account of my refinement.

"The child differs too much from other girls of the same origin for her to be neglected in this way," she said. "I speak frankly, because I feel it is my duty to say this. A human life, the life of your daughter, is at stake. She could grow up to be a lady: it would be a terrible crime to paralyze her finer instincts, to hold her down through self-interest and false pride, when it would be so easy to place her in more suitable surroundings. At her age an example, a word, would be enough to ruin her." (The lady would have felt her arguments confirmed if she had known that my mother always referred to her as "that cow," thinking perhaps of her physical exuberance.)

She made these speeches during the fittings, often scantily clad, and I listened to her inattentively from my corner, all the time gazing fixedly at her buttocks. Then she spoke once more of the boarding school to which she wished to send me, enumerating the nuns, all of them highly qualified, and quoting the names of several girls of good family who had received their schooling from them. Didn't my mother realize that it would be a stroke of luck, a godsend, if they would take me?

At each visit, she reminded my mother that her guilt toward me was increasing every minute. What would she reply when, some day, I asked her why she had missed such an opportunity? How would she dare to look me in the eyes, for the rest of her life, knowing the irreparable harm she had done me and burdened by my conscious reproach?

My mother, still reluctant, partly because she felt I would be unhappy, and partly because of an instinctive aversion to the people with whom I would have to mix, finally said: "I'm not convinced of it, but perhaps this is really a stroke of luck for you."

She suggested a compromise: I should go to the boarding school during the day, for school and recreation, but sleep at home, "as so many girls do," she said.

"But not at such a good school!" objected my benefactress. "In the first place, the nuns don't take day girls; it's a tradition, a rule; they wouldn't alter it, even if the girl were a princess. And they're quite right, because such a good school has to isolate the girls, transplant them into a different atmosphere, so to speak, where they will be protected from all disturbing influences. Why should you, of all people, want to make difficulties and lay down conditions? As though you were doing them a favor, whereas in reality . . ." She stopped there out of delicacy.

"I have little confidence in the effect of this education on Anna, if she is not removed from outside influences. Isn't that the whole object? You should help me, not put obstacles in the way." My mother remained obstinate.

Giving up hope of finding in my mother a disinterested ally against herself and the family into which I had been born, the lady became more explicit: "If Anna were about to marry a man of much higher social station than your own, and this man asked you to retire into the background, what would your conscience tell you to do?"

My mother gave way before this unforeseen argument, but she stood her ground on the matter of the boarding school. She never understood "the duty of parents to sacrifice everything, to disappear from the scene altogether if necessary, for the benefit of their children." Instead she clung positively fanatically to the iron bedstead in which I slept next to her own.

In the end my benefactress was compelled to give in, since she was resolved to save me at any price. She implored my mother, who looked at her with a mixture of obstinacy and deference, but she had to be content with extracting the maximum advantage from the meager concessions my mother was prepared to make. She persuaded the nuns to accept me as a day pupil, no doubt by representing me as an innocent victim whom it was their duty to save by combating my sordid environment.

I was delighted at the thought of going to a boarding school among so many distinguished children, whom I imagined as being fair-haired. At the beginning of the school year my mother provided me with a beautiful new dress, so that I should not look out of place among my elegant companions. She now took my new position seriously and was determined that I should derive the full benefit from it. The vigilance with which she watched over my personal cleanliness and that of my aprons, and even my

underclothes—as if I had to undress at school—became burden-
some to me. Every morning she handed me with my books a
packet containing bread and fruit, or bread and chocolate. As I
was not a boarder I could not have lunch with the rest of the
school but had to bring my food with me from home.

As she handed me the books and food, my mother always wore
an expression of great seriousness, as though transferring to my
shoulders the burden of responsibility which my benefactress had
previously placed on hers. By the solemnity with which she
handed me the books and food, she made me feel how great
would be my guilt if I disappointed the woman who had come to
my aid, and what a grave duty I was assuming, each morning as
I left home, toward my parents, myself, and my destiny. Thus I
used to leave home with the feeling of being weighed down by a
crushing burden that robbed me of liberty and stupefied me; but,
being docile and affectionate, I gave no further thought to this
feeling and accepted it as natural.

Perhaps because of this unheeded weight, or perhaps because
of the attitude of the nuns and my schoolmates, I did badly at
school and remained well below the average. In reality I did not
possess the gifts which the lady had attributed to me. My mother
was right when she said: "Believe me, signora, she's just like any
other girl." It was simply that my silence and reserve were mistaken for intelligence and sensibility. In actual fact, I had an
affectionate nature and longed to be fondled.

After a year's trial my benefactress withdrew her financial support, blaming my failure on my mother for keeping me in my
old environment. "This proves I was right," she said. "You would
have it your own way, but it's all wasted effort if what is done in
the morning is undone in the evening." So she left me to my fate
and the state schools.

But first I endured a whole year of unhappiness in the boarding
school, in the course of which I experienced something I had
never suffered at home—a kind of hunger. To my schoolmates
I was "the day girl," who neither slept nor ate with them, the
lonely butt for their spitefulness. The nuns were hostile to me
and made it clear that I was breathing that air only as a favor

and, to judge by the results, pointlessly. They were quick and practical women, business women rather than women of religion. My slow ways, my childish reserve, and even my longing for affection and my desire to mix with the others, seemed to them an encumbrance and a sign of my lowly origin; the stricter ones among them regarded these as signs of a sinful disposition. They were forever admonishing me to be quicker and more practical and to free my heart from slothfulness.

The baseness of character which I discovered in almost all the teaching staff, their thirst for popularity and approval from the little world within which their lives were confined, drove them to encourage the other children in their attitude to me, to incite them against me—even those who had not made up their minds about me. The moment they noticed my unpopularity they did their best to increase it, confirming unalterably the tendency to shut me out from the corporate life of the school. They drew attention to my scholastic deficiencies and supported the children in their judgment that I was "stupid." In this way I became more and more apathetic and taciturn.

At midday I used to eat my bread and fruit, or bread and chocolate, alone on a school bench, and it left me hungry. True hunger is always hunger for some other food, for other people's food. Such was my hunger. For this reason, now that hunger occupied my thoughts more than ever before, my life seemed entirely dominated, permeated by hunger. I used to want to sit with the others, to drink in their conversation, to sleep among them, to wash with them in the water of the washbasins, to immerse myself in the steam from their soup. Sitting alone on my bench, I imagined them as elegant and with their faces veiled by the steam rising from their soup. This image of their beauty made me incapable of satisfying my hunger with bread, chocolate and fruit. When I returned home in the evening, exhausted, hungry within because I had not partaken of that soup nor inhaled that steam, weak from lack of the only food that appeared to me satisfying, I flung myself on the family stew. My hunger stilled at last, I found repose in my iron bedstead, from which I could hear the breathing of my parents. Going to sleep in that bed I cast off my obsessive longings, because here at least I felt that I belonged to someone.

The birthday of the mother superior was in April, and the nuns planned an entertainment for her. A theatrical performance would cost too much, so it was agreed that the youngest pupils should sing a chorus in the chapel after high mass. I was permitted to take part in this ceremony. We were to be enveloped in tulle veils to make us look like angels, and to wear a wreath of flowers on our heads. The veils were to be made up at the last moment, so as to keep the preparations hidden from the mother superior and not spoil the surprise for her. And as the girls had to stay up and do the work in secret at night and rise very early next morning, I was allowed to sleep those few hours at school. The previous evening, Roberta, one of the pupils, had had a big box of lilies of the valley brought from her garden.

Now before the work began, Roberta was running a slight temperature, which compelled her to retire to bed and withdraw from the festivities. She was slender and had long legs and hair so fair as to be almost white. She too was slow at school, but her backwardness, full of aristocratic disdain, inspired respect and, far from lowering her prestige, actually increased her domination over her schoolmates and the teachers. Whenever I recall her I feel within me a sensation of acid chill, accompanied by a scent like that of spring flowers with their slender stalks and pale green, shadowless leaves.

Twenty of us, with two nuns, set to work secretly in one of the classrooms after the bell had rung for lights out. The long strips of flimsy fabric clung to our knees; the lilies of the valley gave forth scent from their box on the teacher's desk, and this perfume mingled with the other, less pungent but more deeply ingrained, of warm young bodies none too well washed. I immersed myself in that atmosphere; I delighted in it and was full of excitement at being united with the others by the clouds of fabric, by breathing the same stuffy air, by the nimble work of the scissors and needles, by the crackle of the fabric as it was cut. For the first time I had managed to enter into the life of the school by night, and I was living in the ecstasy of at last belonging to the community. I was no longer hungry, I felt replete. When we approached the box to make the wreaths, the scent of the lilies of the valley so excited me that all of a sudden, breaking the deep silence, I started to jump and shout, uttering shrill meaningless cries. This was so surprising in a child who was always taciturn and apparently sullen that the others probably imagined I had suddenly gone mad. One of the teachers immediately seized my arm and hissed in my ear: "You idiot! Do you want to wake the mother superior and give everything away?" Then they all, pupils and teachers, shook their heads, and I heard the word "stupid." But I was happy and felt no humiliation.

After a few hours of sleep, we all washed in the washroom. I had slept and washed with the others and felt myself one of them. Then, having given the finishing touches to our handiwork, we dressed hurriedly a few minutes before high mass. We were all rather pale from lack of sleep, and all fasting because we had to receive communion. I had already put the wreath of lilies on my head and was on the point of putting on the veil, when the door opened and the girl who had been ill entered, tall and fair, followed by a nurse. Roberta, the nurse said, had recovered during the night, knew the words of the song by heart, and had asked to take part in the chorus. One of the nuns said: "Well, that's difficult. . . . There's no material left for another veil and all the lilies of the valley have been used up."

Roberta stood directly in front of us, but she did not look at us. Distant, full of natural fastidiousness, she reminded me exactly of the white highlight on a green leaf, or the cold sap that sets one's teeth on edge. She kept her very long eyelashes lowered over her near-sighted eyes. I felt that she dominated us, even the nun in charge—and to my undoing. For then the nun said: "Unless . . ."

I caught my breath.

"Unless one of the others gives up her place. Roberta has more right than lots of others. Wasn't it she who brought the flowers? And she's a boarder."

I felt everyone looking at me.

"Anna, you're a day girl . . ." went on the nun, giving me a stern look that detached me from the group. She paused for a moment, as though waiting for my spontaneous consent. When this was not forthcoming, as though annoyed by her own hesitations and once more energetic and practical, she cried: "Come along, hurry up, there's no time to lose."

I quickly took off the wreath and, without a word, handed it to my schoolmate. I believe I stared at her wide-eyed. She did not look at me but took the wreath without speaking, as though it were the most natural thing in the world that it should be given to her. It had a pungent scent.

When we moved off to the church, I remained a little behind and tried to slip away, in order to shut myself up all alone in one of the classrooms. But I was stopped by the caretaker, who was carrying a packet in her hand.

"I was just looking for you, Anna. Your mother sends you this."

It was the usual package containing bread and a piece of chocolate. I had hoped that day, after singing with the others, to be allowed to eat lunch with them as well.

"Take it quickly into the classroom and then go to church," said the caretaker, and went away.

I went into the classroom and sat for a moment at my desk. I felt neither anger against my schoolmates, and teachers, nor desire for revenge; but I no longer wanted to share their meal. I was unmoved by the thought of them. Instead, I felt angry with the food which I held between my hands in its wrapping, and wanted to take vengeance on it.

The school had a little garden, damp, always in shadow, uncultivated, and used by no one, neither the sisters nor the children. It was visible from the playground, from which it was shut off by an iron gate that was always firmly closed to keep people out. But I remembered a corridor, deserted at that time of day, which ended in a window overlooking this abandoned garden. I raced along the corridor, swung myself over the window sill, and dropped into the garden. It was a square patch of tangled grass and plants, enclosed on three sides by walls, one of them windowless. Coldly and decisively, as though I were not obeying a fantastic impulse but carrying out some practical task that had been entrusted to me, I crossed the little garden to the blind wall. Close to it grew a few hydrangea bushes and an inky-green yew tree, which had littered the damp soil with its bright red berries.

I dug a hole in the earth with my hands, without any feeling of distaste, took the food from its wrapping, threw it into the hole, and covered it over. Then I trampled the earth over it with my feet. I hated the food and wanted to insult it. That was the only emotion left in me, the only action to which I felt impelled and in which I found any pleasure. My task completed, I climbed in through the window again and waited for mass to finish.

That is the memory which torments me in these days of fear and half hunger. I keep thinking of that yew tree and the damp earth beneath it. It sometimes seems to me as though a part of myself, forgotten while I went on living, had remained in that very spot, amongst those sunless plants. Two or three times I have awakened during the night with the feeling that my hands were covered with mud and I must wash them: as though I had gone out of myself during my sleep and returned to that garden to dig up the soil in search of the bread and the chocolate. ✛

Luigi Pirandello (1867–1936)

THE MAN WITH
THE FLOWER IN HIS MOUTH

Translated from the Italian by
William Murray

THE CAST

THE MAN WITH THE FLOWER IN HIS MOUTH
AN EASYGOING COMMUTER
A WOMAN IN BLACK: nonspeaking

The sidewalk in front of an all-night café in some large city.
At rear, a row of trees lining an avenue, electric lights gleaming through the leaves. On either side, the last few houses of a street that leads into the avenue. In front of the houses at left, on the sidewalk, the tables and chairs of a cheap all-night café; in front of the houses at right, a street lamp casts a cold light. Another lamp shines at the corner of the last house on the left, where the street and the avenue meet. A few minutes past midnight. In the distance, the occasional haunting sound of a mandolin.

At curtain, THE MAN WITH THE FLOWER IN HIS MOUTH *is seated at one of the tables,* THE COMMUTER *at the one next to him. The latter is peacefully sipping a mint frappé through a straw, unaware that he is being closely observed by the other man. A long, silent pause.*

MAN. Well, I've been meaning to talk to you. I hope you won't mind. I suppose you're an easygoing type and—you missed your train?

COMMUTER. By not more than a minute. I rush into the station and it pulls out before my very eyes.

MAN. You could have run after it.

COMMUTER. Of course. It's silly, I know. If I hadn't been loaded down with all those damned packages, bundles, boxes, God knows what else! Like a jackass! But you know women—errands, errands—it never stops! It took me three minutes, believe me, just to get out of the taxi and get my fingers through all those strings, two packages to a finger.

MAN. You must have been quite a sight. You know what I'd have done? I'd have left them in the cab.

COMMUTER. And my wife? Oh yes! And my daughters? And all their friends?

MAN. Let them scream. I'd enjoy it enormously.

COMMUTER. That's because you probably have no idea what women are like when they get to the country in the summer!

MAN. But of course I know. Precisely because I do know. (*A pause.*) They all begin by saying they really won't need anything.

COMMUTER. That's all? They're even capable of maintaining that they're going there to save. Then, as soon as they get to some little village around here, the uglier it is, the poorer and dirtier it is, the more they insist on dressing it up with all the most expensive and useless little fripperies! Ah, women, my dear sir! Anyway, it's their profession. (*Imitating a woman.*) "If you just happen to be going into town, darling, I really could use this—and a little bit of that—and you might also, if it's no trouble"—sweet, that "no trouble," isn't it?—"and while you're there you could stop by so-and-so's. . . ." My dear, how do

The Man with the Flower in His Mouth 319

you expect me to do all these things in just three hours? "Why not, just take a cab, . . ." The trouble is that I planned on being here only three hours and I didn't bring my house keys.

MAN. Oh fine! And so?

COMMUTER. So I left my mountain of packages in the station checkroom and went out to eat in some restaurant. Then, to soothe my nerves, I went to the theatre. It was hot as hell. On the way out I asked myself, "What now? It's nearly midnight and the next train is at four o'clock." For just three hours of sleep it didn't seem worth spending the money for a room somewhere. So I came here. This place stays open, doesn't it?

MAN. It never closes. (*A pause.*) So you really left all your packages in the checkroom?

COMMUTER. Yes, why? Aren't they safe there? They were all nicely wrapped—

MAN. Oh, there's nothing to worry about. (*A pause.*) Very well wrapped, I'm sure of it. With that special skill the young clerks have for wrapping up what they've just sold. . . . (*A pause.*) What hands they have! You see them tear off a great big double sheet of that shiny red paper—a pleasure just to look at it—so smooth you want to put it to your cheek to feel how fresh it is. . . . They spread it out on the counter and then, nonchalantly, gracefully, they put the material you've just bought, all nicely folded, right in the middle. First, from underneath, with the back of one hand, they raise one side of the sheet. Then, from above, they fold over the other one, double-folding it quickly, too, along the edges, that little extra touch for the sheer love of the art. Then they fold up the end flaps into triangles and turn the points under. They reach for the string, pull out enough to tie up the bundle, and knot it so swiftly you hardly even have time to admire their skill before you're handed the package, all wrapped and waiting for you to stick your finger through the loop.

COMMUTER. Well, I can see you pay quite a lot of attention to how they do things in these stores.

MAN. Me? My dear sir, I pass whole days at it. I can spend an hour just staring into a shop window. I forget myself. I feel like—I really would like to be that bolt of silk—that strip of linen—that red or blue ribbon the clerks measure out by the yard. Have you ever noticed how they do it? Before wrapping the thing up, they make an eight with the ribbon between thumb and little finger of the left hand. (*A pause.*) I watch the customer leave the store with his package hanging from his finger or under his arm. I follow him with my eyes until I lose sight of him. I imagine—oh, I imagine so many things! You couldn't guess how many. (*A pause. Then gloomily, mostly to himself.*) It helps. At least it helps.

COMMUTER. It helps? In what way?

MAN. Clinging like this—I mean, in my imagination—to life. Like a vine around the bars of an iron gate. (*A pause.*) I try never to let my imagination rest, not even for a moment. I use it to cling, to cling continually to the lives of others. But not people I know. No, no, I couldn't do that! The mere thought of it disgusts me! Nauseates me! I cling to the lives of strangers on whom my imagination can work freely. But not capriciously, no. I keep careful track of the least little hints I can spot in one person or another. If you only knew how well it works! I see somebody's house and I live in it. I feel a part of it, so at home I can even sniff—you know that particular atmosphere that every house has? Yours, mine? Except that in our own houses we're no longer conscious of it, because it's the atmosphere of our own lives we breathe. Do you understand what I mean? Yes, I can see you do.

COMMUTER. Yes, because—I mean, it must be fun for you to imagine all these different things. . . .

MAN (*irritated, after having thought it over a moment*). Fun? For me?

COMMUTER. Yes, I should think—

MAN. Tell me something. Have you ever gone to a good doctor?

COMMUTER. Me? No, why? I'm not sick!

MAN. Don't be alarmed. I just wanted to find out whether you've ever sat in some good doctor's waiting room.

COMMUTER. Oh, yes. I once had to go with one of my daughters, something to do with her nerves.

The Man with the Flower in His Mouth 321

MAN. Good. I'm not prying. All I meant was, those rooms. . . . (*A pause.*) Have you ever noticed? The sofa's usually dark, old-fashioned looking—those upholstered chairs that hardly ever match—the little armchairs. . . . Furniture picked up here and there, secondhand, stuck in that room for the patients. It doesn't belong to the house. The doctor would never entertain his wife's friends in there. *His* living room is luxurious, handsome. What a contrast between his home and his waiting room, for which this decent, sober furniture seems adequate enough. When you accompanied your daughter, did you pay careful attention to the chair or sofa you sat on?

COMMUTER. No, not really.

MAN. Of course not. Because you weren't sick. . . . (*A pause.*) But even the sick don't usually pay much attention, they're so wrapped up in their troubles. . . . (*A pause.*) And yet how often some of them sit there, staring intently at their fingers as they trace vague patterns on the shiny arms of those chairs! Lost in their thoughts and unable to see . . . (*A pause.*) But what an impression it makes when you're through with the doctor, you're on your way out, and you come face to face with that chair again, the one you were sitting in a little while before, when you were still in ignorance of the verdict! You find it occupied by some other patient, he, too, with his secret illness, or you see it there, empty, impassive, waiting for someone else to sit down. . . . (*A pause.*) But what were we talking about? Ah yes, the pleasures of the imagination. Now how do you suppose I happened to think of a doctor's waiting room?

COMMUTER. Yes, I really don't—

MAN. You don't see the connection? Neither do I. (*A pause.*) It's just that certain seemingly unconnected mental images are peculiar to every one of us. They arise out of experiences and considerations so individual, so private that we simply wouldn't understand each other, if we didn't tacitly agree in everyday conversation to dispense with them. Nothing more illogical than analogies based on such private visions . . . (*A pause.*) But perhaps, in this case, there is a connection. Look, do you think a chair gets any pleasure out of trying to guess who the next patient will be to sit in it? To guess what his trouble is, where he'll go, what he'll do after the visit? No, of course not. And I'm the same way. The patients come and go, and the chair, poor thing, is there to be sat in. Well, I fulfill a similar function. For a while I do this, for a while I do that. At the moment it's your turn. But I want you to understand that I get no pleasure from your story, from hearing about how you missed your train, about your family waiting for you in the country, about all the bother I suppose you've had to put up with.

COMMUTER. It's been a nuisance, all right!

MAN. Thank God it's nothing worse. . . . (*A pause.*) Some people aren't quite so well off, my friend. . . . (*A pause.*) I told you I had to use my imagination to cling to other people's lives, but not for pleasure, not because I'm interested. In fact—in fact, I do it because I want to share everyone else's troubles, be able to judge life as silly and vain. If you can make yourself feel that way, then it won't really matter if you have to come to the end of it. (*With sullen rage.*) But you have to go on proving it to yourself, you know. Continuously, mercilessly. Because, my dear sir, we all feel this terrible thirst for life, though we have no idea what it consists of. But it's there, there, like an ache in our throats that can never be satisfied, because life, at the very moment we experience it, is always so full of itself that we can never actually taste it. All we can really savor is the past, which remains alive within us. Our thirst for life comes from the memories that bind us. But bind us to what? Why, to this everyday foolishness, to these petty irritations, to so many stupid illusions, dull occupations . . . Yes, yes. What now seems foolish to us or boring—I might even say, what now seems a real nightmare to us—yes, sir, who knows how it will all taste to us in four, five, ten years—what flavor these tears will acquire . . . And life, by God, the mere thought of losing it—especially when you know it's a matter of days . . . (*At this point, the head of a* WOMAN *appears from around the corner, at right. She is dressed in black and wears an old hat with drooping feathers.*) There—see that? Over there, at the corner—see that woman's shadow? There, she's hidden herself!

COMMUTER. What? Who—who was it?

MAN. Didn't you see her? She's hiding.

COMMUTER. A woman?

MAN. Yes. My wife.

COMMUTER. Oh, your wife?

(*A pause.*)

MAN. She keeps an eye on me, from a distance. And sometimes, believe me, I could kick her. But it wouldn't do any good. She's like one of these stray bitches: the more you kick them, the closer they stick to your heels. (*A pause.*) You can't imagine what that woman is suffering on my account. She doesn't eat, she doesn't sleep. She follows me around day and night, like this, always at a distance. If only she'd at least dust off those rags she wears . . . She doesn't even look like a woman any more, just dusty rags. Dust all over her, on her hair, at her temples. Permanently dusty. And she's barely thirty-four. . . . (*A pause.*) She annoys me so, you can't imagine. Sometimes I jump on her, I shout in her face: "Idiot!" I give her a shaking. She takes it all. She stands there and stares at me with eyes—eyes that, I swear to you, make me want to strangle her. It does no good. She waits for me to move away before taking up the trail again. (*Again the head of* the WOMAN IN BLACK *appears around the corner.*) There, look —that's her peering around the corner.

COMMUTER. Poor woman.

MAN. What do you mean, poor woman? You see, she'd like me to stay at home. Calmly, quietly. So I could benefit from her most loving and tender care. So I could bask in the perfect order of all the rooms, the spotlessness of the furnishings, that mirrored silence that used to characterize my house, measured by the ticking of the big clock in the dining room. That's what she wants! Now I ask you, just so you'll appreciate the absurdity—no, not absurdity!—the macabre ferocity of this pretense, I ask you whether you think it possible that the houses of Messina or Avezzano, knowing they were about to be smashed by an earthquake, would have contently remained where they were, lined up along the streets and squares, ever obedient to the rules and regulations of the town real-estate board? No, by God, these houses of wood and stone would somehow have managed to run away! Try to imagine the citizens of Avezzano or Messina placidly undressing to go to bed, folding up their clothes, putting their shoes away, and snuggling down under the covers to enjoy the freshness of clean white sheets, knowing all the time that in a few hours they'd be dead. Does that seem possible to you?

COMMUTER. But perhaps your wife—

MAN. Let me finish! Wouldn't it be nice, my friend, if death were merely some sort of strange, disgusting insect someone might unexpectedly find on you. . . . You're walking down the street and some passer-by suddenly stops you. Carefully, he extends just two fingers of one hand and he says, "Excuse me, may I? You, my dear sir, have death on you!" And with those two fingers he plucks it off and flicks it away. . . . That would be wonderful, wouldn't it? But death isn't like some horrible insect. Many of the people you see walking around happily and indifferently may be carrying it on them. No one notices it. And they're calmly and quietly planning what they'll do tomorrow and the day after. Now I—(*He rises.*) Look, my dear sir. Come over here. . . . (*He makes the* COMMUTER *get up and leads him over to the street lamp.*) Under this light . . . Over here . . . I'll show you something. . . . Look here, here, under the mustache. . . . There, you see that pretty violet nodule? Know what it's called? Ah, such a soft word—softer than caramel—Epithelomia, it's called. Pronounce it, you'll feel how soft it is. Epithelomia . . . Death, you understand? Death passed my way. It planted this flower in my mouth and said to me, "Keep it, my friend, I'll be back in eight or ten months!" (*A pause.*) Now you tell me if, with this flower in my mouth, I can stay calmly and quietly at home, as that poor woman would like me to do. (*A pause.*) I scream at her, "I suppose you'd like me to kiss you!"—"Yes, kiss me!"—You know what she did? She took a pin last week and she scratched herself here, on the lip, and then she grabbed my head and tried to kiss me—kiss me on the mouth. . . . Because she says she wants to die with me . . . (*A pause.*) She's crazy. . . . (*Then angrily.*) I will not stay at home! I feel the need to stand at shop windows, yes, to admire the skill of the clerks. Because, you understand, if I found myself for one moment faced by the void inside me—Well, you understand, I could even, like nothing at all, snuff out the life in some total stranger. . . . Pull out a gun and kill someone who, like you, has unfortunately missed his train . . . (*He laughs.*) No, no, don't worry, my dear sir! I'm only joking! (*A pause.*) Well, I'm going now. (*A pause.*) I would kill myself if I ever—(*A pause.*) But these wonderful apricots are in season now. . . . How do *you* eat them? With the skin on, don't you? You break them in half, you squeeze them in your fingers, slowly. . . . Like a pair of juicy lips . . . Ah, delicious! (*He laughs. A pause.*) Give my regards to your wife and daughters in the country. (*A pause.*) I imagine them dressed in white and blue, standing on a lovely, shaded, green lawn. . . . (*A pause.*) And do me a favor. Tomorrow morning, when you get there. I suppose the village is some little distance from the station, isn't it? At dawn you might easily want to walk it. The first little tuft of grass you see at the edge of the road, count the blades for me. As many blades as you can count, that's the number of days I still have to live. . . . (*A pause.*) Be sure you pick me a nice fat one. (*He laughs.*) Good night, my dear sir. (*And he strolls off, humming to the sound of the distant mandolin. He starts for the road at right, but then he remembers that his wife is probably hiding around the corner, waiting for him. Quickly he turns and scurries off in the opposite direction, followed by the appalled gaze of the* EASYGOING COMMUTER.)

Curtain

Vasco Pratolini (1913–)

THE REMOVAL

Translated from the Italian by
Pamela Swinglehurst

GRANDMOTHER AND I MOVED from via de' Magazzini to via del Corno, in the autumn of '26. The two of us had been left "alone on the face of the earth," as she used to say; and via de' Magazzini, in the centre of the city, had, with the passing of the years, bestowed a new value on its buildings, and one by one the apartments had been sold. A business man and his wife had bought the one in which we were living: they came from Turin and needed the house, for meanwhile they were living in a hotel; they were planning to renew the flooring, to put up a partition for the bathroom, between the entrance and the kitchen; they offered us compensation money which grandmother refused. The eviction order was suspended for three months. Now we felt ourselves besieged: the old tenants of the block had left us (and Masi the tailor, anarchist and octogenarian, had died there just in time, at peace with God, of a broken heart) making way for the new owners of the property: the engineer from the first floor was personally directing the installation of electric light and gas, and the modernization of the building. We continued to hold out, alone and isolated, with our oil lamp, our coal stove, receiving looks of reproof, of irony, threats all down the stairs: by somehow refusing it, we were hindering the construction of a modern cesspool. And grandmother, obstinate and with such apparent naïveté, used to repeat to them:

"My husband had the house valued, but then they had second thoughts and didn't want to sell it any more. If now they've made their minds up to it, here are the twelve hundred lire of the estimate."

"Thirty years ago," they told her, "but now it costs twenty thousand. You were the first to be given the option and you let it go."

"Haven't I perhaps paid out twenty thousand lire in rent during these thirty years?"

"You'll lose the compensation money, if you resist the eviction order. With the compensation you'd find somewhere else to settle down, you and your grandson."

"We're comfortable where we are," she would answer. "I've been at home here for over thirty years, and raised children and. . . . Anyway, there aren't any places to be found at a rent to suit my purse. With the compensation money I'd be able to pay for a year or two, and then? Whereas here there are limits to how much they can raise my rent. I've already had to sell the parlour furniture so as to have something put away, in case I need it."

"There you are, you see?" they would say to her. "In fact all you need is one empty room with use of kitchen. And your compensation money would guarantee you a room, a modest one, with use of kitchen, for at least five years."

"But herded together with others, with no freedom any more, and who knows where, who knows in what street, and among what kind of people. I've been living where I am for more than thirty years, my children have been born and died here, my husband died here . . ."

And invariably, by now a kind of stock phrase, and as an argument as final as it was childish:

"For thirty years I've listened to the Palazzo Vecchio [1] chiming the hours."

In this way we went on resisting, with our oil lamp, the coke brazier and the doorbell you had to pull which no longer served any purpose. They had fixed the plate with the electric doorbells on the street door, the doors on the staircase had been varnished, the name plates were of polished brass, the stairs themselves freshly whitened, the glass panes of the skylight renewed. And our door, all scratched from wooden boots, the small card on which I'd printed Casati, the iron grille thick with the dust of years, these were an eyesore, an insult—until the morning when the engineer caught me scraping coal against the staircase wall. Two days later, taking advantage of a Court order which granted the rights to the new owner, bricklayers invaded our home, and began in the parlour by making a glass door there. We had to shift into the bedroom the settee, the table, and the two chairs which still remained of the furniture. And by now the second three months had passed, and it was a freezing November. Behind the locked shutters the chimes of the Palazzo Vecchio had a long sepulchral echo, the silence of the streets was frightening those nights, and grandmother's sighs sounded like a smothered agony: I stayed awake listening to her, boy that I was, with the haunting fear that, when her moaning stopped, she might sink into the sleep that would hand her over to death.

Then it was the 24th November and the bailiffs arrived, and granted us a further six days' grace, and since grandmother refused once more to accept the eviction notice, they pulled out one of the drawing pins and stuck the paper on the door above the little card. The bricklayers stood around watching.

"If you'll forgive my saying so," one of them offered, "I don't think you altogether appreciate the situation."

He was a man of about forty, with a local accent, his moustache cropped short at the corners of his mouth, and he wore a hat while he worked.

---

1. *the Palazzo Vecchio,* "the old palace," once the meeting place of the Signoria, the ruling body of Renaissance Florence.

"You'll find yourself in the street with your bed, what else do you expect?"

Grandmother was leaning on her shoulder at the window, gazing round her at the demolished wall and the missing floorboards, biting her lower lip between her gums.

"I moved into this house soon after I was married. It's because I'm an old woman alone with a young boy."

"It's because they're within their rights," said the bricklayer. "Have they bought the place or haven't they?"

"My husband also wanted to buy it . . ."

"Sure," said the bricklayer. "In the days when one and one made two."

And he offered to help us, he knew of a vacant room, "with use of kitchen," where one of his relations was living, in the via del Corno, among decent folk.

"It doesn't cost much," he said. "They're not grasping."

"So out of the way," said grandmother.

The bricklayer smiled.

"You've been living here for so many years and you don't know where via del Corno is. It's only a stone's throw from here, you just go down the via de' Gendi and you're there."

"Ah," grandmother exclaimed, "I know, let me think it over."

In the evening, quite out of the blue, breaking the silence as we lay in our beds, she said to me:

"Via del Corno isn't the kind of street for us. . . ." Then she added: "We mustn't leave them alone in the house any more, those bricklayers."

But it wasn't necessary: in the knowledge that we would anyway have to get out by the end of the week, work was suspended. The next day I wanted to have a look at the via del Corno, so near and unknown also to me: it was a short alley where traffic could not enter, but bustling, noisy, deafening compared with the via de' Magazzini, stinking of horses and with the washing hanging from the windows. There was a men's urinal on the corner, and it seemed to me that this could be reason enough to stand living there.

In the end, as the bricklayer had predicted, our bits of furniture found themselves lined up on the pavement, and the younger of the two bailiffs, a fair-haired man, asked us to thank him for saving us the expense of a porter.

"It feels like a deserted house" he remarked as we were all moving the cupboard. He turned to grandmother and added: "It isn't our doing, it's the law."

Grandmother shook hands with him. She had been hoping for a new delay, "as long as we don't sign, they'll never put the eviction order into force" she would say to me, but meanwhile she had paid a deposit on the place in via del Corno. We were going to have to adapt ourselves to the street, willy-nilly, after searching throughout those six days, and no feasible or better bargains having presented themselves.

Now I was coming back with a hired handcart, and the two bailiffs helped us to load our stuff onto it.

"We can't do any more," said the fair one, "we're late," and they left us, the two of us alone now in the middle of via de' Magazzini, with the barrow laden with all our belongings, just about as much as it would hold. Grandmother held under her arm the "enlargement" of my mother, with the photograph facing her bosom. She was outwardly calm, too much to be really so, her eyes were dry, her movements unhurried, as if now that the moment had come her anguish was sated; not even her voice betrayed any unwonted emotion. She tugged at the cords which held the household effects, making sure they were securely tied and that nothing was missing.

"It's all here," she said. "The two small beds, the linen chest, the table, the cupboard. We can do it in one trip. I did well to sell the ottoman, we couldn't have got it into this room of ours. We'll put the chairs on top when we move off, I've got the picture of your mother, good. . . . And now?"

"Now we'd better get going," I said.

"Yes, yes, of course," she went on. "The ropes will hold, we'll be there in a few minutes, I've got the money in my pocket, there's the box of pans, there's. . . . But will you be able to manage?"

"It's evenly loaded, and not heavy."

"It's our entire household," she said. "And now we're off to live in a street. . . . Remember now, good morning, good evening and no more, they're people with whom we have nothing in common, it's ill luck that takes us in their midst but it won't be for long, a month at the most. With a whole month ahead of us, we'll find something better, at least in a street such as this one of ours was for so many years, amongst decent folk."

It was ten o'clock in the morning; the via de' Magazzini silent and deserted, with its sliver of sky between the houses, the air numbing our hands, the occasional passers-by turning to glance at us and proceeding on their way, a cyclist ringing his bell as he passed our load.

"I have never been able to understand," said grandmother, "why there are always so few people passing here, right in the centre as we are, with the corner on via Condotta which is a constant bustle."

"But because it's only a side street, you'd need to have a reason for coming along it, it isn't a short cut, don't you think that's why? Rather like via del Corno. It's noisy there on account of the stables and because the people are different, you've said so yourself."

"Yes, yes, they can't be well bred like they are round here, they live in the street, they do a hundred different jobs, and what jobs. Well then, that's everything."

"Yes, that's the lot," I said, "and anyway we aren't exactly going to the ends of the earth."

"True true," she kept repeating. She was looking up at the windows, talking as if she'd returned after a long absence. "You were born there see? The open one, on the right near the drainpipe, it was at eleven in the morning, just about this time. . . . We've left both our windows open. . . . All the others are closed, of course," she answered herself, "it's cold already. I hadn't noticed that they'd put up the net curtains. It's darker inside the rooms, at this time of year, with the net curtains drawn. Your mother never would understand it. 'Does old Masi keep them like that?' I used to ask her. 'With the work he does, he'd be switching on the lights at two o'clock in the winter.' "

"It's for you to say the word," I told her.

I had grasped the two shafts and pushed the handcart forward. It was easy to move, as I'd expected. Grandmother was clasping the portrait to her breast, walking alongside of me. She didn't look back any more, on the contrary she walked faster and drew level with the cart, resting her hand on it to protect the load. In this manner we departed from our street for the new one, downhill, going down via de' Gondi, crossing a short stretch of the Piazza della Signoria, hugging close to the houses.

Just a few minutes previously I had been reflecting that via de' Gondi ran downhill, that I wouldn't be able to control the load by myself and that it would suit me better, although it would make our way longer, to go behind the Badia, along via del Proconsolo and across Piazza Sanfirenze; but then grandmother's behaviour, disturbed as I was by her words, had distracted me. And via de' Gondi seemed to come upon me without warning, unexpectedly, scarcely had we turned the corner.

Suddenly the load went out of control. The shafts were breaking my wrists, and I slithered but managed to hold on tightly to the shafts, my body doubled over the small chain which linked them, and thereafter it became a flight, absurd but nonetheless responding to some kind of physical law: the load was dragging me along and I was managing to keep it on a straight course, on an even keel, to the point of steering it to go gliding, there's no other word for it, up via dei Leoni, miraculously free of passers-by, cars, trams—until the final attempt, once more on level ground, to take the corner into via del Corno. At this point the left wheel went and jammed itself between the base and the metal screen of the little monument, uprooting it, the load turned over, the ropes broke, and all our poverty spilled over the pavement.

The inhabitants of via del Corno came running up, set me on my feet and supported me. The smith was ready with his bucket of water, and a woman made her way through waving a towel, before grandmother arrived on the scene and sank down at my side. Someone thought of picking up the chairs, which by now we were both glad to sit on, and already the incident was causing merriment. Unhurt but stunned, I was slow to appreciate all the commotion.

"The boy's a bit grazed, and the old woman's better than before," shouted a voice to someone above.

"They're Carresi's new tenants."

"It's nothing serious, they only came off the rails a bit."

And already our load was upright again, complete with all the junk which had tumbled out of the cupboard drawers; already grandmother was explaining that the lady in the photograph was her daughter, the boy's mother; already she was gladly accepting a drop of sweet wine to help her recover from the excitement. A woman was saying to her:

"In your room it'll seem as if you have the clock of the Palazzo Vecchio on your bedside table." ❖

Salvatore Quasimodo (1901–1968)
AND SUDDENLY IT'S EVENING

Translated from the Italian by
A. Michael de Luca

Each of us stands alone upon the heart of the earth
transfixed by a beam of sunlight:
and suddenly it's evening.

A REFUGE OF NOCTURNAL BIRDS

Translated from the Italian by
A. Michael de Luca

High on a cliff there's a twisted pine;
intently it listens into the abyss
with its trunk curved down like a crossbow.

A refuge of nocturnal birds,
5 in the deepest hours of night it resounds
with the swift fluttering of wings.

Even my heart has a nest
suspended into the darkness, and a voice;
it, too, lies awake listening at night.

HOMECOMINGS

Translated from the Italian by
A. Michael de Luca

Piazza Navona,[1] at night, on your benches
I would lie on my back in search of quiet,
and my eyes tracing straight lines and curving spirals
linked together the stars,
5 the same ones I followed as a child
stretched out on the dry stone bed of the Platani [2]
while I scanned my prayers in the dark.

"Homecomings" by Salvatore Quasimodo, as translated by A. Michael de
Luca (originally published in *Tutte le Poesie*) from SELECTIONS FROM
ITALIAN POETRY by A. Michael de Luca and William Giuliano. Copy-
right © 1966 by Harvey House, Inc. Reprinted by permission of Evelyn
Singer Agency.

1. *Piazza Navona,* a square in Rome. 2. *Platani,* a river of southwest Sicily.

I would clasp my hands under my head
and remember my homecomings:
10 odors of fruit drying on wicker mats,
of wall flowers, ginger, and lavender;
when I thought of reading to you, but softly,
(just the two of us, mother, in a dimly lighted corner)
the parable of the prodigal son,
15 which pursued me always in moments of silence
like a rhythm resounding in me persistently,
even against my wishes.

But the dead are not allowed to return,
and there is no time even for your mother
20 when you hear the call of the road:
I would then set out again, hidden by the night
like one who fears he will never leave if dawn comes.

And the road gave me my songs
which taste of grain ripening on stalks,
25 of the white olive grove blossoms
that mingle with blue flowers of flax and with jonquils;
rumbling sounds in the whirling road dust,
monotonous chants of men and creaking carts
their dim lanterns swinging,
30 scarcely as luminous as fireflies.

SOLDIERS CRY AT NIGHT

Translated from the Italian by
A. Michael de Luca

Neither the Cross nor His childhood image,
not the hammer of Golgotha,[1] nor His angelic
memory will suffice to obliterate war.
Soldiers cry at night
5 before dying; they are strong; they fall
at the feet of words learned
serving in the army of life.
Loving ciphers, soldiers,
anonymous outpourings of tears.

"Soldiers Cry at Night" by Salvatore Quasimodo, as translated by A. Michael de Luca (originally published in *Tutte le Poesie*) from SELECTIONS FROM ITALIAN POETRY by A. Michael de Luca and William Giuliano. Copyright © 1966 by Harvey House, Inc. Reprinted by permission of Evelyn Singer Agency.

1. *Golgotha,* Calvary, the spot where Jesus was crucified.

TO THE NEW MOON

Translated from the Italian by
Allen Mandelbaum

In the beginning God created the heaven
and the earth; then in His exact
day He set the lights in heaven,
and on the seventh day He rested.

5 After millions of years, man,
made in His image and likeness,
never resting, with his
secular intelligence,
without fear, in the serene sky
10 of an October night,[1]
set other luminaries like
those that turned
from the creation of the world. Amen.

---

1. *October night.* On October 4, 1957, the Russians launched Sputnik I, the first man-made earth satellite.

Giose Rimanelli (1926–   )

A MARRIAGE CONTRACT

Translated from the Italian by
Ben Johnson

WHEN ROSARIA WAS BORN, Seppe Melfi vowed it would be his last trip to America. He had made eight, one for each of his children, and now he was worn out. He said to himself, "I'll go and make enough to cover the dowry for this girl child. Then, never again. I'll buy me a field here, near the house, and watch the wheat grow out the window."

A field near home had been the dream of his life, a field where he could raise wheat and corn, and also have a modest stand of mulberry or fig trees, and—in a kitchen garden plot hoed alongside the well—grow roquette, eggplant, and other vegetables for the family. But when he returned from his last trip to America, the field he got was located a fifteen-kilometer walk away, or rather thirty, what with going and coming, and his wheat, while still sprouts, was got at by various goatherds who drove their animals into the field to browse. Seppe had to bring suit to put a stop to the outrage, and he saw his money eaten up in lawyers' fees. The affair made for bad blood, not to mention the drain on his earnings. But in return he saw his daughter grow before his eyes, a burst of flesh and blood, and a regular worker.

"Giuseppa, these creatures grow into females overnight," he said to his wife one evening. "What can it be inside them, can you tell me?"

"They shoot up fast, all right," the old woman answered. "Rosaria's already made herself three new dresses this year."

"Three new dresses? What in creation for?"

Old Giuseppa sighed and said, "Seppe, the time has come for this, too. And in a year, if no one's come forward, we'll have to take a measure of wheat to Picone. He'll handle the rest, he'll find her a fine young man, a husband."

"Ah, so that's it, eh? But it's early yet, it's early," he said. "And if it's only the asking part of it, Rosaria will have askers aplenty. Is there some way she doesn't come up to scratch? Are you trying to compare her with all the dry sticks in the cities?" He chuckled contentedly.

"No," the old woman said, "this girl of ours isn't lacking anything. She's white and red like a big apple. Even so, it's best to look ahead. There's no telling about the future."

The first suitor, however, was not long in coming. He was a peasant who worked a field bordering on the Melfis' land. He started by asking if he could have a drink from Seppe's well.

"My water tastes of tar," he called one day from his side of the boundary marker. "Somebody's been up to practical jokes."

"If it's only a drink you want, why, sure, help yourself," Seppe said. "You'll find the bucket hidden off the path in the third carrot row."

"To the right or left of the path?" the young man asked.

Old Seppe ran on, "You see, I've got to keep it hidden like a pearl or something; otherwise they'd steal it off me. People'd steal anything, even a bucket, seeing as nobody except the blind nowadays can make any money, and they just ask for it outright." He lifted a hand to his brow, against the sun, and yelled to his daughter, who was hoeing round the reed supports in the middle of the row of tomatoes, "Rosaria! Our neighbor Matteo

Tirchinelli is crossing over. He wants a drink of water. Get him the bucket. He'd never find it himself, there in the carrots."

"All right, Papa," the girl answered.

After that day, the young man crossed the boundary line many times and took to meeting Rosaria by the well. He told the old man that the water in his well must be special, because the more he drank the more he wanted to drink.

The official engagement followed soon after, and for the occasion Seppe wanted to do things up in grand style. He had already married off seven children, counting sons and daughters, but Rosaria was the last, and he wanted her engagement to be something to remember. Money was no object, proof of which was ten bottles of homemade rosolio [1] pressed by his womenfolk with the best extra-fine sugar, a basketful of salted cookie rings, another of sweet cookies, two quintals [2] of wine . . .

Seppe even hired a small orchestra at so much the evening, a fiddle, guitar, and trumpet, the kind of jazz group that only skilled workers could afford: the town was going to know that Seppe Melfi, peasant though he was, was not on his uppers and was getting his daughter engaged to the music of modern and difficult instruments.

"Country louts, yes, but also good workers," he said. "One's duty is one's duty, and nobody can say I scrimped by playing records."

But even with engagements that look to be the best made, things often happen that can't be explained. Inside three months the young man had broken it off. He wrote home from where he was serving in the army that it was all over between him and Rosaria, that uneducated girl whose letters to him were written by a married sister; he wrote that she didn't come out well in photographs; that at best she was only good for bearing children; and that, lastly, he had found himself a little Torinese dressmaker where he was serving who didn't wear her hair in a bun and didn't use old-fashioned hairpins. Therefore he was asking his parents and sisters-in-law to return the presents

---

1. *rosolio*, a sweet cordial. 2. *two quintals*, slightly over fifty gallons.

they had received from the Melfis and to get back the engagement ring and a silk kerchief, a foulard, he had given Rosaria as a love pledge.

Giovanni Tirchinelli wrote to his son, "No, you dog's son, I don't stoop to this sort of thing. The girl's a fine girl and I didn't throw her at you. Now, you marry her."

"I won't marry her," Matteo Tirchinelli answered. "And if you, dear Father, make threats at me—all right, I just won't come home. I'll sign up for five years and then maybe even get myself sent off to a war, seeing there's always one someplace in the world."

Young Matteo was adamant. And since the elder Tirchinelli needed his son's strong arms for work in the country, and since, at the thought that he might have himself sent off to war "someplace in the world," in his love for him he was frightened, he decided to undertake the recovery mission to Seppe Melfi's house.

"But one's word is one's word!" old Seppe stormed. "My daughter's a good girl, and if he doesn't marry her there'll be trouble!"

"Well, he wrote that he's got his reasons, for which he doesn't aim to marry her any more," Matteo's father said lamely.

"What d'you expect—*me* to marry my daughter? Was I the one always going over to talk to her back behind the well, with the excuse that the water there was so special?"

Matters threatened to grow worse and Giovanni Tirchinelli tried to change the subject by recalling the old bonds of friendship between the two men. He went on, "Look, Seppe, we're both old men, and old-fashioned men; stupid maybe, but honest; and for us our word is our word. We went to America together so's to give our young'uns a position, and we sweated blood and hopes. People who're born rich can't understand what we've done, and these youngsters can't understand, either. Remember that time in St. Paul, Minnesota, when the boss he came to us and said, 'Let's have a beer, boys, we've put up eight feet today'? Remember that?"

Seppe said Yes, he remembered the boss and the beer.

"That's water over the dam," he said. "But how is it your son gets engaged and then breaks the engagement? That's the question. How's that?"

Tirchinelli drew a breath. He felt abashed. He said that he personally wasn't able to give an answer to those questions. And what was more, the questions shouldn't even be raised. Young folks today are strange; they get all het up over nothing. They go to movies, they have passions and desires—and often, very often, dreams—and they notice things like if a girl is shorter or taller than another girl, or if she wears her hair in a bun and walks fifteen kilometers in the morning and fifteen in the evening with a hoe on her shoulder, or if another is a seamstress in a dressmaker's shop in the city and takes care of her fingernails and wears lipstick and maybe even comes out pretty in photographs. Can you ask questions about this sort of thing?

"Do you see, Seppe, in our day—" he started to go on, in a persuasive tone; but the old man cut him short. Seppe had realized it was all over and not even the threat of a dozen gunshots would help to put things right again. He got to his feet, striking a pose that could not help looking theatrical.

"Rosaria," he said, "open the door for our friends. And when they've left, don't close it right away. We've got to let out that stink they've brought in here."

Rosaria didn't cry, neither did she go to pieces. She was twenty and there was time enough for marriage. In fact, she made herself another dress, fire-engine red, and one that, every time she put it on, had the young bloods in the town looking at her with gloating slit-eyes.

"Now don't go making a hussy of yourself," her mother warned her. "I can't have people talking about us."

"Carmelino Ricagno has a low-cut green one and she's not a hussy," Rosaria countered.

"Except that you've got blood like the dress you've made yourself," said the old woman. "It makes me giddy to see you with it on. Just remember that young men are funny: they like things that are fine and out of the ordinary, but they marry girls who haven't put themselves on display, girls no one except them has had time to desire."

"All right, Ma, if you call it putting myself on display," said Rosaria, and she decided to wear her red dress only on Corpus Christi [3] and the few other official high feast days.

In the beginning, when she learned that Matteo Tirchinelli had thrown her over, she thought she would die of despair—she had grown used to having a fiancé. She did not cry and did not go to pieces when she had to give back to Matteo's father the ring and the other gifts, but at the same time she did feel as though she ought to wear black, as for the death of a child of hers. Her red dress was meant as a new window of hope opened on the future, and, for that matter, before long she had completely recovered from the hurt of her first love. Also, there was Carmelino Ricagno, her old friend with the low-cut green dress, who was always singing at her a local verse that went: *First love is fine, but second love is finer still* . . . And Rosaria inwardly set herself for another wait.

But matters at home took a critical turn—in fact, grew downright intolerable—when a second young man turned up to ask for her hand and, after a time and for no apparent reason, dropped plumb out of sight.

Seppe fumed, "Madonna, can it be that this girl of mine came so late that I'm doddering and can't blast somebody's back apart?"

"No, Seppe, you mustn't curse. What do we gain by cursing?" said old Giuseppa in a forbearing tone.

"Heaven—we gain heaven!" old Seppe shouted back, continuing to vent his fury. And from that evening on, for months, he stopped speaking to his daughter.

The Melfis now suspected that if things weren't working out, it was obviously not because of ill will on the young men's part, for they had come; but rather, it must have been Rosaria's fault:

---

3. *Corpus Christi,* a Christian festival in honor of the Eucharist, observed on the Thursday following Trinity Sunday.

whatever was wrong was couched deep down inside her, in her character.

"Otherwise," explained a brother-in-law of the girl, a man who considered himself to be "in the know," "it just doesn't figure that a girl gets engaged and then she's unengaged, just like that."

"That's true," old Giuseppa conceded. And turning to her daughter, she said in a voice that was almost gentle, "Rosaria, are you trying to drive me to my wit's end? Is that why you say nothing? Tell us, just for once now, why this Salvo fellow has gone and disappeared? Why did he drop you?"

"I don't have anything to say," the girl said stubbornly.

"Rosaria, a young man just doesn't run off if you haven't done something to him."

"I didn't do anything to him, either. Not a thing."

"Impossible! Why do you lie? Maybe you don't remember exactly what happened that night. You don't rightly remember, or else you don't want to say. But you *must* know what it was, hear?"

"Oh, Mamma, stop it!"

"All right, then. No more questions. But what's clear is that it's your fault, it's all your fault. A fine young fellow with book learning just doesn't pick up and leave for nothing."

And, in an access of bitterness, the old woman drove her hands into her hair and began to rock her head. In a chanting tone, like a lullaby, she started to repeat to herself, "What an unlucky mother I am! She wants to leave me a mother with a husbandless daughter. I got all her bridal linen ready and put it away in the bureau, and I sewed new dresses for her secretly so her father wouldn't find out, and if anyone put the slightest curse on her, I charmed it away, I, her mother; and what is my reward? A strange daughter, witless, growing older and costing me money, and still she wants to be left husbandless!"

Day after day, till it became obsessive, old Giuseppa repeated this chant. In the end, Rosaria burst out in a fit of exasperation, "I'm going to become a nun then! I won't be any more bother to you."

"What in heaven's name are you saying, daughter? Bother?" the old woman said. But she was racked by anguish.

Rosaria would not have taken the veil even if she had been on the brink of desperation; but, in bed at night, she wept, and she implored God to send her a husband, any husband, even a cripple or a drunk for a husband, a brute or a fool, to send her a man, and, if she didn't deserve a man, to send her half a man, *half* of a half a man, so long as he could be a husband for her.

"What have You got to lose, God, if You do me this favor?"

It was not that she could not do without a man: but she wanted a man now, even a quarter of a man, to escape the nightmare of spinsterhood and a state which at home had turned into blame, blame which was hers.

She had not slept for many nights; and as she lay awake she thought back over what had happened, remembering her first and second engagements. She had become convinced, from having it dinned into her head, that blame could be traced to her conduct with her fiancé. But for all the effort she put to finding reasons and causes, reasons and causes she could not discover. "I am not to blame!" she said finally to herself. "Or can it be that I *am* to blame, because I behaved properly?"

Her last fiancé had been a house painter, or rather a "painter," as he put it, giving himself the airs of a skilled worker. In the evening, when he came to the Melfis', he would sit by the fire, smoking and chatting, and occasionally sent out for a bottle of wine, which he and old Seppe drained. The painter addressed the old man as "Don Giuseppe," and little did it matter that Rosaria's father warned him, "Remember now, you're marrying the daughter of a peasant and not a don's daughter." But since he swore, among other things, that once Rosaria was his wife he'd make a lady of her, and that she wouldn't do any more hoeing, Seppe began to show toward him the first signs of opposition.

"This one here," he told his wife, "he's going to have us hogtied and helpless in no time, you just wait. I don't cotton to braggarts."

"He's not bragging," retorted the old woman, who for her part liked the painter. "This one here, in the work he's in, he can really make a place for himself. And Rosaria will share his place with him. And if they have children, he's the sort of father who'll make them study; and we, peasants that we've always been, will have grandsons who are professional men, some who'll even be doctors like Don Vincenzo Rinaldi."

"I'll be dead and buried and won't see any grandsons who're professional men," Seppe Melfi said dryly, faintly irritated.

Yet despite all the young man's fine talk, he always behaved correctly. Except one evening, Rosaria suddenly remembered. It had grown late, she remembered, and her parents had turned in. They were asleep in their big bed, which stood on trestles in the spacious kitchen, where, to have a fire in the hearth at that time of year, it was enough simply to stir the ashes a little with the andirons. To the young couple, the two oldsters in their bed looked like decomposed forms, diluted by the blankets, lying distant one from the other. The painter kept forgetting the old couple in the bed, who were raised on high, as on a catafalque, and were able to observe him. Not so Rosaria. Hunched over on the bench, her feet a bare span from the coals, she listened to him talk, and lazily, without perceptible movements, rolled her eyes toward the two forms immersed in the blankets, checking to see if the sharp eyes of her parents were on her.

That evening he drew shapes in the ash, and she woolgathered. She thought it was the fire warming her knees so, and the pleasure she felt was one of repose mingled with sleep. But it was the painter who, suddenly coming to life, had laid a warm hand on her thigh, as if by inadvertence somehow. He could feel her naked flesh through the coarse material of her skirt and he waited for her to rebel. And seeing that she didn't he thought that she, too, had been caught up in the weblike silence of the room and in that tantalizing game that flayed the senses, making them throb dully. Suddenly, overpowered by temptation, he threw his arms around the girl. Rosaria started up. Quickly the painter tried to calm her near the wall. The slap fell flat and loud like a gunshot against his puffy face; his expression wrinkled instantly into amazement. At that instant, as lust gave way to fear, he saw Rosaria as a stranger, an enemy even.

Seppe awakened, sitting up in bed.

"What happened?" he asked.

Rosaria trembled at the sound of his voice; but she found strength enough to reply, "Nothing, nothing. A chair fell over. Ciccio was just leaving."

Deep down, the old man felt the rekindling of an old anger. But he did not raise his voice. When daughters are engaged, fathers often pretend to shut an eye to things which would otherwise make them blush—fathers be they young or old, for in what happens to their daughters calls up their own never-confessed covetous desires.

"Go home now, it's late," Seppe said to the young man. "When she's your wife, you can spend all the nights of your life together, but this is my house, hear?"

The painter heard, and so perfectly that without so much as a parting word he gathered up his overcoat, went out and off, never to be seen again. Word later had it that he had moved to distant parts.

Winter wore into spring. And autumn, with its cold winds, came again, and the Melfis were still waiting for a fiancé for their daughter. The eligible young men, however, went to knock at the doors of other girls: two fiancés who have proved failures, vanishing without good reason, bring discredit on a girl. Rosaria in the meantime had grown slenderer, and she looked taller, almost beautiful. But she paid no attention to this beauty of hers, which arose from her very affliction, and she neglected herself more and more. She had come to believe, from having it dinned so into her ears, that it was entirely her fault if she didn't get married, that she was really to blame, so that on Sundays she took no care of her youth with a view to being admired by men, and out in the field plunged desperately into work, as if bent on harming herself, on working herself to death. Gradually she was becoming resigned to her misfortune.

But one person who did not resign herself to it was her mother. And one day, without a word to her husband, she took a measure of wheat to Picone, the matchmaker.

"I saw somebody's been grubbing in the grain bin," Seppe

Melfi said later, one evening. "Who'd you give all that wheat to?"

"Really, 'all that wheat'! You're always exaggerating, in everything," the old woman answered, pretending indifference. "Fra Caspio came by and I gave him barely an apronful, out of devoutness. Do you expect me to show disrespect for the saints? Do you want me to have the neighbors calling me stingy, all for an apronful of wheat?"

Seppe could feel it in his throat, his rage, when it was provoked, and now, as always, he couldn't spit it out; he remained silent, resigned, the man who knows that in his own home he has long since lost all power and domination. He didn't want people to account him tightfisted, and neither did he want to be disrespectful of the saints by denying alms to their custodians, the mendicant friars; but he was positively sure now that if that fat Capuchin friar turned up again and he was present, he'd throw him out of the house. Mendicant friars, in the villages of the Italian south, are like common beggars—filthy, insistent, at times irascible. Now they don't even have the silver snuffbox to give you a pinch in exchange for your offering, for the monasteries have deprived them of that, too.

However, one day—the Melfis were eating—Picone came to call; with him was a lanky, rawboned youth dressed in a cheap suit of plain grisaille, without pleats and with his trouser cuffs caked with mud.

"Here is a husband for the little Melfi," the matchmaker said, introducing the young man. "Seppe, won't you offer us a drink?"

Old Seppe barely lifted his head from his plate; a tremor, only just perceptible, coursed through his hands; instinctively he cast a glance toward the grain bin in the corner. This time, Caspio had had nothing to do with it. Even so, Seppe did not show any enthusiasm, partly because he had ceased to believe in his daughter's ever finding a fiancé. He had already held one party for her, when young Tirchinelli had declared his love, and new faces couldn't interest him. Having once squandered quintals of wine, now he didn't feel like offering so much as a glassful.

"What with all these engagements and marriages, my vineyard's gone dry," he said snappishly. "It's been a long, hard struggle. In the end, vineyards dry up."

Picone understood, but his trade no longer permitted him to blush.

"You mean to say, Seppe, that you don't honor your last-born daughter?"

"What's that?" broke in the old woman. "Seppe's out of sorts today. That hail yesterday smashed down the vines, and the vineyard was a river; and it nearly washed the straw hutch into the Cigno. That's why he's out of sorts. But do sit down, sit down. You're not of the town, my good young man, are you?"

"Montelongo," the youth answered as he took a seat. "And you must excuse me if I've tracked a little mud into your house. I've walked seventeen kilometers to come and see you here."

"This is Rosaria," said the old woman. "Do you know her?"

"I saw her once in a red dress, at the Marian Fair in May, and I said to myself then that she was a fine-looking girl. Then, only a week back, Picone spoke to me of a marriage deal with her."

"My daughter's a deal, all right, and the man who marries her raises a rose on his balcony," the old woman asserted smiling. "Well, then, what are you asking for her?"

"What's usually put down in writing is what's right. No more."

"We'll draw up a regular contract," Picone said. "And if the girl's already got a little dowry, all the better. Times are what they are and families aren't built on serenades; you need a bedrock foundation. Love is a fantasy of the rich."

"I can't say you're wrong. . . . Now you're beginning to talk," the old woman said. "We'll draw up a marriage contract."

The young man, whose name was Vincenzo Trecase, was a day laborer on the railroad. A serious fellow, Picone said, honest, a worker. What's more, he didn't drink, smoke, or swear.

"And these are virtues worth more than gold," Picone added.

"And my daughter, too, is serious and a worker. So then, when will we have this marriage?"

"Far as I'm concerned, I'm ready now," Trecase said. "I've got all the furniture stored at the carpenter's, and he's just waiting for me to set up house. Walnut; fine work. Does she, does Rosaria, like walnut furniture?"

He looked at her. And she, for the first time in the evening, looked at him, responding with a forced smile she found an intolerable strain, almost like a wound. She did not like him; yet at that moment, when their eyes met, she realized that this man sitting before her was her husband-to-be, the husband fated to her all these many years; and now, at their first meeting, he aroused in her neither fluster nor joy nor regret. She was without feeling.

The next week Picone drew up a duplicate copy of the marriage contract between Rosaria Melfi and Vincenzo Trecase. For the occasion, all of Rosaria's trousseau was spread about the room, on chairs and on the old couple's bed, so that Trecase could see it and the go-between could make a list of it. This formality took an hour, and then Picone read the marriage list, which, for the two parties concerned, would have the validity of a notarized document. He read:

"MATRIMONIAL NOTE OF ROSARIA MELFI, PEASANT, *daughter of Giuseppe Melfi and Giuseppa Puglisi, wife-to-be of Vincenzo Trecase, laborer, born at and resident of Montelongo in the Province of Campobasso.*

"Before me, Armando Picone, marriage broker and real estate agent, the following matrimonial note, valid for the sole purpose of marriage between the aforesaid couple, is hereby recorded:

  4 *sets of sheets;*
  8 *sets of pillow cases;*
12 *bath towels;*
14 *nightgowns, two of them trimmed with silk lace;*
  1 *bolt of yardgoods;*
  1 *basketful of diapers;*
  1 *set of white table linen for twelve;*
  1 *set of pink table linen for six;*
10 *white napkins;*
  1 *white combination;*
  1 *pink combination;*

1 *yellow combination;*
1 *flannelette combination;*
4 *skirts;*
6 *skirts;*
6 *pairs of panties;*
1 *blanket trimmed with handmade white lace;*
1 *blanket of Berlin wool;*
1 *copper amphora, capacity* 10 *liters of water;*

as well as assorted personal effects not hereinabove listed which the bride will remove to her husband's domicile on the act of marriage.

"Before me, Armando Picone, it is further noted that Rosaria Melfi brings to the marriage a dowry of 50,000 *lire cash, now deposited in her name in a bank, the passbook of which is in my possession and will be given over to Vincenzo Trecase on the act of marriage together with a* tomolo *of land located at Lama, in the Commune of Casacalenda, which Rosaria Melfi also brings to the marriage as dowry.*

"Read and hereinbelow signed . . ."

There followed the signatures of Trecase, the broker, and Seppe Melfi. Not listed was a quilt coverlet, and since buying a new one was an expense the Melfis could scarcely afford then or even after the harvest, when the wheat would be marketed, the old woman decided to deprive herself of her own and give it to her daughter. Vincenzo Trecase did not protest.

"New or old," he said, "just as long as it's there, like it's supposed to be."

After that, every weekend Vincenzo Trecase came to visit his intended, making the trip by foot whether there was rain or wind. He moved about the house at his ease, and knew where to find the comb, the mirror, the shoebrush, the broom from which to snatch a millet thread to pick his teeth after meals. He came into the family with the air of a person who had always been a member.

"What about Ciccantonio Delli Veneri?" Seppe asked him. "How's he holding up?"

"Oh, he's on his last go-round—he's at the old folks' home. He's had tough luck is how they reckon it in Montelongo. Everything he owned went down the drain on account of a son that wanted to become a lawyer. They were supporting him in Naples."

"And Jacurti, the son of Gemma Natabene—Jacurti with the goatee like Victor Emmanuel—'s he alive or dead now?"

"He's gone back to America. He's got a widowed sister in Montelongo, but they don't write."

"Eh, America. What's he expect he's going to do in America, old as he is? He must be living off his son, and it's no fun in America having to count on others when you can't earn a day's wages yourself any more. What's he doing back there?"

"He's back there, though. One day, two years ago, he put on his hat and took the bus to Campobasso. He said, 'I'm taking the boat from Naples and going back to America, seeing as I'm a citizen there.' And he actually went back."

Seated in a corner, Rosaria listened to their talk and sewed. She was sewing her wedding gown.

And she was beautiful on her wedding morning, when she put it on. She sat silently, a little haggard round the eyes after a sleepless night, letting the nimble fingers of the embroidery teacher fuss about her, arranging the lace, the train, and the orange blossoms, which every now and then, like electric wires, refused to stay in place in her hair and formed about her head a kind of halo for an Immaculate Conception.

"I've brought some lipstick, too," the teacher said. "Now if you'll only just sit still a minute, Rosaria, I want to put a little on your lips."

Rosaria instinctively screwed up her mouth, but her kinsfolk who were present broke in, "It's nothing to be ashamed of. Try it, Rosaria, it even tastes good."

"It's putty," Rosaria said. "I don't like it."

"It's good. Why do you think all the city ladies wear lipstick?"

Eventually brought around, she even submitted to being painted, because the embroidery teacher could only have had her own good at heart: in all the years she had taught needlework, she had dressed as brides more than three hundred pupils, and they had all made good impressions with a little lipstick on their mouths.

Now they were waiting for the groom. Seated in the middle of the room with her white patent leather pumps in her lap (when she stood in them those new shoes had proved to be veritable scissors), Rosaria was looking out beyond the door at the sky brushing the treetops and packed with menacing rain clouds, and her mind was a blank. She could also see the chicken-wire boundary fence beside the field, and the expanse of cardoons—thick, bristling tendrils—and a cat with a crazy-quilt coat; but her mind was a blank as the din of her kinsfolk rose and fell round about her as they all, then, began to feel the first signs of weariness.

Some boys had been sent to the highway as lookouts. From time to time one of them would burst into the house and shout, "No one in sight." A spell of silence. He liked the bride sitting there like a statue in the middle of the room, mute, saying nary a word, with those white shoes in her hands.

"Nobody yet," he would say.

"Go back and look again," old Giuseppa would say, hustling the boy out.

It began to drizzle. The appointment in church had been set for eleven o'clock. Now eleven had already struck through the rain from the church tower, and still neither hide nor hair of Trecase or of his witnesses was to be seen. In those who had been waiting in their Sunday best since early morning, weariness began to give way to a dull, pulsing sense of panic. Only the bride appeared to be calm as she sat unstirring, with unseeing eyes focused on her new patent leather pumps. Then a tear, but such a sliver of a tear that it was virtually impossible to see, started from her eye and down her cheek, trying to snake its way through her powder. "He's never coming again—I should've known it," Rosaria thought. And instantly a short-lived idea—the uncovered well in the field—crossed her mind: the well where (she had been a child at the time) Michelina the washer-girl had gone and thrown herself because of some personal grief on the eve of her wedding. Except that Michelina had not been dressed in her bridal gown, and she was; but running through the door, past the boundary fence out to the well—the gate, which always stood wide open, was to the left, and around it, perhaps, the ground was all a puddle of mud now—would only take an instant, running with the shoes in her hands.

The children burst in suddenly, the whole troop of them.

"They're coming!" they cried.

The witnesses were dressed in black; Trecase, however, was in his everyday clothes, the suit with the eternal crust of mud on his trouser cuffs. They closed their umbrellas as they stepped inside, holding them in their hands to drip.

"Are you thinking of going into church looking like that?" the old woman demanded, almost flying at Trecase.

The young man darted a glance at old Giuseppa and rapidly around at the assembled relatives; then he averted his eyes. He had caught a glimpse of his betrothed, but just out of the tail of his eye; now the white, composed mass of Rosaria blurred before him like a cloud bank.

He said, "I'm not marrying."

Gasps—a confused roiling—and then the bride leaped suddenly to her feet and just as suddenly, forlorn, moaning, collapsed all in a heap back onto her seat, still clutching her patent leather shoes in her hands. Nothing more happened and Trecase waited for the crack of rifle shots. Then, after a few seconds— how much larger and emptier the room seemed now!—one of Rosaria's sisters-in-law, a woman whose husband was on overseas duty with the army and who lived in the most respectable quarter of the town, crossed toward him and said, "Why not?"

Trecase shook his head.

"Why not?" the sister-in-law shouted still louder, right beneath the young man's chin, glaring at him as though she wanted to claw his eyes out.

"The marriage contract," one of Trecase's witnesses spoke up, "has not been respected."

"What's missing?" demanded the sister-in-law.

"Here," said Trecase, fishing a crumpled sheet from his pocket and pointing to a line. "This is missing, and I think there's something crooked going on."

"Why?"

"It says here:

'One copper amphora, capacity 10 liters of water.' That's what it says and that's the way it's got to be," said Trecase. "Instead there isn't any, it's missing. How come?"

"My son," the old woman then said, "is it for such a silly little thing that you don't want to get married?"

"I like things on the up and up. I made a check this morning and there was no amphora. Since it's listed here, I want it, and if you don't mean to give it to me, then I'm not getting married," said Trecase.

"But it's an oversight, my son," said the old woman, well aware that it had been an intentional oversight and she had hoped he would not notice it. "That can be straightened out," she said. "I'll give you mine. Go and get it. It's the one I myself brought in marriage as part of my own dowry. Go and get it. This girl must go to the church!"

"I want the one listed in the contract. I've already taken your quilt, I can't take your amphora now."

"But I'm giving it to you."

"I want the one promised me in the contract."

The relatives stood all together in a corner of the room, with bated breath. Then they saw Seppe Melfi rise up from his seat; they saw him cross to an old dresser, open it, and rummage through the linen into the pockets of the black suit he had prepared for his death day. All that was missing from the outfit was a pair of patent leather shoes, and the old man had been laying money aside to buy the shoes. One goes to heaven in black, with shoes on, just the way one goes to be married. Seppe was getting out that money. Gripping it tight in his fist, he thrust it out to Trecase.

"With this," he said, "you'll be able to buy yourself a fine amphora."

Trecase looked at the money clenched tense in the fist and again shook his head.

"I don't want it," he said. "I can buy an amphora with my own money."

"Take it!" the old man urged. "It may be money for my funeral shoes—put aside with much time and hard work, two lire a month, because even a peasant's got to have shiny shoes when he's dead—but now . . . now they can even bury me barefoot."

He was gripping the money tight in his fist in front of Trecase's tanned face.

"Well, are you going to take it?"

They could hear the rain outside, thin and glistening in the pale sun; and the relatives could be heard—their shoes, an occasional cough. Outside in the rain, a small boy—visible through the doorway, bareheaded—threw his arms up happily and suddenly shouted, "Hooray for the bride!"

The shout had the effect of drawing Trecase's eyes back to Rosaria, who was sitting ashen and sullen in her place; and the tension in him relaxed. He gestured helplessly and moved toward her.

"Let's go," he said. "Haven't you put your shoes on yet?"

Under opened umbrellas, the bridal procession set out down the Corso, which led to the church. Indolent, busy people came to their windows to peer into the street from behind closed shutters. But when they saw the small, bedraggled procession coming forward as though begging the houses' pardon, they closed their windows again. Only the butcher, planted among quarters of beef hooked to grappling irons, his arms crossed on his chest—only the butcher bowed and smiled at the couple, and said in a strong voice, "Good luck, and may you have male children! Good luck!"

And when the procession entered the church, even the rain let up, and the sun turned yellower, almost warm. ✤

Umberto Saba (1883–1957)

BEGINNING OF SUMMER

Translated from the Italian by
A. Michael de Luca

Pain, where are you? I do not see you here;
everything I view is hostile to you. The sun
is gilding the city, it is glimmering on the sea.
Vehicles of all kinds on the shore front
5 are carrying something or someone here and there.
All is in joyful motion, as if
it were happy to be alive.

Ignazio Silone[1] (1900–   )

THE PARTING OF THE WAYS

Translated from the Italian by
Barbara Loeb

PIETRO SPINA'S APPOINTMENT with Battipaglia, interregional secretary of the Party, was set for an afternoon in Rome in a small church on the Aventine.[2] When Pietro arrived, he found his comrade already there, pretending to be reading a church notice fixed to the wall near the door. He had not seen Battipaglia for many years and prison life had plainly aged him, for he had grown somewhat stooped and his hair had turned gray. Pietro stood beside him for a moment, and, to attract his attention, leaned close to the wall, peering at the notice as though nearsighted. Then he went through the door.

The church was unfamiliar to him. A double row of arches, resting on the shafts of variously proportioned ancient columns, divided it into three parts. The columns, which were without bases, rose straight up from the floor, and each of the roughly chiseled capitals was different from the others. The stone floor

1. *Silone* (sē lô′ ne). 2. *the Aventine,* one of the seven hills of Rome.

was almost entirely overlaid with mortuary slabs, and, at the end, the high altar, surmounted by a crucifix of black-painted wood, with four candlesticks, looked like a simple tomb. Only two women were in the deserted, gloomy interior, kneeling under a burning lamp before the altar of the Sacrament. Pietro stopped near the door, beside the holy-water stoup. Battipaglia followed him in, but first made a slow tour of the church before going up to him.

"I've had money to give you for over a month," Battipaglia said in a guarded tone. "And I've got a new passport for you. Is your health better?"

"The passport's of no use to me now," Pietro said. "I'm not leaving the country again."

"That's your business," said Battipaglia. "As you know, you're responsible directly to Foreign Headquarters, not to me. I'll send you the passport by Fenicottero. By the way, who's the girl you've been sending to us from Fossa with your information?"

"Her name's Bianchina. She's the daughter of an innkeeper."

"Is she a Party member? How long has she been one?"

"She's not one, but we can still trust her. She doesn't know my true identity or the real purpose of her trips."

"Isn't that risky?"

"Even if she found out, she wouldn't give me away."

"Your business. It's not my job to lecture you. Is she your mistress?"

"No."

"Your business. You're not responsible to me, as you know. The girl mentioned some rabble-rousing priest who must be in your mountains, somebody called Don Paolo. D'you know him?"

"No."

"You ought to contact him. He might be useful to you."

In the meantime a sacristan had come in through the sacristy door and lit two candles on the high altar. Announced by the sound of a bell, a priest in his sacred vestments appeared from the same low door and stopped to pray before the lowest step leading up to the altar. A scuffling of feet outside the church preceded the arrival of the faithful, among whom were a few nuns. They dipped their fingers in the stoup, crossed themselves, and then moved quickly toward the altar.

"Did you make any headway in the south?" Battipaglia asked.

"The peasants down there are a hard lot," Pietro said: "they have more feeling for Gioacchino da Fiore than for Gramsci. 'Liberation of the South' is a bourgeois utopian dream."

"Since there's been no direct contact with you," Battipaglia said, "Foreign Headquarters has asked me to get an answer from you at once on the last Party resolution. It's a formality more than anything else, you know."

"I'm not much good at formalities," said Pietro. "You know that."

"Naturally, no one thinks you'll hesitate in declaring your solidarity with the majority of the Russian Communist Party," said Battipaglia. "You're an old comrade and we all respect you."

"To tell you the truth," Pietro said, "I really don't know what it's all about. It's hard enough for me to understand my home town, let alone my region. How can you expect me to pass judgment on agrarian policy in Russia, approve certain opinions and disapprove others? It doesn't make sense, you know."

"Did Bianchina bring you those three reports?"

"Yes. But I haven't read them yet."

"And when do you think you'll get around to it? Foreign Headquarters wants an answer from you right away."

"I don't know when I'll be able to read all that rubbish," Pietro said. "I don't even know if I'd be able to understand it well enough to form a serious opinion about it. I've got something else—the situation here and now—to worry about." And, making a great effort, he added: "Look, I'm not going to pretend. I'll tell you the truth. I burned those reports. I would have been running a useless risk carrying them about on me, and besides, quite frankly, they don't interest me."

"What you've done is pretty serious," Battipaglia said. "You realize that, don't you?"

"To put it briefly," Pietro ran on, "I don't feel capable of judging questions I have no experience of. I'm not going to submit to any sort of conformism. I can't condemn or approve without seeing for myself."

"How dare you call our condemnation of Bukharin [3] and the other traitors conformism? Are you crazy, by any chance?"

"Always to be siding with the majority is pure conformism," said Pietro. "Don't you think so? Every one of you was for Bukharin when he had the majority with him, and you'd be for him now if he had the majority with him. How can we destroy Fascist slavery if we deny the spirit of criticism? Answer me that, if you can."

"Do you mean to suggest that Bukharin isn't a traitor?"

"I really don't know," said Pietro. "All I know is that he is now in the minority. Furthermore, I know that that's the only reason you dare to oppose him. Just answer me one question: Would you all be against him if he had the majority with him?"

"Your cynicism is going a little too far," said Battipaglia, scarcely able to contain his indignation.

"You haven't answered my question. Try and answer it sincerely, if you can."

"If it were left to me, I'd expel you from the Party here and now."

Battipaglia was shaking with emotion, and after a long silence, unable to give vent to his feelings in the church, he left, without a word of parting. Pietro did not move; he remained standing motionless, with his back against the stoup. The service was still going on. In the dim candlelight, the gold of the monstrance glittering on the altar formed a luminous crown round the priest's white head. At last the ceremony came to an end and the handful of worshipers started toward the door. One of the nuns, touching her fingers to the holy water to cross herself, was suddenly struck by Pietro's distraught look. She stopped and looked at him intently.

"Do not despair," she said quietly, with a smile.

---

3. *Bukharin,* Nikolai Ivanovich Bukharin (1888–1938), Russian Communist leader and active Marxist propagandist. Bukharin was executed in 1938 for allegedly participating in counterrevolutionary activities.

"What do you want?" Pietro demanded.

"Take heart," said the nun. "Do not be discouraged."

"Who are you?" asked Pietro. "And what do you want?"

"Do not be discouraged. The Lord never tries anyone beyond his powers of endurance. Can you pray?"

"No."

"I'll pray for you. Do you believe in God?"

"No."

"I will pray to Him for you. He is the Father of us all, even of those who do not believe in Him."

The nun hurried away to rejoin her companions. Shortly after, Pietro left the church, too. Evening had fallen. ✛

David Maria Turoldo (1916–   )

THE SECRET OF CAIN

Translated from the Italian by
Margo and Anthony Viscusi

Now I am
a man without mystery.
Already
in the first burnt noon
5 I saw the face of God.
Now I am
absolute emptiness:
a frightful evening desert
with nothing but the bitter joy
10 of meeting myself
no more.

Now night hangs heavy over me
but I still walk vigorously
only to leave tracks
15 on the burning dune;
and have them say, "Even beyond there
he went exploring . . ."

"The Secret of Cain" by David Maria Turoldo (trans. Margo & Anthony Viscusi) from MODERN EUROPEAN POETRY (originally published in *Io non ho mani*). Reprinted by permission of Casa Editrice Valentino Bompiani & Co.

Oh! if I had stayed
with the beasts I love most
20 to plow the fields, and then tired,
to sleep sound on any heap of stones,
would this
perhaps
have contented me?

25 Tortures of my heart
set me on my shepherd brother,
to pity him;
the voluptuous pity of testing
what it was to kill; then
30 to run away
from the tortures of God.

I didn't kill
to be alone (my solitude
is the putrid seething of a rivermouth
35 clogged by the filth
of rotten seaweed).

Howling
to drown the absurd silence
that dogged me
40 I fled the woods
to build cities.

I didn't kill
from envy of God:
holding out to Him the first fruits,
45 stubbornly
I hid my face.

Nor that I might see
beast leap at beast; I remember

all was still calm,
50 immersed in deep peace
like a sleeping virgin.
The world
still wore
an innocent smile.

55 Suddenly my veins
turned black, a mysterious being
danced in me.
The unbearable balance at last
was shattered. The silence
60 of the soul's life shattered
at last
by Cain.

And from that moment
my own hands dug my ditch
65 but I did not die:
in there the immense roar
of all those memories tracks me.
Now I seek the infinite silence
and I wait to be hurled in
70 by someone.

WINDY DAY

Translated from the Italian by
Margo and Anthony Viscusi

I have no pity
for this naked heart of mine;

just as one windy day
a tree was beating the glass
5 with insane arms
the sea was one huge sob;

and there on the shore
foam-covered stones
were scarcely breathing,
10 and there was wreckage
of boats and branches
and a shoe tossed among pebbles
and the tatter of a dress;
and I from my cell window
15 watched laughing.

"Windy Day" by David Maria Turoldo (trans. Margo & Anthony Viscusi)
from MODERN EUROPEAN POETRY (originally published in *Chelsea*).
Reprinted by permission of Casa Editrice Valentino Bompiani & Co.

Giuseppe Ungaretti (1888–1970)

Translated from the Italian by
William Giuliano

MORNING

I am enlightened
By the immenseness of immensity.

NOSTALGIA

When
night is about to fade away
a little before springtime
and rarely
5 does someone pass

Over Paris thickly floats
a gloomy color
as of weeping

In a corner
10 of a bridge

I contemplate
the infinite silence
of a young girl
sylph-like

15 Together
our maladies
are fused

And as if carried away
we remain

I AM A CREATURE

Translated from the Italian by
Lowry Nelson, Jr.

Like this rock
of San Michele [1]
so cold
so hard
5 so desiccated
so impervious
so utterly
unspirited

Like this rock
10 are my tears
you cannot see

Death
we redeem
by living

"I Am a Creature" by Giuseppe Ungaretti, as translated by Lowry Nelson, Jr., from CONTEMPORARY ITALIAN POETRY, edited by Carlo Golino (originally published in *L'allegria of Giuseppe Ungaretti*). Reprinted by permission of The Regents of the University of California.

1. *San Michele* (sän mē ke′ le), an island in the Venice lagoon.

Giovanni Verga (1840–1922)

THE ORPHANS

Translated from the Italian by
D. H. Lawrence

THE LITTLE GIRL appeared in the doorway twisting the corner of her apron between her fingers, and said, "I've come."

Then as nobody took any notice of her, she began to look timidly from one to the other of the village wives who were kneading up the bread, and added: "They told me, 'You go to Neighbour Sidora's.' "

"Come on, come on," cried Goodwife Sidora, red as a tomato as she turned from the oven-hole. "Wait and I'll make you a nice breadcake."

"That means they're bringing the extreme unction [1] to Neighbour Nunzia, if they've sent the child away," observed the Licodia goodwife.

One of the women who was helping to knead the bread turned her head round, keeping on working with her fists in the kneading-trough all the time, her arms bare to the elbows, and asked the child:

1. *extreme unction,* the anointing of the dying, in Roman Catholic ritual.

"How is your step-mother?"

The child didn't know the woman, so she looked at her with wide eyes, and then lowering her head again, and rapidly, nervously twisting the corner of her apron, she mumbled in a low tone:

"She's in bed."

"Don't you hear there's the Host [2] in the house?" replied the Licodia woman. "Now the neighbours have begun to lament round the door."

"When I've got the bread in the oven," said Neighbour Sidora, "I shall run across for a minute myself to see if they're not wanting anything. Master Meno will lose his right arm if this wife dies as well."

"There's some who have no luck with their wives, like others who are always unlucky with their cattle. As many as they get they are bound to lose. Look at Goodwife Angela!"

"Last night," added the Licodia woman, "I saw Neighbour Meno standing on his doorstep, come home from the vineyard before Ave Maria,[3] and he was wiping his nose with his handkerchief."

"Yet you know," added the gossip who was kneading the bread, "he's a blessed good hand at killing off his wives. In less than three years this makes two daughters of Shepherd Nino that he's finished off, one after the other! Wait a bit, and he'll do for the third one, and then he'll get everything that belongs to Shepherd Nino."

"But is this child here Neighbour Nunzio's daughter, or is she by the first wife?"

"She's by the first wife. And the second one was as fond of her as if she was her own child, because the little orphan was her niece."

The child, hearing them speaking about her, began to cry quietly in a corner, to ease her aching heart, which she had kept still up till then by fidgeting with her apron.

---

2. *Host*, the consecrated bread used in the Christian sacrament of Holy Communion. 3. *Ave Maria*, the recitation of the Angelus at noon.

"Come here then, come here," said Neighbour Sidora again. "The breadcake is all nice and done. There, don't you cry, your mamma is in Paradise."

Then the child wiped her eyes with her fist the more readily because Neighbour Sidora was just setting about to open the oven.

"Poor Neighbour Nunzia!" a neighbour woman came saying in the doorway. "The gravediggers have set off just now. They've just this minute gone past."

"Save us from it! I am a daughter of Holy Mary!" exclaimed the goodwives crossing themselves.

Goodwife Sidora took the breadcake from the oven, dusted the ashes off it, and gave it fiery hot to the child, who took it in her pinafore and went off with it very quietly, blowing on it.

"Where are you going?" Goodwife Sidora shouted after her. "You stop here. There's a bogey-man at home, with a black face, and he runs off with folks."

The orphan child listened very seriously, opening wide her eyes. Then she answered with the same obstinate little voice:

"I'm going to take it to mamma."

"Your mother's gone away. You stop here," repeated the neighbour. "You stop here and eat your breadcake."

Then the child squatted on the doorstep, so unhappy, holding her breadcake in her hands without thinking about it.

All at once, seeing her father approaching she got up quickly and ran to meet him. Neighbour Meno entered without saying anything, and sat in a corner with his hands hanging between his knees, long-faced, his lips white as paper, not having taken a mouthful of food since yesterday, he was so broken-hearted. He looked round at the women as if to say: I'm in a sad way!

The women, seeing him with his black kerchief round his neck, surrounded him in a circle, their hands still white with flour, sympathizing with him in chorus.

"Don't talk to me, Neighbour Sidora," he repeated, shaking his head and heaving his shoulders. "This is a thorn that'll never come out of my heart! A real saint that woman! I didn't deserve her, if I may say so. Even yesterday, bad as she was, she got up to see to the foal that is just weaned. And she wouldn't let me fetch the doctor so as not to spend money nor buy medicine. I shall never find another wife like her. You mark my word! Leave me alone and let me cry. I've reason to!"

And he kept shaking his head and swelling his shoulders, as if his trouble was heavy on him.

"As for finding another wife," added the Licodia woman to cheer him up, "you've only to look round for one."

"No! no!" Neighbour Meno kept repeating, with his head down like a mule. "I shall never find another wife like her. This time I'll stop a widower. I'm telling you."

Goodwife Sidora lifted up her voice:

"Don't you talk rash, it doesn't do! You ought to look round for another wife, if for no other reason but out of regard for this poor little orphan, else who's going to look after her, when you're away in the country! You don't want to leave her in the middle of the road?"

"You find me another wife like her if you can! She didn't wash herself so as not to dirty any water, and she waited on me in the house better than a manservant, loving and so faithful she wouldn't have robbed me of a handful of beans from the shed, and she never as much as opened her mouth to say, 'You give me this!' And then a fine dowry with it all, stuff worth its weight in gold! And now I've got to give it back, because there are no children! The sexton told me just now he was coming with the holy water. And how fond she was of that little thing there, because she reminded her of her poor sister! Any other woman, who wasn't her aunt, would have cast the evil eye on her, poor little orphan."

"If you take the third daughter of Shepherd Nino everything will come all right, for the orphan and the dowry," said the Licodia woman.

"That's what I say myself! But don't talk to me, for my mouth is bitter as gall."

"That's not the way to be talking now," seconded Goodwife Sidora. "Better take a mouthful of something to eat, Neighbour Meno, for you're at your last gasp."

"No! no!" Neighbour Meno kept repeating. "Don't talk to me about eating, I've got a knot in my throat."

Neighbour Sidora put before him on a stool the hot bread with black olives, a piece of sheep's cheese, and the flask of wine. And the poor fellow began to munch slowly, slowly, keeping on mumbling with his long face.

"Such bread," he observed, becoming moved to tenderness. "Such bread as she made, the poor departed soul, there wasn't her like for it. It was as soft as meal, it was! And with a handful of wild fennel she'd make you a soup that would make you lick your fingers after it. Now I shall have to buy my bread at the shop, from that thief of a Master Puddo, and I shall get no more hot soup, every time I come home wet through like a new hatched chicken. And I shall have to go to bed on a cold stomach. Even the other night, while I was sitting up with her, after I'd been hoeing all day breaking up the lumps on the slope, and I heard myself snoring, sitting beside the bed, I was so tired, the poor soul said to me: 'Go and eat a spoonful. I've left the soup for you warm by the fire.' And she was always thoughtful for me, at home, mindful of whatever there was to be done, this, that and the other, so that she could never have done talking about it, telling me her last advice, like one who is setting off for a long journey, and I hearing her all the time murmuring when I was half asleep and half awake. And she went happy into the other world, with her crucifix on her breast, and her hands folded over it. She's got no need of rosaries and masses, saint that she is! The money for the priest would be money thrown away."

"It's a world of troubles!" exclaimed the neighbour woman. "And now Goodwife Angela's donkey, just close here, is going to die of indigestion."

"My troubles are worse than that!" wound up Neighbour Meno wiping his mouth with the back of his hand. "No, don't make me eat any more, for every mouthful goes down into my stomach like lead. Better you eat, poor innocent child who don't understand anything. Now you'll have nobody to wash you and comb your hair. Now you'll have no mother to keep you under her wing like a mother hen, and you are lost as I am. I found you that one, but another step-mother like her you'll never have, my child!"

The little girl, all moved, pushed out her lips again and put her fists in her eyes.

"No, you can't do no less, I say," repeated Gossip Sidora. "You've got to look for another wife, out of regard for this poor little orphan who'd be left on the streets."

"And me, how am I left? And my young foal, and my house, and who's going to see to the fowls? Let me weep, Neighbour Sidora! I'd better have died myself, instead of that poor soul who's gone."

"Be quiet now, you don't know what you're saying, and you don't know what it means, a home without a master!"

"Ay, that's true enough!" agreed Neighbour Meno, somewhat comforted.

"Just think of poor Goodwife Angela, if you like! First she's lost her husband, then her big son, and now her donkey is dying as well!"

"If the donkey's got indigestion, he'd better be bled under the girth," said Neighbour Meno.

"You come and look at it, you understand about it," added the goodwife, "You'll be doing a work of charity for the soul of your wife."

Neighbour Meno got up to go to Goodwife Angela's, and the orphan ran after him like a chicken, now she had no one else in the world. Gossip Sidora, good housewife, reminded him:

"And what about the house? How are you leaving it, now there's nobody in it?"

"I've locked the door; and then Cousin Alfia lives just opposite, to keep an eye on it."

The ass of Neighbour Angela was stretched out in the middle of the courtyard, with his nose cold and his ears drooping, struggling from time to time with his four hoofs in the air, while the pains contracted his sides like a big pair of bellows. The widow, sitting before him on the stones, with her hands clutching her grey hair, and her eyes dry and despairing, watched him, pale as a dead woman.

Neighbour Meno began to walk round the animal, touching its ears, looking into its eyes, and as he saw that the blood was still flowing from the side, black, drop by drop, collecting at the ends of the bristly hairs, he asked:

"Then they have bled him?"

The widow fixed her gloomy eyes on his face without replying, and nodded her head.

"Then there's nothing more to be done," concluded Neighbour Meno, and he stood there watching the ass stretch itself out on the stones, rigid, with its hair all ruffled like a dead cat.

"It's the will of God, sister!" he said to comfort her. "We are both of us ruined, both of us."

He had seated himself on the stones beside the widow, with his little girl between his knees, and they were silent all of them watching the poor creature beating the air with its hoofs, from time to time, just like a dying man.

When Gossip Sidora had finished taking the bread from the oven she too came into the courtyard, along with Cousin Alfia, who had put on her new dress, and her silk kerchief on her head, to come for a minute's chat, and Gossip Sidora said to Neighbour Meno, drawing him aside: "Shepherd Nino won't be willing to give you the other daughter, seeing that they die like flies with you, and he loses the dowry if he does. And then Santa is too young, and there's the danger that she'd fill your house with children."

"If only they were boys, never mind! But what there is to fear is that they'd be girls. I'm a downright unfortunate man."

"There's always Cousin Alfia. She isn't so young as she was, and she's got her own bit, her house and a piece of vineyard."

Neighbour Meno turned his eyes on Cousin Alfia, who was pretending to look at the ass, with her hands on her hips, and he concluded:

"If that's how it is, we can talk about it after. But I'm a downright unlucky man."

Goodwife Sidora up and said:

"Think of those that are worse off than you, think of them."

"There aren't any, I tell you! I shall never find another wife like her! I shall never be able to forget her, not if I marry ten times more! Neither will this poor little orphan forget her."

"Be quiet, you'll forget her. And the child as well will forget her. Hasn't she forgotten her own true mother? You just look at Neighbour Angela, now her donkey is dying! And she's got nothing else! She, yes, she'll always remember it."

Cousin Alfia saw it was time for her to put in too, with a long face, and she began again the praising of the dead woman. She had arranged her in the coffin with her own hands, and put a handkerchief of fine linen on her face. Because she had plenty of linen and white things, though she said it herself. Then Neighbour Meno, touched, turned to Neighbour Angela, who never moved, no more than if she was made of stone, and said:

"Well, now what are you waiting for, why don't you have the ass skinned? At least get the money for the hide." ✣

DISCUSSION QUESTIONS

Alfieri: THE FREE MAN *(page 27)*

1. What does "His countenance is bare, but the rest of him is armed" (line 4) mean?

2. Is the poem too romantic, too idealized, to have any relevance for free men today?

3. Alfieri's "The Free Man" and William Wordsworth's "London, 1802" are both sonnets in the Italian tradition. (The English Romantics made great use of the Italian sonnet, did very little with the Shakespearean.) Compare these two poems for tone and content.

Alvaro: THE RUBY *(page 28)*

It is commonplace that we frequently do not recognize our most prized possession, and instead overvalue the inferior.

1. "The shopkeeper, who was a boy at heart, often imagined that the pen nibs were of pure gold and he cherished them as a small boy cherishes tinfoil-wrapping off chocolates." Discuss the contribution of this sentence to the story.

2. Although the Italian does not recognize the monetary value of the ruby, he does obtain satisfaction in possessing the "lump of red crystal." Explain his appreciation of it, and explore the meaning of this appreciation for the story.

Basile: THE CAT CINDERELLA *(page 34)*

1. Almost every folk tradition has its Cinderella story and, in each case, the story conforms, at least in some ways, to a pattern: Cinderella, kind, gentle, guileless, is drudge of the house, dirty with housework, while her sisters attend fine balls. Then a fairy arranges for Cinderella to attend one of the balls, too. A prince falls in love with her and finds her by means of a slipper which she drops and which fits no foot but hers. The story is usually told with a great deal of seriousness, its moral being that meekness and virtue are rewarded in the end. In what ways is Basile's tale typical of the traditional Cinderella story and in what ways is it not?

2. The story opens, "In the sea of malice, envy always exchanges ruptures for bladders. . . ." What is the meaning of this metaphor and how is it related to the story?

Betti: CORRUPTION IN THE PALACE OF JUSTICE *(page 41)*

Is justice possible in a corrupt world? This fundamental question seems to be posed by Ugo Betti's strange and haunting play.

1. What does Betti gain by his vague setting: ". . . a large severe room in the Palace of Justice" in "a foreign city"?

2. The play has some of the aspects of a mystery drama. Wherein lies its suspense?

3. Early in the play Erzi says "It is a leper we're looking for." Who is the leper? Why is *leper* a particularly apt epithet to describe this sort of criminal?

4. After Cust's inadvertent confession, the dying Croz says: "That's why we judges are all hypocrites, all of us stuffed with stale rancid sausage-meat. That's what the real corruption in these courts is, the whole place stinks terribly of it; I can't wait to be free of it" (page 103). Discuss this speech in its context and in the context of the entire play.

5. Consider Croz's role in the play. Explore the reasons why he, at the crucial moment, declares himself guilty. What is the meaning of his message to Cust that "every man has to scratch his own scabs by himself"?

6. Elena loves her father with what Betti calls a "pure love" —she loves him not as a possession, a thing, but as a human being. Explain her role in the play. Was her death an accident or suicide, or is it important that we know? Discuss the effect of her death on the incidents that follow in the play.

7. What happens to Cust between the report of Croz's death and the end of the play?

8. As the play ends, Cust opens the door which leads to the office of the Lord High Chancellor "which has hitherto remained unopened" and starts *up* the long staircase. What is implied by this action?

9. It is very plausible that a man in Cust's circumstances would grab at the chance to escape punishment, and many mod-

ern playwrights, having given a character that opportunity, would allow him to take it. But Betti calls such an approach to the theater nihilistic. Drama, he says, must affirm man's capabilities for goodness, not destroy them. He states that ". . . in the soul of the judge who betrays justice, we will discover that, in the end, he himself cannot breathe or survive without justice." He holds that man's need for love and forgiveness will finally overcome the most hardened bitterness. Does Betti make a convincing case for this viewpoint in the drama, or do you find the final scene artistically false?

10. In both *Hamlet* and *Corruption in the Palace of Justice* images of disease, death, and corruption run like a thread through the play. What reasons can you find for this use of similar imagery?

Boccaccio: FEDERIGO'S FALCON *(page 113)*

1. "Federigo's Falcon" appears to be a tale told, not to illustrate life, but to illustrate a principle. What are some of the antirealistic elements in the story? What is the principle illustrated?

2. What is the function of Monna Giovanna's son in the tale?

3. "Federigo's Falcon" anticipates O. Henry's "The Gift of the Magi" by over five hundred years, yet there is a marked resemblance between the stories. Point out the elements that are similar.

THE ONE-LEGGED CRANE *(page 119)*

Wit. Craft. Cunning. These are the tools of the trickster and Chichibio possesses them all.

1. The narrator describes Chichibio as "a bit of a fool." Is he? Why might the narrator have called him one?

2. Chichibio is typical of one of literature's most popular heroes: the man who lives by his wits. Discuss the appeal of this type of character.

3. To what extent are Currado, Chichibio, and Donna Brunetta types and to what extent are they individuals? What difference does the form their characterization takes make in this tale?

4. What makes this story amusing?

TORELLO'S HOSPITALITY *(page 122)*

1. The plot of this tale is shaped in crucial places by coincidence and fantasy. Are these a weakness in the story or do they tend to make it more enjoyable? Explain.

2. Though not bound to reality, does the tale contain any moral truth? Discuss.

3. A critic has written about this tale: " 'Torello's Hospitality' consists of a series of disguises and revelations, suggesting, perhaps, that deep within lies an identity that is sometimes suppressed by form and tradition." Discuss the disguises assumed, the motivation for the disguises, and the consequences. What does the quoted statement as a whole mean? Do you agree or disagree with it?

PATIENT GRISELDA *(page 139)*

1. Is Griselda a well-rounded or a one-dimensional character?

2. In the frame that encloses the story (paragraphs 1–4) the tale-teller expresses his attitude toward Gualtieri. What is this attitude? If this frame is removed, how is the story affected?

3. The tale-teller concludes: "What more is to be said, save that divine souls are sometimes rained down from Heaven into poor houses, while in royal palaces are born those who are better fitted to herd swine than to rule over men?" Explain the meaning of the statement in terms of the characters in the story. Is the tone of the sentiment expressed more closely related to the frame-story paragraphs or to the narrative itself?

4. Chaucer in the "Clerk's Tale" of the *Canterbury Tales* also tells the story of Patient Griselda. Read and compare.

Bontempelli: MIRRORS *(page 150)*

Bontempelli relates his tale of some highly unusual events with the easy familiarity of the oral storyteller.

1. What details in the opening paragraphs of the story help to create the impression that it is being told orally? What are the advantages in this presentation? Find indications that the speaker is amusing himself as well as his audience in spinning his tale.

2. In the last sentence of the story, the speaker describes him-

self (and his image) as "indifferent and tranquil." Why isn't he disturbed by such fantastic events? Find other incongruities between the nature of events and the reactions of the speaker. What do they suggest about the way the reader should react to the tale?

3. ". . . it is not an uncommon thing (even if science has not yet explained it) to find a lost article in the very place where one has looked for it many times before." Is this observation meant merely to be comic, or is it a comment on human nature?

4. Speaking of mirrors, the narrator says that the moment people (especially women) "pull themselves away . . . from the mirror into which they are looking, they feel a slight sense of discomfort." Is this statement simply a part of the fantasy and humor, or is there some psychological justification for the "discomfort" described? And why "especially women"?

5. An old saying contends that there exists an "innate hostility in inanimate objects." Are the objects in this story hostile toward the narrator? What comment might the author be making in portraying the objects as he does? Can you describe some frustrating or annoying or mysterious event involving objects that resembles the tales of the umbrella and the mirror?

Buzzati: SEVEN STORIES (*page 154*)

1. What is the nature of Guiseppe Corte's disease? Would our reaction to the story be different if we were told that the disease was tuberculosis or cancer?

2. Is Corte transferred down because he's dying, or does he die because he's transferred down? What two very different meanings do these two interpretations of his death give the story?

3. An early description of the nursing home tells us: " . . . the patients were divided into seven progressive castes. Each floor was like a little world in itself, with its own rules and special traditions which were meaningless on other floors." What does this passage (and similar ones throughout the story) suggest about the symbolism of the nursing home? What are some of the possible reasons for there being *seven* stories, thereby giving the title to the story?

4. In one of the closing paragraphs, the author says: "And thus, by virtue of a monstrous error, he [Corte] arrived at the last station. . . . The situation was so grotesque, really, that he felt at times a desire to roar with laughter." Explain the "monstrous error" and discuss Corte's reaction to his situation.

Carducci: THE OX *(page 171)*

1. The ox's eyes dominate the poem, appearing in three of the four stanzas. What is it about the eyes that attracts Carducci? What do they seem to reflect?

2. What attitude toward life does the poem express?

ANCIENT LAMENT *(page 172)*

This is a very personal poem, written to a dead child (the poet's son who died at three), the "blossom of my tree."

1. Does the poem's subjectivity make you feel close to the poet, as if he were an old friend sharing a deep and terrible sorrow with you? Or does the poem, with its emphasis on the internal, exclude any universal application that might make it appealing? Must a writer always remain objective in order to communicate?

ALPINE AFTERNOON *(page 173)*

1. Here Carducci has as much painted a picture as written a poem. Mentally shift the poem to canvas. Are the images blurred? sharply defined? Is the scene overwhelming? awe-inspiring? inviting? Does it make you want to be part of it? If not, how does it fail?

2. A technique question: What is the subject of the single sentence in the first stanza? What is the effect of its placement?

Cellini: *from* THE AUTOBIOGRAPHY *(page 174)*

Benvenuto Cellini was talented, handsome, energetic, ingenious, a little cracked-brained, and always aware of his own supremacy.

1. Based on the portion of *the Autobiography* that you've read, do you think the string of adjectives used above to describe Cellini is entirely accurate? Why or why not? If you were making your own list, what would you add?

2. Using for a basis the incident in which Lucagniolo and Benvenuto compete to see whose work makes the most money, discuss the ways in which Cellini reveals more than he means to about himself.

3. Many readers go to Cellini's *Autobiography* not to learn about Cellini so much as to learn about his time. Judging from the portion you have read, assess its value as a commentary on the period.

D'Annunzio: THE END OF CANDIA *(page 192)*
   1. The following lines are from Shakespeare's *Othello:*

   Who steals my purse steals trash; 'tis something, nothing;
   'Twas mine, 'tis his, and has been slave to thousands;
   But he that filches from me my good name
   Robs me of that which not enriches him,
   And makes me poor indeed.

Discuss the relevance of this quotation to "The End of Candia."
   2. Early in the story Candia is described as having "the head of a bird of prey mounted on a turtle's neck." What other animal images are used to describe her? How do these affect your attitude toward her?

   3. When the townspeople accuse Candia, we are told that she "was all the more keenly stung by the unjust charge, because she knew herself to be capable of the action they attributed to her." Explore the soundness of this psychological observation.

   4. Guy de Maupassant's "A Piece of String" also deals with someone who is unjustly accused of theft. Read the story; then try your hand at a brief essay in comparative literature.

D'Annunzio: THE RAIN IN THE PINE GROVE *(page 203)*
   1. What is the dramatic situation which structures this poem?
   2. What is the relationship between the man and woman and the natural scene described?

   3. The Italian poet Carducci (see page 185) had a marked influence on D'Annunzio's poetry. Can you find anything reminiscent of Carducci's work in this poem? What in the poem makes it fresh and original?

Deledda: THE SARDINIAN FOX *(page 206)*

1. On his first visit, the doctor believes that Zana and her grandfather are undernourished and therefore poverty-stricken. What does the author accomplish by reporting the doctor's mistaken impression?

2. Why does the doctor yell "fox" at the end of the story?

3. To whom does the title of the story refer? Is there more than one fox?

4. "The Sardinian Fox" may be considered a local-color story. Compare it with a story by one of the American local-color writers, for example Bret Harte, Mary Wilkins Freeman, or Sarah Orne Jewett.

Erba: THE INATTENTIVE *(page 219)*

1. What is Erba describing: actual people? the most vulnerable part of a child's spirit—the part ultimately destroyed by life? imaginary creatures who symbolize the life of the imagination? What do *you* think Erba is writing about?

2. Erba's friends, as he calls them, are all children. Is this significant? Discuss.

3. What might the "pitiless fevers" that destroy the friends be?

4. To what is the "I don't know" of line 34 an answer?

5. Who are the "inattentive"?

Leopardi: THE INFINITE *(page 221)*

1. In the two closing lines, the poet refers to his thought being "drowned," and to himself as "Foundering in that sea." Explain this metaphor.

THE EVENING AFTER THE HOLY DAY *(page 222)*

1. At the end of the poem the speaker hears someone singing, and gradually the singing dies in the distance. Relate this episode to the rest of the poem.

TO THE MOON *(page 224)*

1. This poem embraces two experiences, the experience of "a year ago" and the present one. In both the poet climbs a hill to view the moon. Reconstruct the first experience as imaginatively as you can, and relate the second to it.

Machiavelli: THE DEVIL TAKES A WIFE *(page 225)*

There is a tradition going back to Pandora's box of woes and Eve's eating of the apple that lays the blame for the world's troubles on women.

1. The story opens with Pluto determined to test the accusation that most men who ended up in Hell were led there by marriage. Does the rest of the tale affirm or deny the truth of the accusation? Explain.

2. Machiavelli's satire exposes the vices of society at the time he wrote. Describe them and discuss their relevance to today's world.

3. The story of the man clever enough to outwit the wily old devil himself is common in literature. Perhaps America's most popular contribution to this tradition is Stephen Vincent Benét's "The Devil and Daniel Webster." Read this story. Then try your hand at a brief essay in comparative literature.

Machiavelli: *from* THE PRINCE *(page 235)*

1. Machiavelli frequently seems to take a position contrary to expectation, or even a paradoxical position, and then to demonstrate its practical application or truth. Explain the following statements in Machiavelli's terms:

a. "A prince ought to have no other aim or thought, nor select anything else for study, than war and its rules and discipline" (page 235, line 1).

b. "Therefore, a prince, not being able to exercise this virtue of liberality in such a way that it is recognized, except to his cost, if he is wise he ought not to fear the reputation of being mean" (page 238, paragraph 2).

c. "Therefore a prince, so long as he keeps his subjects united and loyal, ought not to mind the reproach of cruelty" (page 240, paragraph 2).

d. "Nevertheless our experience has been that those princes who have done great things have held good faith of little account, and have known how to circumvent the intellect of men by craft, and in the end have overcome those who have relied on their word" (page 243, paragraph 2).

2. American politicians today have no handbook such as this one, but it might be interesting to compare Machiavelli's work with some of the ideas in one of Theodore White's books on the making of a president.

Moravia: THE SECRET *(page 246)*

1. Moravia uses first-person narration, letting the truck driver tell his own story. The narrator is thus placed in the position not only of telling what happened, but also of analyzing and explaining his feelings. Discuss the advantages and disadvantages of this point of view in this particular story.

2. When, after the confession of the hit-and-run behavior of the truck driver, the girl is pressed to tell what she is thinking about, she confesses to be thinking about a shoe sale. How does this revelation affect the truck driver?

3. At the movie the girl is moved to tears. Discuss the irony of this incident.

4. Did you like the truck driver of the story? Did you find him deserving of sympathy? Why or why not?

Ortese: A PAIR OF GLASSES *(page 253)*

"A Pair of Glasses" is about seeing, but there are two kinds of seeing: physical seeing and spiritual seeing, sight and insight.

1. Compare and contrast the details in the domestic scene that opens the story with Eugenia's first view of the world through her new glasses (page 255, paragraph 1). Why is it important to the story that Eugenia first "see" the world on the Via Roma?

2. What kind of person is Zia Nunziata? How do you account for the apparent contradictions in her actions?

3. What function does the Marchesa D'Avanzo serve?

4. What makes Eugenia sick, the shock of strong glasses or the sights she sees?

5. The story is notable for the vividness and profusion of details describing the setting. Why might the author include such sharply observed scenes in a story about a blind child?

6. What elements of this story might lead you to consider it a social protest? Does the inclusion of such elements necessarily lessen its value as a piece of literature?

Palazzeschi: BISTINO AND THE MARQUIS *(page 272)*

The motif of the immutable niche in the social order is common in literature, but Palazzeschi gives it an inverse variation.

1. Discuss the influence of class on the behavior and values of each of the three principal characters.

2. Is this simply a story of a caste system or is it also about brotherhood—does each character do what he has to do to make another's (as well as his own) life more tolerable? Explain.

3. In connection with the above, comment on the following: "The story focuses on the relation of Bistino and the Marquis, who in effect change places: Bistino at first served the Marquis; the Marquis now serves Bistino. The old relationship persists only in hollow form; the Marquis is used by both Nunzia and Bistino to fulfill their psychological needs."

4. This story is full of little rituals important to the characters that populate it. What do these rituals tell you about Italian life?

Petrarch: POEMS TO LAURA *(page 295)*

Time and distance alter many things, but they have little effect on human emotions. Writing six hundred years ago, Petrarch expressed the same emotions—the ecstasy, the agony, the melancholy, the inspiration—that lovers sing of today. The poems to Laura are divided by time into two periods: those written while she was alive and those composed after her death.

1. Read the nine sonnets to Laura printed in this anthology. Sonnet 3: "It Was the Morning," describes the poet's first sight of Laura. Trace the poet's changing moods as the love affair continues. Which sonnet marks the death of Laura? How does the poet react to her death?

2. What was the "blessed day/Whereon the Sun in pity veiled his glare" (Sonnet 3)? Read the different things the poet says about Love. By what other term is this personification of Love known? Explain the difference in origin between the allusion in

the first quatrain and the allusions to Love. Trace the allusions to Love through sonnets 36 and 47.

3. The standard Petrarchan—or Italian—sonnet consists of fourteen lines divided into an octave and a sestet, the first rhyming *abba abba* and the second usually *cde cde*. The octave is frequently a presentation to which the sestet is some kind of resolution (a problem followed by a solution, a complaint followed by an explanation, etc.). Choose one of the sonnets and examine it along the lines suggested above.

4. What is the thought pattern followed in each of the stanzas of "It Is the Evening Hour"?

5. This poem, like the sonnets, is written to Laura. Where would you place it in the sequence of sonnets you have read?

6. Sir Thomas Wyatt (1503–1542) and Henry Howard, Earl of Surrey (1517–1547) probably introduced the Petrarchan sonnet into England. During the reign of Elizabeth various forms of the sonnet evolved and many sonnet sequences were written. Among the most famous are Sir Philip Sidney's *Astrophel and Stella,* Edmund Spenser's *Amoretti,* and William Shakespeare's *Sonnets.* Read some of the earlier sonnets by Wyatt and Surrey or sample one of the sonnet sequences. Compare the form and idea with Petrarch's.

Piovene: THE DRESSMAKER'S DAUGHTER *(page 307)*

1. Discuss the process of reasoning by which the aristocratic lady came to the conclusion that Anna was somehow above her background. How does her reasoning characterize the lady herself?

2. Roberta reminds Anna "exactly of the white highlight on a green leaf or the cold sap that sets one's teeth on edge." Later in life, when Anna recalls her, she feels "a sensation of acid chill, accompanied by a scent like that of spring flowers with their slender stalks and pale green shadowless leaves." Explore the meaning of these images and sensations. Do they seem an apt description of Roberta?

3. Why does Anna despise and bury her food?

4. Why is the story entitled "The Dressmaker's Daughter"?

Pirandello: THE MAN WITH THE FLOWER IN HIS MOUTH (page 318)

If a man learns when he is going to die, how will he spend the time remaining to him? Many writers have attempted answering.

1. What is the effect of the title, "The Man with the Flower in His Mouth"? Why is the man never identified or given a name?

2. What is the role of the Commuter in the Man's life? Does the Commuter act as you expect him to? As he probably *should* act? Discuss.

3. Near the end of the play, the Man talks of a series of things; for example, after saying, "I would kill myself if I ever . . ." he immediately begins to talk about the wonderful flavor of apricots. Use this example (or another) as a springboard for exploring the state of mind of the Man.

4. Explain the Man's attitude toward his wife.

5. Compare Pirandello's Man with the narrator in Buzzati's "Seven Stories" (page 154). Are both writers saying essentially the same thing? Discuss.

Pratolini: THE REMOVAL (page 327)

One's life can become so deeply attached to a place that to move means a kind of death.

1. The story ends in a disaster which turns out to be the ultimate success. Explain.

2. The Grandmother concludes her arguments with: "For thirty years I've listened to the Palazzo Vecchio chiming the hours." How does this statement characterize the old lady? What do the chimes serve to symbolize later in the story?

3. Despite its background of poverty, this story is warm, gentle; the move is made to seem almost an adventure. What does the point of view contribute to this feeling?

4. Like "The Removal," Anna Maria Ortese's "A Pair of Glasses" (page 253) has as its subject the poor and poverty. Compare the two stories for mood and tone.

Quasimodo: AND SUDDENLY IT'S EVENING *(page 335)*

1. In this poem about the brevity of life, what does evening symbolize?

2. Judging from Quasimodo's choice of words and images, speculate on his attitude toward existence and its end.

A REFUGE OF NOCTURNAL BIRDS *(page 335)*

1. In what way is this poem a comment on poetry?

2. Poetry and its creation is a favorite subject of poets in their verse. Does Quasimodo give any fresh insights into the poetic process that make this poem worth knowing? Discuss.

HOMECOMINGS *(page 336)*

1. What two periods of his life does the speaker link by his mention of the Piazza Navona and "the dry stone bed of the Platani"? On what does his memory dwell?

2. Explain the opening line of the third stanza: "But the dead are not allowed to return."

3. Why do you think the title uses the plural form of *homecoming?*

SOLDIERS CRY AT NIGHT *(page 338)* and TO THE NEW MOON *(page 339)*

1. God plays a role in both these poems. How does Quasimodo view Him?

2. Is Quasimodo anti-man in either of these works? Explain.

3. Compare these two poems (both written after World War II) to "Homecomings" (written early in the poet's life) and tell what you learn about the changes that time made in Quasimodo, both as a man and as an artist.

Rimanelli: A MARRIAGE CONTRACT *(page 340)*

The arranged marriage, in which a young girl is little more than a commodity, is a sad but common fact of life in many societies.

1. How do you account for Rosaria's lack of success in attracting a suitor?

2. When Vincenzo Trecase is first brought to Rosaria by the marriage broker, he is described as a "lanky, rawboned youth

dressed in a cheap suit." What in his behavior indicates the kind of man he is and the kind of marriage in store for Rosaria?

3. What sort of person is Rosaria? Why, even after his insulting behavior on her wedding day, does she marry Vincenzo?

Saba: THE BEGINNING OF SUMMER *(page 359)*

1. What details does the speaker cite as characteristic of the summer scene?

2. Is he in tune with this scene? Explain your answer.

Silone: THE PARTING OF THE WAYS *(page 360)*

1. At one point Spina asks Battipaglia, "How can we destroy Fascist slavery if we deny the spirit of criticism?" Explain Battipaglia's reaction to the question. Discuss the meaning of the question as a thematic statement of the story.

2. The church service is described at the end of the story, followed by Spina's chance encounter with a nun. Analyze the effect of this ending.

Turoldo: THE SECRET OF CAIN *(page 365)*

1. When is the "now" with which the poem opens?

2. Why, according to Cain, did he kill Abel?

3. Compare "The Secret of Cain" to the version in *Genesis*. Discuss their similarities and differences.

WINDY DAY *(page 368)*

Explain the connection between the first two lines and the remaining ones. Is this a happy poem? Discuss.

Ungaretti: THREE POEMS *(page 369)*

1. Relate the title of the poem "Morning" to the poem itself. What is gained by the extreme brevity of this poem?

2. In "Nostalgia" the "gloomy color" of Paris is described "as of weeping." Explore the meaning of this metaphor. What details extend the idea?

3. The last stanza of "I Am a Creature" is a reversal of the usual view that Christ's crucifixion redeems our life at death. What view of life does Ungaretti set forth in the first two stanzas? How does this lead to the concluding reversal?

Verga: THE ORPHANS *(page 372)*

Goodwife Sidora tries to lessen Neighbor Meno's grief by uttering a universal platitude: "Think of those who are worse off than you, think of them." And Neighbor Meno answers in kind: ". . . I shall never be able to forget her. . . ."

1. The shrewd goodwife tells Meno: "Be quiet, you'll forget her. And the child as well will forget her. Hasn't she forgotten her own true mother? You just look at Neighbor Angela, now her donkey is dying! And she's got nothing else! She, yes, she'll always remember it." What does this speech reveal about the lives of the people in the story? Has Goodwife Sidora made a valid observation about human nature, or only about the characters in the story, or merely about her own character? Discuss.

2. Why is the story of the donkey included, especially in such vivid terms (we see it actually die)? The last line of the story is given to the potential worth of the donkey's hide. What value does Verga stress by ending the story this way? Why might he have chosen Meno to point out this value? What does Meno's interest in the hide suggest about his future: will he continue to grieve the loss of his wife, or will he marry Cousin Alfia?

3. (In English, the word *orphan* is usually applied only to a child whose mother and father are dead, but its Italian equivalent is used to describe a child who has lost only one parent by death as well as those who have lost both.) The title of the story is plural, yet only one child has been orphaned. Who is the other orphan, and why is he considered one?

BIOGRAPHIES OF AUTHORS

Vittorio Alfieri (1749–1803)

Remembered primarily as Italy's greatest tragic dramatist, Alfieri was also a military figure, a fighter for freedom, a satirist, a memoirist, and a lyric poet. Among his most interesting lyrics, for American readers at least, are five odes grouped under the title *L'America libera* [*The American Liberation*] which were written during various stages of the Revolutionary War.

Dante Alighieri (1265–1321)

Dante Alighieri (usually called Dante) was born in Florence into a family of the lower nobility. The most important event of his youth was his seeing a Florentine girl, Beatrice, when he was nine and she was eight. It was not until some nine years later that she first spoke to him. Overcome with his feelings for her, Dante began the composition of his first work, a series of love poems. He remained quite remote from Beatrice, worshipping her from afar, until her death in 1290, when Dante was twenty-five. Although the identity of Beatrice has remained in dispute, her reality in Dante's imagination clearly grew and endured. When for complicated political reasons Dante was exiled from Florence for the last twenty years of his life, and he turned to the writing of his masterpiece, *La Commedia* [*The Divine Comedy*], he introduced Beatrice as the spirit of love guiding him through Paradise. In this greatest of all Christian allegories, Dante portrays himself, led by the Latin poet Virgil, as progressing through Hell, Purgatory, and ultimately into Paradise. The poem appears to be the sum of all medieval theology and mythology, and includes a great many topical references. In *The Divine Comedy* Dante produced the greatest poem of the Medieval period, and one which continues to this day to awe readers and inspire poets.

Corrado Alvaro (1895–1955)

Alvaro was born in Calabria in southern Italy. He fought in World War I and afterwards became both a journalist and novelist. He worked for a series of newspapers until his death, but at the same time turned out novels that were praised as being evocative and lyrical. Among his best known works is *Revolt on the Aspromonte* (1930), which combines elements of realism with something of the fabulous to create an effect uniquely Alvaro's.

Giambattista Basile (1572–1632)

Like many writers, Basile became famous for the work which he did not take seriously, while his serious work lies forgotten. He collected fairy tales as they were told around his native Naples, and thought so little of them that he published them under a pseudonym, Gian Alesio Abbatutis—an anagram of his real name (using the same letters, but scrambling them). He called his work the *Pentameron*, to suggest it was half-*Decameron* (see page 113); his storytellers go on for five days, while Boccaccio's talk for ten. Basile's fairy tales combine realism and fantasy in strange mixtures, and they are told with earthiness and imagination.

Ugo Betti (1892–1953)

Ugo Betti was a professional magistrate and used the courts and the judiciary as the setting for a number of plays which point to the larger social responsibility for crime and evil. He published a total of twenty-six dramas, many of which seem to have been written more for reading than for production. Among the best of his plays are *The Queen and the Rebels* (1949), a revolutionary drama which emphasizes the ironies and ambiguities of idealistic social upheavals, and *Corruption in the Palace of Justice* (1944). Despite often frightening themes Betti's work displays a strong belief in man's basic goodness, a love of God, and a recognition of His power and benevolence.

Giovanni Boccaccio (1313–1375)

Boccaccio, poet and humanist, friend of Dante and Petrarch, is to Italy what Chaucer is to England. Indeed, Chaucer read Boccaccio and used many of his plots and techniques. Almost nothing is known of Boccaccio's early life except that it was spent largely in Naples. In 1340 Boccaccio went to Florence and was there during the great plague of 1348. He used the plague as the background for his masterpiece, the *Decameron*. The one hundred stories range widely in length, mood, and effect; but they tend to be earthy in nature and to emphasize the role of fortune and fate in men's lives and to demonstrate the triumph of shrewdness and endurance.

Massimo Bontempelli (1878–1960)

Massimo Bontempelli began as a teacher, but after a few years he devoted his entire time to writing. In 1926 he helped to establish a new magazine, entitled *900*, for which James Joyce served as a foreign editor. Bontempelli was in rebellion against conventional nineteenth-century realism. He adopted as his position what he called "magical realism," which, he said, was an attempt to "discover surreality in reality." He is best remembered for his short stories.

Dino Buzzati (1906–1972)

A Milan newspaper man, Buzzati began publishing strange stories in 1933 and readers could not tell for sure whether they were children's stories or morality tales for grown-ups. His symbolic novel, *The Tartar Steppe,* appeared in Italy in 1940 at a time when the political situation (Mussolini was in power) made honest realism hazardous. But Buzzati's strength is in his short fiction, his "metaphysical fables" that create an unrealistic but frighteningly real world similar to that in the fiction of Franz Kafka. Critics charged him with following Kafka too closely, and his later work (as in *A Love Affair,* 1963) was more conventional.

Giosué Carducci (1835–1907)

Critic, scholar, teacher, and legislator, Giosué Carducci is best remembered now as a poet. Throughout his career, Carducci strongly supported the unity and freedom of Italy. He combined a classical outlook and romantic feeling in his poetry. He received the Nobel prize in 1906.

Benvenuto Cellini (1500–1571)

Benvenuto Cellini, the celebrated Italian goldsmith and sculptor, had a life that reads like an adventure story. Hot-headed and quick-tempered, proud and intense, Cellini lived life to the full, moving from art work to art work as passionately as he moved from scrape to scrape. He was born in Florence at the height of the Renaissance, at a time when such painters as Leonardo da Vinci, Michelangelo, and Raphael dominated art. He studied their work as he cultivated his own fine talent. He was forced to flee Florence at the age of twenty-three because of a brawl largely of his making, and he went to Rome where he was eventually employed by Pope Clement VII. He spent his life in the great cities of the Renaissance—Florence, Rome, Venice, Naples, Bologna, Pisa, Paris. And he devoted himself, under a succession of patrons, to the creation of works of art of bold design and exquisite beauty. Not the least of his creations is his *Autobiography,* which he dictated to a young amanuensis (writing clerk) near the end of his life. Its earthy prose and vivid picture of the life of Renaissance Italy have attracted many readers since its first publication in 1730.

Gabriele D'Annunzio (1863–1938)

Gabriele D'Annunzio is a dominant figure in Italian literature and history. He was a poet, dramatist, novelist, and soldier, and he distinguished himself in all fields. He was also a romantic figure, whose love affair with the actress Eleonora Duse inspired many legends. In fiction he is considered one of the founders of Italian realism. His poetry, at its best, is delicate and filled with vivid imagery.

Grazia Deledda (1871–1936)

Born on Sardinia, Grazia Deledda spent the first part of her life among the peasants and simple people of the island. She began to write when only thirteen and had published stories by the time she was twenty. From the beginning her fiction dealt with the primitive life of people close to the land. Even after her marriage and move to Rome, she continued to write of the people of Sardinia, mixing romantic descriptions with a strange sense of fatalism. Her best work is haunting, evocative, and poetic, as in *Ashes,* published in 1904. She was awarded the Nobel prize in 1926.

Luciano Erba (1922–   )

Born in Milan, Luciano Erba went to Switzerland during the German occupation of Italy in World War II, and he has lived in France and America. His poems appear to be straightforward statements, but leave a residue in the mind to puzzle and haunt.

Giacomo Leopardi (1798–1837)

Leopardi is considered by many critics as the greatest Italian poet of the nineteenth century. In his youth he studied language, including the classics, and by the time he was eighteen he had mastered Greek, Latin, French, and English. He had made himself into a brilliant scholar, but he had also impaired his health. More and more he turned to poetry as the creative outlet for his genius. His first poems tended to present patriotic themes, but as he developed, his work became darker and more pessimistic, showing man at the mercy of an indifferent nature.

Niccoló Machiavelli (1469–1527)

The man who gave his name to sinister and underhanded behavior (Machiavellian) devoted his active career to serving the great Florentine Republic. He spent much of his time on diplomatic missions which brought him close to centers of power, and in the presence of princes who wielded the power for good or ill. The man who impressed him most was Cesare Borgia, who lived a life of intrigue and crime in desperate attempts to gain and hold power. In 1512 Machiavelli was dismissed from public service in Florence, retired to a farm, and used Cesare Borgia as a model in writing *The Prince*. The book has served as a political handbook ever since and has been both praised and condemned. In it Machiavelli explains that he intends to describe not what ought to be but what is, and in this he seems to have been perfectly honest. Machiavelli also wrote other political treatises as well as histories, plays, and amusing and satirical pieces.

Alberto Moravia (1907–   )

Probably the most widely read contemporary Italian novelist in translation, Moravia was deprived of a formal education because of a youthful illness. But he read voraciously, and early in life found his talent as a writer. He published his first novel, *The Time of Indifference*, in 1929, and in it he presented strong criticism of contemporary Italian life and society. The novel greatly upset the then ruling Italian Fascists headed by the dictator Mussolini. As Moravia continued to write fiction implicitly critical of the ruling regime, he ran into problems of censorship, and he more and more turned to indirect, surrealistic ways of achieving his ends. With the end of World War II and the overthrow of the Fascists, his work changed once again as he concentrated in depth on man's basic psychological and sexual nature.

Anna Maria Ortese (1914–   )

Known as one who has remained aloof from the literary world, Anna Maria Ortese was born in Rome and has lived for long periods in Naples, Genoa, Venice, and other Italian cities. She established her reputation in a series of volumes of short stories, including *The Sea Is Not Naples* (1953), which won the literary award *Premio Viareggio*. It contained "A Pair of Glasses" and other stories which demonstrate an eye for vivid detail and feelings of strong compassion.

Aldo Palazzeschi (1885–1974)

A native of Florence, Aldo Palazzeschi is a poet whose poetry reads like prose and a novelist whose prose reads like poetry. He was influenced by the poet D'Annunzio (see page 192) in his poetry and the storyteller Boccaccio (see page 113) in his fiction. At its best his fiction combines a gentle humor with lyrical descriptions to give a vivid picture of Italian scenes and life.

Francis Petrarch (1304–1374)

Francis Petrarch ranks with Dante as one of the two greatest poets of Italy. He wrote in Latin as well as in Italian, and he did much to interest his contemporaries in the power and beauty of classical antiquity.

Petrarch was the son of a Florentine exiled from his native city the same year as Dante. He spent years at Avignon in southern France, then the residence of the popes. There he saw for the first time his beloved Laura, source of his enduring poetic inspiration. Some critics have identified her as Laura de Noves, but others have assumed that she was largely a figment of Petrarch's poetic imagination. Whatever the reality of Laura, there is no denying the greatness of Petrarch's 366 lyrics, odes, and sonnets written to and for her. Written in the tradition of chivalry, in which the lover remains separated from his beloved, this body of love poetry has been a major influence ever since, particularly on the Elizabethan poets.

Guido Piovene (1907–1974)

Piovene attended the University of Milan and soon after began a journalistic and literary career. His first novel, *Letters of a Novice* (1941), revived the epistolary form of the novel, a form that permitted the kind of discursiveness congenial to Piovene's temperament. In this and later novels Piovene incorporated social criticism, particularly of the aristocratic rich. Piovene is also the author of two travel books, one of America (*De America*, 1953) and another of his own country (*Viaggio in Italia*, 1957).

Luigi Pirandello (1867–1936)

Luigi Pirandello introduced techniques and explored themes that are still relevant in today's theater. He was born in Sicily, and married the daughter of his father's business partner. When the fortunes of his and his wife's parents were wiped out in a flood, Pirandello was thrown back on his own meager resources to support his growing family. The financial difficulties resulted in his wife's breakdown and final insanity, and Pirandello drove himself to make enough money to provide her with care at home. Out of all these hardships and tribulations, Pirandello drew the material for his stories and plays. The most famous of his plays are *Six Characters in Search of an Author* (1921) and *Henry IV* (1922); both explore the thin line of separation between reality and illusion. Pirandello was awarded the Nobel prize for literature in 1934.

Vasco Pratolini (1913–)

A son of the working class, Pratolini worked at a variety of jobs before becoming a writer, and he served the resistance movement against Mussolini and the Fascists during World War II. After the war he established his reputation as a novelist with such works as *A Tale of Santa Croce* (1945) and *A Tale of Poor Lovers* (1947). His fiction portrays working people sympathetically and movingly; at the same time it probes deeply the injustices of modern society.

Salvatore Quasimodo (1901–1968)

A native of Sicily, Quasimodo early gave up technical training to study Greek and Latin. The classics helped to give shape to his poetry. His first volume of poems, *Waters and Lands,* was published in 1930, and many volumes followed, including *Day after Day* (1947) and *The Incomparable Earth* (1958). In 1959 Quasimodo was awarded the Nobel Prize. Quasimodo's early poetry, like other poetry of the time, was sometimes obscure, even surrealistic. But after World War II, his work began to show more concern with reality.

Giose Rimanelli (1926–)

Giose Rimanelli was born at Casacalenda (Campobasso) in southern Italy. He is considered one of the most promising of postwar Italian writers. Two of his novels, *The Day of the Lion* (1953) and *Original Sin* (1954), have been enthusiastically received.

Umberto Saba (1883–1957)

Saba was a great admirer of Petrarch. The most traditional of modern Italian poets, his work was little affected by the various poetic movements of the early twentieth century. Collections of poems like *Il Canzoniere* (the title Petrarch also used for his collected poems) have a note of bitter sadness about them.

Ignazio Silone (1900–   )

Ignazio Silone is one of those writers who have greater reputations abroad than at home. In his youth he helped to found the Italian Communist Party; and when Mussolini rose to power during the 1920's, the young revolutionary went underground to fight Fascism. He adopted Ignazio Silone as a pseudonym (his real name is Secondo Tranquilli) to protect his family from persecution. He broke with the Communists in 1930 and settled in Switzerland, where he turned to writing fiction. His first novel, *Fontamara* (1933), is intensely anti-Fascist and propagandistic. It was with his second novel, *Bread and Wine* (1936), that he established his reputation. The book is clearly autobiographical; it tells the story of the revolutionary Pietro Spina who gradually becomes disillusioned with Communism. The story "The Parting of the Ways" represents one episode in Pietro Spina's tale.

David Maria Turoldo (1916–   )

Turoldo decided early on a life of religious service and entered the Order of the Servi at the age of twenty-four. His first book of poems, *I Have No Hands* (1948), introduced him as one of the sensitive new voices in the post-World War II period. Other books followed, all filled with a deeply religious but original and vivid poetry.

Giuseppe Ungaretti (1888–1970)

From his youth, Ungaretti showed *avant garde* tendencies in his poetry. He placed great emphasis on the evocative power of the single word, and waged a battle against sentimentality. Like other experimental and rigorous poets, he was accused of obscurity and deliberate confusion. But his poetry at its best has a lucidity and simplicity seldom matched in modern verse.

Giovanni Verga (1840–1922)

Verga was born and died in Catania, Sicily, and his greatest fiction is set in his native land. He is best in dealing with the cruel and painful struggles against poverty among the peasants of Sicily, but his interest is psychological as well as social. Verga is perhaps the preeminent Italian novelist, and his fiction has strongly influenced recent Italian literature. His best works include *Cavalleria Rusticana,* the play that forms the basis of Mascagni's opera of the same name, *The House by the Medlar Tree,* and *Little Novels of Sicily,* both fiction.

PRONUNCIATION KEY

The pronunciation of each word is shown after the word, in this way: **ab bre vi ate** (ə brē′vē āt). The letters and signs used are pronounced as in the words below. The mark ′ is placed after a syllable with primary or strong accent, as in the example above. The mark ′ after a syllable shows a secondary or lighter accent, as in **ab bre vi a tion** (ə brē′vē ā′shən).

Some words, taken from foreign languages, are spoken with sounds that otherwise do not occur in English. Symbols for these sounds are given at the end of the table as "Foreign Sounds."

a	hat, cap	o	hot, rock	ə represents:
ā	age, face	ō	open, go	a in about
ä	father, far	ô	order, all	e in taken
		oi	oil, voice	i in April
b	bad, rob	ou	house, out	o in lemon
ch	child, much			u in circus
d	did, red			
		p	paper, cup	
e	let, best	r	run, try	
ē	equal, see	s	say, yes	**foreign sounds**
ėr	term, learn	sh	she, rush	
		t	tell, it	Y as in French *du*. Pronounce
		th	thin, both	ē with the lips rounded as
f	fat, if	ŦH	then, smooth	for English ü in **rule.**
g	go, bag			
h	he, how			œ as in French *peu*. Pronounce
		u	cup, butter	ā with the lips rounded as
i	it, pin	u̇	full, put	for ō.
ī	ice, five	ü	rule, move	
				N as in French *bon*. The N is
j	jam, enjoy			not pronounced, but shows
k	kind, seek	v	very, save	that the vowel before it is
l	land, coal	w	will, woman	nasal.
m	me, am	y	young, yet	
n	no, in	z	zero, breeze	H as in German *ach*. Pro-
ng	long, bring	zh	measure, seizure	nounce k without closing the breath passage.

The pronunciation key is from the *Thorndike-Barnhart High School Dictionary,* copyright 1968 by Scott, Foresman and Company.

INDEX OF AUTHORS AND TITLES

405

INDEX OF TRANSLATORS

407